FROM NARRATOLOGY TO COMPUTATIONAL STORY
COMPOSITION AND BACK

Dissertations in Artificial Intelligence

Artificial Intelligence (AI) is one of the fastest growing research areas in computer science with a strong impact on various fields of science, industry, and society. This series publishes excellent doctoral dissertations in all sub-fields of AI, ranging from foundational work on AI methods and theories to application-oriented theses.

Editor-in-Chief:
Professor Dr. Ralph Bergmann
Department of Business Information Systems II, University of Trier,
54286 Trier, Germany

Volume 353

Previously published in this series:

ISSN 0941-5769 (print)
ISSN 2666-2175 (online)

From Narratology to Computational Story Composition and Back

An Exploratory Study in Generative Modeling

Leonid Berov

IOS Press · AKA

ISBN 978-3-89838-769-9 (AKA, print)
ISBN 978-1-64368-382-9 (IOS Press, print)
ISBN 978-1-64368-383-6 (IOS Press, online)
doi: 10.3233/DAI353

Bibliographic information available from the Katalog der Deutschen Nationalbibliothek (German National Library Catalogue) at https://www.dnb.de

Dissertation approved by University of Osnabrück, Germany
Date of the defense: 3 December 2021
Supervisor: Prof. Dr. Kai-Uwe Kühnberger

Publisher
Akademische Verlagsgesellschaft AKA GmbH, Berlin

Represented by Co-Publisher IOS Press
IOS Press BV
Nieuwe Hemweg 6B
1013 BG Amsterdam
The Netherlands
Tel: +31 20 688 3355
Fax: +31 20 687 0019
email: order@iospress.nl

LEGAL NOTICE

The publisher is not responsible for the use which might be made of the following information.

In loving memory of Elena Livchits (✱ 1960, ✝ 2022) and Alexandra Leitman (✱ 1929, ✝ 2022).

Abstract

There are two disciplines that are concerned with the same object of study, narratives, but that rarely exchange insights and ideas, let alone engage in collaborative research. The first is Narrative Theory (NT), an analytical discipline from the humanities that attempts to analyze literary texts and from these instances derive a general understanding of the concept of narrative. The second is Computational Story Composition (CSC), a discipline in the domain of Artificial Intelligence that attempts to enable computers to autonomously compose fictional narratives in a way that could be deemed creative. Several reasons can be found for the lack of collaboration, but one of them stands out: The two disciplines follow decidedly different research methodologies at contradistinct levels of abstraction. This makes it hard to conduct NT and CSC research simultaneously, and also means that CSC researchers have a hard time validating whether they use NT concepts correctly, while NT scholars have no use for the outputs created by work in CSC. At the same time, a close exchange between the two disciplines would be desirable, not only because of the complementary approach to their object of study, but also because comparable interdisciplinary collaborations have proven to be productive in other fields, like for instance linguistics.

The present thesis proposes a research methodology called *generative modeling* designed to address the methodological differences outlined above, and thus allow to conduct simultaneous NT and CSC research. As a proof of concept it performs several cycles of generative modeling, in which it computationally implements concepts and dynamics described in two frameworks from NT, namely Marie-Laure Ryan's possible worlds approach to plot, and Alan Palmer's fictional minds approach to characters. In detail, the first cycle attempts to implement Ryan's possible worlds semantics and the resulting dynamics of plot, but falls short in a way that suggests that the first principles laid out in the theory are not sufficient to capture an example plot, for a number of reasons. The second cycle resolves these hypothesized problems by extending Ryan's plot understanding with affective dynamics based on Palmer's understanding of fictional minds. With plot dynamics completed, the third cycle implements Ryan's concept of tellability, which represents a quantifiable measure of the structural quality of plots. The last cycle implements a Genetic Algorithm based search heuristic that is capable of searching the plot space spanned by the employed formalism for plots high in tellability, which provides additional insights on properties of tellability. The resulting implementation is an in-depth computational representation of plot ingrained into the CSC System *InBloom*, which is capable of autonomously composing novel plots and evaluating their quality.

The study reported in this thesis demonstrates, how implementing narratological theories as generative models can lead to insights for NT, and how grounding computational representations of narrative in NT can help CSC systems take over creative responsibilities. Thereby, it shows the feasibility and utility of generative modeling.

Acknowledgment

LIKE ANY DECENT STORY, the arc of this hero's (scientific) journey would have been much less enjoyable (and probably, rather impossible) without numerous associates and companions. To them, I owe a great debt of gratitude.

My adventure started with a (quite recent) tractate—undersigned with a mysterious and foreign-sounding name—that captivated my imagination and gave me a key to the magical lands of machine storytelling and creativity. Little did I know, how soon I would come to meet Pablo Gervás, the author of this treatise. He would occasionally appear, at unexpected times and places, to offer me wise words of advice, and when the road turned rough he invited me to his castle in Madrid to lift my spirits. Dear Pablo, thank you for being my mysterious wise wizard, for piquing my curiosity and for the conversations accompanied by good food and drink.

My quest was of my own choosing, and yet I had a sender who was the first to provide me with a scientific traveler's equipment, and who gave me a prophecy along the way. Right at the start, Mark Turner warned me of the length of the journey that I was attempting. Of course, like any foolish young adventurer, I payed his warning no heed. Now, many years later, I know that he was right. Dear Mark, thank you for getting me on this way, and for connecting me with so many other, much more experience travelers than myself.

On my journey I visited two different kingdoms. In the first, Peter Schneck handed me the scientific equivalent to the Lonely Planet's guide to the lands of narratology—with its numerous quarreling factions and rulers—where I saw many wonders, and even myself tried to forge new alliances. Dear Peter, thank you for showing me this way, and for encouraging me to not take it in as a passive observer but to attempt to contribute myself. In the second kingdom, Kai-Uwe

Kühnberger adopted me into his motley band of heroes, and sent me on quests deep into the random forests and recursive caverns of artificial intelligence. There, I fought heinous bug monsters, and created generations of small societies of virtual critters. Dear Kai-Uwe, thank you for taking me in, and for incessantly supporting me with all the small and big challenges that I encountered. This meant the world.

The road ahead remains, as it should, uncertain. But here my thanks go to Jonas Kuhn, who showed me visions of a potential future and invited me to explore it with him.

My story would not be complete without all of the other travelers who, busy on their own journeys, shared a part of the way with me. Dear Vinicius Silva, Wiebke Ahlers, Filipa Correia, Philipp Wicke, João Cunha, Christian Guckelsberger and all the others: thank you for telling me your own stories, going with me through highs or lows, or just sharing a laugh on the wayside. These are the things that keep a wanderer sane.

Foremost, thank you Sabrina, for coming into my life and staying there throughout everything.

Contents

List of Figures

List of Tables

*Call me Ishmael. Some years ago—never mind
how long precisely—having little or no money in
my purse, and nothing particular to interest me
on shore, I thought I would sail about a little and
see the watery part of the world.*

Herman Melville, 'Moby-Dick'

1

Introduction

THIS DISSERTATION ATTEMPTS TO CROSS THE SPACE BETWEEN
TWO DISTANT SHORES, the disciplines of narrative theory (NT) and
artificial intelligence (AI). At first glance, these two have not much
in common. NT is an analytical discipline from the humanities that
attempts to analyze literary texts and from these instances derive a
general understanding of the concept of story. AI deals with digital
problem-solving machines and attempts to understand the concept of
intelligence by recreating it, being thus wedged in between computer
science and psychology. However, I firmly believe that this appearance of detachedness is misleading. As I will outline shortly, stories
are an integral part of human nature, and might one day turn out
to be one of the keys towards unlocking a machine's ability to make
sense of the surrounding world. At the same time, stories are made
by the human mind and are concerned predominantly with the human mind, so their understanding should benefit from a clearer view
of the principles that constitute minds. I encountered the wittiest
summary of this interconnection early in my voyage, when literary
theorist Víctor Bermúdez succinctly quipped that "literature is the
data of consciousness" at the 2016 Symposium on Narrative, Cognition and Science held at the University of Erlangen-Nürnberg (per-

1

sonal communication). My thesis will cross the waters between AI and NT several times, and while the trips are not intended to uncover the Great whale of consciousness it is an attempt to demonstrate how both disciplines can benefit from trading ideas. The concrete project on which I will conduct my demonstration is a computational plot composition system I called InBloom, yet it is not the final system in which I see my thesis' main contribution. Instead, I see it in the repeated cycles of design grounded in NT, and implementation using AI technology, as well as the insights that are garnered along the way.

In the following, I will first motivate my work by further outlining the benefits of an exchange between NT and AI, which will lead to the formulation of three research questions. I will continue with short introductions of NT and computational creativity in order to provide readers with differing backgrounds with a shared common ground. Then, I will outline related work on computational story composition (CSC) to allow readers to place this thesis in context. The chapter will conclude with a reader's guide intended to describe the structure of the rest of this thesis, and, more importantly, disclose the rationale behind this structure.

1.1. Motivation

Narratives are an ubiquitous part of our every day life, be it as books, films, or small talk. But under this surface, they also play a more crucial role than mere entertainment. We make sense of our experiences by organizing a continuous stream of concurrent perceptions in the form of events connected by a meaningful structure, that is, in narratives. As cognitive scientist Mark Turner writes: "Narrative imagining—story—is the fundamental instrument of thought. Rational capacities depend on it. It is our chief means of looking into the future, of predicting, of planning, and of explaining. It is a literary capacity indispensable to human cognition generally" (M. Turner, 1996, p. 4f). Another line of argument for the central role of narratives in human cognition focuses on its role in interpreting the behavior, and by that merit basic understanding, of other humans, as cultural theorist Phoebe Sengers (2000, p. 3) agues: "Narrative psychology shows that, whereas people tend to understand inanimate objects in terms of cause-effect rules and by using logical reasoning, intentional behavior is made comprehensible, not by figuring out its physical laws, but by structuring it into narrative [...]". Paradoxically, this seems to apply not only to others, but even to understanding oneself. Philosophers have argued, that the notion of the self—that is how people conceptualize and locate themselves in existence—has an important narrative constituent (Schechtman, 2011): the stories we tell ourselves about ourselves define who we are. Quite naturally, such definitional narratives also play a role in close dyadic settings. Lasting bonds between romantic partners have been argued to be connected to the presence and type of shared narratives adopted in the relationship (Bühler & Dunlop, 2019). Narratives also organize the interactions of humans at a much grander scale. According to the historian Yuval Harari (2014) it was an important part of the cognitive revolution—which was central to the evolutionary success of homo sapiens—that humans learned to create reliable bonds between members of large groups based on shared narratives: we call these narratives religions, nations or the free market. So pervasive is the role of narratives in human matters, that evolutionary psychologist Jonathan Gottschall (2012) called homo sapiens "the storytelling animal".

Why should this be relevant to the discipline of AI? According to one of the canonical introductory books on AI, two main traditions exist in the discipline (Russell & Norvig, 2010): the engineering approach studies how individual tasks that usually require intelligence to be performed can be solved using computers, while the cognitive approach is the empirical study of the mind. For the AI engineer, the ability to create and understand narratives might be a secondary but still relevant problem: if humans have evolved to communicate via narratives then computers should also be able to employ this medium in order to improve human computer interaction. Nobody likes to read spreadsheets. However, it is for the AI cognitive modeler for whom narrative intelligence should be a central concern. If human level general intelligence has only been observed in correlation with strongly developed narrative capabilities that also seem to serve important functions, then AI should be interested in them.

Narrative capabilities come in two forms: understanding and generation. Personally, I find the second type more fascinating since it involves another elusive component of human general intelligence: creativity. In fictional narratives, non-existent but believable characters have to be developed (or assembled from stereotypes and filled with individuality). They have to be credibly ensnared in a network of made-up events, and the resulting interactions have to convey meaning. Even in factual narratives this structure and meaning imposed on a sequence of events is never a given, but a result of imagination and interpretation. The composition of narratives (a term I prefer to generation, in this context, due to its connotation of creativity) is thus a topic especially worthy of cognitively minded AI research because it provides the chance to study two relevant parts of human intelligence at the same time.

As I outlined above, the composition of fictional narratives leaves more room and freedom for an algorithm than the composition of factual ones, which are constrained by a set of events that need to be reported. It might be this freedom, or perhaps the questionable impression that it reduces the complexity of an already daunting task, that lead to a focus on fictional narratives early on in AI research.[1] While these narratives seem to play a lesser role than their factual brethren, and are not commonly associated with notions like the self or the evolution of society, the great regard that we place on them in incarnations like literature or film still makes them a relevant research topic. Another great benefit of focusing on fictional narratives is the existence of a venerable and long-standing tradition of research on literature, going back as far as Aristotle's *Poetics* around 335 BC. This body of work means that researchers interested in generating fictional narratives do not necessarily need to first personally conceptualize an artefact far outside the usual scope of their studies, but can instead cherry-pick from the work of specialists.

One of these specialist fields is NT. The focus of NT, which sets it apart from fields like Literary Criticism, is on what defines narratives as a genus, as opposed to the meaning making strategies of individual narratives (Prince, 2003, p. 66). Does this mean that the computational composition of narratives is just an application of insights from NT, or can AI also contribute back to that field? The case is much harder to make than the reverse, since I know of no instances where insight from story composition changed what theorists think about narratives. However, I believe that there is indeed great un-

---

[1]The earliest system attempting this task was recently discovered by an ongoing digital archeology project (J. Ryan, 2017) and dates back to 1963, only seven years after the Dartmouth workshop that is often regarded as the founding event of AI as a field.

tapped potential. NT is an analytical discipline, that performs theory building by analyzing canonical instances of narratives and deriving general frameworks[2] of what constitutes narratives, through abstraction. The computational composition of narratives opens a complementary approach: implementing the first principles and dynamics described by a narratological framework as a generative model, and deriving insight from the outputs it generates. One type of insight can come from judging these outputs individually. If they do not appear valid and well-formed instances of the genus narrative, or if certain effects—which the underlying framework purports to represent—fail to appear, then the first principles that constitute that framework are not sufficient. The other type of insight comes from comparing composed narratives to each other. This allows to do something that is impossible in an analytical setting: study the effect of individual parts of a framework in isolation, by varying an individual parameter of the model while keeping all others constant. From the outputs, the influence and effect of a single part of the framework on the structure and dynamics of a narrative as a whole can be observed; something that cannot be done based on narratives 'in the wild' because no two existing narratives can be guaranteed to differ only in one trait. I am aware that to those who are well acquainted with the complexity of narratives and the vagaries of narratological theories this might sound abstract, and impossible to achieve in practice. But I take courage from the fact that such an approach is by now quite established in another discipline from the humanities, in linguistics, where the study of computational natural language generation is an established field that plays its part in the overarching quest of linguistics for a theoretical understanding of language.

Researchers working on CSC commonly take one of two approaches. One is to use an established technology from AI and see how it can be used to model some of the constituent parts of narratives. This seems to be the case for many planning based approaches like Bahamon and Young (2013), Brenner (2010), Meehan (1977), Riedl and Young (2010), and Ware and Young (2014) or many multi agent simulation approaches like Klein et al. (1973), Riegl and Veale (2018), Swartjes and Theune (2008), and Wadsley, Ryan, et al. (2013). The other approach is to depart from cognitive theories of writing or cre-

---

[2]I use the plural here, since no unified framework holds sway over the field, but rather a multitude of 'narratologies' that coexist (Meister, 2014).

ative thought, and to implement these via any technological means. Representative instances of this approach are, for instance, the works of Akimoto (2019), Pérez y Pérez and Sharples (2001), and S. R. Turner (1993). This distinction aligns well with the two general approaches to AI research (engineering and cognitive modeling) I discussed above, and its reification in computational creativity research (Pérez y Pérez, 2018). What these approaches have in common is that they treat narratives as a secondary phenomenon: they either focus on a technology or a process model, and consequently subordinate their computational representation of narratives to whatever requirements these foci bring with them.[3] Given my interest in how NT can benefit from the exploits of CSC, my ideal is to follow an inverse route. The research agenda of my thesis is to 1) depart from a promising narratological framework, 2) based on this, implement a computational representation of narrative (with little regard to technological purity), and 3) consider any process that can operate on this representation in search of narratives with particular properties a system for CSC (no matter its cognitive plausibility). This allows the formulation of two general research questions, that permeate the present thesis.

RQ 1: Can NTs be computationally implemented using generative models? How can narratological theories benefit from such modeling? Answering this question involves solving a range of more specific sub-questions, and the problems they represent: Can a narratological framework be identified that is formulated in a way that is amenable to computational generative modeling, at all? Can such a framework be sufficiently formalized and specified in order to be implemented, despite of parts that are described at a level of abstraction that is substantially above the algorithmic, without distorting the underlying ideas beyond recognition? Can such an implementation be used to generate artefacts that are recognizable as instances of the genus narrative, and do variations of the parameters of such an implementation result in narratologically meaningful dif-

---

[3]Claiming that there are only two approaches in the field is of course a simplification. For instance, Gervás (2016) also departs from a narratological theory outlined by Russian folklorist Propp. And even those approaches that do not focus on NT do not operate in total disregard for its ideas. My main point is that neither are interested in contributing the insights of their work back to NT, which I consider a lost opportunity.

ferences in these outputs? Can insights about the properties of the underlying narratological framework be drawn based on the observation of such outputs?

RQ 2: Can CSC be modeled as the manipulation of a computational representation of narratives grounded in NT? What are the benefits of grounding the modeling process in NT? Again, several sub-questions are involved in addressing this question: Can a narratological framework be identified that supports all tasks that are involved in the computational composition of narratives, especially generation and evaluation? Does an implementation of such a framework provide sufficient parameters such that a search space of narratives can be explored based on them? What constitutes a meta-algorithm that can manipulate such a search space? Are the artefacts that are created by such a search recognizable as narratives, and is there sufficient variation in such a search space to support a semblance of creativity?

Both of the original research questions contribute to answering a central, meta-research question: **RQ 3: Is a scientific/scholarly exchange between NT and CSC possible and productive? How can such an exchange be facilitated?** While it might sound trivially true at the beginning, I believe that this question could lead to insights that allow to address some of the reasons that, so far, have limited the exchange between these two disciplines. From the outset, I see several problems that impede this exchange: One is a fundamental difference in methodology, whose effect I felt immediately when I first developed an outline for this dissertation. Practical research in AI commonly follows a linear course: 1) one starts with a task that needs to be solved by the machine and where success can be measured and compared to other approaches, 2) based on theoretical or empirical considerations one formalizes a model and ideally demonstrates theoretically that it can solve the task at hand, 3) one implements the formalization in parameterizable algorithmic form and, in the end, 4) empirically establishes the best parametrization as well as its performance in comparison with previous approaches based on task-specific metrics. Practical research in NT, in contrast, commonly follows a helical course: 1) one identifies a concept whose scope seems to be in need of refining,[4] 2) analyzes its use and presence in a small set of

---

[4]Originally, I envisioned this process to start with the identification of a concept that is lacking (in a particular theory). After running this first version past

canonical texts, 3) derives an improved understanding of the concept, 4) revises the initial analysis of the texts and perhaps expands the corpus to contain more varied texts, 5) revises and extends the adopted understanding of the concept to account for newly gained insights, 6) returns to the corpus... and so on. Both approaches are based on the scholarly traditions of the respective fields and were developed to account for their respective challenges. Work on the interface of these two disciplines needs to find a way of honoring both.

However, even once procedural questions like these are cleared out of the way, the situation does not get easier. Applying AI methodology to narratological frameworks is not straightforward. Concepts from NT are specified at a high level of abstraction and are analytical or interpretative in nature, which means that their operationalization is a complex reasoning task in itself. This holds to such an extent that specialists often disagree on how a concept should be operationalized and, what is worse, even given one particular operationalization and the same text to apply it to, different specialists can be expected to disagree on instances of the given concept in the given text. This is not mere conjecture on my side but was recently demonstrated in a fascinating series of workshops, where groups were invited to formulate annotation guidelines for the concept of narrative levels, and these guidelines where then used to annotate a corpus of short stories (Gius et al., 2019).[5] Given how a formalization of concepts that would be reliably usable for humans eludes the grasp even of domain experts, it is highly problematic to expect computer scientists to be able to perform such formalizations in a way that is sufficient for machines. To make matters worse, there are no established quantifiable metrics that measure the quality of instances of such concepts in a (computationally generated) narrative, and no universal metric of the quality of a narrative either, so also the empirical evaluation step, that is fundamental to AI research, is not readily applicable to this domain.

Dr. Janina Jacke—a narratologist at the Institute for German Studies of the University of Hamburg—she pointed out to me that in NT research the introduction of completely new concepts is rare. Instead, most work revolves around the refinement and re-contextualization of existing concepts (Janina Jacke, personal communication).

[5]Eight different guidelines where submitted, and the resulting inter-annotator agreement ranged from 0.05 to 0.30, where 0 indicates below chance level agreement and 1 indicates perfect agreement.

Furthermore, the other way around, there also is no intuitive application of generative models from AI in narratological studies. Including computationally generated narratives into a corpus is theoretically questionable since it is not clear whether they are proper instances of the genus narrative at all, and practically questionable since the state of art in CSC has not yet reached a point where performance is close to human. While I have sketched one way out of this situation in my remarks on NT on p. 5 above, so far, it remains hypothetical and has never been successfully carried out in practice. If the present thesis can demonstrate the feasibility of this hypothetical way by generating viable narratological insights then I would consider the mere fait accompli an important stepping stone in NT/CSC exchange, and, at the same time, a step towards answering my third research question.

Before continuing this introduction with more details about the context of my work, a general technological reservation is in order. When I started my work in 2016, computational linguistics was not in a state to provide outsiders with out-of-the box capabilities to generate natural sounding language, let alone narrative prose. Rare individual forays into prose generation existed (see e.g. Callaway & Lester, 2002) but were closely tied to idiosyncratic systems for content generation. It did not seem like the field would mature enough in the decade to come, so I made the decision to focus my work on composing the content plane of narratives (like plot or character) and leave the presentation plane (like discourse or prose) to future work, a separation that has been quite common in the field (Gervás, 2009). Only four years later, by 2020, the deep neural network architecture GPT-3 (Brown et al., 2020) demonstrated the ability to generate prose that is hardly distinguishable from human[6], including a remarkable aptness for varying the style of its output. However, even this advanced system is not capable of generating prose about a given content, which would be the requirement for attaching it to a story composition system like the one envisioned here. For this reason, from now on, my use of the term 'CSC' will remain restricted to the task and the field of computationally creating the *content* of

---

[6]One of the use cases was an automatically generated article for the British newspaper The Guardian, where GPT-3 was tasked with arguing that it does not pose a threat to humanity: https://www.theguardian.com/commentisfree/2020/sep/08/robot-wrote-this-article-gpt-3.

narratives.

1.2. Narrative Theory

Above, I outlined that NT is concerned with the study of what constitutes narratives as a genus, that is, with the theory of narrative representation. However, NT can also be regarded a methodology for studying instances of narrative, for instances as a first step of interpretation (Meister, 2014). Since the post-classical turn in the 1990s, the state of NT has been described as one where no unifying, universally accepted framework exists, but instead a "multitude of compound or 'hyphenated' narratologies" (Meister, 2014) coexist. Different schools have proposed differing theories, and while most theories agree on the general type of the phenomena involved in narrative representation, they still markedly differ in how they analyze their concrete functioning, interaction, and relevance. For instance, a Proppian formalist approach analyzes characters as mere functions subservient to the teleology of plot (Propp, 1968), while a cognitively informed approach like Palmer's (2004) puts the focus on the mimetic properties of characters as fictional beings reconstructed from the discourse; just to demonstrate the potential gamut of differences. For this reason, NT is best considered neither a theory nor a methodology but a discipline in its own right (Meister, 2014). The goal of this section is not to provide an overview of the current state of this discipline, as this would probably require a thesis in its own right. Instead, it will attempt to opportunistically distill a (more or less) uncontroversial understanding of the field's subject of study, in order to demonstrate the breadth and complexity of the type of thing a creative AI system would have to generate. It is also intended to provide a common ground for readers from different backgrounds.

1.2.1. Definition of Narrative

The barest viable definition of narrative I came across is "the representation of an event or a series of events" (Abbott, 2002, p. 12). Maintaining that narratives are representations defines them as semiotic constructs, while requiring them to signify events distinguishes narratives from descriptions[7] or arguments. Taken together this means

---

[7]Abbott (2002, p. 12) explicates the distinction between descriptions and narratives by contrasting "My dog has fleas" with "My dog was bitten by a flea":

that there are at least two phenomena that comprise narratives: a content plane that encompasses the events that are narrated, and a presentation plane that encompasses the way they are mediated to the reader. The notion of a 'series of events' additionally implies that on the content plane also the phenomenon of temporality plays a role. While representing the broadest possible consensus among theorists (Herman et al., 2005, p. 347), the above definition omits important phenomena and would, for instance, also classify historical annals and chronicles as narratives. A slightly more specific definition expands the understanding of that which is represented in narratives to "the transition from one state to another state, caused or experienced by actors" (Bal, 1997, p. 182). This adds two more phenomena to the content plane: fictional characters that are capable of action as well as perception, and character-mediated causality as a central relationship between the narrative's events. The notion of character carries with it the phenomenon of a story world (i.e. spatiality) of which they, like other existents, are part, while character-action, in turn, implies motivation and conflict. As becomes apparent, already these seemingly innocuous definitions import at least as much implicit elements as they explicate. However, there is still one major phenomenon missing. Above, I explained that narrative differs from argument and description because it represents events, and from chronicle and annal because it is concerned with characters. Herman et al. (2005, p. 347) argue that this can be generalized: narrative differs from other text types by its ability "to evoke a certain type of image in the mind of the recipient", stressing that it is the nature of the evoked images that distinguishes text types. The crucial part is the explication that all these phenomena (the spatial, temporal, mental and causal dimensions) require a reader, in order to be realized in the form of mental models and through that to unfold their discriminatory effect. A definition that, in my opinion, brings all these parts together best, has been proposed by the narratologist Monika Fludernik:

> A narrative is a representation of a possible world [...], at whose center there are one or several protagonists of an anthropomorphic nature who are existentially anchored in a temporal and spatial sense and who (mostly) perform goal-directed actions (action and plot structure). It is the experience of these protagonists that narratives focus on, allowing readers to immerse themselves in a different world and in the life of the protagonists.
>
> (Fludernik, 2009, p. 6)

In the following, I will present a rough overview over each the four phenomena that are central to this definition: plot, discourse,

---

the former "is a description of my dog, but it is not a narrative because nothing happens".

character, and reader. Then, I will sketch their interactions because they only constitute narrative when taken together.

1.2.2. Constituent Phenomena

Story and Plot

At the heart of each narrative is a temporally ordered series of events, which is often referred to as *story* (Herman et al., 2005, p. 435). These events can be of two types: those that have no agent but only patients (*happenings*) and those that are caused by an intentional agent (*actions*). They take place in a spatial realm referred to as *story world*, which is comprised of two types of *existents*: those that have the potential to act and perceive (*characters*) and those that do not (*settings*). An interesting paradox is that in contrast to the real world the story world is at the same time incomplete and over-determined; incomplete, since a finite story can never present all details that would be perceivable in the real world, and over-determined since some details can be presented that could not be known in the real world (Lahn & Meister, 2013, p. 200), like for instance the thoughts of all characters when reported verbatim by a hetero-diegetic (sometimes called 'omniscient') narrator. A particular type of over determination is that the events that form a story are known to have been selected and assembled in a certain way in order to achieve an intended effect. To describe this aesthetic structuring that underlies stories, the concept of *plot* has been introduced. It can be best understood as a mental configuration that draws out a meaning from a series of events (Ricoeur, 1984, p. 65)[8]. Two perspectives can be taken on plot: a *post-closure view* that imposes a rigid structure over a known series of events to imbue them with a certain meaning, and a *pre-closure view* that sees plot as the fluid development of all the possible, superimposing structures that could be applied to an ongoing series of events, whose final teleological organization has not yet fully emerged (Dannenberg, 2008, pp. 9, 45). In both cases, the organization achieved by plot can be conceptualized as a network of

---

[8]Consider, how the same sequence of events could be taken to represent the overcoming of a monster, or a tragedy, depending on whether one empathizes with the experiences of the 'hero' or the 'monster'. Sometimes, a series of events can also seem completely unconnectable at all, in which case there would be no plot, a setting that is sometimes explored in post-modern fiction

causality that permeates the story world.[9]

Discourse

While story and plot describe the content plane of a narrative (i.e. what is told), *discourse* is used to describe the presentation plane (i.e. how it is told) (Prince, 2003, p. 21). A central notion for this is the *narrator*, a textually inscribed entity that recounts the events of the story or presents the properties of the story world, to an equally inscribed narratee. Narrators can be *overt*, in which case they establish a distinct personality and occasionally foreground the diegetic situation, or *covert*, in which case they recede behind the content and appear to simply transmit information (Prince, 2003, pp. 66f). An interesting paradox is that in fictional narratives it is only through discourse that story and story-world come into being, but, at the same time, discourse can be seen as subordinate to story because it appears to be a reorganization and selection, that is just the mediation, of story. This finds its culmination in the phenomenon of *unreliable narration*, when it becomes clear that the presentation of the story is biased, misleading, or incomplete, which can happen when the telling contains inconsistencies, contradictions to the ontology of the story world, or even just endorses questionable moral norms (Herman et al., 2005, pp. 495f).

In general, Genette (1983) distinguishes between three aspects of discourse: voice, mode, and tense. *Voice* investigates the ontological position of the narrator with regard to the story. Two types of voice are distinguished. A *heterodiegetic voice* is not itself part of the story world that it narrates, and consequently can have reliable access to characters' thoughts or feelings, future or past events, and is not subject to the physical laws of the story world. On the other hand, a *homodiegetic voice* belongs to a character of the story it recounts (although it might be in retrospection), so that it does not

---

[9]Causality is a difficult and philosophically contested notion whose discussion lies far outside the scope of the present thesis. After reviewing the gamut of possible philosophical notions of causality for the application to narrative, Currie (2010, Sec. 2.1) identifies the interventionist understanding as the best candidate, but finds also fault with that. Suffice to say that I follow his analysis and its final position that "[i]n saying that the representation of causation is central to narrative, we are saying something about the centrality of represented relations which we would, in our philosophically unreflective moments, think of as causal" (Currie, 2010, p. 29).

have privileged access to other characters' inner world and speaks in an individuated manner. The *mode* (also called perspective) is an epistemic criterion about how the narrator knows what it recounts, and three types can be distinguished. *Zero focalization* implies that no restrictions exist on the narrators viewpoint, which is often also a strong indication of a heterodiegetic voice. In *internal focalization* the perspective is identical to the viewpoint of one particular focalizer character at a time, so that everything that that character sees, knows or feels is known to the narrator. Potentially, the reported perceptions appear to be filtered through the fictional consciousness of the focalizer, which, for instance, in the case of a small child or a deranged character results in unreliable narration. In *external focalization* the view-point follows one particular focalizer character at a time, but takes a perspective 'from without' that character, so that no access to its internal states is granted. The final aspect, *tense*, focuses on the representation of time in the narration. Here, the criterion *order* investigates whether the temporal sequence of events in the story is preserved in the telling (*chronological order*) or whether they are reordered (*achronological order*). Possible reordering operations are *flash-backs* (when events from the past relative to the time of the narrated now are revisited) and *flash-forwards* (when events from the future relative to the narrated now are foreshadowed). The criterion *duration* investigates the relation between how long the fictional events take (*story time*) and how long it takes to narrate these events (*discourse time*). Several options exist to describe this relation, for instance *scene* (both are equal), *summary* (discourse time is shorter), or *stretch* (discourse time is longer). It is common for duration to switch often throughout the narrative text. The *frequency* criterion investigates the number of discourse references to a story event. This can be either *singulative* (an event takes place once and is recounted once), *repetitive* (a single occurrence is referred to several times) or *iterative* (an event takes place several times but is referred to once). Thus, Genette's aspects provide a toolkit to analyze the relationship of story and narration.

Character

Fictional characters are anthropomorphic existents of the story world that possess agency. There are two dominant approaches to conceptualizing character.

The mimetic approach treats characters as non-actual individuals that are located in space as well as time, and are characterized using traits from three dimensions: *physical, behavioral,* and *mental* (Herman et al., 2005, p. 53). This can take the form of *explicit characterization,* when a character is ascribed certain properties by the narrator or other characters, or *implicit characterization,* when traits can be derived from certain behavioral or emotional patterns of the character. Unlike actual individuals, fictional characters are incomplete, which means that some of their properties are not determined by the text. Some of these gaps can be filled in based on general world knowledge, whereas others are fundamentally open. For instance, the number of legs Lady Macbeth has is never explicitly mentioned in the text of the near-eponymous Shakespeare (1623) tragedy, however, Gricean pragmatics and common sense knowledge allow to assume she had two. This is the case because gaps in character representation can be filled by readers by importing knowledge about actual persons, like for instance about human physiology, social stereotypes, or behavioral scripts. Alas, a comparable inference is impossible in order to determine the number of her children (Knights, 1933), since this particular gap cannot be filled from general common sense knowledge. Central to the mimetic view is that characters posses an interiority that is comprised by mental phenomena like goals, emotions, or seemingly stable dispositional traits (also expectations imported from common assumptions about actual persons). Although they are presented through a series of events, characters' interiority is assumed to be continuous, so that when a character is encountered in a narrative after some story time has elapsed, its mental state can have changed in comparison to the last encounter. The actions of a character are intended to achieve its goals, and can be influenced by its emotions.

An alternative perspective on character is the non-mimetic approach, which focuses on the textual, functional and semiotic properties of the narrative discourse representing characters (Herman et al., 2005, p. 56). Here, characters are understood as proper nouns that are ascribed with properties through referring expressions resulting in a *web of semes* (Barthes, [1970] 1974), and derive their meaning from standing in opposition to other characters. The analysis of characters as instantiations of a *plot function,* like e.g. the protagonist, the antagonist or the foil, is also a non-mimetic stance.

Reader

Narrative theory distinguishes two types of reader concepts: the actual or *empirical reader*, a real person who in the process of consuming a text constructs mental models and can be researched using methods from psychology, and *reader constructs* that are textually inscribed, abstract addressees (Herman et al., 2005, p. 482, for examples see below).

As argued above, the nature of the mental models produced by the empirical reader is one of the criteria distinguishing narrative from other text types. It is hypothesized, that readers' mental models are built up gradually in working memory and integrate information over time. During bottom-up processing, new information from the text is entered into working memory without necessary integration into a holistic model. During top-down processing this content of working memory is expanded by importing text-external knowledge from the reader's long-term memory, which is activated by association to the current content, or is required to fill gaps. This can lead to categorization, when the information in the working memory is consolidated into a holistic mental model, which might come at the cost of rejecting contradictory pieces of information. In the case of mounting evidence contradicting a mental model, later bottom-up processing can result in decategorization and consequently reconstruction of parts of the model (Schneider, 2001). Empirical research has shown that readers can be emotionally affected during the consumption of narrative fiction (see e.g. Keen, 2013). Scholars have argued that the two central readerly emotions are *sympathy*, that is, feeling for a character, and *empathy*, that is, feeling with a character (Caracciolo, 2016; Eder, 2006).

Different abstract reader constructs have been used by theorists to highlight differing properties of narratives. An influential concept is the *implied reader*, which can be seen to fulfill two functions (Schmid, 2014): As the *presumed addressee* it encompasses the "linguistic codes, ideological norms, and aesthetic ideas" that the implied author seems to assume to govern her audience. As the *ideal recipient* it functions as an image of an audience that "understands the work in a way that optimally matches its structure and adopts the interpretive position and aesthetic standpoint put forward by the work". This difference becomes relevant in ideological works that propose an uncommon way of thinking, and where, consequently, the presumed addressee differs strongly from the ideal recipient. Reader constructs should not be confused with the narratee, who is the intra-diegetic recipient of the narrator's fictional speech acts.

1.2.3. Models of Narrative

The idiosyncrasies of narrative originate not only in the properties of the above phenomena seen in isolation, but also in their interactions and how they are structured when seen in combination. While there appears to be a fairly broad consensus about which phenomena are relevant, their combination and relative relevance are already a contested domain. Peter Wenzel's (2004) introduction opens with two complementary, overarching models.

The communication model (pp. 6f, 10f) conceptualizes narrative as a Russian doll of fundamentally different layers of communication (see Fig. 1.1). The outer-most layer is the layer of non-fictional

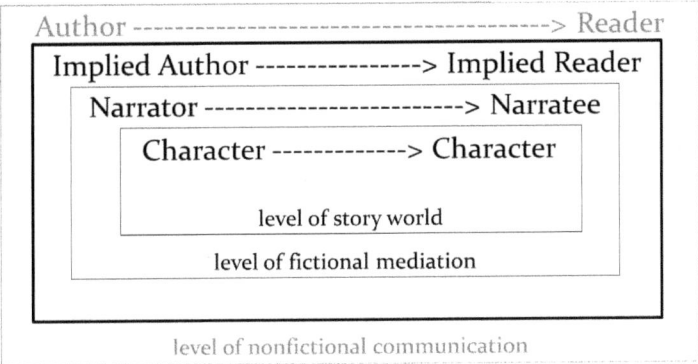

Figure 1.1: The communication model of narrative, based on (Wenzel, 2004, p. 12).

communication, between an author who composed the narrative in order to achieve a certain effect, and an actual reader who consumes it and is affected by it. This is a strictly text-external communication situation, and details about it should not be inferred from the narrative text (although it can be studied, by e.g. psychological experiments on subjects during the process of reading).

Text internally, the outer-most (and hence, most authoritative) layer of communication is that between the textually inscribed implied reader and the textually inscribed implied author, neither of which is individuated as a person. A key phenomenon that requires the postulation of this layer of communication, at this position, is unreliable narration. If a narrative text contains clues that indicate that its narrator is not mediating the fictional truth, then this information must be communicated at a layer that is superior and more authoritative than the narratorial layer. It is clearly directed to the implied reader as an ideal recipient, and thus the sender has been dubbed the implied author for symmetry reasons. For instance, in Edgar Poe's (1843) short story *The Tell-Tale Heart* the narrator explicitly and repeatedly explains that he is not mad, yet the frantic and disrupted way these assertions are phrased (and the very fact that they need to be made, at all) communicates to the reader that the narrator is, indeed, mad and thus cannot be reliable. The implied author subverts the narrator, by crafting his pleas for sanity in a way that discloses his insanity.

As already indicated, the next layer is that of fictional mediation, where a narrator communicates to a narratee. This communication can be more or less covert; with the narrator either just relaying information that has been perceived in the story world by a focalizing instance, or describing events using a clearly individuated voice while drawing attention at the diegetic situation through commentary, as the two opposite sides of the spectrum. The inner-most layer is that of the story world that is described by the narrator, where characters communicate with each other through direct speech or action. It is an interesting feature of this model that it can be infinitely recursive because characters can tell each other stories, resulting in nested narratives that in turn have the same structure as the actual narrative.

The two-level model (pp. 7f, 15f) follows a structuralist approach, in that its constituent phenomena are delineated through binary contrasts (see Fig. 1.2). The first dichotomy is that between the layers of story and discourse—that which is told in a narrative as opposed to how it is being presented—which was already discussed above. On the story side, a general distinction is made between events and existents. The former are dynamic components, which means that events act as the driver of the story. Events can be further distinguished into either actions (events that have an agent) or happenings (events that have a patient but no agent). Existents capture the stative components of a story that can be categorized as either characters (anthropomorphic agents) or parts of the story world (entities incapable of action, physical and societal rules governing the fictional space).

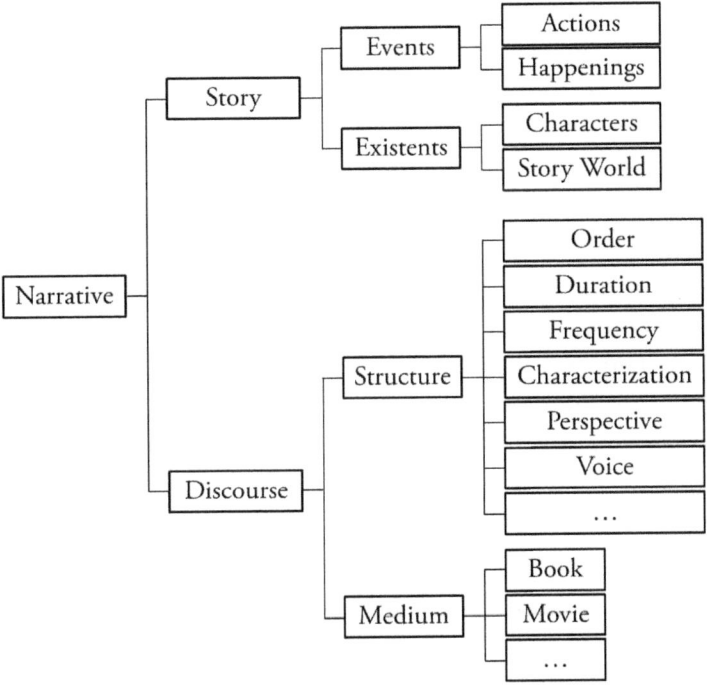

Figure 1.2: The two-level model of narrative, based on (Wenzel, 2004, p. 15).

These components comprise the states that define the narrative and can be changed by events. On the discourse side, a distinction is made between structure and medium. The layer of structure contains literary devices that can be used to present the story, like the different types of perspective or characterization discussed above. The layer of medium, on the other hand, describes the material and technique that is used to implement these devices. For instance, perspective in books is implemented using written text, while in film perspective can be implemented using visual frames.

While the first model describes the structure of the communication that brings narrative into being, and the second model opposes narrative phenomena with each other to sharpen their profile, personally, I also find it relevant to outline how these phenomena interact with each other when they come together as constituent parts of a narrative. The model I propose is depicted in Fig. 1.3.

Here, all phenomena are shown to interact with each other in different ways, which is one of the reasons for the complexity of modeling narrative. Without implying a rank order, I will start untangling this knot from the concept of reader. The actual reader consumes the narrative discourse, and from that reconstructs a series of events that form the story, and forms mental models of the characters as well as the   story   world.

Through interpretation he posits a structure that permeates and connects these components into a meaningful whole, the plot. In a fictional narrative, characters and story do not actually exist, which means that they are brought into being only through the fact of being mediated by a discourse. The dis-

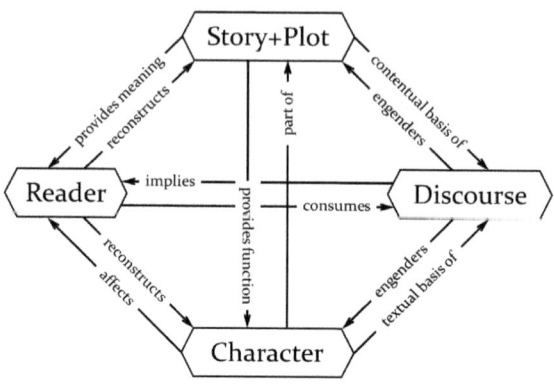

Figure 1.3: An interaction model of narrative.

course also implies a certain image of an abstract reader construct, be it in the form of a presumed addressee or an ideal recipient. Story is the contentual material from which the discourse is assembled because the discourse is considered a temporal rearrangement and an aspectual mediation of the events and the existents of the story. The plot part of story provides functional roles (like, for instance, protagonist or foil) that certain characters can fill. It also provides meaning to the actual reader by suggesting a structure that holds the narrative together. Characters also affect the actual reader, but emotionally, and by that merit keep her engaged with the events of the story. They are constituent parts of the story world, and their actions (driven by characters' intentions) as well as happenings (as perceived and appraised by characters) are the material over which the plot weaves its structure. Finally, in a homodiegetic narrative the discourse is produced by a character that acts as the narrator, while in a heterodiegetic narrative the characters' direct speech, thoughts, and perceptions are the textual material from which the discourse is comprised.

1.2.4. Perspectives on Narrative

Narratives are not only multi-faceted phenomena by virtue of their constitution, but also because they can be seen and analyzed from multiple perspectives.

One simple distinction of two perspectives that I find very compelling is proposed by the philosopher Gregory Currie (2010, Chap. 3). The *internal perspective* focuses on the narrative, as if its events and existents were actual, even though they are known to be fictional. While taking this perspective, it is plausible to analyze a characters intentions or emotions, to feel sympathy for their ordeals, or to ponder whether they are behaving logically (all while knowing, that they do not actually exist). The *external perspective*, instead, focuses on the whole of a narrative as an intentional artefact that was crafted by an author in order to achieve certain effects and which stands in relation to the norms of a society in which that author is embedded. While taking this perspective, one would be rather inclined to analyze whether a character is believable, the plot coherent, or a stylistic device appropriate to achieve a certain effect. Currie summarizes:

> The interaction of these two ways of seeing and thinking is crucial to understanding how narrative works. Our expectations about a narrative, our desire for explanation of what happens, and our sense of what is satisfactorily explained, are all a product of the interaction between these two factors. By getting us to adjust the resources we allocate to the two different perspectives, narratives manipulate our expectations, affect our sense of what is probable, and shape our willingness to grant plausibility to events within the story. (Currie, 2010, p. 49)

A more specialized distinction is proposed by the film scholar Jens Eder et al. (2010), who suggests to analyze fictional characters using the four aspects: artefact, fictional being, symbol and symptom. Eder restricts his analysis to characters, however, I do not see why the same aspects that underlie characters should not also be at the core of all narrative. My following suggestion is based on Eder's work, with a slight difference in terminology to account for this widened scope. The first is the *synthetic aspect*, which focuses on the properties of the narrative as an artefact: by what means is it constructed, which artefactual properties does it have, how does it achieve certain aesthetic effects. The *mimetic aspect* focuses on the properties of the story world as if it was actual: what happens to whom and why, what emotional reactions could this elicit in readers. The *symbolic aspect*, in turn, focuses on indirect meaning that is transported through the narrative: symbols for concepts or entities from the actual world, morals conveyed by the plot, or general themes of the human condition raised by the story. Finally, the *symptomatic aspect* focuses on the role of the narrative in a socio-cultural context: the effects a narrative can have on real audiences, the forces and causes that led to its creation, or the structures of power that underlie its meaning-making mechanisms.

It is worth pointing out a few observations, here. The most general is that the mimetic aspect seems to correspond one to one to Currie's internal perspective, while only the synthetic, symbolic and symptomatic aspects taken together correspond to a holistic external perspective. Another one is that these aspects are cross-cutting concerns with regard to what I called the narrative phenomena above. In his reading of the fictional character Rick Blaine from the 1942 film *Casablanca*, Eder et al. (2010) demonstrate, how Rick's mimetic and synthetic properties come together to allow a (symbolic) interpretation of him as a symbol for the United States at the beginning of the second world war, and allow a (symptomatic) analysis of the image of masculinity promoted by this acclaimed performance. However, such an interpretation along the four aspects could also be performed on the plot of this film, or its implied reader. A last observation refers back to the comparison I made between NT and linguistics in Sec. 1.1, when I pointed out how the analytical approach of classical linguistics has been combined with the generative approach of natural language generation. Also in linguistics, language (as the object of study) is analyzed using different aspects: morphology, syntax, semantics, and pragmatics. This ability to break down a complex concept into different levels of abstraction was of great importance for enabling the exchange between classical and computational approaches. It thus seems worthwhile to also keep such a distinction close at hand for this exchange in NT.

1.3. Computational Creativity

Before I will come to the concepts that drive work on computational creativity (CC) I think it is important to provide a brief glance on the human side of creativity that fuels the interest of AI researchers in this topic.

1.3.1. Human Creativity

In everyday language, creativity is a widely applicable tag: great works of art like de Cervantes's (1605) novel *Don Quixote* are considered the results of creativity, but also activities like playing the Chinese game of Go can be said to demand creativity, and even everyday acts of petty problem solving, like fixing a bike without proper tools, are often referred to as creative. What is more surprising is that also the scientific community, despite empirically studying the concept and even developing tools to assess creativity in humans, could not agree on a common definition. In *The Cambridge Handbook of Creativity*, Plucker and Makel (2010, p. 48) write that "[d]espite the abundance of definitions of creativity and related terms, few are widely used and many researchers simply avoid defining the relevant terms at all". In their preface to the Handbook, the editors attempt to bring together three components that are common to most definitions:

> First, creative ideas must represent something different, new, or innovative. Second, creative ideas are of high quality. Third, creative ideas must also be appropriate to the task at hand or some redefinition of that task. Thus, a creative response is novel, good, and relevant.
> (Kaufman & Sternberg, 2010, p. xiii)

The problem with this attempt is that it focuses on ideas, that is the outcome of a creative act, but does not make any assertions about the cognitive process that produced this outcome. An influential distinction called "the Four P's of creativity" (Rhodes, 1961) refers to this as one of the four facets of creativity it posits. The facets are: product, process, person and place. As we have seen, the *product* facet focuses on properties of the outcomes of creativity, be it fully realized works of art or merely ideas that still need to be executed. The *process* facet focuses on the nature of the cognitive mechanisms and representations that occur during, and contribute to, creative thought. Another facet, *person*, focuses not on the process of creative thought, but rather on the properties and traits that are common in creative thinkers. Finally, the *place* facet focuses not on the traits of individuals but on properties of the settings that enable interactions between persons and environments that foster creative thought. These facets are useful labels to group related strands of research together, and explain differences between unrelated strands. However, it should be remembered that they are all views, from different directions but on the same phenomenon, which consequently should be considered a superposition of the individual views.

Another distinction of views considers the magnitude of creativity (see e.g. Kozbelt et al., 2010). The *Big C* perspective derives insights from focusing on unambiguous instances of creative thought (like the novel Don Quixote), outstanding people that repeatedly succeeded in producing such instances (like the Russian writer Lev Nikolayevich Tolstoy), or particular places that created environments where creative thinkers could strive (like the cafés of Paris during the Belle Époque). In contrast, the *little c* perspective focuses on more subjective experiences of creativity accessible to anyone in every day life, but again cross-cutting the facets person (like a development in the painting style of an amateur painter), process (like the reaching of a new developmental stage by a child), person (like the traits common to handymen) and place (like institutions that enable effective learning or problem solving). Sometimes, this dichotomy is also referred to as *H-creativity* (as in historical creativity, an idea new to mankind) versus *P-creativity* (as in psychological creativity, an idea new to a person), where the former is of course a special case of the latter (Boden, 2004, p. 2).

An influential position has been taken by the cognitive scientist Margaret Boden, who derives three different types of creativity from the three different meanings the adjective 'surprising' has (which is one of the properties products are commonly expected to exhibit, in order to be considered creative):

> An idea may be surprising because it's unfamiliar, or even unlikely—like a hundred-to-one outsider winning the Derby. This sort of surprise goes against statistics. The second sort of surprise is more interesting. An unexpected idea may 'fit' into a style of thinking that you already had—but you're surprised because you hadn't realized that this particular idea was part of it. Maybe you're even intrigued to find that an idea *of this general type* fits into the familiar style. And the third sort of surprise is more interesting still: this is the astonishment you feel on encountering an apparently *impossible* idea. It just *couldn't* have entered anyone's head, you feel—and yet it did.
>
> (emphasis as in Boden, 2004, p. 3)

The first type of surprise, according to Boden, is directed at results of *combinational creativity*, which appears when familiar concepts and ideas are combined in a new way. A natural example of this is analogy, like for instance seeing the atom as a solar system, which has become known as the Rutherford-Bohr model in atomic physics. The second type of surprise arises from perceiving *exploratory creativity*, which appears when new concepts and ideas are discovered by following established conventions of the domain or accepted stylistic rules. This can lead to masterful results that surprise by the virtue that it is possible to create them by following conventions in certain ways. An example for this could be George Eliot's (1871) novel *Middlemarch* that is considered one of the greatest works of literary realism, a genre whose conventions and central tenet (that objective reality can be perceived by the senses and described in language) had been established early in the 19th century, long before the publication of that novel. The third type of surprise, finally, is aroused by *transformational creativity*, which appears when the rules and conventions that are accepted in a field or genre are altered in a way that allows the creation of concepts that were previously impossible. This can be exemplified by the rise of literary modernism, a genre that overturned the previously accepted tenet of a perceivable objective reality and replaced it with the idea that reality is merely a subjective construction by individuals. This lead to the development of novel stylistic devices like unreliable narration or the stream-of-consciousness, and allowed the creation of contentious novels like James Joyce's (1922) *Ulysses*.

The metaphor that serves as the foundation for these three types of creativity is that of the *conceptual space*. Conceptual spaces are culture-dependent "structured styles of thought" (Boden, 2004, p. 4), which define how one idea or concept can be created from another idea. Based on such traversal rules certain regions of a conceptual space are quickly explored by a culture and become common knowledge, resulting in a network of (unsurprising) ideas. Consider the conceptual space of literary devices for expressing abstract themes, in which poets operate when they compose. In such a space, one common style of thought would be to describe situations that are connected to, or evocative of, a theme. For instance, to express longing one could describe a lover's reminiscence of a deceased partner of a lifetime, or portray an expatriate recalling memories of his distant home. While strongly evocative, these ideas have been explored countless times and might be of limited interest to a poet, who would forgo them because they have become trite, and rather look for novel ways of expressing this theme. Creativity, as we can see, can be understood as search for novel and valuable ideas in an appropriate conceptual space. Combinational creativity, then, is the combination of ideas in a well explored region of the space, that by themselves would either not be novel or valuable, but taken together result in a new idea. Our poet, if she were combinationally inclined, could combine the two ideas above and express longing by describing the memories of a person thinking about an exiled lover. This results in a blend that equates exile with death and reverses the focus from the one deported to the ones left behind, thus exposing uncommon sides of two seemingly well-known clichés. The second type, exploratory creativity, corresponds to following the established traversal rules of the conceptual space until they end up in a previously unexplored region of the space. In our example, one candidate situation that could be considered by the poet to evoke longing is that of a train leaving the station and speeding towards the horizon. While in modern times this, too, might be considered trite, for someone during the age of the industrial revolution this situation in itself would have been completely novel and its connection to longing unexplored. This demonstrates the ability of conceptual spaces to grow and incorporate new ideas, resulting in an abundance of potential for exploratory creativity despite the constant exploration performed by creative thinkers. The last type, transformational creativity, is associated with the introduction of new traversal rules into an existing space. This results in its transformation into a completely new space because it allows the enmeshment of concepts that were impossible to reach previously. The space of literary devices for expressing abstract themes, that we considered so far, only allowed to "describe situations that are connected to, or evocative of, a theme", which, effectively, restricted it to a space of situations. A transformational insight for a poet could be that longing can be evoked not only representationally, by descriptions of situations, but also by means of form—like grammar or syntax—which results in the addition of a novel "style of thought" allowing the consideration of grammatical devices inducing longing in a reader, which fundamentally alters the nature of ideas available in that conceptual space and allows the fortunate poet to discover the value of overly long parenthetical sentences (like the present) in triggering a reader's longing for conclusion by a delay of the use of punctuation. In contrast to exploratory creativity, the transformational type is not a search over concepts but a search over conceptual spaces; in particular for spaces that allow to find previously inaccessible ideas.

1.3.2. Computational Forays into Creativity

Instances of H-creativity are widely revered by mankind and humans often engage in P-creativity, so it is no wonder that the phenomenon has sparked ample interest in AI. This has led to varied experimental research, typically through the engineering of systems that are capable of solving tasks that require creativity in humans. Indeed, machines have repeatedly demonstrated their ability to generate creative outputs. For instance, Google Translate[10] can deliver high-quality translations of texts, that were not used during its training, into many different languages (an act that would be considered P-creative in humans), and in 2016 DeepMind's Alpha Go beat the human world champion in a five-game match of Go (something that could well be considered H-creative in itself, but especially so because Alpha Go's style of playing has been described as surprising and unconventional[11]). However, in the general public there still remains a wide spread conviction that computers cannot be genuinely creative. Boden presents some of the arguments made in support of this position:

> For instance, it's the programmer's creativity that's at work here, not the machine's. The machine isn't conscious, and has no desires, preferences or values, so it can't appreciate or judge what it's doing. A work of art is an expression of human experience and/or a communication between human beings, so machines simply don't count.
>
> (Boden, 2004, p. 7)

AI researcher Simon Colton (2008) experienced similar reactions to his CC systems and summarized them into three avenues of criticism: *skill, appreciation* and *imagination*, from which he inferred that in order to appear creative a system needs to "exhibit behavior which could be described as skillful, appreciative and imaginative" (a notion he called the *creative tripod*) although without being able to outline which concrete properties could make a behavior qualify as one of these three. Another set of objections was described by AI researcher Dan Ventura (2019), after analyzing three surveys about the possibility of CC conducted among different audiences. His conclusion was that a system needs to demonstrate *intentionality* and *autonomy* in order to be judged creative. These are all notoriously slippery

---

[10]https://translate.google.com/

[11]For instance, European Go champion Fan Hui commented on the decisive move 37 of game two, made by the system: "I've never seen a human play this move. So beautiful." (https://www.theatlantic.com/technology/archive/2016/03/the-invisible-opponent/475611/)

concepts, but what they imply is that in order to earn the label creative, machines need to pursue a goal or objective when they generate outputs, that they need the ability to evaluate to what extent their output satisfies that goal, that they need to have some measure of freedom in the goals they pursue and the means they select to obtain them, and that all of this needs to be done well. It seems that when it comes to creativity, algorithms are held to a somewhat higher standard than human individuals, in whom many of these properties are simply presupposed.

In fact, it should not come as a surprise that it is hard to convince the public that a machine could be creative, given that there exists no accepted definition of what constitutes creativity in humans. This led the field to two conclusions. The first is that a focus on the product aspect of creativity in CC research is simply not enough: the *mere generation* of (perhaps even large numbers of high quality) outputs for the programmer to curate and the audience to judge does not plausibly warrant the use of the label creative. Instead, generation needs to be coupled and influenced by an awareness of the quality, novelty, and utility of the generated output. The second conclusion is that CC cannot just be a scientific and engineering discipline, but must also be a philosophical one, because it targets a phenomenon that so far cannot be grasped only by empirical means. This resulted in the adoption of the following self-conception by the field: "The philosophy, science and engineering of computational systems which, by taking on particular responsibilities, exhibit behaviors that unbiased observers would deem to be creative." (Colton & Wiggins, 2012) It should be noted, that this manifesto does not explicitly mention the study or implementation of human means for creativity. While a certain amount of overlap can be expected in any case, in order for the "exhibited behaviors" to be recognizable as creative by "unbiased observers", this leaves the door open for processes that are not inspired by human creativity. For this reason, AI researcher Rafel Pérez y Pérez (2018) suggested the use of a *computational creativity continuum* in order to judge whether and how different CC systems can be compared. On the one side of the continuum is the *cognitive-social approach*, whose adherents focus on the study of human creativity using technology from AI to implement and test models of creativity. They typically judge the success of their approaches not by the quality of the artefacts generated by their systems, but by how well certain phenomena can be reproduced that have been observed in naturally creative situations. On the other side of the continuum is the *engineering-mathematical approach*, which applies when existing computational optimization or problem-solving techniques are adapted and transferred to creative domains. Here, success is judged based more on the merits of the generated outputs and the projectability of certain adjectives on the process by which they were generated. As it is natural to continua, most actual systems do not fall squarely onto one end or the other, but are best located somewhere in between.

1.3.3. Important Responsibilities for Creative Appearances

CC systems need to be more than sophisticated tools like Adobe Photoshop, which can produce surprising effects but have no intentionality or autonomy. In order to do so, according to the above manifesto, CC systems need to take on particular 'creative' responsibilities. Under the acronym FACE, Colton et al. (2011) have suggested four main types of responsibilities that play a role in creative acts and thus should be implemented in a CC system. These responsibilities are called: framing, aesthetic evaluation, concept generation and expression of concept. Their interrelation is schematically depicted in Fig. 1.4, and will be outlined now.

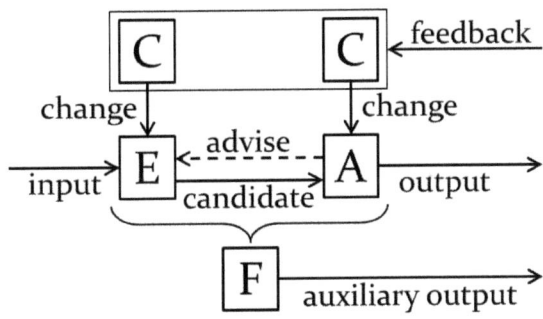

Figure 1.4: Interrelation of creative responsibilities in a CC system. The responsibilities, represented as rectangles, are: framing, aesthetic evaluation, concept generation and expression of concept.

Expression of concept, in this terminology, means the generation of a candidate output based on an algorithm, which can potentially take inputs and is parametrizable, such that the output can be varied by the system. As I explained above, this can be seen as a search in a conceptual space, but not yet quite seems to fit the moniker exploratory creativity because the system has no way of determining whether it found a satisfying concept.

Aesthetic evaluation can be understood as the application of a function that takes as input the candidate output of an algorithm responsible for expression of concept, and computes a numerical value representing its appropriateness. The candidate is considered a valid output only if it passes a certain threshold. Appropriateness needs to be determined depending on the domain of the system, but in general it should be geared towards assessing the properties that we above described as important for creative products: quality, novelty, and utility. The interaction between E and A can be understood as a mere generate-and-test procedure that filters out bad candidates, but it could also be a more complex iterative process where E generates more and more elaborate drafts which it revises and expands based on feedback from A. Both these approaches, however, would be regarded instances of exploratory creativity according to Boden.

Concept generation stands for the ability to create executable algorithms, or at least make changes to existing algorithms that go beyond mere parameter manipulation. In particular, this means the autonomous ability to change how the system performs aesthetic evaluation or concept expression, for instance based on feedback that the system receives from its environment. This expands the system's creative responsibilities to a meta level, where it is also responsible for autonomously adopting the ways it is creative, a capability that is central in order to counter the line of criticism that sees CC systems only as expressions of a human programmers creativity. Since changing the way candidates are generated and evaluated alters what types of outputs the system can generate, this corresponds to a modification of the traversal rules in a concept space in Boden's terminology, and can be considered transformational creativity. It is not exactly clear, whether learning[12] can be considered an approach to concept generation or not. On the one hand, expanding a systems knowledge base does result in a fundamental change to what types of outputs can be generated, and if previously generated outputs by the system are taken into account by the learning algorithm it does operate on a meta level. On the other hand, GOFAI learning does not change

---

[12]Here, I refer to learning in the Good Old Fashioned AI (GOFAI) sense, which means expanding the system's knowledge base, as opposed to learning in the machine learning sense, which, in its barest essence, means changing parameter values. This distinction is important to make, since changes of parameter values clearly correspond to responsibility E, expression of concept.

the procedures that are employed in generation and evaluation, so it does not really fit the description of concept generation. In any case, learning based on feedback from the environment can go a long way in enhancing the system's appearance of creativity.

Framing is the ability to generate natural language information that discloses details about some parts of the creative act. These can include, but is not limited to, the intention that initially guided the generation, details about decisions made during the generation, properties of the output that lead to a positive evaluation, or how any of this relates to previous outputs. This becomes necessary because without framing information the workings of a CC system remain opaque to the audience, who only can consume its outputs and might as well assume these to be the result of a random process instead of an algorithm that takes up creative responsibilities. In fact, human artists often come up with framing information (Charnley et al., 2012), which is another reason to regard this as a valid creative responsibility. An interesting consideration is that with human artists, it is not always clear whether such framing information contains valid descriptions of their creative process (which might be partially subconscious), or intentional fabrications to project a certain persona. Equally, it would be possible to enable a CC system to generate fake framing information that enhances its appearance of creativity. However, the ethical side of such an approach would have to be carefully reflected.

Apart from a useful way for comparing CC systems that operate in different domains, the FACE framework can also act as a guideline for the development of such systems. Each aspiring creative system starts out with some capabilities, while responsibilities outside these capabilities are usually taken up by the developer. For instance, an early story composition system might generate murder mysteries, but the developer would have to carefully curate those that are coherent in order to publish a paper in a prestigious journal. A more advanced system might be capable of generating the stories and then discarding those that are nonsensical, but if the developer were now inclined to have a folktale generated instead, they would have to implement additional domain knowledge and different plot structures. The suggested developmental principle is referred to as *climbing the meta mountain*, and calls for developers to carefully observe which responsibilities they take up in conjunction with their CC system, and to strive to enable the system to perform these tasks on its own.

1.4. Computational Story Composition

There exists an abundance of computational systems that generate narratives[13], but little theory that could unify these works into a coherent field. A first, very general, distinction can be made based on the field from which a system stems: Story composition systems *from computational creativity* focus on enabling a computer to generate any number of narratives, as long as these narratives are 'good', and by that merit allow to view the composing system as creative. Work of this type is presented at the annual International Conference for Computational Creativity. Composition systems *from interactive digital storytelling*, in contrast, focus on telling one particular narrative while allowing readers as much meaningful influence over it as possible. The two main venues for work of this type are the annual International Conference on Interactive Digital Storytelling and the annual conference on Artificial Intelligence and Interactive Digital Entertainment. Unfortunately, collaborations between these two fields are rare. Since my focus is on the interaction of concepts from NT and their implementation using AI, I do not regard this distinction a particularly important factor, and think that both fields could benefit by an increased exchange over their shared interest: how narrative can be represented computationally. When looking at computational representations of narrative, a more interesting distinction between systems can be derived from the way they handle the trade-offs necessary when operationalizing NT concepts. One particularly influential distinction is that between strong story systems and strong autonomy systems (see e.g. Riedl & Bulitko, 2013), which should be viewed as a continuum between these two poles.

As a last general remark before exploring this continuum, I want to point out that most (if not all) CSC systems borrow freely from NT in order to find representational formalisms for narratives (see

---

[13]The latest attempt to collect the existing systems was published by Kybartas and Bidarra (2017) and is based on a monumental review of more than 100 references. By 2020, it lacks several new systems, and historical research by James Ryan also uncovered several older systems that are not included in this review. This is by no means a shortcoming on the side of the authors, but rather a testament to the Sisyphean nature of the task.

e.g. Cavazza & Pizzi, 2006), but, to the best of my knowledge, none of the work on generative models was intended to contribute back to NT, or explore the nature of narrative per se. As I argued in Sec. 1.1 on the motivation of my thesis, I view this as a missed opportunity, and attempt to explore the feasibility of using generative models to explore the dynamic properties of narratological theories.

1.4.1. Strong Autonomy Systems

Strong autonomy systems can be seen as grounded in an internal perspective on narratives, and put their focus on modeling fictional characters as agents that have varying intentions, stable traits and values, and an internal state that is affected by their environment. These characters act autonomously in order to realize their intentions, and plot emerges from their interactions with each other and the story world. For this reason, this paradigm is also referred to as *emergent narrative* systems. The strength of this approach is that it results in believable characters, whose actions appear to be plausible and goal directed.

A major drawback, however, is that such a lack of global guiding principles usually results in plots that lack structure and coherence, simply because plausible character goals rarely coincide with authorial goals from the external perspective: Authors, in general, are interested in a thickening network of conflicts during the beginning phase, and their gradual resolution towards the end of a narrative[14], whereas characters are interested in resolving conflicts as quickly and easily as possible, with no regards for tension, symmetry, or the elegance of the resulting interactions. Since character believability and plot coherence are both important properties for a narrative, but are seemingly at odds with each other here, this can be called the *emergent narrative paradox*.[15] In his dissertation, James J. Ryan (2018,

---

[14]This is, of course, a generalization and oversimplification of dramatic structure, and exceptions can be easily found. Most notably, all open-ended plots leave some conflicts unresolved and thus do not follow the described recipe. However, I would claim that is a form of baseline structure that readers have come to expect, and deviation from which results in heighten readerly attention or surprise.

[15]The emergent narrative paradigm was originally suggested as a solution to another paradox in interactive fiction by Aylett (2000). This so-called "narrative paradox" lies in the incommensurateness of scripted characters (that are required for a coherent plot) with user autonomy (that is required to make a narrative truly interactive). It thus seems appropriate to me to refer to the resurgence of this problem in its intended solution as the emergent narrative paradox.

p. 12) argues that "emergent narrative actually works more like non-fiction than fiction". This can be observed quite well in the output of early strong autonomy systems like Meehan's (1977) Tale-Spin, which generates fable-like animal stories. One (in)famous instance goes:

> John Bear is somewhat hungry. John Bear wants to get some berries. John Bear wants to get near the blueberries. John Bear walks from a cave entrance to the bush by going through a pass through a valley through a meadow. John Bear takes the blueberries. John Bear eats the blueberries. The blueberries are gone. John Bear is not very hungry.
>
> (Gervás, 2009, p. 53)

Ignoring the obvious problems with regard to prose, this text also seems to hardly qualify as a narrative due to a lack of plot: there is no structure, no tension and no point. In fact, it seems more like a chronicle of events than like a story that would have the potential to be told.

One solution the proponents of the strong autonomy camp came up with is the introduction of a specific module—variously called *drama manager* or director—that analyzes the events that are emerging from character interactions and can exert some sort of influences on them in order to steer the interactions in a narratively more productive direction. In the Oz-project system (Kelso et al., 1993) and the Façade system (Mateas & Stern, 2002) the drama manager acts prescriptively, in that it can provide characters with new goals that are likely to result in behaviors that come together in a plot. In the Virtual Storyteller system (Theune et al., 2003) the drama manager is limited to acting proscriptive, in that characters choose their goals on their own but are required to get the drama manager's permission for their actions so that it can prevent events that would be detrimental to plot. The additional guidance, naturally, comes at the cost of a decrease in character autonomy, and depending on its execution moves systems further towards the strong story side along the continuum.[16]

In contrast, J. Ryan (2018) suggests in his dissertation that the solution is not to find a balance between emergence and guiding interventions, but instead to double down on the autonomy of story

---

[16]In particular, presenting Mateas and Stern's (2002) Façade system under the caption of strong autonomy makes me feel uneasy since the drama manager provides characters with whole beats to play out. However, the authors themselves refer to their characters as "behavior-based autonomous agents", which probably means that Façade should be located around the center of the continuum.

world and characters. Since meaningful structures are not very likely to emerge from the simulated interactions of characters, he argues, the simulation needs to be more complex in order to provide enough interactions so that some of them will form a plot by sheer chance. The more characters interact, the more dynamics are guiding these interactions, and the longer a simulation runs, the more potential there is to detect interesting configurations of events in the chronicle of everything that happened. Hence, an emergentist system must first run complex simulations, and then sift through the abundance of generated material to identify configurations that fit a meaningful structure. He summarizes his position in the tag-line "overgenerate and curate" (J. Ryan, 2018, p. 227), and accordingly calls his approach *curationist emergent narrative*. This is also the reason why he prefers to see emergent narratives as non-fiction and computational storytelling more as historiography in the sense of Hayden White (1981).

As will become apparent in the coming chapters, the story composition system that I developed in my project, too, falls into the category of strong autonomy systems. In my conclusions presented in Chap. 6 I will return to Ryan's position, in the hope to demonstrate that emergent narrative systems can also be grounded in NT, and still address the emergent narrative paradox. In order to have a catchy label to go along with Ryan's, and also provide a cliffhanger that keeps readers engaged, I will here only dub the approach developed in my thesis *creationist emergent narrative*, and flesh the name out in the concluding chapter.

1.4.2. Strong Story Systems

Strong story systems commonly model the events and the plot that is comprised from them. They focus on artefactual goals like maintaining coherence, a strong sense of organization and the potential for an emergence of secondary meaning. That is, considerations important to the external perspective on narrative. For this reason, characters are primarily understood as second-order entities: necessary effectors of plot events that have no dynamic internal states that might be causally responsible for their actions. This is also the major drawback of this approach because it is hard to project believable character behavior without genuinely modeling notions like intention or personality.

One way to ensure the coherence of a plot is to rely on a formal grammar, that uses production rules to describe how events can proceed from one another, or how higher order plot functions can be instantiated by lower order functions and events. A recent example is Gervás's (2016) Propper system, that implements a story grammar of Russian folktales as described by the formalist Vladimir Propp (1968). Plots, in this formalism, are described as a succession of interdependent character functions (like "villany" or "villain punished"), that can appear in a clearly defined order and that offer roles (like "hero" or "villain") which stand in for characters.

Another approach is to rely on an explicit modeling of the story world, which has a predefined start state and one or several desirable end states (which are desirable because they achieve some authorial goal). Plot, then, can be seen as a sequence of state transitions that can transform the start state into an end state, where each transition is effectively an action that is executed by a character. The computation of such valid transition sequences can be achieved using classical reasoning techniques like forward chaining or backward chaining. One particular line of research is especially interesting here because it attempts to address the main drawback of strong story systems. Riedl's (2004) planing system IPOCL uses backward chaining to come up with an action sequence that transforms the start state into the goal state, but with the additional constraint that an action can be only assigned to a character if it also works towards achieving an intention that this character has. Intentions can be assigned to characters arbitrarily by the planer, but once assigned have to be respected for the rest of the planning branch. This contributes to an appearance of goal directed behavior. A recent extension of this paradigm was introduced by Bahamon's (2016) system Mask, which was designed to portray character personality along the trait agreeableness. Whenever several actions exist that the planning system can choose from to effect a desired transformation, these actions are evaluated as agreeable or non-agreeable by checking whether they interfere with other characters' intentions or not. If the evaluation shows that there is a choice available between actions that portray different expressions of this traits, then the system picks one in accordance with the executing character's personality (or assigns the character a personality by choosing randomly, if it previously had none). This allows Mask to increase character believability by creating an impression of consistently 'good' or 'bad' characters, and demonstrates that strong story approaches can be constrained in a way that also allows a measure of character autonomy. It is particularly heartening, that the empirical evaluation reported in Bahamon's (2016) dissertation shows that such an action selection based on underlying character traits can result in plots that convey the correct impression of this underlying trait to an audience.

In Chap. 3 I will report how the story composition system that I developed in my project models characters' personality along the traits openness to experience, conscientiousness, extraversion, agreeableness and neuroticism. Since my approach, as mentioned above, is located in the strong autonomy camp, the way this is realized is markedly different from the one reported here since it cannot rely on the detection of choice-situations by a macro planer. Instead, personality is conceived as one of the relevant character phenomena, which interacts with other such phenomena, like emotions or moods, and results in an dynamic internal state that affects how characters reason and act. The empirical evaluation I will report in that chapter is based on the one conducted on Mask, and I am grateful for this inspiration, as well as the opportunity to demonstrate how very different intellectual positions and technological means can be used to computationally model the same narratological phenomenon.

1.4.3. Cognitive Approaches

The distinction between strong autonomy and strong story is mainly based on technological considerations and the trade-offs that have to be made when computationally modeling narrative. However, it seems that also human authors are privy to such problems, at least anecdotally. In an interview with the British newspaper The Guardian, the novelist George R.R. Martin presented his trade as having two basic dispositions:

> I think there are two types of writers, the architects and the gardeners. [...] The architects plan everything ahead of time, like an architect building a house. They know how many rooms are going to be in the house, what kind of roof they're going to have, where the wires are going to run, what kind of plumbing there's going to be. They have the whole thing designed and blueprinted out before they even nail the first board up. The gardeners dig a hole, drop in a seed and water it. They kind of know what seed it is, they know if they planted a fantasy seed or mystery seed or whatever. But as the plant comes up and they water it, they don't know how many branches it's going to have, they

find out as it grows.

(Flood, 2011)

This description so acutely echoes the distinction I presented before that I would not have been surprised to find it in a scientific publication to the ICCC instead of The Guardian. It brings to the fore the idea, that perhaps some difficulties encountered by the field are not only due to technological limitations, but also to the cognitive affordances of the task of composing narrative. This perspective is what lies behind a third type of approach to CSC, which focuses on modeling the cognitive processes that are assumed to implement creative writing in human authors. Since also human authors, by necessity, have to think about plot coherence and character believability, this approach is not completely detached from the distinction discussed above. They should rather be seen as cross-cutting concerns.

One of the first notable systems to go this way is S. R. Turner's (1993) Minstrel, which explores case-based reasoning. It operates in two stages: a (first) planning stage that operates on authorial goals, which can be either decomposed into sub-goals or passed on to the second stage that is focused on problem solving. Problem solving is performed by querying an episodic-memory like knowledge base that contains fragments from which previous stories were built. If no fragment fitting precisely to the query can be found, the query is made successively more and more abstract through a chain of transformations, until a fitting fragment can be identified, which is then adapted back to the present situation by applying the reversed chain of transformations. The creative potential of the Minstrel system lies in the ability of these transformations to identify not easily recognizable matches, which correspond to unexpected solutions to authorial problems.

Another approach is taken by Pérez y Pérez's (1999) system MEXICA, which implements a psychological model of creative writing in which phases of engagement—where material is generated in order to satisfy authorial constraints—interchange with phases of reflection—where the generated content is analyzed and new constraints are formulated—in a cycle. Plot is represented as a sequence of networks of emotional links between characters, from which the tension arc of the plot can be computed, and the actions that were taken to transform one network of the sequence into the next one. The system has a library of known narratives represented in this format, as well as an ideal tension arc that plots should follow. Starting from a user-selected action during engagement, MEXICA first expands the plot by searching its library for actions that were taken in the same (or, if none are to be found, in 50% similar) networks and applying them to the present state of the plot. After repeating this step for several times, or running out of options, the system switches into reflection mode, where it evaluates whether all the preconditions for the selected actions were met, whether the plot follows a desirable tension arc, and how similar it is to already known narratives. From this evaluation, it can add individual actions at any step of the plot in order to satisfy any open preconditions, and issue guidelines for the subsequent engagement step, which affect what actions are preferred when querying the knowledge base.

1.5. Reader's Guide

To decide on the structure of a thesis at the intersection of NT and CSC is not a straightforward task. As I discussed when presenting my RQ 3 in Sec. 1.1, research methodologies in AI and NT differ, and both methodologies have their own benefits and drawbacks which are rooted in the different challenges that are posed by the two disciplines. In particular, the linear succession of theory-implementation-evaluation of AI research provides the structure that is necessary to concretize abstract concepts into executable code, and then verify that the code indeed addresses the original problem. However, it is hard to transport this methodology into the narratological domain, which does not formulate quantifiable metrics of success and operates in concepts that are specified at a high level of abstraction. On the other hand, the hermeneutically grounded iterative interaction of theory formation and text analysis of NT is well suited for the development of concepts from a complex and diverse subject matter like narrative, but has no place for the generative type of models that I am interested in. This makes it clear why, for the present thesis, it is not sufficient to simply follow one of the two research styles. Instead, I will now outline an approach I call *generative modeling*, which attempts to merge the styles in a way that solves the above drawbacks, and that I adopted as the guideline for my work as well as the structure of my thesis. This means that, in essence, my thesis itself is intended to be an answer to RQ 3, by way of demonstration that generative modeling is a suitable approach for the exchange between NT and CSC.

The proposed generative modeling methodology is schematically represented in Fig. 1.5. The starting point is a narrative theory, that

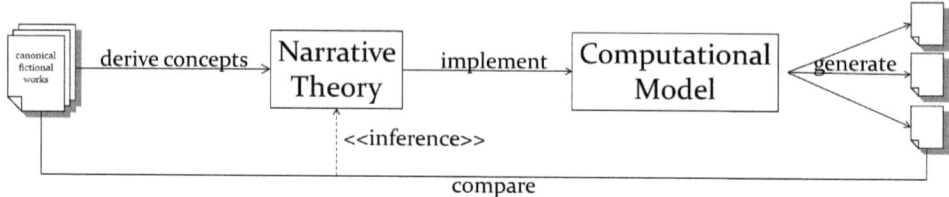

Figure 1.5: The proposed generative modeling methodology for NT and CSC.

is either personally developed or adopted from prior work. In both cases, the theory can be assumed to be grounded in a set of canonical fictional works. Then, a first pass is made at implementing that theory in a generative computational model, while concretizing underspecified concepts as one goes along. When the implementation is complete, the model is used in an attempt to reproduce a set of canonical works. The outputs can then be compared to the original works, and if differences between them become apparent, insights can be drawn on the shortcomings of the employed theory and its implementation. This concludes one cycle of generative modeling. In practice, as I mentioned above, concepts from NT are not likely to yield easily to implementation, so that multiple cycles will become necessary, in which the implementation and the theory are expanded until the generated outputs sufficiently resemble their canonical counterparts. At this stage, additional canonical works can be added to the corpus, and the process can be continued.

The proposed methodology has several benefits: First, it circumvents the problem of missing numerical evaluation criteria in NT, by instead relying on a comparison of generated artefact to existing ground truth narratives. Second, it proposes a way for drawing narratological insights from generation instead of analysis. It does so by relying on the assumption that if the first principles posited by a narratological theory are sufficient to describe the structure of a narrative, then the narrative should be reproducible from these first principles. If, in practice, such a reproduction does not succeed, then the first principles must be insufficient and the theory needs to be expanded in order to account for the problems.[17] Third, the methodology retains the hermeneutical approach of an iterative revision of the theory based on exposure to the material, which has been demonstrated to work well in the literary domain. Finally, the generative computational model that has been developed to implement a narrative theory can not only be used to recreate existing works, but also to generate new works by exploring alternative parameter settings. It thus can be employed as a part of a creative CSC algorithm, especially taking over responsibilities for the expression of concepts and the aesthetic evaluation of candidates (see Fig. 1.6 for a visual representation of this overlap between NT and CC).

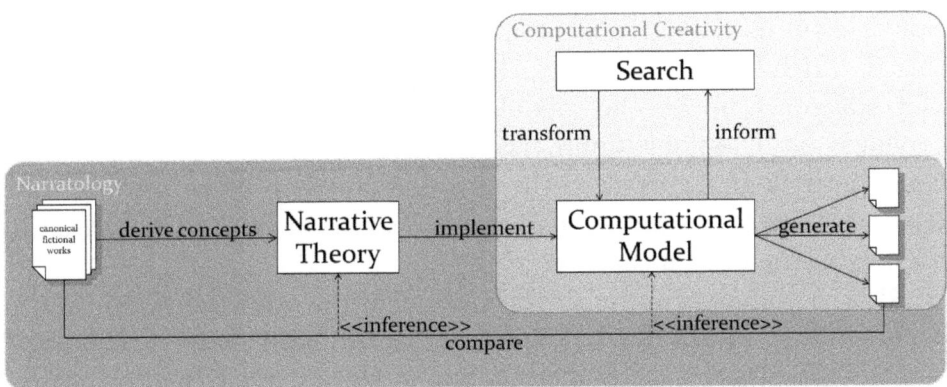

Figure 1.6: A schematic representing how generative modeling brings together NT and CC. While NT contributes an approach to improving computational models of narrative, CC assists in searching for unconventional outputs that can be generated by this models.

As I pointed out above, the rest of the present thesis is organized based on this methodology. Each chapter represents one cycle of generative modeling. This means that each chapter will be divided in the parts: theory, implementation and case study, where the case study will lead to an evaluation of that cycle. In Chapter 2, I will introduce Marie-Laure Ryan's possible worlds theory of plot, implement it using a multi-agent simulation system, but ultimately fail to reproduce

---

[17]A complicating factor, here, is that a failure to reproduce a narrative might not be caused by the narrative theory in question but by its implementation. Consequently, I would not claim that one cycle of generative modeling is always enough to demonstrate the shortcomings of a theory. Instead, multiple cycles might be necessary to improve the computational model, until the problems cannot be traced to technical details of the implementation anymore.

the plot of a popular folktale using that implementation. Based on this result, in Chapter 3, I will propose an extension of Ryan's theory based on Alan Palmer's concept of fictional minds, which I will implement using an affective reasoning architecture, and demonstrate that the resulting implementation can reproduce the plot of the folktale from my case study. In order to surpass mere generation, I will continue in Chapter 4 by introducing Ryan's theory of tellability as a measure of plot quality, implement it using graph analysis algorithms and evaluate it based on a variety of alternative versions of the folktale from my case study. In Chapter 5, I will have to part ways with NT, in order to demonstrate that the benefits of my approach are not limited to the narratological domain, but that the resulting models can also be used for the generation of plots in a CSC system. For this, I will introduce Genetic Algorithms as a means to explore the plot space set up by the models developed so far. Chapter 6 will conclude my thesis by summarizing the final system, presenting the contributions of my work to the two domains it bridges, and by that means attempt to address the three research questions I proposed in the beginning of this chapter.

Before commencing with the next chapter, and the cycle that it constitutes, I would like to offer a conjecture and make a request. I can imagine that, as a reader, it might feel unsatisfying to have to read through Chapter 2 while already knowing that it is bound to fail, indeed, to repeatedly have to mentally switch between theory, implementation and evaluation without first knowing the complete picture. My request is this: to read this thesis not as the manual to a ready-made and well-formed (conceptual) gizmo, but rather as the narrative of an intellectual journey, that is, to curiously go along with the flow and judge the experience at the end, when the overall shape has revealed itself.

I consider that a man's brain originally is like a little empty attic [. . .]. Now the skillful workman is very careful indeed as to what he takes into his brain-attic. He will have nothing but the tools which may help him in doing his work, but of these he has a large assortment [. . .].

Arthur Conan Doyle, 'A Study in Scarlet'

2

The Narrative System

WHEN SETTING OUT TO enable the computational composition of narratives, an important concern is to understand what a narrative is. In a computational setting this requires a deconstruction of this complex concept into its constituent phenomena and their interactions. Such a reconstruction has to be rigorous, as any phenomenon missing in the analysis cannot be represented by the computational model and hence will be either completely missing in the generated narratives, or worse, will emerge unintended from an interaction of the represented parts and each individual reading process.

A classical example for such formally unwarranted emergence has been documented by Heider and Simmel (1944), who presented participants with a short cinematic sequence depicting "three geometrical figures [. . .] moving in various directions and at various speeds" (p. 244, for one frame see Fig. 2.1). When asked to report what they saw, all but one participant described the scene in terms of social, animated beings partaking in anthropomorphic interactions like fights or love-making, that is, they described it using a narrative form. What is more, when prompted, participants even ascribed the geometrical shapes with anthropomorphic traits like "bad-tempered", "a fighter" or "female" just based on their shape, size and movement, demon-

43

strating the mind's immense propensity for superimposing a narrative structure on its raw perception stream. Reports like these led psychologist Jerome Bruner to go as far as elevating narrativized thinking[1] to one of two fundamental modes of cognitive functioning (Bruner, 1986, Chapter 2).

At first sight, this willingness to find narratives in chaos might seem like an alleviating factor for computational systems aiming at generating them because it implies that less strict standards are necessary for their outputs to be recognized as such. However, even if unrepresented phenomena *can* emerge during the reading of a narrative, their effect can by no means be accounted for, controlled or affected by a generating system. Since the aim of a CSC system is not to just create any narrative but to create a good narrative, while at the same time conveying the impression of intentionality

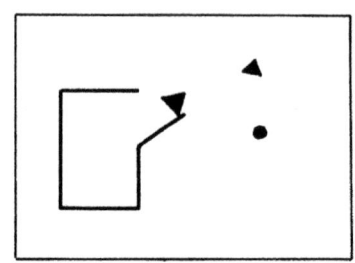

Figure 2.1: A frame from the cinematic sequence Fritz Heider and Marianne Simmel presented to their participants. The triangles and the circle are commonly perceived as characters, while the broken square is seen as a house. Figure from Heider and Simmel (1944).

(for the rationale behind this, see Section 1.3), such arbitrariness is not conducive.

A second constraint on the deconstruction of narrative into phenomena is the required low level of abstraction, since both the structure and the dynamic properties of a phenomenon need to be implemented in computer code. All underspecification or recourse to higher level concepts result in ambiguities which have to be resolved ad-hoc by the system designer in order to even just get a first result from the system. While such gaps are unavoidable, their number and size affect how complicated, in the case of a failure, it will be to infer the responsible ad-hoc solution from an undesired output (i.e. an output that does not resemble a natural narrative). Thus, the deconstruction of choice has an immense impact on the performance of the result-

---

[1]Bruner describes the narrative mode as interpreting events via "human or human-like intention and action and the vicissitudes and consequences that mark their course" (Bruner, 1986, p. 13) and opposes it with the "logico-scientific" mode.

explicitly specify all properties of its TAW. Yet still, readers are often found capable of answering questions about such gaps. Recall from Sec. 1.2.2, that, asked about the number of legs in command of fictional Mr. Bloom, any reader will insist to know the answer for two—despite the fact that the truth value of this proposition is never mentioned by the text. Ryan explains this situation with another central tenet of the phenomenology of reading, which she dubs the *Principle of Minimal Departure*. This principle states that gaps in TAW will be filled by readers by tacitly importing knowledge from AW, unless such an import is explicitly countermanded by the text, intertextual conventions, or genre conventions (M.-L. Ryan, 1991, p. 51). Whether this implies that TAWs are ontologically complete—that is that all possible logical propositions about a TAW are either true or false—has been a topic of debate. As we have seen, a question often used to illustrate this situation is how many children Lady Macbeth had in Shakespeare's (1623) near eponymous tragedy. Since an answer to this question cannot be provided by AW-based common sense logic it remains an ontological gap even in the face of the Principle of Minimal Departure. While some argue that such gaps are of relevance for a texts aesthetics, like e.g. its "texture" (Doležel, 1998), others propose that for each possible reification of a gap simply a distinct TAW should be postulated (M.-L. Ryan, 1991). This debate is mentioned here because of its relevance for the theory, however, for generative purposes like the present it can be safely left unresolved since all phenomena generated by a computational systems must be explicitly covered by its knowledge base anyway.

2.1.2. Structure

The two principles introduced above imply that the nature of this postulated system is recursive. If mental acts—like counterfactual thinking or narrative telling—in the AW set up PWs (fictional recentering), and the functioning of characters in TAW can be mostly inferred from the functioning of actual individuals[3] (minimal departure), then the mental acts of characters should also be analyzed as setting up textual possible worlds (TPWs), branching from the center that is the TAW. M.-L. Ryan (1991, p. 111) suggests three types of mental operations that set up different categories of character's

---

[3]This thesis will be discussed extensively in Section 3.2 on fictional minds.

private (textual) possible worlds: epistemic, axiological and deontic thought acts, resulting in the creation of knowledge, wish and obligation worlds.

- *Knowledge (K) World*: contains all propositions regarding a character's beliefs about the complete system, that is, the TAW or other character's private worlds. While K-Worlds can be incomplete, or conflicting with regard to other worlds, for a character they form their subjective, complete reality. All other private worlds of a character are defined in relation to its K World, and all of a character's thinking as well as planning is performed on propositions from this world.

- *Wish (W) World*: "capture[s] how a character would like the [TAW] to be" (M.-L. Ryan, 2013), it contains propositions the character wants to be true (or false), like, for instance, desired events or undesired states. A W World can be inconsistent within itself, when a character's wishes are mutually exclusive, or in conflict with other worlds, when propositions in those worlds have a different truth value than desired.

- *Obligation (O) World*: represents "[...] a system of commitments and prohibitions defined by social rules and moral principles" (M.-L. Ryan, 1991, p. 116). It contains propositions that are mandated to be true (the obligatory) or false (the prohibited), and can also be in conflict with other worlds or inconsistent within itself.

This embedded referential structure, K Worlds centered around TAW, and W/O Worlds centered around each characters' K World, is metaphorically referred to as *narrative universe* (see Fig. 2.2), and provides the background from which other narrative phenomena are derived: "Narrativity resides in a text's ability to bring a world to life, to populate it with individuals through singular existential statements, to place this world in history through statements of events affecting its members [...]" (M.-L. Ryan, 1991, p. 112).

Summarizing, the TAW represents a narrative's factual domain: "[...] a succession of different states and events which together form a history. [...] TAW also comprises a set of general laws that determine the range of possible future developments of the plot out of the present situation "(M.-L. Ryan, 1991, p. 113). Based on this, characters' private possible worlds unfold their narrative significance from a juxtaposition with the 'actual facts' of TAW, and by how they affect TAW states, over time, through characters' actions, which are motivated or guided by the respective propositions of their private worlds.

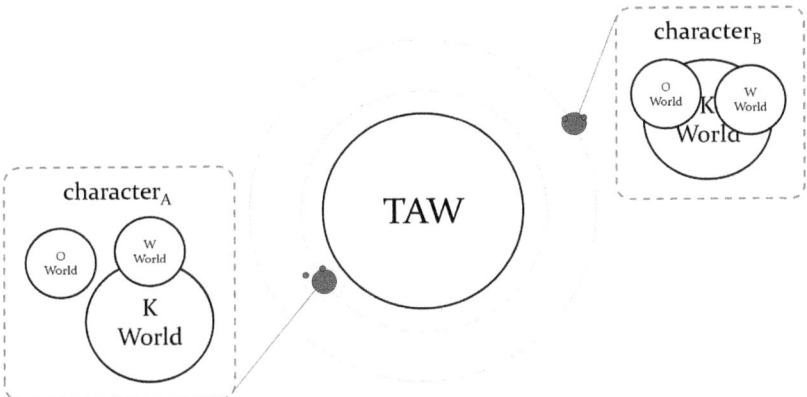

Figure 2.2: The embedded referential structure of the narrative universe: TAW represents the factual domain. Character's K Worlds are subjective representations of TAW and can be more or less in conflict with it ('closer or further away' from being accurate representations). W and O Worlds are representations of the characters' desired state of TAW as represented by their respective K World (in turn 'closer or further away' from being satisfied by their subjective reality). Here schematically: a narrative universe with character A, an unhappy realist, and character B, a content 'errorist'.

2.1.3. Conflict

M.-L. Ryan (1991, p. 119) expounds that "[f]rom the viewpoint of its participants[4], the goal of the narrative game—which is for them the game of life—is to make TAW coincide with as many as possible of their private worlds". This goal is meaningful only if no complete coincidence is given from the outset, that is, at least one *conflict* exists between TAW and a character's private world. Thus, Ryan's understanding of conflict is fairly unconventional:

> Conflict is not simply the complication or thickening of the plot that occurs between exposition and resolution, but a more or less permanent condition of narrative universes. The dénouement of a narrative is not the elimination of all conflicts, since the resolution of the hero's problems usually creates conflicts in his opponent's domain, but only

---

[4]i.e. characters, footnote mine.

the disappearance of the productive ones. A conflict is productive when its experiencer is in a position, and is willing, to take action toward its resolution.

(M.-L. Ryan, 1991, p. 120)

Crucially, this implies a transitive nature of conflict. Let p be a true proposition in TAW (e.g. character A possesses a magical ring). Another character B's W World could be in conflict with TAW due to proposition w_B (say, it desires the possession of the magical ring owned by A). Assume now, that, at the same time, character A's O World is in conflict with TAW due to proposition o_A (say, society demands the destruction of said ring). Because the propositions w_B and o_A cannot be satisfied in the same TAW (assuming a semi-realist ontology where an object can't be destroyed and owned at the same time) this means that they are also transitively in conflict with each other. This demonstrates, that conflicts can also exist between characters' private domains. In fact, there is no restriction that these worlds need to belong to different characters: It is absolutely conceivable that above wish w and obligation o could pertain to the same character. Both, the former *inter-character conflict*, as well as the latter *intra-character conflict*, are for instance extensively portrayed in Tolkien's (1954) magnum opus *Lord of the Rings*; one by the inner struggles of protagonist Frodo Baggins, the other one by the opposition of Frodo and Gollum.

Taking into account the mediating nature of K Worlds, M.-L. Ryan (1991, p. 122) also makes a distinction between *objective conflicts*, which relate to properties that hold in TAW, and *subjective* (also called second-level) conflicts that are grounded only in an epistemological conflict (i.e. a conflict based only on a character's lapse of judgment). A prime example is Shakespeare's (1603) tragedy *Othello*, where the eponymous protagonist erroneously believes his wife Desdemona to be unfaithful (K World conflict), which leads to a subjective conflict between his W and O Worlds since he feels a "gentleman's" obligation to punish her as well as a lover's wish to not hurt her[5]. This conflict is subjective because it results from a belief that is not warranted by the facts of TAW.

This all goes to show that Ryan's focus, when describing characters, is their use for the teleology of the plot. They are completely described by the propositions of their private modal worlds, as these

---

[5]Ryan's own example.

lay the foundations for their goals, and the knowledge for their plans, which lead to the actions that shape the plot. Consequently, character and conflict are the catalysts of plot: "The relations among the worlds of the narrative system are not static, but change from state to state. The plot is the trace left by the movement of these worlds within the textual universe" (M.-L. Ryan, 1991, p. 119).

2.2. Understanding Plot Through Possible Worlds

The last section was mainly concerned with the structure of textual possible worlds, and their relation to each other: it presented the concept of narrative universe. Plot, per se, is not a building block of such a system, but rather a phenomenon that emerges from the dynamics that occur when a particular universe is 'let loose' to follow its own rules; a "trace left by the movement of [...] worlds" in Ryan's words (ibid.), or the runtime behavior of an execution-run in more computational parlance. This means that, while the unit of consideration so far has been the proposition, it will now become the state transition, i.e. the event.

2.2.1. Events and Event-structures

M.-L. Ryan (1991, p. 129) distinguishes between two main types of events: happenings and actions. A *happening* is an event that is accidental and has no animated agent, only patients. Example happenings are chance encounters, natural forces or failures of action-execution. From an internal perspective (introduced in Section 1.2), happenings appear to be random (or, in pre-realist fiction, perhaps divine) events that coincidentally happen to affect characters in a relevant way. From an external viewpoint, of course, happenings are anything but random; they are teleologically motivated by the changes they induce and their contribution to the plot[6].

An *action* is an intentional event that has an agent, which executes it to realize a goal, usually as part of a plan. Not all actions are of the same narrative significance. Some are just dictated by the underlying logic of the narrative universe (like having to rest regularly during an arduous trip to a fiery mountain), while others are directed at

---

[6]This understanding will become relevant in Chap. 5 to propose a solution for the emergent-narrative paradox, which was introduced in Section 1.4.

solving an important character goal, often connected with a chance of failure (ibid.). In this context, deliberate non-action (sometimes called 'passive action') can also be regarded as a type of action if it serves to further a character's goals.

Goals can be understood to form a direct link to the structure of the narrative universe as analyzed above. They are "[...] established by selecting one of the propositions through which some private world departs from the actual world: a desire to fulfill, an obligation to satisfy, an enigma to solve" (M.-L. Ryan, 1991, p. 130). A *plan*, then, is a sequence of events that is intended to lead from the present state of TAW to the goal state. It is a projection into the future of TAW because it involves not only selecting actions but also predicting the results of these actions on the state of TAW. Some plans even contain a transfer of control from the main planing agent to a subagent, in cases where the planner requires assistance. While in cooperative circumstances this transfer is straight forward for the main agent—it usually just has to ask the subagent to fulfill some shared sub-goal—in competitive circumstances the main agent's goals are conflicting with the sub-agent's ones, so that the transfer has to be deceptive (M.-L. Ryan, 1991, pp. 142).

Apart from prospective constructions, also retrospective constructions influence the structure of plans. Beliefs about the history of TAW can be incomplete or false, leading to further complexities in plan execution. In the example of Othello, the protagonist kills Desdemona with the goal of punishing her for adulterous behavior. While his action succeeds, his goal can be seen to fail, as the assumption of her guilt is based on a false reconstruction of the narrative past—instead of delivering justice Othello becomes guilty himself.[7] This demonstrates how plans can, and often do, fail if a character's projections fall short of the textual reality. Yet even when a plan does not come to fruition, its presence as causal-intentional structure is important as it turns physical gestures into interpretable actions. From the bird's eye view of the plot in Othello, the deed of smothering Desdemona is the unfathomable murder of an innocent loved one. It is as part of Othello's subjective plan, that it becomes explainable as

---

[7]The tragedy Othello is also a prime example of a deceptive transfer of control, as Othello's plan is, in fact, a sub-plan of Iago's, who has been subversively plotting Othello's downfall by his own hand (example from M.-L. Ryan, 1991, p. 146).

an action towards the goal of punishing an intimate betrayer.

2.2.2. Plot as a Network of Possibilities

Fictional mental constructs, be they pro- or retrospective, are important for plot. Ryan explains that:

> [...] they link states and events in a temporal sequence, and [by that merit] present the same structure as the narrative of which they are a part. [...] Whether they are verified by the actual events or remain purely virtual, these private embedded narratives weave their strands into the texture of the plot and turn it into a layered structure, a bundle of possible stories.
>
> (M.-L. Ryan, 1991, p. 147)

Classically, plot is understood as consisting only of the things that physically happen: actual events and their causal interconnection (see the overview in Sec. 1.2.2). The statement above explicitly includes the domain of the virtual into plot: Mental events, which capture prospective and retrospective story-like constructs that may never be realized, are accepted as necessary for understanding the actual events of classical plot. They are included into its causal structure and turn plot into a network of possibilities, instead of a linear chain of events.

Since the implications of this analysis on the understanding of plot adopted by this thesis are immense it is necessary to dwell on it a little longer. The general idea that plot should be understood on more layers than just action is supported by Jerome Bruner (1986, p. 14) when he outlines that "[...] story must construct two landscapes simultaneously. One is the landscape of action, where the constituents are the arguments of action: agent, intention or goal, situation, instrument[...]. The other landscape is the landscape of consciousness: what those involved in the action know, think, or feel, or do not know, think, or feel". The interaction of these two 'landscapes' had been previously also analyzed by Greimas and Courtès (1976). Although their work is dealing with narrative semiotics, their conception of this term is "the analysis of the descriptions of actions and of their concatenations, descriptions which are at the same time the place where events are organized into meaning"; which describes the same phenomenon that Ryan is defining as plot presented from the internal perspective, just viewed from the outside of the external perspective. Greimas and Courtès' insight is that the pragmatic plane of action is inseparably connected with a cognitive plane of knowledge: the beliefs acquired and presuppositions activated by observing other characters act. This is of no significance if both planes overlap

and all characters possess perfect knowledge. However, Greimas and
Courtès observe:

> The producer of the narrative [. . .] can distribute the knowledge dif-
> ferently by attributing it (partially or totally) to certain characters
> and by depriving others of it. In this case, a gap or disjunction is
> produced between the acting subject (the subject of doing) and the
> knowing subject (the cognitive subject), a gap the sudden destruction
> of which can constitute an event of a different order, a *cognitive event*
> with repercussions and peripeteias, *capable of generating a new string
> of events.*
>
> (Greimas & Courtès, 1976, emphasis mine)

What this implies is that the distribution of knowledge between characters is a plotting principle and, consequently, that epistemic virtual
events are a plot driver—just like actions, their pragmatic counterparts. The subtle difference is that Greimas and Courtès' analysis,
coming from a considerably different perspective then Ryan's, argues
that actual events are inseparably connected with epistemic events
so that including the former in the plot necessitates the inclusion of
the latter. Plot, in their understanding, remains a linear structure of
cause-and-effect. Ryan, on the other hand, argues that failed plans,
which might never fully come to fruition as actual events, are crucial
to interpret characters' physical gestures as actions, and that this necessitates the inclusion of the virtual into plot. This, too, involves
(especially false) beliefs, but also prospective constructs like plans.
These are structured like plots themselves, for which Ryan calls them
private embedded narratives, and their inclusion into plot turns it into
a mixed actual-virtual network.

2.2.3. Introducing the Case Study

The folktale "The Little Red Hen" (TLRH), which I will use as a case
study throughout the thesis, will be used to demonstrate the importance of this difference. A few words should be said about this choice
of genre, in order to preempt criticism from those expecting narrative
theory to operate only on works of the likes of Proust (like the seminal Genette, 1983) or Balzac (the equally acclaimed Barthes, [1970]
1974). The irritation, in short, might be that folktales are not prototypical literary masterpieces, which are the works commonly used
as a test-bed for theory. At the same time, it is neither a plot-driven
genre in the same way as e.g. the detective novel, nor do its char-

acters provide particularly interesting cases of conflicting desires or complex mental functioning, like e.g. the psychological novel of the 19th century. Indeed, the main appeal of the folktale, for the present purpose, is not canonicity but instead its shortness and simplicity, which allow for thorough analysis and at times even graphical representation of the phenomena involved. I also want to point out that I do not at all intend to contest a more commonplace reading, which sees the folk-tale's parabolic message as its main driver of action, and its characters as allegoric symbols without deep interiority. All that is required here is to agree that the ensuing possible-worlds reading is one plausible analysis of many; an exercise undertaken not even in order to glean a better understanding of the meaning-making strategies of TLRH, but rather to tease out the dynamic properties of the theory itself. It is a further solace that even a highly acclaimed expert of the narratological trade like Marie-Laure Ryan adopts this genre for most of her analytical heavy lifting.

The version of TLRH I will be employing is the following:

Once upon a time, Little Red Hen lived on a farm with a dog, a pig and a cow. Little Red Hen worked hard every day to grow plants in her garden. The dog, the pig, and the cow did nothing but sleep all day in the warm sun and watch Little Red Hen work in her garden.
One day, Little Red Hen found a grain of wheat. "Who will help me plant this wheat so that we can eat fresh bread?" she said. "Not I" said the dog. "Not I" said the pig. "Not I" said the cow. "I will plant it myself then" said Little Red Hen, and she planted the grain of wheat.
Little Red Hen took good care of her wheat, but the dog, the pig and the cow said they were too tired to help.
By the end of the summer, the wheat grew very tall. It was time to cut the wheat and take it to the mill. "Who will help me cut the wheat and take it to the mill so that we can have fresh bread?"; "Not I" said the dog. "Not I" said the pig. "Not I" said the cow. "Well then, I will take it to the mill myself" said Little Red Hen, and she cut the wheat and set off for the mill.
After the miller made wheat into soft flour, she came back to the farm and asked, "Who will help me bake the bread?"; "Not I" said the dog. "Not I" said the pig. "Not I" said the cow. "Well then, I will bake the bread myself ". And she did just that! She mixed the flour with salt and yeast to make the dough. After the dough rose, she put it in the oven to bake.
When the bread was done, she asked, "Who will help me eat the bread?"; "I will", said the dog. "I will", said the pig. "I will", said the cow. "No, you will not", said Little Red Hen. "You did not help

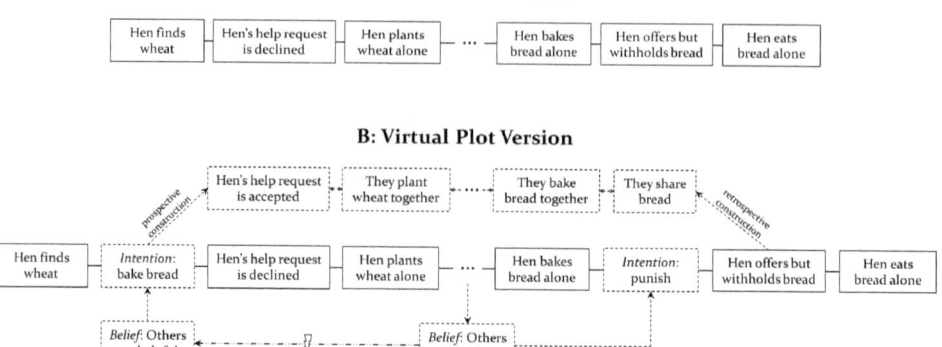

Figure 2.3: A graphical representation of the events of the TLRH plot, following an (A) virtuality-agnostic or (B) virtuality-aware understanding of plot.

me plant the grain, and you did not help me care for it. You did not help me cut it and take it to the mill. You did not even help me make the bread. I will eat it myself." And she did.

Figure 2.3 depicts this plot from a virtuality-agnostic (A) and a virtuality-aware (B) perspective, in a somewhat abridged version. In (A) the story text is analyzed through actual events, in a straight forward manner. Finding wheat is a happening, which initiates a line of action: the hen asks for help with planting the wheat but her request is denied by the animals, which forces her to plant it by herself. The same interaction structure is repeated with the other agricultural proceedings (omitted in the diagram for brevity) until the hen has baked the bread alone. This results in the hen being in sole possession of the bread, which allows her to taunt the other animals by first offering them bread but in the end withholding it and eating it alone.

Of course the TLRH plot can be represented in such a linear structure of cause and effect. However, the chain contains one weakness. Having the bread is causally connected to offering and withholding it, in the sense that it is a necessary condition. But is it also the event that is responsible for the arising of the intention to 'taunt' the animals? This seems unlikely, yet the virtuality-agnostic view conceals any other causality from view, and even speaking of virtual events like "intentions" in the last sentence is problematic in such a perspective.

Version (B) can resolve this problem and offers us a more comprehensive view of the plot's structure. In this view, again, the storyline is initiated by the happening of finding wheat. However, this is seen to first cause a virtual event: the hen's adoption of the goal to make bread. This goal causes the hen to take up a plan to make bread, where she asks the other animals for help, they consent and in the end they all share the labor and its fruits together. Since this process is never actualized in TAW it remains a purely virtual, prospective construction, depicted in the graph by dashed arrows and vertices. It is interesting to note, that such a construction implies that the hen holds (at least an implicit) belief that the other farm animals are of a helpful nature and would consider such a request. This is, again, a virtual state and, in sight of the actual plot, might be considered an incorrect reconstruction of the actual state of TAW, respectively of the characters it contains. During the ensuing negative interactions it can be assumed that the other animals' behavior eventually leads to an adjustment of the hen's belief system. This proceeds by means of a virtual event when she adopts the belief that the other characters are selfish, necessarily terminating her previously held belief about their disposition. That virtual event can be taken to lead to a goal of punishing them for their selfish behavior[8], which can be realized as soon as the hen obtains some bread. Thus, the explanatory gap of version (A) is filled by disclosing the dual causal precursors of the punishment intention.

At the same time, version (B) is able to reveal a structural elegance of the TLRH plot that remained hidden in (A). By 'offering but withholding bread' the hen brings to the foreground of the other animals' (and readers') attention a preferable, unactualized PW where she shared the bread because the other animals had helped her. This happens by way of retrospectively constructing the same virtual course of action that the hen had prospectively constructed in her initial plan, down to her incipient belief (see upper lane of

---

[8]This fairly weak motivation can be analyzed better by relying on a more elaborate psychological model of characters. For instance, one could instead assume that the punishment-intention of the hen is caused by the negative experience of having to suffer from cognitive dissonance in the face of false beliefs. This would make it plausible to adopt a plan in order to teach the others a lesson, with the goal of changing their personality. Such a chain would allow the hen to reinstate her initial belief and thus reduce cognitive dissonance again. While being fairly cumbersome, this interpretations is fully in line with the character meta-goal of increasing the coincidence of their private worlds with TAW.

Fig. 2.3.B). It is such multi-functionality—the same (virtual) chain of events being the motivation for punishment and the means for its attainment—that will be discussed as an important feature of plots' aesthetic appeal in Section 4.1.1.

The advantages of the view adopted here are offset with a drawback, which already manifested itself in the all-permeating subjunctive mood of the preceding paragraph. Not all virtual events of a plot have to be directly reported in the discourse, so that some of them have to be inferred, like e.g. the hen's initial belief that the other animals are helpfully disposed. With no direct access to plot, no guarantee can be given about the correctness of these inferences, or that they are the only possible interpretation. The discussion in footnote 8, whether the hen's intention is to taunt the others in order to reduce cognitive dissonance or in order to simply punish them, is indicative of how underlying assumptions—like e.g. differing cognitive models of character—can change an interpretation of the structure of the virtual realm, with little evidence to decide among competing options. How can plot remain a definitive category if we include such ambiguous virtual structures? Ryan addresses this problem by taking the stance that a virtuality-aware plot is the result of one possible narrative universe, and any one discourse is compatible with multiple possible universes at the same time (M.-L. Ryan, 1991, p. 173). Ambiguities like these are inherent to an analytical approach to plot because it is a deep structure which cannot be directly accessed but must be inferred from the surface, i.e. text.[9]

Analytical reasoning in NT has, by necessity, to depart from text and can thus infer properties about the nature of a narrative only from text. For instance, Genette (1983) investigates, among other things, how different types of discourse create changes in story time, while Palmer (2004) describes how fictional minds are reconstructed by readers from the discourse. It is one of the advantages of generative modeling as undertaken throughout this thesis, that it allows to also investigate the inverse direction of reasoning, that is, how changes in

---

[9]The spatial metaphor of depth has been described as one of two currently prevalent literary methodologies by the professor and critic Rita Felski (2015): "Reading is imagined as an act of digging down to arrive at a repressed or otherwise obscured reality. [...] The text is envisaged as possessing qualities of interiority, concealment, penetrability, and depth; [...]" (p. 53). While her analysis focuses on the discipline of literary criticism, and its quest for meaning, the same metaphor, to me, seems to also underlie much narratological thought.

a deep structure can influence the surface (or at least higher levels). Instead of hypothesizing how different stories can be analyzed by the same abstraction, it demonstrates how varying the parameters of this abstraction can generate differences in stories. The narratological insights garnered by the generative modeling undertaken in this thesis will be presented in the last chapter in Section 6.2.1.

2.2.4. Summary

Summarizing the whole discussion we can distill a working definition of plot:

Definition 1 (Plot). The plot of a narrative is any causal network of happenings, actions and mental events that is consistent with the narrative's discourse. Happenings are events that have no agent but are experienced by at least one patient and thus cause mental events. Actions are events that have an agent and are caused by mental events. Mental events them self include: the adoption or deprecation of beliefs, wishes, obligations or plans. They are the building blocks of prospective as well as retrospective virtual constructs, which have the same structure as the actual parts of plot. These constructs are the private embedded narratives characters have about their narrative universe.

This makes clear that all the constituent parts of plot in this model are defined in reference to character, and especially its mental functioning. In the following, I will therefore refer to it as a *character-centric plot model*. M.-L. Ryan (2013)'s own description of characters as "the [non-actual] individuals whose actions, experience, and destiny form the central concern of narrative fiction" should be a case in point that this view is not unduly reductive.

While Ryan uses the metaphor of the narrative universe, Umberto Eco describes the narrative text as "a machine for producing possible worlds" (Eco, 1984). Under this view, a narrative can be seen as a system whose dynamics, the movement of possible worlds, lead to the emergence of a plot. As plot is a dynamic property of this system, changes in its individual static properties—the parameters and levers of Eco's machine—can result in changes of the plot. Some of these alternative plots are made explicit in the narrative through the virtual and counterfactual constructions of characters, while others remain implicit. To capture this phenomenon I will refer to the compound that makes a concrete narrative, i.e. the TAW it constructs, the APWs of its characters and the plethora of potential plots it spans, as a *concrete narrative systems* (e.g. 'the narrative system of TLRH'). The term *narrative system* as a genus, then, will refer to the abstract concept that was outlined by the two previous sections. This metaphor maintains the structural implications of Ryan's narrative universe, while also importing properties from Eco's machine metaphor. Especially, I intend it to explicate the generative capability of this concept, as well as the insight that changes of parameters in parts of its structure can result in different dynamic properties: the generation of different plots whose potential already lay within the system.

2.3. Implementing the Concept of a Narrative System

As observed before, plot is a phenomenon that emerges from the dynamics that occur when a narrative system is 'let loose'. The concept of a narrative system—as derived from possible worlds semantics—is character-centric, and all events relevant to plot are closely connected to characters. Therefore, my computational implementation of this concept will depart from modeling characters.

2.3.1. Multi Agent Systems

Systems where several goal-directed, autonomous entities interact with each other and an environment can be modeled as *Multi Agent Systems* (MAS) in an AI context (e.g. Wooldridge, 2002).

An *agent* is understood as an entity that "receives stimuli from the environment and carries out actions in the environment" (Poole & Mackworth, 2010, p. 43). The following explanations are based on Chapter 2 of Russell and Norvig (2010), in which a *percept* is used to describe the input an agent receives at any given instant, while the complete history of all input is referred to as the percept sequence. *Actions* are atomic events initiated by agents and potentially affecting the state of the environment. Since agents act in order to achieve goals, they are required to have a *performance measure* that allows them to establish whether their goals are met (or how close they are to this state). Research on MAS is primarily concerned with the question of how to implement rational agents, which are agents that "for each possible percept sequence [...] select an action that is expected to maximize [their] performance measure, given the evidence provided by the percept sequence and whatever built-in knowledge the agent has" (Russell & Norvig, 2010, p. 37).

The *environment* is an entity that encodes the states towards which agents are oriented: their performance measure is based on environment states, and their actions affect environment states. This means that environments have to also encode state transitions, i.e. the dynamics that agents attempt to leverage in order to maximize their performance measure. These dynamics do not need to be re-active, that is, only triggerable by agents. Environments can also encode entirely internal dynamics that result in state changes inde-pendent of agent action. For the present purpose it can be assumed that all agents in a MAS are part of the same shared environment, which allows individual agents to perceive other agents through the mediation of the environment.[10]

Russell and Norvig (2010, pp. 42) outline different dimensions along which environments can be described. To exemplify that con-cept, I provide a subset deemed important here.

- *Fully* vs. *partially* observable: In the former case each per-ception contains the complete environment state at that time, whereas in the latter case parts of the state can remain unknown after an individual sampling step.

- *Deterministic* vs. *stochastic*: The former is true if the next state of the environment is dependent only on its previous state and the agent's action. If the next state can be described only by a probability distribution then the system is stochastic. Partially observable environments can appear stochastic to an agent, if their behavior is determined by unobserved properties.

- *Static* vs. *dynamic*: An environment is described as dynamic for an agent if its state can change while the agent is deliberating.

- *Discrete* vs. *continuous*: Discrete describes an environment where states, time, percepts and actions (if modeled) are rep-resented in a countable way, that is by a set of separate (if po-tentially infinitely many) values they can take. If one of these

---

[10]This must not always hold true. In some cases a purely abstract environment is employed to just encode a task. For instance, a crosswords puzzle environment does not need to represent the playing agent.

properties can take any value within a range, or cannot be deconstructed into atomic constituents, then the environment is continuous in that property.

While all of the preceding terminology is sometimes used to describe embodied agents in an actual environment, throughout this thesis it will only be used to refer to virtual agents and environments.

2.3.2. The Belief-Desire-Intention Agent Architecture

Different agent architectures have been developed to conceptualize the inner workings of rational agents (see e.g. Siebers & Aickelin, 2008). For the present purpose the *Belief-Desire-Intention* (BDI) architecture (Rao & Georgeff, 1991, 1995) is a natural fit since it was derived from possible-worlds semantics. As will become apparent, this allows the representation of many parts of the expounded narrative semantics as first-order entities when modeling a particular narrative system.

The BDI architecture consists of four principal components and an interpreter algorithm, which performs reasoning based on them. These components are:

1. *Belief:* Beliefs encode an agent's informational state by representing its knowledge about the environment, which apart from propositions can include inference rules that generate new propositions from existing ones. This is necessary because goal-directed action needs to be based on information about the environment, but an individual sensing act is not guaranteed to return complete information, which necessitates agent-side knowledge management. Beliefs can be false when grounded in an unreliable perception or inference, and can change over time.

2. *Desire:* Desires encode an agent's motivational state, that is, the objectives it might want to accomplish. Since desires represent all states that are associated with an increase in performance measure, the set of desires can be conflicting. New desires can arise as a reaction to new percepts.

3. *Intention:* Intentions encode an agent's deliberative state, that is, a non-conflicting subset of desires that it is currently committed to.

4. *Plan:* Plans encode information about courses of action that are sufficient to achieve certain desires. Adopting a plan to achieve a desire turns it into an intention. A plan consists of a *goal*, which is the state it achieves, a set of *preconditions* that have to be met in order for the plan to be viable, and a *body* which is a sequence of atomic actions as well as subgoals. This implies that plans are partial. That is, the means for achieving subgoals are not predetermined in the containing plan itself, but are resolved at runtime when plan-execution arrives at the subgoal.

The interpreter algorithm is a loop that is executed for each agent (see Alg. 1). It operates on the agent's internal state and mediates between the maintenance of the four components described above as well as action execution.

Algorithm 1 BDI-interpreter, amended for clarity from (Rao & Georgeff, 1995)

1: INITIALIZE_STATE();
2: **loop**
3:     *// State update*
4:     B = BELIEF_REVISION(event_queue.dequeue(), B);
5:     D = OPTION_GENERATOR(B, D);
6:     I = DELIBERATE(D, B, I);
7:     *// Action selection*
8:     i = SELECT_INTENTION(I);
9:     EXECUTE(i);
10:    *// Sensing the environment*
11:    event_queue += SENSE();
12: **end loop**

At the beginning of each reasoning cycle the interpreter updates its belief base B by processing a number of events, which are organized in a first-in first-out order. Then, the set of desires D is updated based on the current belief base, which requires checking whether previous desires have been satisfied and whether new desires have been triggered. After that, the intention set I is updated. In practice, adopting a desire as an intention means coming up with, and committing to, a plan which has the goal of satisfying that desire, so that I contains a set of plans. Updating I requires checking whether a new desire can be committed to, which is the case when it is satisfiable (a plan exists to attempt it) and not conflicting with the already present intentions. Since, in a dynamic environment, conditions might change and plans might fail, intentions can also become impossible to achieve by means of the selected plan, in which case they have to be removed from I. However, they can remain in D and be readopted during a later cycle. After the internal state has been updated, action selection can commence: From the intentions in I one plan is selected, and its next step is executed. If this step is an action its execution is attempted in the environment. Otherwise it must be a subgoal, in which case an internal event is enqueued in the events queue in order to add it as a new desire. In this case, the current intention is paused until the subgoal is satisfied. The loop finishes by performing a sensing act and enqueueing the newly perceived external events, usually at least containing the outcome of the initiated action—as well as all coinciding but unconnected environment changes—into the event queue. Further internal events that are generated during cycle execution, like e.g. the observation that an intention had to be aborted, can be enqueued at any time during the loop.

The main advantage of BDI is that it allows agents to balance planing, goal-directed action, and reactive behavior, which means that it can operate effectively in dynamic, partially observable environments in real-time. Of importance for the envisioned narrative semantics is that the distinction between intentions and desires allows the representation of conflicting motivational states (e.g. a wish in conflict with an obligation). Furthermore, the ability to adopt multiple intentions at the same time allows to concurrently pursue several goals. This flexibility, however, comes at a cost because it means that neither forward nor backward chaining[11] can be employed during reasoning. Since agents cannot predict the results of their actions they cannot independently come up with new plans in situations when no existing partial plan is applicable. Also, they cannot dynamically re-plan in case of a plan failure, but have to abort plan execution completely even when the goal is still attainable via actions that are

---

[11]Forward and backward chaining are the two main inference methods used in AI systems. Basically, they are build on a repeated forward (respectively backward) application of generalized modus ponens (e.g. see Russell & Norvig, 2010, Secs. 9.2 and 9.3).

not part of the initial plan.

2.3.3. Modeling Narrative Semantics using MAS

With this understanding at hand, the introduced narrative system can be modeled in the MAS framework as follows (see Table 2.1, below, for a summary): The factual domain that is the TAW is modeled as an environment. The environment is initially in a start state s_0, and each subsequent state transition of the environment represents an event in TAW. If the transition was caused by an agent then the event is an action, in the case of a transition that is causally dependent only on environment dynamics it is a happening.

Characters are modeled as BDI agents.[12] A character's APW are modeled by the respective agent's internal state. The K World is comprised by the belief propositions and inference rules in an agent's belief base: $K = \{p|p \in B\}$. Since in a partially observable environment beliefs about parts of the environment might be missing (or initially incorrect), and in a dynamic setting the environment can change in between agents' sense-acts, an agent's beliefs can be(come) incorrect. This allows to model objective conflicts between K World and TAW, as well as subjective conflicts of all types. The W World and O World of an agent are related from a MAS perspective because both contain propositions that determine what the agent wants to achieve. Consequently, both worlds need to be modeled through desires, and a solution is required to keep the respective desires distinguishable from each other. I propose to represent the difference between them through propositions in that characters belief base, making use of the unary predicates $wish/1$ and $obligation/1$. Thus, the O World of an agent is determined by the following set: $\{p|p \in D \wedge obligation(p) \in B\}$, while its W World is given by: $\{p|p \in D \wedge wish(p) \in B\}$. This solution allows to keep the function of D restricted to representing motivational states, while maintaining discriminability between wishes and obligations via B. As a consequence, characters represented this way always posses propositional knowledge about their wishes and obligations, which

---

[12]Note that character and agent are both representations of the same narrative phenomenon. From now, on the term 'character' will be used to refer specifically to its narratological manifestation and the connected semantic field, while 'agent' will refer to its computational counterpart. Since these domains sometimes overlap, some flexibility will be inevitable.

precludes the modeling of subconscious drives. Since in the underlying narrative semantics the main function of W and O Worlds is to be the source from which plan-goals are derived, and planning requires the conscious formulation of target states, this trade-off seems warranted. Because desires that have not yet been selected as intentions can be conflicting, this solutions also does not preclude the representation of intra-character conflicts, e.g. between contradictory wishes and obligations. Note that desires are triggered and satisfied only on the basis of changes in an agent's belief base and do not have direct access to the true state of the environment. This situation reflects the embedded referential structure of the narrative universe described in Section 2.1, where the W and O Worlds are defined in reference to a character's K World, and only the K World is defined in direct reference to TAW.

As mentioned above, conflict is present as soon as an agent's set of desires is not empty because the elements in this set represent wishes and obligations.[13] By iteratively adopting desires as intentions the BDI-interpreter thus implements a strategy to reduce conflict by selecting wishes/obligations as goals, identifying plans to satisfy these goals, and executing these plans. This resonates well with the underlying narrative theory that expounds that characters' meta-goal is to make their private worlds coincide with TAW as much as possible, which in the implementation coincides with a small D. By following this line of reasoning we can conclude that BDI agents not only model characters, but also more specifically, that the BDI-interpreter implements characters' reasoning. This means that the results of such reasoning, character-plans, are directly represented by the outcome of the interpreter-cycle: partial plans selected form the agent's plan library. What is more, when a BDI-interpreter is executed it regularly senses the environment and turns the results into events of perception, which in turn trigger further internal events that together form a trace of the agent's processing of the environment. Hence, these internal events—the acquiring or abandonment of beliefs, the arousal and satisfaction of desires and the adoption and failure of plans—must represent the mental events that have been analyzed in Sec. 2.2

---

[13]This is a sufficient but not necessary condition. Conflict can also be present with $D = \varnothing$ if the agent's B set contains incorrect beliefs. This can be neglected here, as false beliefs do not initiate action unless in connection with a desire to rectify them.

Table 2.1: Overview of how the elements of narrative semantics are represented in the MAS framework.

narrative semantics	MAS framework
character	BDI agent
K world	agent's belief base B
W world	$\{p\mid p \in D \wedge wish(p) \in B\}$
O world	$\{p\mid p \in D \wedge obligation(p) \in B\}$
character plans	agent's adopted partial plans
embedded narrative	internal events of an agent's BDI-interpreter
TAW	partially observable, dynamic environment
action	agent-induced state transition
happening	internal state transition
productive conflicts	union of all agents' desire sets $\bigcup D$
plot	union of actions, happenings and all embedded narratives

as constituting the virtual constructs that turn plot into a mixed actual-virtual network. By that merit the execution of an agent's interpreter continuously generates the corresponding character's private embedded narratives.

Since plot, in the underlying theory, is taken to be the network between the actual events and the private embedded narratives of the characters, we can conclude that, in the MAS framework, plot is represented by the internal events of all agents' reasoning cycles (virtual part) and the actions and happenings that perform the state transitions of the environment.

2.3.4. InBloom: A BDI based MAS Framework for Narrative Semantics

To implement the abstract specifications of the last section in an executable programming language, the BDI framework Jason[14] was selected. Its primary advantages are the following:

- A book-length documentation of the agent architecture, programming best-practices and design decisions is available (Bordini et al., 2007).

- The framework was published more then 10 years ago, so that

---

[14]https://github.com/jason-lang/jason

maturity is guaranteed, and is still under active development so that help requests can be addressed by the authors.

- The implementation is open source, and can be easily extended and adopted to personal needs.

- Jason provides entry points for both agent modeling and environment modeling, and manages their interaction mostly autonomously.

- Advanced features exist that, among others, enable speech-act based agent communication, the handling of plan failure, and strong negation.

Jason needs to be extended in three regards in order to enable the full functionality of narrative semantics: (1) the agent model needs to account for wishes and obligations, (2) the environment model needs to support both actions and happenings, as well as universal narrative phenomena like spatio-temporality, and (3) a dedicated model of plot needs to be created from scratch, as normal MAS do not require this concept at all. **Since the result of this extension can be used to model different narrative systems** (see Fig. 2.4) **it should be considered a BDI based MAS framework for modeling narrative semantics.** To do justice to the character-centered nature of the underlying semantics I dubbed the framework `InBloom`, short for 'inside Bloom'; a homage to Joyce's ingenious character construction of Leopold Bloom. It is made accessible as open source software to the general public at https://github.com/cartisan/inBloom.

The Jason framework

Before outlining my extensions, an introductory overview of Jason proper will be provided.

AGENT-SIDE REASONING   in Jason can be implemented in a declarative paradigm using an extended version of AgentSpeak (ASL). Its full syntax and formal semantics can be found in Bordini et al. (2007, Chap. 10), but I will informally review the basics necessary to parse this thesis.

An agent is comprised by a set of beliefs (its belief base) and a set of plans (its plan base). *Beliefs* are ground atomic formulae, where an

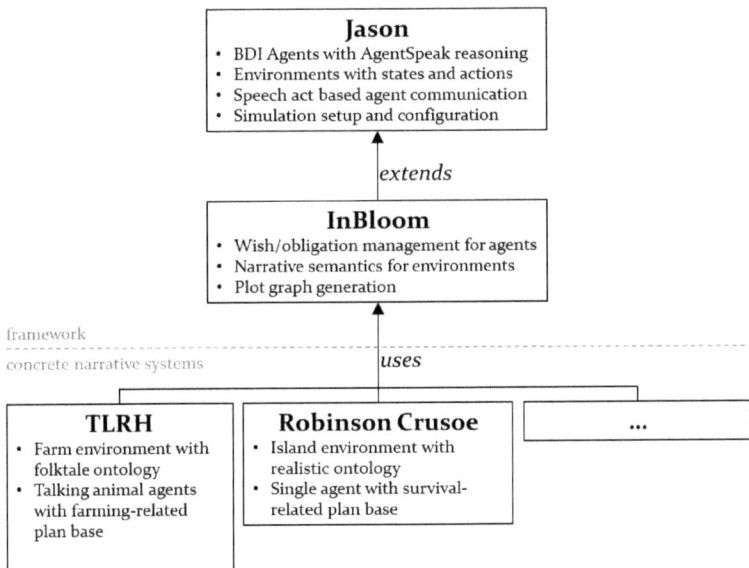

Figure 2.4: Schematic representation of the envisioned architecture. InBloom is a framework that extends the Jason multi agent simulation framework with narrative semantics. Concrete narrative systems, like for instance the TLRH system, can be implemented by using (and further extending) InBloom.

atomic formula is of the form $P(t_1, \ldots, t_n)$ with P being a predicate symbol (starting with a lowercase letter) and t_i being terms (either constants c, variables X, or atomic formulae themselves). Beliefs can also be defined indirectly using inference rules based on (potentially not-ground) atomic formulae, that are unified against the belief base. The belief base and its inference rules encode what an agent holds to be true. Lines 1–3 in Listing 2.1 demonstrate the ASL syntax for this. They encode a belief base in which the agent believes that it is hungry, that it is pleasant to eat bread, and that anything that is pleasant to eat is useful, when one is hungry.

Line 3, at the same time, demonstrates how atomic formulae can be connected and modified using logical operators. The main operators are &, |, and **not** which represent conjunction, disjunction and negation from a Boolean Algebra. Any combination of atomic formulae using these operators is called a *logical formula*. A *literal* is an atomic formula, or its negation. Also, the line demonstrates the use of *variables* (symbols starting with an uppercase letter), which are initially free but can be unified against the belief base, in which case they are bound to a particular value (a constant or an atomic

```
1    hungry .                          // 0-ary atomic formula
2    pleasant(eat(bread)).             // atomic formula
3    // inference rule:
4    useful(Item) :- pleasant(eat(Item)) & hungry .
5
6    // plan statement, belief addition:
7    +has(Item) : hungry & pleasant(eat(Item)) <-
8        -wish(has(Item));            // belief removal
9        ?present(Agents);            // declarative goal
10       !share(Item, Agents);        // achievement goal
11       eat(Item).                   // action
12
13   +!share(Item, Agents) <- // ...   // plan statement: goal add.
```

Listing 2.1: AgentSpeak example code.

formula[15]) throughout their scope. In this case, useful(*bread*) would result in a belief of the agent because unifying Item with *bread* results in the atomic formula pleasant(eat(*bread*)) that can be derived from the belief base, while useful(*cheese*) would not resolve into a belief of the agent because no corresponding atomic formula about *cheese* can be found in the belief base.

An idiosyncratic feature of Jason-flavour ASL are annotations, which can be used to provide additional information about an individual belief, like e.g. its provenance. Annotations are enclosed in square brackets following a literal, and contain a list of atomic formulae. Thus, *hungry* [source(*perception*),intensity(5)], would encode that the agent knows that it is hungry from a perception, and that the intensity of this feeling is 5. While this does not increase the expressive power of AgentSpeak, it is a handy shorthand for conveying meta-knowledge.

Plans are statements of the form **triggering event :   context <- plan body**, which denotes that **plan body** is to be adopted as a plan whenever an agent's BDI-interpreter processes the **triggering event**, under the condition that **context** can be derived from the agent's belief base. A *triggering event* can be either the addition/removal of a belief (denoted as $+af$ or $-af$ with af being an atomic

---

[15]This means that ASL is effectively a higher order logic, which entails certain theoretical problems. However, since it lacks universal quantification, in practice, these problems can be circumvented through reification.

formula), or the adoption/failure of a goal (denoted as $+g$, $-g$ with
g being a goal as defined below). Line 5 in the example demonstrates
a plan that is triggered when the agent processes the addition of a
belief of form `has(Item)`. In this case, the *context*, which can be any
logical formula, is evaluated using the variable instantiation from the
triggering event. E.g. for `+has(bread)`, the context of line 5 would be
evaluated to true in our exemplary belief base. A *plan body* consists
of goals, belief addition/removal or actions. Line 6 demonstrates the
syntax of belief removal. In the example, processing this plan step
generates the internal event `-wish(has(bread))` because in ASL variables are plan-scoped. The event is added to the interpreters event
queue to be processed in due time (when it will remove the atomic
formula `wish(has(bread))` from the belief base, and also could in
turn trigger a new plan). Belief addition functions comparably, but
is denoted using the $+$ operator. Like with beliefs, the addition of
goals (denoted as $!af$ for achievement goals, and $?af$ for declarative
goals) generates internal events. However, with goals, execution of
the active plan is paused until the sub-goal is achieved, and resumed
only after that. Line 7 demonstrates a declarative goal, which generates the internal event `+?present(Agents)` and is achieved if `Agents`
can be instantiated against the belief base (essentially constituting a
request against the agent's knowledge). Line 8 contains an achievement goal, which generates the internal event `+!share(Item, Agents)`,
with appropriately instantiated variables. It is achieved if this event
triggers a (sub) plan, and execution of this plan is successful. Line 9,
finally, demonstrates an action. This step does not trigger an internal
event, but instead attempts to execute the given action in the environment. Plan execution is again paused, until the environment notifies
the agent whether action execution was successful. Remember, that a
BDI-interpreter can concurrently pursue several plans as well as process external events, which means that an agent continues reasoning
while a plan it was executing is paused. This interpreter, responsible
for maintaining agent state and performing reasoning with the help
of ASL agent programs of the above type, is implemented in the Java
programming language. Its functionality is realized in `void jaso`
`n.asSemantics.TransitionSystem#reasoningCycle()`[16] and each
agent has its own reasoning cycle, which is executed in a dedicated

---

[16]References to program code throughout the thesis will follow the convention:
`return-type package.Class#method`.

thread so that agents can run concurrently. For details on the implementation of the reasoning cycle see Bordini et al. (2007, Chap. 4, especially Fig. 4.1).

COMMUNICATION BETWEEN AGENTS can be initiated from AgentSpeak using a mechanism called *speech act* (Bordini et al., 2007, p. 118). A speech act is a predefined action (called internal action) of the form:

    `.send(receiver, performative, propositional_content)`,

where `receiver` is the name (or list of names) of the receiving agent, `propositional_content` is a literal, a triggering event or a plan and `performative` is one of the following message-types, which define the effect of the speech act:

- `tell`/`untell`: adds/removes the literal in the content to/from the receiver's belief base;

- `achieve`/`unachieve`: adds/removes the triggering event in the content as a desire to/from the receiver's desire set;

- `askOne`/`askAll`: the receiver resolves the literal in the content against its belief base and returns one/all variable assignments that make it true;

- `tellHow`/`untellHow`/`askHow`: tells the receiver to add/remove/return a plan from its plan library.

This means that Jason enables information exchange, goal delegation, information seeking and know-how related communication between agents.[17]

THE COMMUNICATION BETWEEN AGENTS AND ENVIRONMENTS is implemented in Java and realized through the base class `jason.en vironment.Environment` that needs to be subclassed to implement a custom environment. A Jason environment is mainly responsible for two tasks: executing agents' actions, and delivering perceptions to them. For this, it needs to maintain a state, which is how it

---

[17]Speech act, here, is loosely based on the classical speech act theory as developed by John Austin and John Searle (see e.g. Green, 2017). Especially, each invocation of `.send` constitutes a locutionary act, and the literal `propositional_content` defines its illocutionary force.

represents the TAW. Whenever an agent requests the execution of an action, the method `boolean jason.environment.Environment#exe cuteAction(String agentName, Structure action)` is triggered, with `agentName` containing a unique identifier of the agent and action containing the name and potentially the parameters of the action, for instance `eat(bread)` in the example above. Custom environments need to override `executeAction`, and by that implement the state changes that are caused by any action available to agents. If, after that process, the environment determines that the action was successful then the method needs to return `true`, otherwise (e.g. the agent didn't posses any bread to eat) it returns `false`, which is reported as action failure to the agent.

Whenever a custom environment determines that an agent should perceive a state (change) it can schedule perceptions using the method `void jason.environment.Environment#addPercept(Stri ng agName, Literal... per)`. Per is an array of individual perceptions p, which are ASL atoms or predicates. Analogously, a perception can also be removed using the method `boolean jason.environment .Environment#removePercept(String agName, Literal p)`. All perceptions currently available to an agent according to the environment are maintained in a list, and whenever the agent's reasoning cycle performs `sense()` all the changes since the last sensing (addition or removal of individual percepts) are conveyed to it as internal events of form $+p$ or $-p$.

A SIMULATION IS CONFIGURED using a multi-agent systems definition file in the custom mas2j syntax (Bordini et al., 2007, pp. 236). This file contains the class name of the custom environment to be used, the location of the ASL file containing the plan library, and a definition of each agent to be executed. The agent definition contains configuration details like each agent's name, the class that will be used by Jason to run the agent (per default:`jason.asSemantics.Agent`) as well as a number of special initial beliefs or goals particular to that agent. The mas2j file is then passed to `jason.infra.centra lised.RunCentralisedMAS`, which performs all tasks necessary for setup and execution. Normally, a simulation runs until it is paused using the GUI, or stopped from inside the simulation.

InBloom: Environment Implementation

After having reviewed Jason, we can now come to the implementation of InBloom performed by me. On the environment side, InBloom implements narrative semantics in a set of classes connected to `inBloom.PlotEnvironment`—which extends Jason's `Environment` class—loosely following the Model-View-Controller (MVC) pattern (see e.g. Buschmann et al., 1996, pp. 125): From an MVC perspective, agents' BDI-interpreters act as views, which receive partial (and potentially subjective) representations of the TAW and regularly request to change it. This objective TAW is encapsulated in the model, of type `inBloom.PlotModel`. It acts as a computational representation of the current state of the TAW, and is responsible for computing how characters' actions affect this state. This means that each action available to agents needs to be implemented as a method in the model. Thus, when the `PlotEnvironment` receives an action request from an agent, its task is to parse this request, identify the method in `PlotModel` that provides the requested operation, and call it with the parameters supplied by the agent. The respective model methods change the state of the TAW according to the action, determine any side effects that need to be reported to observing agents, and decide whether the action was successful. PlotEnvironment, in essence, acts as controller by mediating between multiple concurrent agents, the model, and the plot-graph capturing mechanism (see Fig. 2.5).

As outlined above, InBloom is a framework and provides only domain-independent narrative semantics through the classes introduced in detail below. Custom narrative systems are expected to subclass them in order to extend the system with domain-specific functionality.

PLOTENVIRONMENT subclasses `Environment` via `jason.environm ent.TimeSteppedEnvironment`, which synchronizes agent action execution. It does that by collecting action requests until each agent has requested one action, and only then executing them together. Since agents can take different time to come up with an action request depending on their internal state, it can happen that one agent requests several actions in the same time that another one needs for one.[18] In

---

[18]To prevent deadlocks a timeout of 100ms is set in place, which enforces the execution of all presently scheduled actions thus forcing slow reasoners to take a

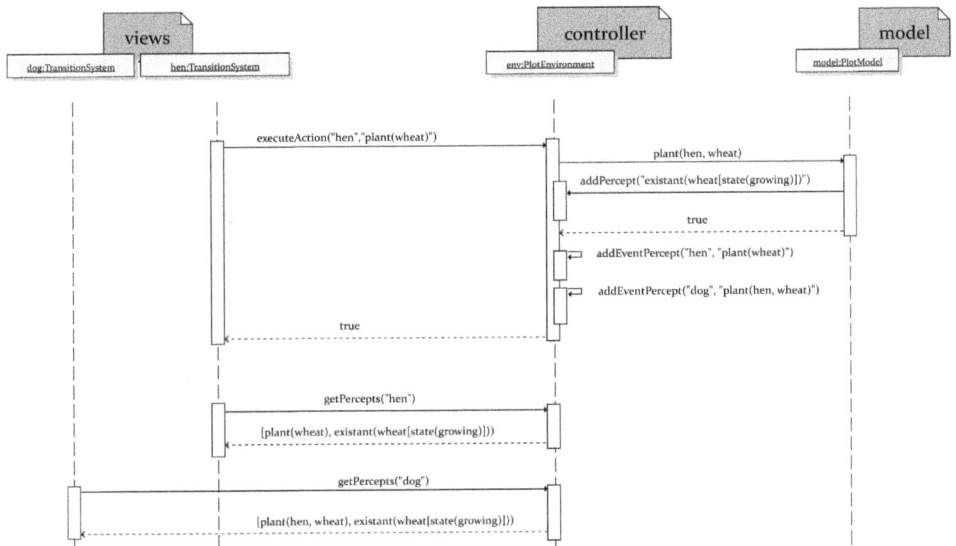

Figure 2.5: Sequence diagram depicting the general MVC style setup of the InBloom framework. The PlotEnvironment (controller) mediates the interaction of the agents (view) and the PlotModel (model). Note, how agents request actions from the controller, which decides which model method implements the required functionality, and how, in turn, the model requests the controller to report a new state-perception to the agents. Also, the PlotEnvironment automatically generates event-perceptions reporting that an action was executed and delivers them to all perceiving agents.

that case, the surplus actions are queued for later execution. Each round of simultaneous action execution increases an internal counter called step. A step is thus delimited by an (excluded) lower-bound at which the previous actions of all agents are executed, and an (included) upper bound at which the new actions are executed. This means that *environment steps* are denoting time intervals in which each character decides on a course of action and executes this action. They can be interpreted as units of story time. The foremost benefit of this discretization is that its units are independent of program execution time, and thus of processor speed, which otherwise would result in the paradoxical situation that the same story exhibits differing temporal properties on different computers.

Jason's `addPercept` mechanisms introduced above is very well suited to notify agents of the state of the environment. However, as I have discussed, most narrative interest resides not in states but in events: actions and happenings. While it would be possible for

---

none-action instead of blocking the entire environment.

agent reasoning programs to infer events from pure state percepts, the reasoning (and ASL programming) load can be lowered by providing environments with a dedicated mechanism for event perception delivery. For this purpose `PlotEnvironment` implements the method `void addEventPercept(String agentName, String perc ept)`, which adds `percept` to the list of perceptions for only one reasoning cycle and removes it again after it has been perceived once. Deciding, when events happen and who is capable of perceiving them is a task of custom models. The only exception concerns events that report the outcomes of actions, which are generated automatically by the InBloom framework: After an agent action is executed by the model, the environment determines which agents are capable of perceiving this event (per default this corresponds to all characters present at the same location) and adds a corresponding event perception for each of these agents. For the acting agent the literal of the perception is equal to the action request it provided to the environment. For the observing agents an additional term containing the acting agent's name is inserted at position 0 of this literal, which allows them to ascribe the action percept to the acting agent (e.g. note the different event percepts in Fig. 2.5). That way, happenings and actions are reported to agents as events, while all other percepts are reported as states.

Apart from that, `PlotEnvironment` is responsible for administrative tasks at the intersection of model, agents, actions and happenings. Due to its central position it can determine when a particular narrative system has reached an equilibrium state, that is, when no noteworthy events are expected to happen anymore. This is for instance the case, when each agent has been repeating the same action sequence for a considerable number of times. Custom environments can further extend these conditions by overriding the method `boolean PlotEnvironment#narrativeEquilibrium()`. When a narrative equilibrium is detected, `PlotEnvironment` pauses the execution of the simulation under the assumption that all productive conflict has been resolved. This allows users to inspect the hitherto created plot, or subsequent processing to initiate. Furthermore, the environment can notify agents of all dynamic common sense knowledge, that is, belief base entries that cannot be hand-coded into ASL files because they depend on the particular model and launcher configuration. The method `void initialize(List agents)` is responsible for this task, and, currently, notifies agents of all available locations and all existing characters. This, too, can be extended by custom environments.

PLOTMODEL provides the actual implementation of the TAW. It implements a weak form of spatiality by representing distinct locations using the `inBloom.storyworld.Location` class. Each location has a unique name, a list of present characters and a list of available items. Characters can enter any location from any other location in one time step, and items can be placed or removed from the location. When a character enters a location, it perceives all items, other present characters as well as their visible belongings. One default location is created during start-up, which is used as initial location for all existents unless the subclassing custom environment specifies otherwise.

Characters are implemented in the model using the `inBloom.storyworld.Character` class, and one character is set up for each Jason agent. Each character has a name, a location and an inventory of items it carries. The class implements methods to share, receive, collect or eat items from its inventory.

Items are non-agentive existents that characters can interact with. The abstract class `inBloom.storyworld.Item` can be subclassed to implement custom item types, and makes sure that all item types have a name and define whether they are edible or not.

All three classes: `Location`, `Character` and `Item` represent existents of the TAW that are perceivable to characters. In order to enable this functionality, they extend the abstract class `inBloom.storyworld.Existent` that implements the method `Literal literal()`. Per default, this method creates a `jason.asSyntax.Literal` from the generic `String toString()` representation, and can be used by any method to generate an ASL-compliable perception about the respective existent. Subclasses are responsible for implementing their own toString method in an appropriate manner.

HAPPENINGS are events that have no agent but affect at least one patient. By that merit they have to be understood as environment-internal state changes. Since they are state changes, happenings require at least two properties: an *effect* they have on the model, and a *trigger* that causes their occurrence. These are maintained via the class `inBloom.storyworld.Happening<T extends PlotMo del>`. The effect is a function that takes as input a custom model (that is, an instance of any possible class `T`), and performs a set of manipulations on that model. The trigger is also a function, but one that takes as input a custom model, and returns true if specific triggering condition are met by this model. Since version 1.8, this can be implemented in Java using functional interfaces, which allow the representation of functions as objects—in this case of type `java.util.function.Consumer` and `java.util.function.Predicate`, respectively. Listing 2.2 serves to demonstrate how the happening 'finding a grain of wheat' could be implemented.

At first sight, it might appear tempting to incorporate randomness into the triggering function in order to capture the apparent coincidental nature of happenings. However, as was discussed in Section 2.2, happenings appear random only from the internal perspective, while from an external perspective they serve a function for the plot. This means that happenings that appear random (i.e. not caused by changes in model state) still happen at a definite point in time, which can be implemented using a triggering condition that is dependent on the environment step e.g. `model.getStep() > 3`. This has the added benefit that simulation runs remain deterministic, which leaves experiments with inBloom reproducible.

While trigger and effect describe the happening itself, its function is to affect a patient. For that, it further needs to specify a patient, as well as a percept that will be delivered to the patient as an event perception. In the example of Listing 2.2 the patient would be the **hen** and the percept would be *"found(wheat)"*, which need to be defined before the happening instance is operational. Note, that it doesn't have to be the case that the entity affected by the happening's effect (e.g. see code lines 13/14) is also the patient. Imagine Cinderella loosing her slipper: it's Cinderella's inventory that is changed by the event, but in her haste she does not even perceive this state change. It is the prince who, perceiving *"lost(girl, slipper)"*, is the patient of this happening.

Happenings are scheduled with a triggering condition in mind, and in advance of a simulation run. This means that it cannot be guaranteed that all happenings will, in fact, be executed, because for some the triggering conditions might never be met. The management of happenings is performed by the class `inBloom.storywor`

```
1    Happening<FarmModel> findCorn = new Happening<FarmModel>(
2        // trigger:
3        new Predicate<FarmModel>(){
4            public boolean test(FarmModel model) {
5                if(model.FARM.farmingProgress > 3)
6                    return true;
7                return false;
8            }
9        },
10       // effect:
11       new Consumer<FarmModel>() {
12           public void accept(FarmModel model) {
13               Character chara = model.getCharacter("hen");
14               chara.addToInventory(new FarmModel.Wheat());
15           }
16       }
17   );
```

Listing 2.2: Happening: A hen finds a grain of wheat after some farm work has been done.

1d.ScheduledHappeningDirector, of which each model has an instance. A happening can be scheduled by using the method void sc heduleHappening(Happening h). At the beginning of each step, before considering the execution of scheduled actions, the environment will delegate to the model to check whether any happenings have been triggered using the method void checkHappenings(int step). The model queries its ScheduledHappeningDirector, which iterates over its list of scheduled happenings and for each one checks whether its trigger-function returns true. It removes all triggered happenings and returns them to the model, which for each happening executes the corresponding effect function and schedules the happenings perception to be delivered to its patient as an event. This means, that each happening is executed only once after it gets first triggered. Recurring happenings need to be scheduled multiple times.

ATTENTIVE READERS might have noticed a whiff of event-related causality relationships wafting around the mechanism of happening triggering. Listing 2.2 encodes that 'finding corn' is triggered when the field farmingProgress of location FARM passes a certain threshold—one might say that it is causally dependent on the state of this field (on the notion of causality, review my comments in foot-note 9 on p. 13). The state of this field itself is, in the same way, dependent on previous events, which have affected it. In the example above, `farmingProgress` would be increased above the threshold by an execution of the action `farmWork`, which by rule of transitivity can be considered the event that triggers our serendipitous happening— is causally responsible for it. Since all states and events are realized through the model, it is well equipped to track such causality re-lations. To capture the state of the TAW, `PlotModel` maintains a cache of relevant fields of model, location and character instances, mapped to their current values. The decision which fields are rele-vant for TAW state representation is a responsibility of the user of the framework; it can be indicated to the framework by annotating the respective field with the custom annotation `@ModelState`. Dur-ing model initialization, and whenever new locations and characters are added, `PlotModel` uses Java's reflection capabilities to detect all annotated fields and store them (with their respective containing ob-jects and current values) in `Table<Field, Object, Object> Plot Model.fieldValueStore`. After each action or happening e that is executed, the model is requested to note state changes, which it can do by iterating over the entries of its `fieldValueStore` and com-paring the stored values with the current ones. If it finds a value change, then it can note that event e caused the change by sav-ing this connection in the field `Table<String, String, String> PlotModel.causalityTable`. With one additional step this allows identifying the causes of happenings: Each happening has a field `String Happening.causalProperty`, which can be set manually by the framework user. It represents the name of the field whose state change triggers the execution of the happening (as per it's trigger-ing condition). When the `ScheduledHappeningDirector` determines that a particular happening was triggered, it can look up `causal-Property` in `PlotModel`'s `causalityTable`, and that way determine which previous event caused the triggering field-value change. This information will become relevant later on, when causality relation-ships between events will be used in order to find units of functional significance in plot graphs (see Section 4.1.1).

Together, the environment and the model classes realize an ontology that covers basic versions of spatio-temporality,

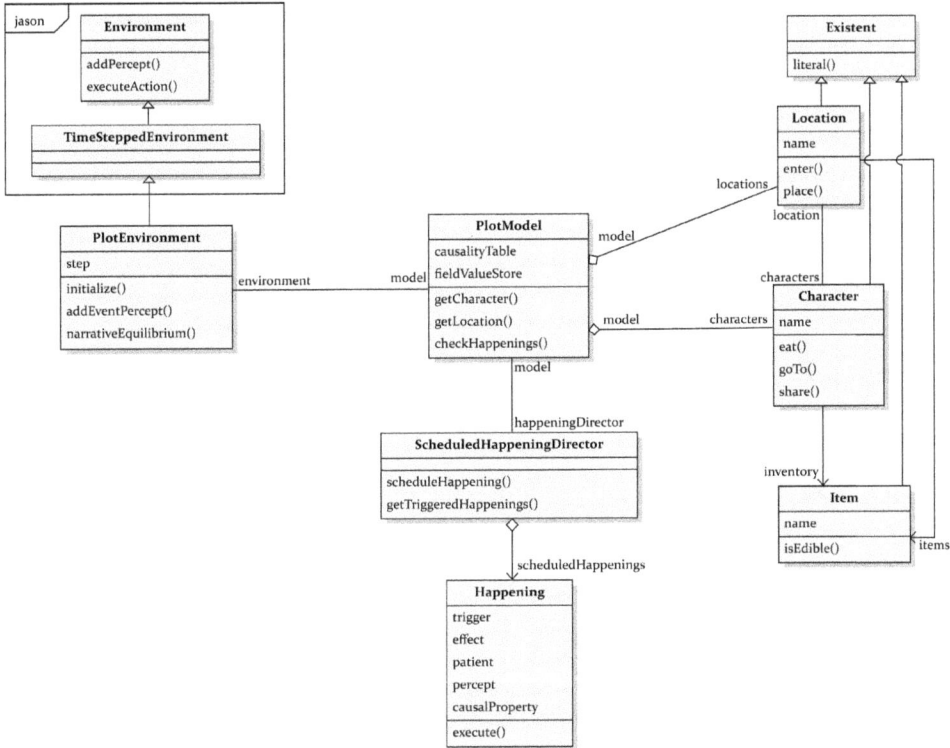

Figure 2.6: An abridged class diagram representation of the narrative semantics architecture in InBloom. For brevity reasons attributes are represented without types and methods without parameters or return types.

causality, agency and ownership (for an overview see Fig. 2.6). This selection, and the degree to which it was implemented, was guided primarily by the needs of the case-studies implemented so far, and can be further extended by custom models.

InBloom: Agent Implementation

On the agent side, InBloom implements narrative semantics using a custom AgentSpeak formalism for wish and obligation management, encoded in `agent-desire_wish_management.asl`. It can be imported in all custom ASL files to include its functionality.

As outlined in Sec. 2.3.3, wishes and obligations are representable in a BDI setting by a belief-desire combination, e.g. a $goal_1 \in D$ can be considered a wish only iff $wish(goal_1) \in B$. Naively, this could be achieved by triggering a desire to achieve $goal_1$, whenever the agent program adds a statement $wish(goal_1)$ to its belief base, utilizing the

```
1   // adding a 'wish-belief' creates a second-order desire
2   // to achieve it --> wish(Goal) established
3   +wish(Goal) <-
4       !wish(Goal).
5
6   // attempting to achieve the second-order desire by attempting
7   // to achieve embedded first-order desire
8   +!wish(Goal) <-
9       !Goal;
10      !wish(Goal).
11
12  // on failure reintroduce second-order desire, keeps wish active
13  -!wish(Goal) <-
14      !wish(Goal).
15
16  // removing a wish-belief removes all associated desires
17  // --> wish(Goal) removed
18  -wish(Goal) <-
19      .drop_desire(wish(Goal));
20      .drop_desire(Goal).
```

Listing 2.3: Implementation of narrative semantics of wishes using AgentSpeak.

second-order plan-statement: +wish(Goal) <- !Goal., where *Goal* is a variable that contains goals like eat(*bread*). However, this solution quickly falls short. As soon as the Jason BDI interpreter processes the internal desire-addition event +!Goal, it attempts to match a plan to achieve this. Yet, in most cases pertinent to narrative semantics this has to fail, as narrative interest (at least partially) resides in the long-range maintenance of such conflict. In such cases, Jason will be unable to identify a matching plan, and as a consequence remove the unsolvable goal from its desire set while creating an internal desire-removal event -!Goal. According to the above definition this is tantamount to removing wishes after only one failed attempt at achieving them, which doesn't make for modeling very interesting stories. The solution is to leverage the desire-removal event to reintroduce the wish. However, the naive solution of simply reintroducing the goal via -!Goal <- !Goal. would again be inadvisable as it would result in a blind adherence to *all* goals an agent might ever commit to, and not just wishes. This impasse can be broken by a provident utilization of second-order plans to allow the distinction of mundane goals from wish-goals, as depicted in Listing 2.3. A mediating second-order desire `!wish(Goal)` is introduced by the belief addition instead of the actual goal. It contains the sub-goal of achieving the actually wished state, which, like above, is likely to fail. However, its failure now also causes the failure of the second-order goal and the creation of an additional internal desire-removal event `-!wish(Goal)`. This can finally be leveraged as per lines 13, 14 of Listing 2.3 to reintroduce the wish-goal, while not being sensitive to other goals. Note, that line 10 effects a similar reintroduction of the wish-goal even in the case that the sub-goal is successfully achieved. The resulting behavior is that wishes remain active even after they were satisfied. In order to remove a wish the respective belief has to be removed from an agent's belief base as per lines 18 and following. This design decision was made to maintain consistency with the mechanism of wish-addition, and preclude inconsistent states where $wish(goal_1) \in B \wedge goal_1 \notin D$. Note, that the initially proposed formalization has to be slightly updated:

Definition 2 (Wish). A character is said to have a wish to achieve $goal_1$ iff for its corresponding InBloom agent the following holds: $wish(goal_1) \in B \wedge wish(goal_1) \in D$, where B is the agent's belief base and D its desire set.

Obligations are represented and managed accordingly:

Definition 3 (Obligation). A character is said to have an obligation to achieve $goal_1$ iff for its corresponding InBloom agent the following holds: $obligation(goal_1) \in B \wedge obligation(goal_1) \in D$, where B is the agent's belief base and D its desire set.

InBloom: Plot-Graph Generation

Per Def. 1, plot is a causal network of actions, happenings, and mental events, which emerges from the interaction of characters in a TAW. As has been discussed in Sec. 2.2.2, significant narrative interest resides in the virtual parts of plot: the private embedded narratives of the individual characters. So far, the computational representation of plot has not been discussed, since common MAS do not require modeling comparable phenomena. A custom data structure needs to be developed for InBloom, which can support all operations that a storytelling system might conceivably perform on plot.

Throughout the second part of her book, M.-L. Ryan (1991) resorts to graphs to illustrate the points she makes about plots, and in

her Chap. 10 she introduces two formal representations by means of
directed graphs. Since the system introduced in this thesis will have
to part with Ryan's framework starting from Chap. 3, a scrupulous
implementation of one of these formalisms is not expedient. However,
the general approach to plot representation using graphs remains very
appealing, since graphs are extensively researched computational data
structures. The details of the graph formalism deployed here are heavily influenced by the work of Lehnert (1981)—one of the approaches
mentioned by Ryan—which will come in handy in Chap. 4, when plot
quality will need to be estimated. At the same time, the present solution adapts and expands Lehnert's suggestions liberally, based on
technological affordances and conceptual needs.

IN GENERAL, a *plot graph* is comprised of vertices that represent
the events of a story, and edges that indicate how these events are
connected. Since InBloom models different types of events, different
vertex types need to be distinguished:

- I: to represent intentions;

- P: to represent perceptions, which could be happenings, the
  actions of other agents, or the occurrence of internal events;

- A: to represent actions;

- S: to represent the sending of speech acts;

- L: to represent the reception of speech acts.

The semantics of the event represented by a vertex (e.g. the content
of a speech act, or the particular state of affairs that an intention
aims at achieving) are called the *propositional content* of that vertex,
and will be represented by an ASL event (in informal graphs, I will
resort to single words or a short phrases in English, instead).

Events are generated by the BDI reasoning cycles of individual
agents (or are, in the case of actions, at least initiated by them).
This means that they are subjective representations of the TAW and
can be taken to capture (parts) of the characters' private embedded
narratives. Thus it makes sense to organize the plot graph into *character subgraphs*, each of which contains the events generated by the
reasoning cycle of only one agent. To denote this in the plot graph,
another type of vertex is introduced:

- *R*: to represent root vertices, and containing the respective characters' name as propositional content

In a plot, events can stand in different types of relations to each other so that Lehnert's formalism introduces several edge types in order to represent this distinction. For representing Ryan's narrative semantics, however, this is not relevant so that for now[19] edges can be simply taken to always represent a total temporal ordering.

Definition 4 (Character Subgraph). A character subgraph is a directed, vertex-labeled graph $G_c = (V_c, E_c, l_v, prop)$ comprised by a set of vertices V_c, a set of directed edges $E_c \subseteq V_c^2$ as well as the label function $l_v : V_c \to \{I, P, A, S, L, R\}$ and the propositional content function $prop : V \to Asl$, where Asl is the set of valid expressions in the AgentSpeak language. Each character subgraph contains exactly one root vertex v_0—with $l_v(v_0) = R$ and $prop(v_0) = c$—which has no predecessors in the subgraph: $|E_{v_0}^-| = 0$.[20]

Thus, for readability purposes c can be assumed to be the name of the corresponding character, which will be also the propositional content of the root vertex when the graph is displayed by InBloom.

Definition 5 (Plot Graph). A plot graph is a directed graph $G = (V, E)$ that is comprised by disjoint character subgraphs such that $V = \bigcup V_{c_i}$ and $E = \bigcup E_{c_i}$ for all $c_i \in C$ and C being the set of all characters participating in a plot.
The plot graph can be said to contain the character subgraphs from which it is comprised, shorthand notation: $G_{c_i} \in G$. It thus holds that: $\forall G_{c_i}, G_{c_j} \in G : i \neq j \Rightarrow V_{c_i} \cap V_{c_j} = \emptyset$.
The type of a vertex $v_i \in V$ in a plot graph is a short hand way of referring to the label of that vertex in the character subgraph to which it belongs: $type(v_i, G) = l_v(v_i)$ where $l_v \in G_c$ with c such that $v_i \in V_c$ and $G_c = (V_c, E_c, l_v, prop) \in G$.

From Definition 5 follows that each vertex of a plot graph is contained in exactly one character subgraph: $\forall v \in V \forall G_i \in G : v \in V_v \land G_v \neq G_i \Rightarrow v \notin V_i$. It is also worth noting that, following the above definitions, plot graphs only represent the subjective domains of individual characters. Although these domains may sometimes overlap because e.g. the action of one character is perceived by another one,

---

[19]This formalism will be extended with the edge types: motivation, actualization, termination, causation and cross-character in Chap. 4 in order to enable specific aspects of plot-quality estimation.

[20]Let E_v^- denote the set of incoming edges for the vertex v.

the resulting picture does not necessarily represent an objective total. The system and formalism would effortlessly support the addition of an objective domain, i.e. events representing state changes occurring (only) in the environment, by insertion of an additional subgraph for the TAW. However, no added benefit from this could be identified so far, so that an implementation remained unnecessary.

As a noteworthy aside, I would like to point out that plot graphs are generated by InBloom during the execution of narrative systems, and their vertices are temporally ordered in accordance with the order of the events of the system. From a computer science perspective, they could be regarded as the *execution trace* of a simulation run, a tool used by software engineers to debug the dynamics of complex programs. The developer and poet Richard Gabriel, who attempted to implement a computational system for poetry generation based on his personal writing style (Gabriel, 2016) noted, that execution traces of his system allowed not only the debugging of the system itself, but also could be subverted to assess and frame the aesthetics of the poem that was generated by that execution. As mentioned, in Chap. 4 I will face a similar problem, and I too will resort to the execution trace (in its instantiation as plot graph) in order to solve it. Whether this is a coincidence, or a yet under-investigated affordance of CC software I do not dare to say.

For the convenience of the system's users, another auxiliary subgraph is added to plot graphs, whose vertices are not of any of the previous type but contain environment step numbers. This subgraph acts as a temporal axis, and when the plot graph is displayed vertices from character subgraphs are visually distributed in a way that enables a quick identification of synchronous events and the associated environment step. A toy plot graph, generated and visualized by the system, can be found in Fig. 2.7. Note, how the agents develop beliefs about each other through mutual perception, and how action-perceptions like `+wipe(barbara,glass)` are delivered and removed in quick succession by the environment, as they represent fleeting events and not permanent states. Also, a collection of dynamic common sense knowledge (about locations and characters) is digested by each agent in the beginning, as has been described in Section 2.3.4.

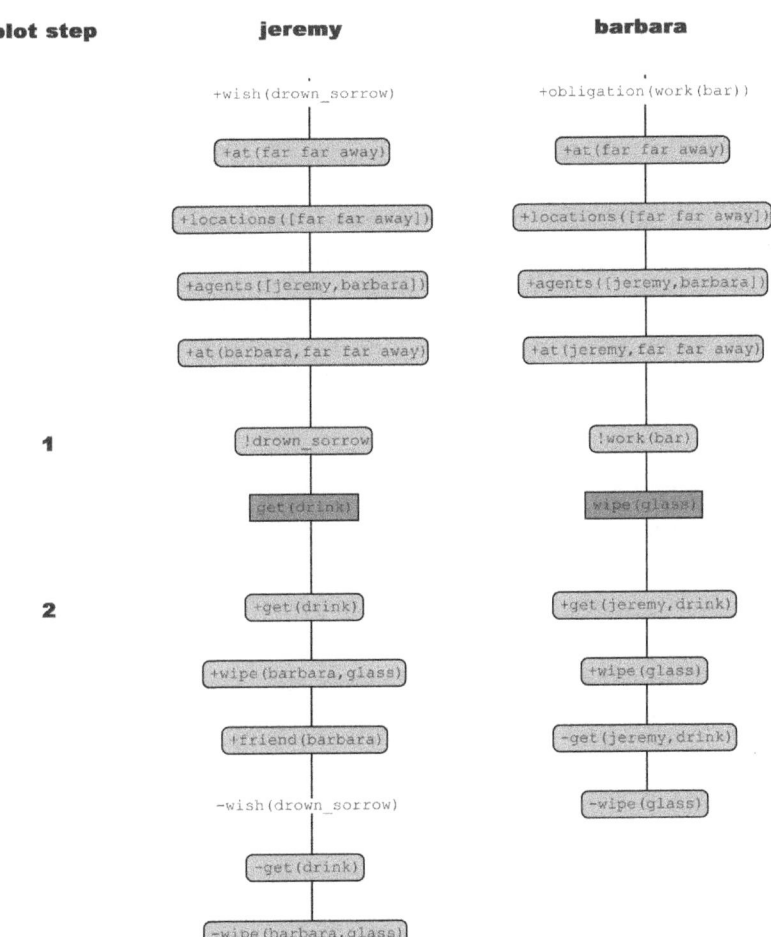

plot step	jeremy	barbara
	+wish(drown_sorrow)	+obligation(work(bar))
	+at(far far away)	+at(far far away)
	+locations([far far away])	+locations([far far away])
	+agents([jeremy,barbara])	+agents([jeremy,barbara])
	+at(barbara,far far away)	+at(jeremy,far far away)
1	!drown_sorrow	!work(bar)
	get(drink)	wipe(glass)
2	+get(drink)	+get(jeremy,drink)
	+wipe(barbara,glass)	+wipe(glass)
	+friend(barbara)	-get(jeremy,drink)
	-wish(drown_sorrow)	-wipe(glass)
	-get(drink)	
	-wipe(barbara,glass)	

Figure 2.7: Example plot graph generated by InBloom. Actions (A-type vertices) are visualized by dark-gray color, while virtual events are visualized by light-gray color: Intentions (I-vertices) start with an !, perceptions (P vertices) start with + or − (denoting belief addition or removal). The addition or removal of wishes and obligations are a special type of virtual event, and for that reason do not appear inside a box. Content-wise, the graph represents a plot with two characters, located at a bar called Far Far Away. Barbara is a bar keeper, busying herself by wiping a glass. Jeremy patronizes the establishment with the intention of drowning his sorrows. He gets himself a drink, and watches barkeeper Barbara wipe the glass. Presumably already inebriated, he decides that Barbara is his friend, and feels his sorrows ease.

THE PLOT GRAPH IS IMPLEMENTED   using the JUNG framework[21].
The class `inBloom.graph.PlotDirectedSparseGraph` implements
methods to add events to the graph, which are translated into vertices (`inBloom.graph.Vertex`) and edges (`inBloom.graph.Edge`).
For this it maintains `HashMap<String, Vertex> lastVertexMap`, a
mapping from character names to the last vertex added to this character's subgraph (initially, the root node). When a new event is
added, a `Vertex` instance is created whose label contains the full
event literal, and whose type is a representation of the type of the
occurring event (an enum with the options: `ACTION`, `PERCEPT`, `SPE
ECHACT`, `LISTEN`, `INTENTION`, `ROOT`, `AXIS_LABEL`). The new ver-
tex is connected via a new `Edge` instance to the last vertex of the
experiencing character's subgraph, and replaces its new-found parent
vertex in `lastVertexMap`. The method simultaneously maintains the
previously mentioned temporal axis, by checking whether the newly
added event was experienced at a new environment step, and attaching a `Vertex` instance of `AXIS\_LABEL` type to the subgraph of the
temporal axis if this is the case.

This graph is managed and built by the class `inBloom.grap
h.PlotGraphController` in real-time, while a simulation is being
executed. The `PlotGraphController` is designed following the
singleton pattern (see e.g. Gamma et al., 1995) such that the
static method `PlotGraphController#getPlotListener()` provides
the whole system with access to an instance of `PlotGraphControlle
r`. This instance can be used to add events to the graph using the
method `void addEvent(String character, String event, Vert
ex.Type eventType, int step)`. Once a simulation is completed
(usually, because `PlotEnvironment` identified a narrative equilibrium
and paused the execution) it is again the controller's responsibility
to create the centered, character and step aligned column layout[22]
that was devised to visualize the graph (refer to Fig. 2.7 for an ex-

---

[21] "A software library that provides a common and extendible language for the
modeling, analysis, and visualization of data that can be represented as a graph
or network" (http://jung.sourceforge.net/).

[22] Since a graph is an abstract structure that is defined only by which vertex-
pairs are connected, a plethora of different layouts can be used to illustrate the
same graph. Thus, a layout is a function $f : V \to \mathbb{N}^2$ that transforms plot graphs
into legible plot graph drawings by computing for each vertex $v \in V$ a point that
can be used as the upper-left corner for a visual representation of this vertex.
Edges can then be inserted as straight lines accordingly.

ample). This is done by the method `PlotGraphController#visu alizeGraph()` via the class `inBloom.graph.PlotGraphLayout`. For this purpose, `PlotGraphLayout` iterates twice over the whole graph. In a first run it computes the x-position of each character subgraph (which is dependent on the maximum vertex-width in the previous subgraph), and the y-position of each step (which is dependent on the maximum number of vertices in the previous step). In the second run it determines the position of each individual vertex depending on its step and subgraph affiliation. Lastly, the `PlotGraphController` is also responsible for creating the UI that visualizes the graph on screen and allows user-interactions with it.

In order to use the functionality of the `PlotGraphController`, Jason needs to be extended so that vertices are added in the following situations:

1. an agent requests the execution of an action,

2. an agent sends or receives a speech act,

3. an agent processes an internal or external (perception) event.

As has been described previously, the first functionality is implemented by the method `PlotEnvironment#executeAction`, which can be easily extended to include a call to `PlotGraphController`'s `addEvent` method.

Sending and receiving messages, in the setup under which Jason is employed throughout this thesis, is implemented by the class `jason.infra.centralised.CentralisedAgArch`. It is extended by `inBloom.jason.PlotAwareCentralisedAgArch` so that the method `void sendMsg(Message m)` can be overridden to include a call to `PlotGraphController` to create a new SPEECH-type vertex. This is followed by an execution of the method `void receiveMsg(Mess age m, Vertex senderV)` on the `PlotAwareCentralisedArch` instance that runs the receiver of the message, which creates a LISTEN vertex and delegates the rest of the message-reception to it's superclass. Jason can be configured to use the new agent architecture during simulation start, which will be described in the next subsection.

The third situation can be captured by attaching a listener to each agent's `TransitionSystem`. The listener gets notified by the Jason framework each time an event is added during the agent's

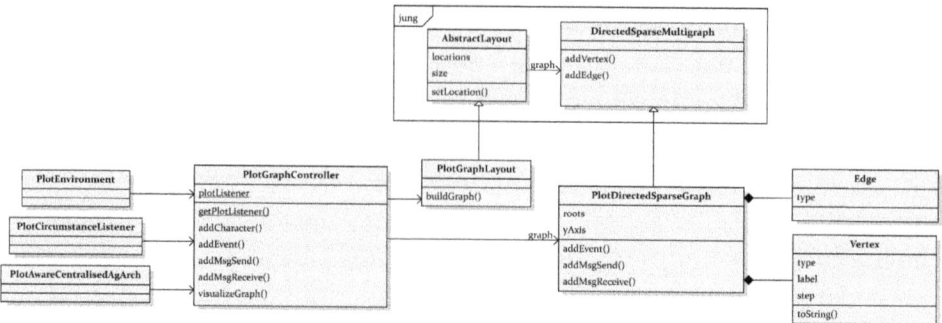

Figure 2.8: An abridged class diagram representation of the plot graph architecture in InBloom. For brevity reasons attributes are represented without types and methods without parameters or return types. Static members are underlined.

reasoning cycle. This is done by extending Jason's abstract `ja son.asSemantics.CircumstanceListener` class and overriding its method `void eventAdded(Event e)` to include a call to `PlotGrap hController`'s `addEvent` method, which is accomplished by the In-Bloom class `inBloom.jason.PlotCircumstanceListener`. Listener instances need to be added for each agent during initialization, so that the respective listeners are operational when the simulation starts. To accomplish this, Jason allows extending its `jason.asSemantics.Ag ent` class and overriding the method `void initAg()`, which is done by `inBloom.jason.PlotAwareAg`. Jason can be configured to use `PlotAwareAgent` as agent class in the simulation's mas2j file (refer back to Section 2.3.4 for a description of Jason's configuration mechanism).

Summarizing, `PlotGraphController` effectively functions as a tracer that is informed whenever a plot-relevant event is processed by the system, and that constructs a plot graph by ordering these concurrent calls and matching them to the appropriate character subgraphs. The resulting architecture can be seen in Fig. 2.8.

InBloom: Start-up and Configuration

A Jason simulation is typically started by `jason.infra.centrali sed.RunCentralisedMAS`, which reads in a mas2j configuration file and, based on its contents, sets up the agents, the environment as well as the UI. This mechanism is extended by InBloom to make the start-up more dynamic and appropriate for the narrative context in which it operates.

First, the UI needs to be adopted. This is done by `inBloom.Pl otControlsLauncher` which extends `RunCentralisedMAS` and overrides its method `void createButtons()`. This method omits several unnecessary controls created by default, and instead adds a button that can be used to display the current plot graph. The realization of this is straightforward, since the graph and its graphical representation are made available to the whole system by the singleton `PlotGraphController`.

For a better division of concerns the actual setup is encapsulated in a subclass of this launcher class, `inBloom.PlotLaunch er`. This class provides the convenience method `void run()` that starts a simulation, waits until it ends (usually because a user clicked the "end" button) and then finalizes the system before quitting. What is more important, the class also implements the method `void initialize (String[] args, PlotModel<?> mode l, List<LauncherAgent> agents, String agentFileName)` that performs everything necessary to configure an InBloom simulation run. Especially, it automatically constructs the file `launcher.mas2j` based on the list of provided agents and a number of static parameters that declare which classes should be instantiated to represent individual agents (`PlotAwareAgent`) and the environment (any subclass of `PlotEnvironment`). During launch, agents can be configured by instantiating the class `inBloom.LauncherAgent` and appropriately setting the parameters: `beliefs`, `goals`, `inventory` and `location`, which can be used to set up differing initial states for each agent, as well as `name`, which is used as an agent ID throughout the simulation. That way, users of the InBloom framework do not need to manually write or modify configuration files when they make changes to the initial narrative semantics of a simulation, but instead can rely on purely object-oriented methodology.

After creating the config file and using it to initialize the Jason framework, the method proceeds by successively initializing `PlotEnvironment`, `PlotModel` and all `PlotAwareAgents` (in that order) so that all of the newly introduced InBloom functionality is operational on start-up. As a side-note, `PlotLauncher` also has to override the method `void createAgs()` that is used by `RunCentralisedMAS` to setup agents, in order to change the agent architecture class to InBloom's own `PlotAwareCentralisedAgArch`.

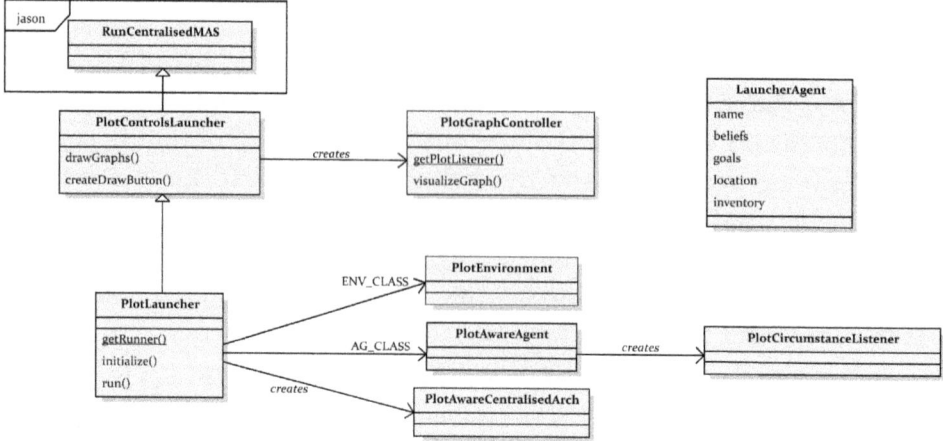

Figure 2.9: An abridged class diagram representation of the launcher architecture in InBloom. For brevity reasons attributes are represented without types and methods without parameters or return types. Static members are underlined.

Thus, all a user has to do in order to start a simulation is to instantiate `PlotLauncher` and perform the following four steps:

1. indicate the custom environment class for the simulation by setting the launcher's static variable `ENV_CLASS`,

2. provide details on the agents that should be created for the simulation via a list of `LauncherAgent` instances,

3. instantiate the custom model class for the simulation and provide it with an initialised happening director,

4. set the simulation in motion by executing the `initialize` and `run` methods of the launcher instance.

This is usually done by extending `PlotLauncher` with a custom launcher class that performs these steps in its `public static void id main(String[] args)` method.

To enable any other system to operate on the active launcher, `PlotLauncher` provides the static method `PlotLauncher getRunner()`, which gives access to the only existing launcher instance in singleton fashion. This is crucial for any meta-process that would like to exhibit creative behavior by iteratively executing and evaluating simulation runs, which will be the focus of Chap. 5. The resulting architecture can be seen in Fig. 2.9.

Overview

Before moving on to a case study, lets quickly recapitulate what has been accomplished with InBloom so far.

The environment and the model realize an ontology that covers basic versions of spatio-temporality, causality, agency and ownership, and by that means model the TAW of a narrative system. An AgentSpeak file implements the management of wishes and obligations via belief addition and removal. By that means it enables an automatic translation of narrative semantics into Jason's BDI logic. The plot graph controller functions as a tracer that is informed whenever a plot-relevant event is processed by the system. It constructs a plot graph by ordering these concurrent calls coming mainly from agent's reasoning cycles, and organizing them in time step aligned character subgraphs. That way it captures plot, which is an emergent, virtuality-aware property of a narrative systems. These extensions of the Jason framework are orchestrated by the plot launcher, which can be used to dynamically set up and run simulations.

As pointed out repeatedly, InBloom ended up a framework rather than a simple application because it implements the abstract rules that govern narrative systems rather than an individual narrative system. It can equally well be used to realize e.g. folktale systems or bildungsroman systems, although their respective TAWs follow markedly differing rules and their characters are subject to differing behavioral patterns. In order to implement a custom narrative system only few steps are required, which involve the implementation of its domain-specific rules. This is done by sub-classing three InBloom classes and creating an ASL file:

1. `PlotModel` needs to be subclassed to implement the state of the environment, the actions available to agents in order to affect it, as well as its internal dynamics leading to happenings.

2. A custom AgentSpeak file needs to be created that includes InBloom's agent-desire_wish_management.asl and implements a domain-specific plan library, common-sense reasoning and basic world knowledge.

3. `PlotEnvironment` needs to be subclassed to perform a mapping from agent actions to model methods.

4. `PlotLauncher` needs to be subclassed to configure InBloom to use these custom classes, setup the initial state of the agents and schedule happenings.

Following this procedure, the next section will attempt to create a narrative system for TLRH using InBloom.

2.4. A Case Study (in Red)

Far from being a mere example, recreating the plot of an existing folktale is an important step in the process of theory building. It is the experimental validation of the implicit hypothesis behind any comprehensive narratological theory: that the first principles set up by this theory are suitable and sufficient to describe the narratives in its target corpus. The default approach of a narratologist to theory validation is the analysis of existing stories. While being the classical tool in the narratological toolkit, the *analysis* is susceptible to several problems: One is, that it has to depart from text, which can lead to ambiguities when dealing with underlying layers like the virtual parts of plot, a problem we have encountered in the discussion of the plot of TLRH in Section 2.2.4. Furthermore, it operates on a high level of abstraction that makes it easy to overlook inconsistencies or omissions on lower levels. Lastly, analysis best affords static descriptions like the classification of phenomena, while making it harder (albeit far from impossible) to describe how the dynamic properties of a narrative unfold from its static components. The computational means described in this chapter can be seen as a belated addition of *generation* to the tool belt of one particular narratologist, namely Mary-Laure Ryan. Her theory can be validated by being put to the test via generation: Are the first principles set up by her theory sufficient to recreate the plot of existing folktales? Using InBloom to recreate one tale, 'The Little Red Hen', can be but the start of such an endeavor.

2.4.1. Implementation

We will walk through the steps required for implementing the narrative system of TLRH one by one.

A CUSTOM MODEL that represents the story's TAW needs to be created. For this purpose, `inBloom.stories.little_red_hen.F armModel` is set up by extending `PlotModel`. It has one location, `inBloom.stories.little_red_hen.FarmModel.Farm` that extends `Location`. The farm can have produce, represented by the field: `Wheat produce`, which is initially empty but can contain a wheat instance as soon as some cereal grain has been planted. The respective class, `inBloom.stories.little_red_hen.FarmMod el.Wheat`, extends `Item` and has a state, represented by the field `Wheat.STATES state`, with the enum type `STATES` allowing the constants: `SEED, GROWING, RIPE, HARVESTED` or `FLOUR`[23]. In order to make the state available to ASL reasoners, it is appended to the default representation created by the method `literal` as an annotation of the form $state(\alpha)$ with $\alpha \in$ `Wheat.STATES`. The farm offers the convenience method `void updateProduceState(Wheat.STATES st ate)` which changes the state of its produce to the requested state and at the same time updates the state perceptions available to all present agents using the `addPercept` method provided by `PlotEnvironment`.

This is used by the `FarmModel` method `plantWheat(Character a gent)`—which checks whether the agent's inventory contains a wheat seed instance and, if so, moves it from the agent's inventory to the farm's produce field—to update the wheat's state to growing. `Farm Model` implements comparable methods: `tendWheat, harvestWheat` and `grindWheat`, to enable the successive transition of the growing wheat from ripe over harvested into the flour state, located again in the inventory of the agent who executed the grinding. It also offers the method `bakeBread(Character agent)`, which destroys one wheat-flour instance in the agent's inventory and adds a newly created instance of `inBloom.stories.little_red_hen.FarmModel.Bread`, which is a generic `Item` subclass with the single deviation that it overrides the `isEdible()` method to return `true`.

To enable this process, the hen needs to find a grain of wheat, around the beginning of the story. This can be accomplished by extending `Happening` with a custom class `inBloom.stories.litt le_red_hen.FindCornHappening` whose `execute` method creates a

---

[23]Representing flour as a state of grain is an ontologically highly questionable decision. However, since in the present narrative system flour only ever appears as an interim stage in the bread-making process it seems acceptable to maintain this simplification.

`Wheat` instance, adds it to it's patient's inventory, and is perceived in ASL as the predicate `found(wheat)`. The `trigger` for this happening can vary. In its simplest form, it can return true when a certain environment step is reached, in combination with the hen being the hard-coded patient. Another, more elegant, route was chosen to show-case the utility of the causality implementation. The story notes the hen's propensity to regular farm work, which can be exploited for our own wicked needs. Thus, the additional method `farmWork(Character agent)` is implemented in `FarmModel`, which allows an agent (located at the farm) to increase the value of the field `int farmingProgress`, which is added to the location `Farm` precisely for this purpose. This can then be exploited by setting the happening's trigger to return `true` when `farmingProgress` reaches a certain threshold (arbitrarily set to 2). In my parlance, this makes the happening causally dependent on `farmingProgress`.[24] Once an action results in the required state change, InBloom's causality mechanism can back-track this connection, and extract the responsible agent to be subjected to the happening in question.

Only a few loose ends remain to be tied up for the model. Characters need the ability to eat, so the method `eat(String itemType)` is implemented in the class character. It succeeds iff the respective character posses an instance of `itemType` in its inventory and that instance is edible, with the effect that the instance is removed from the inventory. Furthermore, the method `relax()` is added to the character class, which (at least for now) has no effect and always succeeds.

A CUSTOM AGENTSPEAK FILE   that will determine the agents' reasoning needs to be created, then. Since all the characters in the story are essentially of the same nature—folktale animals—it seems prudent to assign them the same set of cognitive affordances, that is, common-sense beliefs, potential plans, and so on. For this, the file `agent_folktale_animal.asl` is created.

To enable the main process of the story, plans need to be encoded that allow an agent to make bread from wheat. One possible way of

---

[24]This additionally requires the developer to remember to set the happening's `causalProperty` field to `farmingProgress`, as described in Sec. 2.3.4. This is tedious, but necessary, as Java Reflection is not powerful enough to automatically extract such logical information.

doing that is demonstrated in Lis. 2.4.

```
1  +!create(bread) : has(wheat [state(seed)]) <-
2      !plant(wheat).
3  +!create(bread) : at(wheat [state(growing)], farm) <-
4      !tend(wheat).
5  +!create(bread) : at(wheat [state(ripe)], farm) <-
6      !harvest(wheat).
7  +!create(bread) : has(wheat [state(harvested)]) <-
8      !grind(wheat).
9  +!create(bread) : has(wheat [state(flour)]) <-
10     !bake(bread);
11     .resume(wish(relax));
12      -obligation(create(bread)).
```

Listing 2.4: ASL plans for bread creation

This is a more flexible notation then employing one monolithic plan that is comprised of all individual sub-plans, since it allows agents to decide the appropriate next step based on the state of the environment instead of a blind schema. Note, how the state annotations that the class **Wheat** appends to its literal representations can be leverage by this approach to identify the next plan step independent of whether the wheat is planted or in an agent's inventory.

In order to commence the bread-making, an agent needs to develop either a wish or an obligation to do so. I enable this in Lis. 2.5 in a fairly general fashion to again allow for flexibility.

```
1  +found(X) : creatable_from(X,Y) & is_useful(Y) <-
2      .suspend(wish(relax));
3      +obligation(create(Y)).
4
5  is_useful(A) :- is_pleasant(eat(A)) & hungry.
6
7  creatable_from(wheat,bread).
8  is_pleasant(eat(bread)).
```

Listing 2.5: ASL system triggering bread baking behavior

Thus, the obligation to create something is cued upon finding a thing from which something useful can be created. Apart from requiring a plan statement, this solution brings about the design of a

fledgling common-sense knowledge base that encodes facts (like that
bread is creatable from wheat) but also conceptual knowledge (like
that something is useful, if it is edible and oneself is hungry).

A crucial part of the story is the hen's repeated request for help,
and the repeated refusal of the other characters. Our implementation
in Lis. 2.6 again attempts to generalize as far as possible in order to
create an abstract reasoning template for the schema denied request,
and naturally makes use of Jason's speech acts. The main work here

```
1    +!X : is_work(X) &
2            not complex_plan(X) & not already_asked(X)   <-
3          .my_name(Me);
4          ?present(Animals);
5          +already_asked(X);
6          for (.member(Animal, Animals)) {
7              .send(Animal, tell, request(help_with(Me,X)));
8              +asking(help_with(X), Animal);
9          }
10         .wait(not asking(help_with(X), _), 1000);
11         !X;
12         -already_asked(X).
13
14   +request(help_with(Helpee, Plan)) <-
15         +obligation(help_with(Helpee, Plan)).
16
17   +!obligation(help_with(Helpee, Plan)) : wish(Y) &
18            is_work(help_with(Plan)) <-
19         !reject(Helpee, help_with(Helpee,Plan)).
20
21   +!reject(Helpee, Plan) <-
22         .send(Helpee, tell, rejected_request(Plan));
23         -obligation(Plan).
24
25   +rejected_request(help_with(Helpee,Req))[source(Name)] <-
26         -asking(help_with(Req), Name).
27
28   is_work(help_with(Name, X)) :- is_work(X).
29   is_work(plant(X)).
30   // and so on, for the other the sub-plans for creating bread
```

Listing 2.6: ASL plans for managing help requests and denying them

is performed by the meta-plan in l. 1 of Lis. 2.6, which encodes that
an agent asks all other present agents for help before attempting a

plan that is encoded as work-intensive in its knowledge base. Then, the agent waits a reasonable amount of time for the other agents to answer, before attempting its plan—with or without help. In order to avoid an infinite recursion of help-asking, a short lived mental note `already_asked(X)` is added after the first time the meta-plan is triggered, and removed after the actual plan is executed, so that the next time the plan is attempted the cycle can start again. The help request is transmitted to the other agents as a Jason speech act of type *tell*, which results in the addition of the belief `request(help_wi` `th(sender_name, plan))` to the receiver's knowledge base. Processing this event triggers an obligation to help the sender (l. 13–14).

While, so far, the implementation has remained fairly independent of the current application, the next steps are dictated by the needs of the folktale to have the hen's requests rejected. My solution is to stipulate that an obligation to help someone is rejected by an agent if the requested task is work-intensive and the agent has a wish with regards to something it would rather like to do (l. 16). This rejection is implemented by *tell*-ing the sender that the agent rejects its request and removing the obligation. Processing this event on the side of the original sender results in the addition of a mental note that its collocutor has answered, which enables it to stop waiting for help after everyone has answered.[25]

From the story's main elements, only the capacity for punishment remains open. The most general solution for implementing punishment would see an agent reason about another agent's intentions and desires, as well as means to counteract them. This is a non-trivial task of other-representation based on some sort of theory of mind, which unfortunately remained outside the scope of the possible for this dissertation. Thus, for want of a generic solution, I opted for introducing a story-specific, basic one depicted in Lis. 2.7.

This implementation of punishment works based on a conflation of self and other: The punishing agent works under the assumption that if itself beliefs something to be pleasant of taste, then other agents will do so, too. It then leverages the fact that it posses a 'tasty' item by triggering a desire in the other agents to eat (some of) that tasty item via means of an *achieve* speech act, and then removing

---

[25]The conspicuous absence of a capacity for positive response is due to the narrow requirements of the original story. It can be easily added to the current implementation along the same lines, and will be, in Chap. 3.

```
1  +!punish : has(X) & hungry & is_pleasant(eat(X)) <-
2      ?punishment_targets(Anims);
3      .send(Anims, achieve, eat(X));
4      !eat(X);
5      -wish(punish).
```

Listing 2.7: ASL plans for punishment behavior

it's victims possibility of doing so by visibly destroying that item by ingesting it itself. This, in essence, taunts the other animals with a piece of food, which conventionally is understood as a malevolent act and thus can serve as punishment. As mentioned above, this is a very basic solution because it does not include any reasoning about why such a plan is harmful for the other agent and thus also does not allow any meaningful alteration of the plan to come up with comparable punishment strategies in case of absence of suitable edibles. The ideal solution for this would be the implementation of a theory of mind module based on which punishment plans can be deduced dynamically.

In order to set up the general behavior of the farm animals, some default behavior and machinery has to be put in place as, per Lis. 2.8.

```
1  wish(relax).
2  self(farm_animal).
3  hungry.
4
5  +self(farm_animal) <- +obligation(farm_work).
6
7  +!plant(wheat) <-
8      plant(wheat).
9  //... each action wrapped in dedicated action-execution plan
```

Listing 2.8: ASL setup for default farm-animal behavior

Lines 1 and 5 set up an essential conflict underlying the tale: the wish of (presumably every creature) to relax, versus the obligation of a farm animal to work on the farm. In order for this to have effect, the inhabitants of the farm require the knowledge that they are farm animals, which is accompanied by the belief that they are hungry in order to fulfill the preconditions of the plan for bread creation later during the simulation. Also, in order to enable the help-seeking behavior described above, it is necessary to wrap the actions involved in bread-making in dedicated plans like in lines 7-8. To maintain clarity and comparability of style the decision was made to equip all other actions with such plans, which I call *action-execution plans*. This is a side-effect of the fact that ASL only allows reasoning about plans but not actions.

2.4.2. Discussion of the Case Study

The main goal of the present case study is to put to the test the narratological theory underlying InBloom's implementation. However, before reporting the actual insights gained from this endeavor, I find it important to openly discuss the limitations of the technological execution that lead to them.

Technological Considerations

As discussed in Sec. 1.4, strong-autonomy approaches to plot generation rest on the emergence of unexpected event combinations from the dynamics of the MAS. In order to allow such unexpected interactions the implementation of the environment's internal behavior and the agents' reasoning must be as general as possible. As such, the introduced narrative system does not completely hold up to my personal expectations. Consider the ASL code implementing the obligation to create bread (line 1 in Listing 2.5). It is triggered when an agent that believes to be hungry finds a grain of wheat. However, already in the trivially isomorphic case that an agent, who posses a grain of wheat, *turns* hungry, this obligation is not triggered any more. Of course, this can easily be alleviated by implementing an analogous second case with the new triggering condition. But extending this approach to all conceivable cases would lead to code-duplication and a code base cluttered with conditions that (in the foreseeable future) are never going to be executed.

During another case study, the above narrative system has been extended in order to accommodate the plot of a second folktale. For this it was necessary to enable a piece of cheese to fall out of the beak of a bird that starts singing. In an ideal world, this should be done by incorporating gravitation into the ontology of the narrative system. However, this would require implementing the concept of a surface, meaning that all existents have to be supported by a surface, as well as a general rule that existents fall to a lower surface when they stop being supported. This, in turn, would require incorporating a three-dimensional Euclidean model of spatiality into that system, in order to be able to identify lower surfaces. As if this wasn't enough, the cheese in the target tale actually always remains supported by the underside of the crows beak. However, since it is larger then the beak, it rests in an unstable equilibrium that is maintained only by the force of the upper beak being applied from above. It is the singing-induced lifting of the upper beak that deprives the system of the external force and breaks the equilibrium, which leads to the fall of the cheese. Modeling this would require incorporating at least a subset of Newtonian physics into the narrative system's ontology, as well as a three-dimensional modeling of the constituent parts of existents; a dizzying prospect that led me to the decision to quickly abandon this 'ideal' world. Instead, I chose to implement that the entire inventory of an agent that sits on a tree falls below the tree as soon as the agent sings. Obviously, this is a remarkably inept solution that is at the same time too broad (since e.g. a singing human should not loose a single thing) and too narrow (since singing on e.g. a roof would not produce the desired effect) and thus undermines the systems potential for interesting emergent behavior. Yet, implementing a solution that generalizes better seemed a bad trade-off due to the exorbitant amount of required time.

Problems like these are a fundamental aspect of symbolic, non-embodied approaches, especially in cases where the knowledge base and environment have to be completely manually designed and cannot be reliably learned by the system, which in itself is an open research problem. In fact, problems like these have led to the great wave of disappointment with the AI research program by the end of the 1980s that has been called the AI winter. It has never been the ambition of this thesis to solve, or even just address, these long standing problems, so that all that is left here is to acknowledge them and move on with a meek smile.

Another problematic point can be exemplified by how in the implementation of the environment one action is enough to enable the wheat's transition through the individual stages of its ripening process (note too, how no other produce, possibly with other needs for upkeep, have been realized). This is clearly not a realistic simulation, even of the context of a folktale story world. Instead, it is a simplification that alleviates the need for any downstream composition-processes that performs condensation[26], and facilitates the synchronization of the fates of individual characters. Solutions like this have no merit from an internal perspective on the story world but have to be included into the simulation because of reasons from the external perspective, which is an undesirable intermixture of concerns.

Conceptual Insights

The implementation introduced in the last section covers all phenomena required by Ryan's framework to model the narrative system of TLRH. If the first principles provided by her theory are sufficiently expressive then running the simulation should result in the emergence of the narrative's plot. However, this is not the case, because two questions remain to be addressed before all of the characters' observed behavior can be implemented:

1. Why does the hen normally work on the farm, while the other animals always relax?

2. What triggers the hen's desire to punish the other animals?

THE FIRST QUESTION leads back to the previously mentioned basic conflict between the obligation to work and the wish to relax. Ryan's approach outlines how plot can be analyzed based on the conflicts inherent to the state of a character's private worlds. The dynamics of goal selection in the presence of conflicting private worlds, however, are not discussed by her at all. At the very least, for the sake of consistency, the position must be that comparable characters act comparably in similar states. Specifically, this means that they should select the same goals if they have the same beliefs, wishes and obligations. Yet precisely this appears not to be the case in TLRH: the characters start out in comparable positions, yet their default goals differ: the hen follows the obligation, while the others indulge the wish. One might resolve this problem by assuming that for some reason the hen lacks the wish to relax, and the other animals lack the obligation to

---

[26]The narrative system that is implemented by the MAS, here, is only one component of a complete CSC algorithm. Whether condensation should be considered the responsibility of a plot generation process, which uses the narrative system, or of a later process, which transforms plot into discourse, is left open here.

work on the farm. However, this is undesirable for several reasons. One is that such an interpretation removes two fundamental internal conflicts from the narrative system, thereby stripping its virtual domain bare of some of its characteristic furnishing. Here, it is important to remember Ryan's position, introduced in Section 2.1.3, that conflict should be considered the default condition of the narrative universe. Thus, resolving the problem by removing conflict seems not prudent. Another reason is that such an interpretation does not appear grounded in the logics of the underlying story world. What reason might there be in a folktale world that one in four farm-animals be obliged to work, while others should not be subject to such societal expectations? On the technical side, the issue could of course be easily resolved by implementing the hen's behavior via a separate ASL file. The implication of this would be, however, that the hen is an essentially different type of agent than the other animals, a situation that again is not warranted by the logic of the story world.

THE SECOND QUESTION arises with the need for low-level descriptions that an implementation brings with it. It can be safely assumed that the hen's wish to punish the other animals is a reaction to their actions. But when precisely does it form? Is already the rejection by the first animal enough to trigger the hen's vengeance, or is it only after she was rejected by everyone, that this goal arises? Is one cycle of rejections enough, or does it take several rounds? The text of the story does not specify the precise time nor reason, which would be required to resolve this problem. What is worse, Ryan's framework and the above implementation offer only binary decision mechanisms: either an event occurs and triggers a desire, or it does not. A gradual accumulation of negative disposition that only eventually results in a wish—like what appears to be the case here—cannot be explained with the first principles at the disposal of our theory. Technologically, a possible solution would not be complex: the perception of a rejection could increase a counter stored in a belief. The surpassing of a certain threshold by the counter could be then implemented to trigger the wish to punish the offending agents. But this again raises more questions: Should other events also influence the counter's level, and how to decide which events do? Does its level also fall eventually, and if yes, how and why? How can such a negativity counter be interpreted narratologically? And, finally, should there be more counters of this sort, for instance a positivity counter?

MY CONCLUSION   of the conducted case study is that M.-L. Ryan's (1991) theory does not stand the test of generation.[27] It is not that the plot emerging from an implementation of the outlined first principles is not sufficiently similar to the original plot. The problem is that the provided first principle are not sufficient to resolve questions that need to be addressed before any plot can be generated at all. In short: the theory appears to be underspecified.

This situation might appear a failure of the undertaken approach, but should rather be considered a success. Generative modeling was capable of uncovering problems at the level of theory. All that remains to be wished is that another cycle of theory-building, implementation and generation can also uncover the nature of the underspecification and how it can be resolved. Should another cycle succeed, then this would be a strong indication that generative modeling as approach, as well as InBloom as a concrete operationalization, are valid and valuable. That is, that the problem indeed lies with the theory, and not the tools.

Thus, the next chapter will begin by focusing on the uncovered short-comings and attempt to derive what is amiss at the level of theory. As the culprit seems in both cases to be the hen, its primary lens will be fictional character.

---

[27]To be precise, it is only my operationalization of the theory that has been shown to fall short. However, one of the claims of this thesis is that inferences about the underlying theory can be drawn from such operationalizations.

Mr Leopold Bloom ate with relish the inner or-
gans of beasts and fowls. He liked thick giblet
soup, nutty gizzards, a stuffed roast heart, liver-
slices fried with crustcrumbs, fried hencods' roes.
Most of all he liked grilled mutton kidneys which
gave to his palate a fine tang of faintly scented
urine.

James Joyce, 'Ulysses'

3

Fictional Characters

THE OBSERVATION FROM CHAPTER 2 that currently no unified theory of narrative holds sway over the field of narratology also means
that there is no predominant understanding of fictional character as
one of its main constituent phenomena.[1] The previous chapter introduced characters as agglomerations of beliefs, wishes and obligations,
whose intentions are the main driver of plot: Actions that are undertaken serve characters' intentions, happenings trigger new intentions,
and mental events outline the connection between intentions and actions (for more details refer back to Sec. 2.2.2). Such a character-
centric view is not overly idiosyncratic. Bruner, for instance, puts
the action-intention nexus at the center of his understanding of all
of narrative (as a genus): "I think we would do well with as loose
fitting a constraint as we can manage concerning what a story must
'be' to be a story. And the one that strikes me as most serviceable
is [...]: narrative deals with the vicissitudes of intention" (Bruner,
1986, p. 17). And yet, the case study I introduced in the last chapter has shown that such a view is not sufficient to recreate plot from

---

[1]For an overview of the main approaches and possible perspectives on character see the discussions undertaken e.g. by Eder et al. (2010), Margolin (1990),
and Mead (1990).

character behavior, as it can be observed in existing narratives. What might be amiss?

My overview of the phenomenon of character in Section 1.2 introduced four analytical perspectives that can be taken in order to look for an answer. The symptomatic and symbolic perspectives can be dismissed out of hand, since they operate on too high levels of abstraction: Since Ryan's narrative semantics make no attempt to model the emergence of secondary meaning, like themes or messages, our problem can be neither located nor addressed from the symbolic perspective. And since the theory takes a strictly text-internal stance, the problem can also not be located at the symptomatic level of socio-cultural communication. The synthetic perspective focuses on aspects of characters as constructed artefacts. For us, this would imply a teleological analysis of characters with regard to plot, which makes it a promising candidate to understand why the desired plot fails to emerge from the described characters. The classical approaches in this vein view characters as signs (in the semiotic sense) without interiority but defined by e.g. a function (Propp, 1968) or the actant of a grammar they correspond to (Greimas, 1983). Unfortunately, this is incommensurate with Ryan's approach, since it derives plot precisely from the interiority of characters, so it seems unlikely to find solutions in these more classical works. To recapitulate, Ryan's position on the teleology of characters for plot is that "the plot is the trace left by the movements of [character's private worlds] within the textual universe" which is a result of characters' attempts "to make TAW coincide with as many as possible of their private worlds" (M.-L. Ryan, 1991, p. 119). Thus, whatever is amiss in a plot must be so because it is not supported by a possible worlds understanding of fictional character. In a later summary of her approach, M.-L. Ryan (2013) endorses an understanding of characters as "make-believe life-like persons" or "non-actual individuals". This implies that potential shortcomings must be due to a failure to sufficiently represent 'actual individuals'. Analyzing characters through the lens of how they represent persons is, incidentally, the main avenue of the fourth, the mimetic, perspective. This is a curious realization, since it means that taking the synthetic perspective in the present case implies to rather take the mimetic one. Elaborating what the mimetic perspective entails, Margolin (1990) outlines that "[...] this nonactual individual [...] possess[es] human or humanlike properties and relations of the most diverse kinds: physical, behavioral, social, communicative, and mental (psychological). [It] can also be endowed with [...] a consciousness, interiority or personhood." Ryan's approach, as we have seen, is compatible with such a perspective since it views characters as an agglomeration of beliefs, wishes, obligations and intentions. However, it arrived at this state not because it set out to model the properties of personhood, but the possible worlds semantics of narrative discourse: the importance of deontically, axiologically and epistemically modalized propositions for a comprehensive logical representation of a narrative. Consequently, it did not include any further phenomena that might be associated with slippery, non-formal, concepts like "consciousness, interiority or personhood" (see the Margolin quote above). This hesitation is understandable, but the issues encountered in the previous chapter indicate that it might be problematic, and suggest an exploration of notions of character that are more comprehensive from a mimetic perspective.

In a wistful remark, Currie (2010, p. 187) suggests that "narratives encourage us to make sense of the world by telling of the ways in which the mind controls it. Perhaps narrative encourages us to think of the mind as [...] more robustly in control of circumstances than it really is". This move artfully brings together the above discussion: It explicates Bruner's position that intention is central to narrative, by outlining that the structure of plot derives from intention, while at the same time expanding it to consistently encompass a mimetic approach by replacing mere intention (or even intention combined with wishes, beliefs and obligations) with the more general concept of mind. This chapter will explore why 'mind' can help overcome the first iteration's shortcomings, how it can be thought in a narratological context, and whether it can be substantiated enough to be computationally modeled.

3.1. The Mimetic Perspective

The above discussion was guided by theoretical considerations. To consider whether it is also practically fruitful, we need to revisit the problems uncovered by the case study and check whether they can be traced back to an incomplete modeling of phenomena connected to (an at this moment still pre-theoretic understanding of) mind.

3.1.1. Addressing the Case Study

The first problem was uncovered by the question why the hen in TLRH chooses to follow an obligation, while the other farm animals follow their wishes. Being the same type of character (i.e. folktale farm animal) in the same circumstances (i.e. living on a farm), according to Ryan, they should choose the same goals. From a mimetic position, it is this implication that is problematic. While minds in persons fundamentally do work comparably, simply because they share biological properties, in particular situations even resemblant persons belonging to the same socio-cultural group often behave markedly different: One farmer might treat his animals respectfully, while another might abuse them. This is because persons are subject to strong inter-individual differences. The same can be observed in folktales, which are not commonly regarded as overly concerned with accurate representations of the human mind. For instance in "Three Little Pigs" two pigs quickly build houses from straw and wood which turn out to be unsafe, while the third one takes more time and employs stone to a more stable effect. Clearly, some inter-individual differences must exist between the pigs. Even the moral of the tale—a little extra work can go a long way in ensuring happiness—is reducible to an inference from physical action to psychological essence: laziness is punished, while diligence gets rewarded. A comparable stance would also resolve the TLRH problem. The diligent hen chooses to work on the farm, while the lazy other animals choose to relax. It remains to be seen whether binary traits like laziness and diligence are narratologically desirable properties of the phenomenon mind, but the general idea of introducing some sort of interpersonal difference—as first principles responsible for goal selection—into Ryan's framework seems fruitful.

The second problem was uncovered by the question when precisely the hen forms the wish to punish the other animals. Ryan's framework only supports binary decisions: an occurring event triggers a wish/obligation, or not, while in TLRH some sort of gradual accumulation of negative disposition seems to take place. Additionally, the precise nature of this negativity remains unclear, as well as whether there could be comparable mechanisms at work with e.g. positivity. From a mimetic position, this situation appears much less confusing. In psychology, persons' valenced reactions to external events are being described by the concept of affect. This covers short-term phenomena like the appraisal of individual events through emotions, as well as mid-term dispositions that result from an aggregation of emotions into moods. This is a useful observation because Ryan herself makes extensive use of the concepts of positive and negative affect when, later in the book, analyzing the plot of another folktale, "The Fox and the Crow" (see e.g. p. 223 in M.-L. Ryan, 1991). Curiously, she does not explain what these phenomena are, or how they relate to the rest of the framework she set up. In the case of TLRH, it seems plausible to assume that the repeated rejections that the hen experiences cause negative emotions like anger or disappointment. Over time, these emotions solidify into a hostile mood, causing her to lash out at her earliest convenience.

Affect could also help untangle another issue with the plot. So far, the hen's punishment plan has been introduced as a form of taunting: offering something which is then withheld. Yet, why should this, in fact, be considered a punishment, i.e. what is the negative effect of such a treatment? Consider a Ryanian reasoner's expected reaction: it adopts its belief base concerning the (non-)existence of bread, scraps a wish to eat some bread, and carries on unfazed. Affect, especially in the guise of a negatively valenced reaction like disappointment, would be a good explanans for this situation because it is an a priori negative, involuntary reaction of the experiencing agent. It is this negative emotion that gives this punishment the required sting.

These two exercises in mimetic interpretation support the theoretical argument that Ryan's approach suffers from insufficient modeling of phenomena related to mind. Specifically, it seems that InBloom could be successful in recreating the plot of TLRH if the underlying framework would address affectivity and interpersonal differences in characters. However, before we analyze in more detail what phenomena comprise a mind and could be of use as first principles in a narratological setting, an important objection to the mimetic approach in general needs to be addressed.

3.1.2. Anti-Mimetic Objections

The previous section ascribes characters wishes and obligations, suggests that they exhibit personalities and experience affect—it even boldly claims fictional characters have fictional minds. Does it not run the danger of confusing fictional characters with actual persons by falling into the fallacy of anthropomorphising mere signs?

This position would certainly be taken by Knights (1933) who expressed it in the catchy question "How many children had Lady MacBeth?" about the near-eponymous tragedy by Shakespeare (1623). Naturally, Knights was not interested in the answer, but instead wanted to criticize the then-prevailing approach in Shakespeare criticism to analyze characters as if they were humans. The problem his question exposed was that the text itself offers contradicting evidence and leaves no recourse to close this epistemic gap, since the answer can neither be inferred from the logic of the TAW nor by importing common sense knowledge from the AW (relying on what was introduced as the Principle of Minimal Departure in Sec. 2.1.1). This incompleteness is a fundamental ontological difference to actual persons, who, as inhabitants of AW, are necessarily ontologically complete, even if we normally only have incomplete knowledge about them. The solution, for formalists like Knights, is to treat characters strictly as aggregates of words that are either used to describe them, or are uttered by them, and are understood in opposition to other such word-aggregates. Thus, Weinsheimer (1979, p. 195) writes that: "[...] characters at most are patterns of recurrence, motifs which are continually recontextualized in other motifs" while Barthes ([1970] 1974) observes that 'voices'—a code he introduces to substitute characters with a less anthropomorphic term—are nothing but a web of semes attached to a proper noun. This view has no place for purely conceptual phenomena like fictional minds, or even emotions and beliefs, unless they are explicitly attached to the proper name that is a character, by explicit psychonarration. Positing their existence purely because they exist in people, for the formalist, means ignoring the incompleteness of fictional narratives and naively conflating non-existing paper-beings with actual persons. Literary critic Vermeule (2010, p. x) even insists that "If my profession has a single rule it is that the distinction [between fictional character and real person] has to be honored". A sentiment that was voiced more figuratively by Weinsheimer (1979, p. 187) who postulates that "[...] Emma Woodhouse is not a woman nor need be described as if *it* were"[2]. I find the formalist view of character per se valid and valuable, but remain unconvinced by its petulant insistence on being the only valu-

---

[2]Emphasis mine.

able perspective.

Before I address my reasons for this, I would like to first strengthen the position I oppose, by adding what I would classify as anti-mimetic criticism that does not take a formalist stance itself. These positions were occasionally expressed to me in private communication, for which I am grateful both because of the valuable input as well as the realization that my position needs delicate re-adjusting. R. Michael Young—director of the Liquid Narrative Research Group and Professor in the School of Computer Science at the University of Utah—expressed his anti-mimetic stance in the catchy phrase "Life-like is not like life", while Janet Murray—Professor in the School of Literature, Media and Communication at the Georgia Institute of Technology and author of the seminal *Hamlet on the Holodeck: The Future of Narrative in Cyberspace* maintained the (less severe) position that "[...] there is one thing that computer scientists need to be told over and over again: Creating characters is not about being realistic. It is about abstracting reality in a way that is dramatic". This is not a formalist stance, since it does not prescribe how characters should be conceptualized. However, it is anti-mimetic because it posits that understanding characters as mere representations of actual persons is not sufficient to account for the 'dramatic effect' that they are intended to produce. I find this (broader) position sensible, too, but several reasons lead me to maintain that a mimetic perspective is still tenable by arguing that it is just *one* of the viable perspectives—especially one that is not at odds with a formalist one.

3.1.3. Arguing for Fictional Minds

I shall depart from a formalist position myself, by affirming that in the text of a narrative, characters, indeed, are mere signs without interiority: proper nouns that are further qualified by descriptive statements, and that take their signification from an opposition with other, comparable aggregates. What is important to maintain is that the text is only the mediating part in an act of communication, in which a sender (the author, an entity commonly considered 'dead' to narratologists) intends to encode symbolically charged representational content, such that it is decodable by a receiver (the much more narratologically innocuous reader).

THE PROCESS OF DECODING   fictional characters by readers[3] has
been surveyed from a cognitive perspective by Schneider (2001, 2013).
The central claim is that readers use the clues in a text (what Barthes
would call semes) to construct mental models of the referred-to characters. A mental model is a "holistic mental representation of [a
person's] experience of the world and that, in tasks such as problem
solving, [...] can provide a guideline for the operations of the mental
apparatus" (Schneider, 2001), i.e. a dynamic cognitive structure that
is being continuously and effortlessly deployed by persons to make
predictions about the actual world. This alone is already much richer
than the barren 'proper name cum web of semes' that formalists claim
exhaustively represents characters.

To add insult to injury, Schneider essentially suggests that readers
use the same mental structures to represent fictional characters that
they use to represent actual persons, implying that—to the reader's
mental processing—there is no fundamental difference between an actual person and a fleshed-out character[4], an important pro-mimetic
argument. Schneider also observes that this bottom-up process of
mental model construction is accompanied by a top-down process
of information integration, which opportunistically imports relevant
real-world knowledge that appears to apply to the character, into the
emerging mental model. This dominantly pertains to stereotypical
information, for instance about social roles ('mother'), professions
('lawyer') or class ('rich person'), which allows readers to form expectations about characters' behavior even before sufficient individuating
information has been provided by the text. This results in a further
conflation of the mimetic with the textual because knowledge about
persons in AW is imported into readers' mental character representations.

Keeping in mind the idea that readers represent fictional characters like they represent humans, it does not come as a surprise
that they regularly and predictably develop affective dispositions towards characters: sympathy, that is, feeling for the character, as well

---

[3]Reader in this context refers to actual lay persons as the subject of empirical
study, not abstract reader-constructs like the modal or ideal reader (see Sec. 1.2.2)
that is sometimes put forward by literary scholars like Eco (1984).

[4]A non-fundamental difference between the two would be that the mental
model of a character contains the additional belief that it represents a non-actual
entity.

as empathy, that is, feeling with the character (see e.g. Caracciolo, 2016; Eder, 2006). It is absurd to even speak of 'feeling with' a "pattern of recurrence" or a "web of semes". Empathy is a disposition that is reserved to animate objects and supposes in its target a phenomenological center of experience capable of feeling; one might say: a mind. Thus, if readers are capable of feeling with a character, then they must (at least subconsciously) perceive it as something that has a mind with enough capacity for joy or suffering to trigger an empathetic reaction. An observation that implies the usefulness of a mimetic analytical category in the fashion of fictional mind.

This point is developed further by cognitive narratologist Lisa Zunshine (2006) who makes a convincing case that readers effortlessly apply their real-world Theory of Mind (ToM) capabilities when interpreting fictional characters' actions. ToM is the ability to infer others' (but also one's own) mental states from observable behaviors and physical states; something that comes natural to neurotypical[5] human adults. This ability develops during childhood through exposure to a complex social environment, and is honed well into adolescence. Zunshine's introductory example demonstrates how the very same ToM influences the reception of a novel:

> When Peter Walsh, a protagonist of Virginia Woolf's Mrs. Dalloway, unexpectedly visits Clarissa Dalloway "at eleven o'clock on the morning of the day she [is] giving a party," and, "positively trembling" and "kissing both her hands" (40), asks her how she is, how do we know that his "trembling" is to be accounted for by his excitement at seeing his old love again after all these years and not, for instance, by his progressing Parkinson's disease? (Zunshine, 2006, p. 3)

At first glance the question seems nonsensical since it is hard to conceive of a reader that should make the assumption Walsh's trembling could be caused by Parkinsons' disease or even just cold weather. But it is precisely this pervasiveness of the assumption that physical gesture must be caused by psychological state—which readers carry over from the actual world into fiction—that makes us blind to its existence. As Zunshine puts it, this default interpretational stance rests on "our evolved cognitive tendency to assume that there must be a mental stance behind each physical action and our striving to

---

[5]It is interesting to note that disorders on the autistic spectrum are characterized by (more or less expressed) difficulties with applying ToM, correlated with unusually low interest in fiction and narratives (Zunshine, 2006, p. 8). A correlation that Zunshine suggests is not accidental, but due to the fundamental role mind reading plays in the functioning of stories.

represent to ourselves that possible mental stance even when the author has left us with the absolute minimum of necessary cues for constructing such a representation" (Zunshine, 2006, p.23). For the present discussion these observations mean that readers do not only reconstruct fictional minds from narrative discourse, as I suggested previously, but also that these representations of minds seem to function closely enough to those of real minds that reader's real-world trained ToM can be successfully applied to them.

Summarizing, readers seem to reconstruct fictional characters from narrative discourse by importing real world knowledge into the resulting representation, they respond emotionally in ways that are reserved for animate beings, and per default successfully apply their real world ToM to infer a broad range of fictional characters' properties. These phenomena seem hard to explain from a formalist perspective, but even if it were possible, the principle of parsimony seems to suggest that a more economic theory would be to simply acknowledge the referential, mimetic aspects of their nature. Once a mimetic perspective is established as valid, accepting the tenability of fictional minds is only logical, especially in view of the above argument from ToM.

THE PROCESS OF ENCODING   narrative fiction by an author is, in contrast to its decoding by the reader, rarely the object of scientific study due to the notorious difficulty of finding empirically valid approaches and sufficiently large pools of subjects. It also fell into disrepute as the subject of scholarly argument in the middle of the 20th century, when Roland Barthes (1977) famously declared the 'death of the author'. The main driver for this move was to liberate the text from an authoritative interpretation in reference to an authorial intention, which is unknown, and instead accept that it contains a plethora of meanings that can be uncovered by any individual act of reading. This seems to thwart any possibility to infer properties of fictional characters from their mental representations pre-encoding, like we did from the mental representations post-decoding. However, an interesting opening is provided by creative writing-researcher Lina Varotsi (2016), who essentially makes the argument that, while the mind of an individual author is necessarily opaque, it still remains an instance of the human mind as a genus and thus subject to all and any properties and limitations that pertain to all minds. Thus, we can depart from the assumption that the author as an intentional agent intends to communicate something that originates in the author's experience of the actual world: "Texts are [...] inspired by concepts, perceptual products, and the personal experiences of their originators.

Those experiences reflect upon, or are drawn by, real-life interactions, even if their conveyance is purely conceptual; the correspondence to the prototype is inevitable" (Varotsi, 2016, p. 71). It seems that the formalists' liberation of the text from the author is questionable because it focuses solely on the signifier while neglecting the signified. Yet the nature of the signifier, in narratives, is connected to the signified: "the text does not antagonize the concept; it defines and shapes it, as per the author's aims, and the reader's deconstruction, both of which can be examined [...]" (Varotsi, 2016, p. 72). Thus, Varotsi views "The fictional text [...] as an imprint of the author's consciousness on paper" (Varotsi, 2016, p. 73). When applied to the question at hand this means that the conception and creation of characters is necessarily shaped and informed by the author's phenomenological experience of its prototype, the actual person:

> The novelist invents and discovers her characters through her experience of the human person. Invents, because every textual being is conceived ex nihilo; discovers, because her individual textual elements, both 'physical' and idiosyncratic, will emerge from the author's cognitive informational storage processed by her imagination.
>
> (Varotsi, 2016, p. 74)

A fascinating study of such writerly informational processing of characters, presented by Taylor et al. (2003), revealed a strong prevalence of a phenomenon they dubbed Illusion of Independent Agency (IIA). IIA is defined as the writer's subjective experience of their fictional characters "[...] as having their own thoughts, feelings, and actions. The essence of this conceptual illusion is the sense that the characters are independent agents not directly under the author's control. As a consequence, writing becomes more like passive reporting than active creation" (Taylor et al., 2003, p. 366). The study's authors conducted interviews with 50 writers and found that only 4 report no experience of IIA. Of the 92% of writers who experienced IAA, 22 were classified as reporting mild, 19 moderate, and 5 strong forms. The study's authors also remark that "furthermore, the writers provided vivid examples of their characters who not only had taken over the job of composing their own life stories, but who also sometimes actively resisted the writer's attempts to control the story" (Taylor et al., 2003, p. 376). This quantitative and qualitative findings lend credibility to the many remarks by novelists to this effect, most famously perhaps Edward Morgan Forster's below, which were commonly dismissed by literary scholars as cliche:

> The characters arrive when evoked, but full of the spirit of mutiny. For they have these numerous parallels with people like ourselves, they try to live their own lives and are consequently often engaged in treason against the main scheme of the book. They "run away," they "get out of hand": they are creations inside a creation, and often inharmonious towards it; if they are given complete freedom they kick the book to

pieces, and if they are kept too sternly in check, they revenge themselves by dying, and destroy it by intestinal decay.   (Forster, [1927]
2002, p. 48)

No explanation for the phenomenon of IIA can be derived from a
quantitative study. However, Taylor et al. offer an interesting hypothesis, by drawing an analogy to operating a car. For a novice,
the process is effortful and requires constant attention to the details.
An experienced driver, on the other hand, experiences the process as
quasi automatic: It usually doesn't require much attentional resources
and leaves the driver room to listen to music or have a conversation.
This corresponds to two fundamental modes of thought Kahneman
(2011) calls 'System 1': fast, automatic, unconscious; and 'System
2': slow, effortful, conscious. With prolonged training and increased
mastery, tasks can move from being executed in System 2 to System
1. When applied to fiction writing, this reasoning suggests that also
the process of imagining fictional characters and their interactions
could, in time, be relegated to System 1, which would mean that it
would be executed fast, automatically and subconsciously. A manifestation of this could be phenomenologically experienced as if the
imagined characters were having a life of their own: precisely what
is described by the IIA. The ramifications of this, for the discussion at hand, is that writers at least ground their understanding of
fictional characters in real life, and seem to employ mental representations that are life-like enough for these characters to be perceived as
non-actual individuals with independent agency. Clearly, no mental
model is perfect, and any writer has (at least in theory) full control
of her writing process. Consequently, Varotsi suggests that "the nature of the correspondence between character and the real person is
defined as much by the similarities between the two poles, as by their
fundamental differences" (Varotsi, 2016, p. 77). But even speaking
about the differences between characters and persons presupposes a
mimetic, referential perspective from which these entities first become
comparable.

SUMMARIZING   the previous section, it seems appropriate to state
that the opposition of a formalist versus a mimetic perspective is a
gratuitous dilemma. The two perspectives merely view different sides
of the same coin: formalists restrict their study to the properties of
the signifier, while mimeticists focus on the signified. The advantage

of the formalist view is that it operates on the only reified part of the act of narrative communication, the immutable piece of writing that is the result of an encoding and the source of any decoding. The advantage of the mimetic view is that it focuses on the beginning and the endpoint of this narrative communication act, thus allowing a more teleological approach.

The observation that both perspectives can be valid at the same time also allows to address the second class of criticism reported previously, which objects that a mimetic perspective does not allow to account for the dramatic effect of fictional character. These non-mimetic parts of a character-representation can be captured in a formalist analysis, while phenomena that can not be accounted for from a formalist perspective—like empathy or applying ToM to characters—are captured by a mimetic analysis. Furthermore, I would argue that a dramatic effect can arise from a non-mimetic representation precisely because readers' default assumption is that a character will appear mimetic. The heightened sense of awareness that results from this defied expectation allows the realization of the character's aesthetic constructedness.

With this argumentation in place the suggestion to approach the TLRH case study's problems by introducing the notion of fictional minds appears finally vindicated. If characters are written and read like persons, then their narratological constitution in relevant regards should be comparable. This includes the property of seemingly being determined by a mind.

3.2. Fictional Minds

The concept of fictional minds was introduced by the narratologist Alan Palmer (2004), who takes a mimetic position quite like the one developed above: "narrative fiction is, in essence, the presentation of fictional mental functioning" (Palmer, 2004, p. 5). His work, however, starts from a different perspective. Palmer states that narrative theory has mostly equated mental functioning with characters' thoughts, and dealt with it in two ways: by classifying relevant parts of the narrative discourse based on several categories of thought report, and by grounding assumptions about their mental states in explicit psycho-narration. However, he also observes that even in narratives that do not provide much access to characters' interiority, like for instance

Hemingway's quasi-behaviorist novels, readers are capable of extracting a great deal of fictional mental functioning. Palmer concludes that there must be more to fictional mental functioning than mere thought report, and suggests that fictional minds could be reconstructed by readers even just from action descriptions because actions are completely determined by minds. Accordingly, the main difference is that Palmer departs from the reconstruction of fictional minds from discourse, while my discussion above was motivated by how fictional minds are causally related to the events that comprise the plot. Since these two approaches are connected through their shared focus on minds, Palmer's insights will be also valuable for us. Such an application of his work can be seen as licensed by Palmer when he writes that his is "a functional and teleological perspective that considers the purposive nature of characters' thought in terms of their motives, intentions, and resulting behavior and action" (Palmer, 2004, p. 12). A teleological perspective to characters' minds, in the end, must be one that leads to the purposive nature of these minds in the overarching organizational principle of the plot.

The main approach of Palmer (2004, Chap. 4) is to review what he calls the cognitive science discourse on actual minds, and outline how it applies to the fictional minds reconstructed from narrative discourse. Since Palmer operates in an analytical setting he presents cognitive phenomena conceptually and at a high level of abstraction, which is reflected in the fact that he grounds his thoughts in the works of big-picture thinkers like Dennett, Pinker and Damasio. In the following subsections, I will follow Palmer's lead and summarize his observations on a selection of topics: functionalism, disposition, emotion and action. These will become the constituent phenomena that make up the concept of fictional mind for this thesis. Since for the present work it is necessary that this concept is operationalizable in a generative model, I will expand Palmer's view with insight from the applied side of the cognitive sciences, wherever it is opportune to demonstrate how mental phenomena are quantifiable and operationalizable.

I want to caution that the following sections might produce a feeling of jarring discrepancy, since mathematical descriptions of cognitive phenomena will appear alongside Palmer's high-level literary considerations. Being able to think phenomena both ways at the same time is one of the inherent challenges (but also chances for cross-fertilization) that come with interdisciplinary efforts like the present.

3.2.1. Functionalism

To understand why Palmer puts forward a teleological approach to fictional minds that allows to integrate his ideas so well into this thesis, I will first summarize his view on functionalism. He subscribes to a weak form of functionalism, which he summarizes like this: "[...] the functional view of the mind [...] analyzes what it does and what it is for, rather than asking what the brain is made of" (Palmer, 2004, p. 88). In a narratological setting, this corresponds to the position that I already outlined: fictional minds should be analyzed not only through the thoughts that are reported (what they are 'made of' in a story), but also how they shape characters' actions and reactions (what they 'are for')—its teleology. In analogy to the computational theory of mind that is at the basis of the work of thinkers like Dennett or Pinker, Palmer observes that also fictional minds can be analyzed as (representations of) processes of information processing. To exemplify how this perspective can be applied to a novel, I will relay Palmer's own brief analysis of Charles Dickens's (1861) *Great Expectations*:

> Pip's mind processes the information that he receives from the other minds around him and from other aspects of his physical and social environment. He learns, in particular from Estelle and Miss Havisham, that he wants to be different. He develops goals, such as wanting to be a gentleman, that conflict with his current situation. He then learns from Herbert, Mr. Jaggers, and so on how to adapt and how to become a gentleman. His mind adapts differently to all of the various minds with which it interacts. Finally, he learns the most difficult lesson of all—that becoming a gentleman is not enough and that he has another goal: he has still to learn how to be a good person.
>
> (Palmer, 2004, p. 90)

3.2.2. Dispositions (From Cognitive and Literary Perspectives)

Dispositions, for Palmer, are not events that take place in the mind, but rather a sort of state that affects how and which events *usually* take place in a particular mind: "These are states of mind or dispositions that, Damasio claims, are 'records which are dormant and implicit rather than active and explicit, as images are' (2000, 160). [...] Daniel Dennett calls them 'mind-ruts' (1991, 300)" (Palmer, 2004, p. 109). To continue the metaphor: these mind-ruts channel a

Table 3.1: The five personality factors and a sample of adjectives associated with the high pole of the respective dimension; abridged version from (McCrae & John, 1992).

Factor	Adjectives (high pole)
Openness	Artistic, curious, imaginative, insightful, original
Conscientiousness	Efficient, organized, planful, reliable, responsible
Extraversion	Active, assertive, energetic, enthusiastic, outgoing
Agreeableness	Appreciative, forgiving, generous, kind, sympathetic
Neuroticism	Anxious, self-pitying, tense, touchy, unstable

person's stream of thought in common ways, which results in tendencies to act in certain ways—pronounced enough to allow observers to form expectations about that person's behavior. These expectations are then perceived by both parties as *personality*, and even allow to distinguish persons from each other. "Antonio Damasio describes the differences between immediate, single mental events and states that continue over time in terms of two selves: 'the seemingly changing self and the seemingly permanent self' (2000,217)" (Palmer, 2004, p. 109). Hence, the 'changing self' corresponds to a person's sense as locus of experience, while the 'permanent self' corresponds to that person's sense as diachronically stable essence manifested in a distinct personality.

In psychology, personality is commonly operationalized using a set of fixed and distinct traits which can be empirically demonstrated to have predictive value. One of the most influential trait theories is the Big Five model (McCrae & John, 1992) that proposes the five basic factors (i.e. domains of traits) *openness to experience, conscientiousness, extraversion, agreeableness* and *neuroticism* (OCEAN) to comprehensively capture an individual's personality. Each factor is associated with clusters of related adjectives used as trait terms in natural language (see Table 3.1), and derived rating scales that contrast these adjective groups. McCrae and John (1992, pp. 195–198) attempt to distill factor definitions but fail to provide a succinct wording. The following provides a short explanation while grossly simplifying the original discussion:

- Factor O captures the broad domain of aesthetic sensitivity, intellect and a need for variety, which could be seen as lack of focus or unpredictability, at the high end of the dimension. At the low end, it corresponds to conservatism, perseverance, and pragmatism.

- Factor C, at the higher end, can be understood as either an inhibitive tendency to control ones impulses, or the proactive tendency for planning and organization. Thus, at the lower end it corresponds to flexibility but also impulsive tendencies.

- Factor E, at the high end, corresponds to a tendency for positive affect, which also captures the complex of warmth-dominance because "cheerful people consistently tend to be dominant, talkative, sociable, and warm" (McCrae & John, 1992). Low E corresponds to independence, but also retiring and quiet behavior. It should not be confused with high negative affect (corresponding to high N) or what is folk-psychologically referred to as introversion (high introspection).

- Factor A captures a tendency for altruistic cooperation and a concern for social harmony at the one end of the dimension. At the other, it captures self-centered antagonism, but also strength of will.

- Factor N, at the high pole, is understood as the tendency for negative affect and low stress tolerance. The low pole denotes the opposed tendency for calmness and serenity, but also low emotional reactivity.

Personality is assessed using standardized questionnaires. Most commonly, this is done via self-report, when a person is requested to rate how strongly several statements apply to them. However, valid scores can also be obtained by asking observers to provide the necessary information about that person (Eysenck, 2004, p.455–457). This is felicitous because self-report data is not readily available for the study of fictional characters, while third-person ascriptions can be requested from readers[6]. A recent questionnaire, that has been successfully used for self-report as well as observer ratings, is the Berkeley BFI instrument (John et al., 1991, 2008). The whole instrument consists of 44 items in the form of "short phrases based on the

---

[6]One might argue that third-person ascriptions are even more reliable in the case of fictional characters than they are in actual individuals because narrative discourse often provides readers with direct access to characters' thoughts—a privilege that in AW is not available even to one's closest relatives.

trait adjectives known to be prototypical markers" (John et al., 2008) that are answered using a 5-point Likert scale. An excerpt of which can be found in Lis. 3.1.

The OCEAN personality score of a person has been shown to have predictive value for a broad range of behavioral (see e.g. Ozer & Benet-Martinez, 2006) and affective (see e.g. Komulainen et al., 2014; Revelle & Scherer, 2009) tendencies. However, it is important to point out that, apart from personality, also context has an important effect on a person's behavior. In fact, the debate on whether the former or the latter has the stronger influence is still not settled. A fascinating case in point has been made by Darley and Batson (1973), who demonstrated the role of time pressure on helping behavior. Their experiment was conducted on seminarians, who were asked to give a 5 minute talk on the vocational careers of seminary students based on a short passage of text. After some time for preparation, each subject was told to go to another building. In the low-hurry condition the subject was informed that the facility would be ready in a few minutes and that they could wait there. In the high-hurry condition the subject was told that they were already expected a few minutes ago so they should better hurry. When passing through the alley between buildings, all subjects encountered a collaborator who had seemingly collapsed, sitting slumped in a doorway, coughing and groaning. If personality were a strong predictor of helping behavior one would expect time pressure in an insignificant assignment to have no effect on behavior in such high stake circumstances, i.e. that the amount of help observed in

---

I see myself as someone who...
... is talkative.
... is reserved.
... is full of energy.
... tends to be quiet.
... has an assertive personality.
... is sometimes shy, inhibited.
... is outgoing, sociable.

Listing 3.1: The BFI items used to asses the factor extraversion.

all conditions would be the same. The observed results were quite sobering: In the low-hurry condition 63% offered some sort of help, against 10% in the high-hurry condition.[7] This demonstrates that context can have a dramatic effect on behavior and seems to be able to override intrinsic dispositions.

In the context of narratological study, personality has been behind one of the first generally accepted approaches to classify fictional characters: E.M. Forster's ([1927] 2002) distinction between "flat" and "round" characters. Forster, who was not only a writer but also an accomplished literary critic, maintained that flat characters are "constructed round a single idea or quality" (Forster, [1927] 2002, p. 48); one might say they are built around one strongly pronounced personality trait. Round characters, on the other hand, are "capable of surprising in a convincing way" (Forster, [1927] 2002, p. 55), which means that they either have conflicting traits, undergo a marked development, or are capable of acting 'out of character'—not in accord with their personality.

The personality of characters has been mainly analyzed by annotating passages of narrative discourse that perform *direct characterization*: remarks by either the narrator or other characters that directly ascribe certain properties to a character. These are further distinguished by whether they appear en bloc, or interspersed. More interesting, in this context, is the approach of *indirect characterization*, which allows the analyst to derive properties of a character's personality from its actions: "Given the sort of disposition that this particular character has, how will he or she react in this specific situation? The answers to this question will then modify to a greater or lesser extent the initial hypotheses that we have formed regarding that character" (Palmer, 2004, p. 112). While this makes no claims about underlying personality dimensions or the set of possible personality traits, it at least presupposes that a causal connection exists between fictional minds (and especially their dispositions) and characters' actions, which allows to infer the former from the latter.

It is important to keep in mind that 'mind-ruts' apply not only

---

[7]It's a notable twist, that half of the subjects were given the parable of the Good Samaritan as basis of their talk, while the others received a task-related text. Whether subjects read the parable, or another text, turned out to have no significant effect on helping behavior.

to actions, but also to emotions, which often modify how actions are performed. This connection, too, has been utilized by narrative theory. "It is not so much what a character does and says that is important, but how s/he behaves or speaks: in a leisurely way, agitatedly, preachily, shrilly, looking at the floor in embarrassment etc. The adjectives and adverbs used in the course of a text often contribute more extensively to characterization than a detailed, one-off description of a person's appearance or disposition" (Fludernik, 2009, p. 46). While Fludernik's remarks focus on the discursive surface of a narrative text, they also demonstrate that personality can be derived from a character's displayed emotions. Hence, a causal connection is presupposed also from personality to affect. This demonstrates how the concept of fictional minds has been implicitly present even in more classical approaches to narratology, via the concept of personality.

An example of personality at work (and how it is analyzed) in literature can be found in the introduction of Leopold Bloom in Joyce's (1922) *Ulysses*, which served as this chapter's epigraph (on p. 107). Bloom's introduction does not ascribe him any traits directly but, instead, compiles a long list of his dietary predilections. These are in and of themselves dispositions; but taken together they also allow to infer a general tendency: Bloom is a man of prodigious appetites, someone who takes great pleasure in the satisfaction of his bodily needs. The mention of his relish of the 'faint tang of urine' in his favourite food demonstrates that he is unruffled even by the less savory of bodily phenomena and can be taken to imply a certain vulgarity. This complex disposition manifests and guides the protagonist throughout the novel. To name but a few (from the innocent to the vulgar): In the chapters 'Lestrygonias' and 'Circe' great detail is provided on Bloom's mental dealings with food, the chapter 'Calypso' contains a vivid description of the protagonist enjoying the mundane process of moving his bowel, and 'Nautica' describes him masturbating on a beach while watching the bathers. On a more fundamental level, Bloom's attitude towards physicality can be considered the main (mimetic) driver behind the plot of the novel. He is described as incapable of intercourse with his wife, Molly Bloom, ever since the death of their son, Rudy, more than a decade before the day on which the novel takes place. Molly has taken a lover, Blaze Boylan, to compensate for this lack. Leopold Bloom's Odyssey through Dublin can be seen as an attempt to flee (and eventually come to terms with) the evidence of his own inability to satisfy the physical needs of a loved one. Thus we can state that his actions and emotions project a distinct personality which is consistent with the expectations created in his introductory characterization.

3.2.3. Emotions (From Cognitive and Literary Perspectives)

Emotions were mentioned above as one type of mental events that can vary depending on dispositions. However, the distinction is not so clear-cut. As Palmer points out: "Emotions last for varying periods of time. When they are short-term, they are emotional events; medium-term, they tend to be called moods; as long-term states, they are closer in nature to dispositions" (Palmer, 2004, p. 114). Indeed, some theories refer to personality as long-term affect (see e.g. Gebhard, 2005). To make the distinction clear, I will use the term emotion only to refer to short-term affect. To refer to the whole temporal continuum described by Palmer, I will use the term affect.

It is important to stress that the folk-psychological notion of an opposition between affectivity and rational thought is not appropriate. Emotions are often the precondition of rational thought:

> According to Damasio, 'the presumed opposition between emotion and reason is no longer accepted without question. For example, work from my laboratory has shown that emotion is integral to the processes of reasoning and decision making' (2000, 40–41). Patients who have 'lost a certain class of emotions' have also 'lost their ability to make rational decisions' (2000, 41)
>
> (Palmer, 2004, p. 116).

However, emotions can not only serve as an enabler of rational thought, but can also arise as a result of it. As Palmer succinctly puts it: "Cognition causes emotion" (Palmer, 2004, p. 116). This elucidates that rational thought and emotion are closely intertwined instead of opposing modes of cognition.

Palmer mentions several ways of categorizing emotions, one of which is the distinction between primary and secondary emotions. The former are considered immediate, unreflective and universal reactions to events. Commonly, four or six emotions are considered primary: *fear, happiness, sadness, anger*, and sometimes also *surprise* and *disgust*. Secondary emotions are learned and thus can sometimes be specific to the culture in which a person grew up. They are deliberative and social, which means that they can arise as the result of a reasoning process and serve a function in social interaction. Elgin (1999, Chap. V) presents an insightful example for the learned, deliberative and fine-grained nature of secondary emotions. She explains that regret is an emotion that arises as a reaction to misfortunes, and remorse differs from regret "only by incorporating a belief that one is responsible for the misfortune it concerns" (Elgin, 1999, p. 148). This is interesting because we do not have specialized emotions for many other types of misfortunes, like for instance those happening on Mondays. She claims that the reason for this is that it is socially encouraged to develop an awareness for one's responsibilities with regard to misfortunes, while not with regard to days of the week.

Several taxonomies exist that outline the differences between emotions, and an overview is outside the scope of this thesis. One popular approach, which will be the one to be computationally adopted in Sec. 3.3, is the theory of Ortony et al. (1990, short: OCC). OCC is an appraisal theory, which means that it conceptualizes emotions as valenced reactions to some aspects of the environment: either events, agents or objects. The diagram in Fig. 3.1 outlines which emotion corresponds to which appraisal in OCC. For instance, if an event is appraised with a focus on its consequences for one self and the prospects of this event are irrelevant, then a positive appraisal would elicit the emotion of joy, while a negative appraisal would elicit distress. Overall, the taxonomy is comprised of 22 different emotions, which is significantly larger than the set of basic emotions. However, in a literary context, where often great sensibility is displayed towards affective phenomena[8], this might prove a meager selection, and even in a cognitive science context at least the lack of surprise as a distinct emotion is questionable.

Medium-term affect, i.e. mood, has also been the object of psychological investigation. In contrast to emotion, mood is not taken to be bound to one particular event, but is rather a stable and pervasive affective state whose changes can correlate with emotional events. Psychologist Albert Mehrabian (who refers to mood as temperament) defines it as the "average emotional state across a representative sample of life situation" (Mehrabian, 1996b). Because it is not possible to

---

[8]A fine example of the sensibility with which authors dissect affect can be found in the preliminary studies that were conducted and preserved by Gustave Flaubert on his classic novel Madame Bovary (Leclerc, 1995). They include the author's analysis of characters' states using emotions as specific as *feeling of emptiness, poetic feelings* or *jealousy-curiosity.*

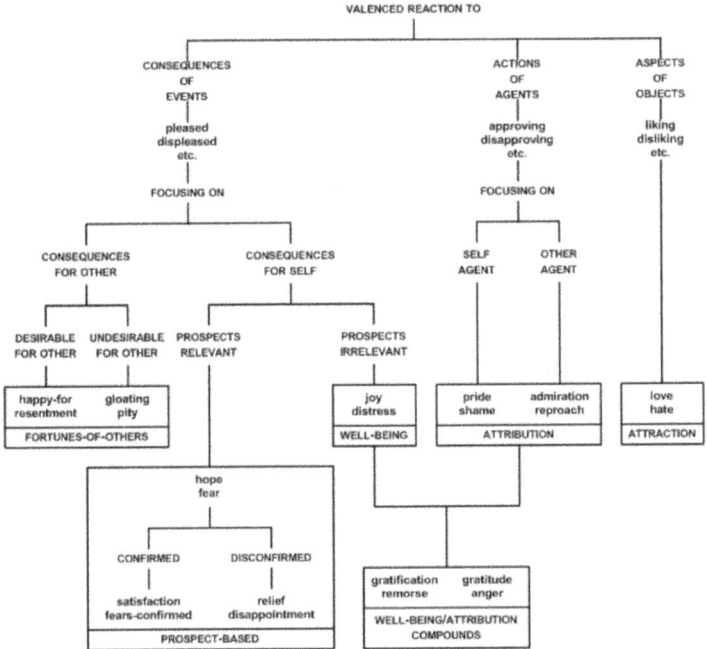

Figure 3.1: The OCC taxonomy of emotions, from Ortony et al. (1990).

compute an average over a set of discrete emotion-events[9], Mehrabian presents three basic dimensions along which moods and emotions can be quantified: *pleasure* (P), *arousal* (A), and *dominance* (D):

> The Trait Pleasure-displeasure Scale (Mehrabian, 1978a; 1994a) indexes the relative predominance of positive versus negative affective states across a representative sample of life situations. [...] The Trait Arousability Scale (Mehrabian, 1977; 1994b; 1995a) is a measure of how easily a person is aroused by "high information" (i.e., complex, changing, and/or unexpected—Mehrabian & Russell, 1974b) stimuli and how slowly his/her arousal returns to baseline levels. [...] The Trait Dominance-submissiveness Scale (Mehrabian & Hines, 1978; Mehrabian, 1994c) assesses a person's characteristic feelings of control and influence over his life circumstances versus feelings of being controlled and influenced by others or events.
>
> (Mehrabian, 1996b)

This allows to understand mood instances as points in a three dimensional space with the axes P, A, and D. Mood changes, for instance caused by the onset of an emotion, are then con-

---

[9]To illustrate this point one might for instance ask oneself what the average of the emotions: anger, pity and pride would be.

ceptualized as a movement of this point in the PAD space. To further classify moods, Mehrabian suggests to dichotomize each of the axes of the PAD space and assigns a label to each of the resulting octant-segments which enables a discretization. Figure 3.2 presents the resulting PAD space with the octants: *exuberant* (+P +A +D), *dependent* (+P +A -D), *relaxed* (+P -A +D), *docile* (+P -A -D) as well as: *hostile* (-P +A +D), *anxious* (-P +A -D), *disdainful* (-P -A +D) and *bored* (-P -A -D). Thus, a

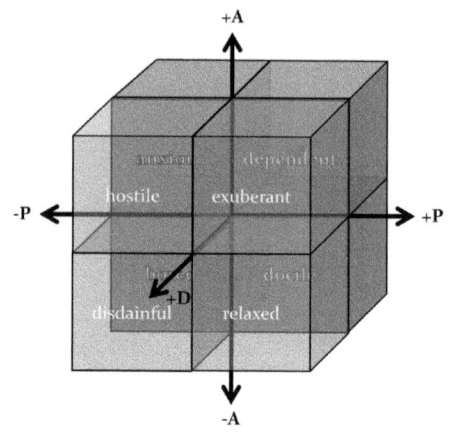

Figure 3.2: The mood-octants of the PAD space.

subliminal mood change would correspond to a movement inside an octant, while a noticeable, categorical change of mood corresponds to a transition from one octant to another.

In the context of narratological study, Palmer notes, affect has been accepted as an important motivational factor but has not been thoroughly theorized. The main approach is to distinguish between how affect is presented to the reader: "Emotions can be explicitly labeled or inferred from mental events that appear to embody an emotion such as anger. For example, if one character says of another, 'He's angry,' this has a different status from a direct presentation by the narrator of a stream of angry thoughts" (Palmer, 2004, p. 114).

As an example Palmer analyzes a short passage from Austen's (1815) novel *Emma*, which describes the young protagonist Emma Woodhouse's reaction at being reprimanded by the respected gentlemen George Knightley for an unkind jest she made about Mrs. Bates:

> He had misinterpreted the feelings which had kept her face averted, and her tongue motionless. They were combined only of anger against herself, mortification and deep concern. She had not been able to speak; and, on entering the carriage, sunk back for a moment overcome—then reproaching herself for having taken no leave, making no acknowledgement, parting in apparent sullenness, she looked out with voice and hand eager to show a difference, but it was just too late. He had turned

away, and the horses were in motion [...] She was vexed beyond what
could have been expressed—almost beyond what she could conceal.
Never had she felt so agitated, mortified, grieved, at any circumstance
in her life. She was most forcibly struck. The truth of his representation there was no denying. She felt it at her heart. How could she
have been so brutal, so cruel to Miss Bates!

(Austen, 1815, p. 309)

Palmer (2004, p. 113) uses this passage to demonstrate several narratological observations about fictional affectivity. One is how emotions are presented using thought report. Sometimes they are directly
labeled ("agitated, mortified, grieved"), and sometimes transported
indirectly through the content of the thoughts ("How could she have
been so brutal", here e.g. in the form of free indirect discourse). Another is that the internal affect reported through thoughts also causes
behavioral changes that are observable to other characters. Even if
the underlying emotions are sometimes misconstrued (which is for
instance the case with Knightley) it allows these characters to form
opinions about the interiority of the thinker. A third observation is
that affect and thinking are closely intertwined: Emma's emotions
arise as a reaction to her beliefs[10], and in the end lead to a decision
to change her behavior. Palmer's last observation is that affectivity
can have teleological value. In *Emma*, the affective conflict creates a
rift between Emma and Knightley, whose elimination leads to their
marriage that concludes the novel.

3.2.4. Actions (From Cognitive and Literary Perspectives)

For Palmer, the classical understanding of an action as an event that
has an agent, only apprehends the tip of the iceberg:

Action arises when an agent wants to change some aspect of their
environment and believes that an action will successfully bring about
that change. The agent sees both the world as they believe it to be
and also the world as they desire it to be. Action is required when
there is a disparity between the two, and it is necessary to align the
world as it is believed to be with the world as it is desired.

(Palmer, 2004, p. 118)

---

[10]It is interesting to note the nature of these beliefs. Her vexation is directed
at the belief that Knightley's beliefs about her emotions are mistaken. One might
say it is a 3rd-level mental phenomenon: a belief about someone's belief about
someone else's thoughts. This demonstrates vividly how the embeddedness and
referentiality of fictional minds and the associated phenomena like affect allow to
create complexity and conflict.

This picture is somewhat reminiscent of Ryan's possible worlds approach outlined in Chap.2. However, it also departs from it in that the observable event—i.e. a physical doing—is seen as just the endpoint of a larger mental process that involves a desire that is not met according to the agent's beliefs about the current state of the environment, all of which should also be considered part of the action. As Palmer points out, the crucial difference between a mere doing and an action is that the latter is brought about intentionally. This means that for Palmer beliefs, desires and intentions form a necessary part of the concept action. Although he only vaguely refers to "philosophy of action" as the source of his understanding, the decomposition into constituent phenomena and the descriptions Palmer employs for them are a clear indicator that he adopts a BDI approach. This is a valuable insight because it implies that his general framework is compatible with the practical approach to character reasoning that was developed and adopted during the previous chapter. Because the concepts belief, desire and intention where already introduced there (see Sec. 2.3.2), I will refrain from repeating myself.

Seeing how actions can be hardly separated from the thought processes causing them, Palmer prefers to speak of a *thought-action continuum* (Palmer, 2004, pp. 212) in a narrative context. He demonstrates what he means by this, masterfully, in a discussion of one simple statement from Evelyn Waugh's (1930) novel *Vile Bodies*:

> The three statesmen hid themselves. (86)
> This is a description of an action, but it goes further in identifying the accompanying mental processes than a statement such as "They stood behind the curtain," that leaves more work for the reader to do in deciding why they are standing there. It can be decoded in consciousness terms as follows: the three agreed that it was in their interest to conceal themselves from someone, realized that it was possible for them to do so, and decided together to take the action of hiding.
> (Palmer, 2004, p. 211)

Two points are worth expanding here. One is that an action verb like 'hide' implies certain epistemic and intentional, i.e. mental, positions that are presupposed in the fictional mind of the hiding character. Without them, the same physical gesture would be a mere 'standing behind the curtain'. This should be taken as an indication that actions are indeed comprised of physical gestures and the mental events that cause them. The other is the relation between 'hide' and 'stand

behind the curtain', which are two ways for a narrator to describe
the same physical gesture. The action of hiding, as we have seen, discloses a great deal about the accompanying events in a fictional mind.
The action of 'standing behind a curtain' is much more opaque with
regard to thoughts. This illustrates well what Palmer means, when
he suggests to speak of a though-action continuum: The former is located closer to the thought end of this continuum, while the latter is
located closer to its action end. One might ask why 'standing behind
a curtain' is located on the continuum at all, if it doesn't disclose any
thoughts. I suggest two possible explanations. One is that, read in
the appropriate context, many readers would still be able to decode
a hiding intention from such an action description, especially since
we have established above that the default reading assumption seems
to be that fictional action is caused by fictional minds. An opaque
description just demands more work when decoding. The other is
that it might indeed be the case that some readers do not decode any
mental phenomena from this description. I would argue, however,
that in that case the statement ceases to be an action description at
all, and turns into a state description. If 'standing behind a curtain'
is not connected to any intention, and not based on a belief that it
achieves a certain effect, then it simply is not an 'event that has an
agent' but becomes a passive, thoughtless maintaining of a contingent
state.

3.2.5. Implications

The previous subsections have described the phenomena that make
up the mind for cognitive science, and how these phenomena are
conceptualized and operationalized. It also described how they have
been implicitly employed by narrative theory, without realizing that—
or how—they realize whole fictional minds. This subsection will now
present the implications that Palmer draws from his new, holistic
understanding of fictional minds.

A first, general, implication follows from the ways in which personality, affect, intentionality, and action are intertwined: "[...] narratological examinations of fictional action need not involve just the
study of physical actions on the story level, it should also entail
the systematic analysis of presentations of mental action in the discourse" (Palmer, 2004, p. 174). This suggests that my argumentation
so far has been on the right track: it departed from an analysis of plot

(i.e. action on the story level) and arrived at the concept of fictional minds (i.e. mental action). However, it also uncovers the limitations of a purely analytical approach to theory building like Palmer's. For the analyst, mental action has to remain a phenomenon limited to the discourse level, a mostly hidden dynamic that has to be more or less effortfully reconstructed from action. In a generative setting, this artificial separation of physical action on the plot plane and mental action on the discourse plane can be removed because it allows to directly study how mental action causes physical action. In a generative setting, a change in personality can be realized through the change of a single parameter, which will cause a change in affectivity, which will cause a change in action, that is, in plot. Hence, to contrast Palmer's quote above, I will claim that also the reverse is true: Narratological examinations of mental action need to involve not just the study of the presentation of mental events in the discourse, they should also entail the systematic analysis of the effect of mental events on physical actions on the plot level.

A more specific implication of postulating fictional minds is what Palmer calls the *continuing-consciousness frame*: "The reader collects together all of the isolated references to a specific proper name in a particular text and constructs a consciousness that continues in the spaces between the various mentions of that character" (Palmer, 2004, p. 176). Just like actual minds don't stop functioning the moment we stop observing, also fictional minds continue functioning when the narrator is not describing them. The understanding of this comes so natural to readers that even mentioning it here might appear trivial. However, it is useful to still do so in order to point out that it is a readerly strategy that facilitates integrating the various mentions of a character into a coherent whole, by interpolating the blanks as (unknown) processes of mental functioning.

What are the results of this mental activity that is continuing throughout a story? Each character constantly observes a small part of the story world, integrates these observations into an aspectual world view, develops desires based on the world, plans to achieve them and intermittently adjusts these plans to changing circumstances. It's not a coincidence that this description closely echoes our previously developed understanding of plot: Ricoeur (1984, p. 65) writes that "emplotment is the operation that draws a configuration out of a simple succession", that is, plot is the meaning that can be derived from observed events. As such, the result of characters' attempts to make sense of the unfolding, overarching plot they witness can as well be called a plot. These aspectual, character made, plots are an essential but encoded part of all narratives. They are what a reader reconstructs when she decodes the continuous functioning of fictional minds from sparse references and periodic action descriptions. Palmer (2004, pp. 183) proposes to call the result of such a reconstruction *embedded narrative* to draw out that it is an aspectual narrative inside the narrative (and about the narrative). This term will be familiar to readers of this thesis, as it has been introduced in Subsection 2.2.2 as a concept that Ryan uses to describe the virtual branches in her plot understanding. Indeed, Palmer adopts her terminology, but extends it in subtle ways:

> It is Marie-Laure Ryan's notion of embedded narratives, which I am extending by applying it to discourse analysis and using it to mean the whole of a character's mind in action: the total perceptual and cognitive viewpoint; ideological worldview; memories of the past; and the set of beliefs, desires, intentions, motives, and plans for the future of each character in the story as presented in the discourse.
>
> (Palmer, 2004, pp. 183, 184)

The crucial part here is the identification of embedded narratives with the whole of the fictional mind in action. This includes all the phenomena that comprised private embedded narratives for Ryan, but further extends it via generalization with regard to fictional minds: all internal events that take place within them (which, as we have seen, extends into the actions taken as a result of these events) while they function continuously throughout the whole of the story. A second adaptation is that of viewpoint, alluded to above: Ryan, as well as this thesis, is interested in how embedded narratives shape, and are part of, the plot, while Palmer focuses on how they can be reconstructed from discourse. The two viewpoints, however, work hand in hand: "Fictional minds are semiotic constructs that form part of an overall narrative pattern. They are elements in a plot as well as centers of consciousness" (Palmer, 2004, p. 191).

Finally, I would like to suggest an implication of my own: Fictional minds, in most regards, can be understood to function like real minds. This statement needs some clarification. Fictional minds do not literally function, in the same way as real minds function, since they are just words on a page. However, the previous sections argued that they are representations of such functioning, and are read as if they were the same; which is why I write 'can be understood'. The equalization of fictional and actual mental functioning undoubtedly has limits. One obvious difference is in ontological status: the latter are actual, while the former are not. Yet more intricate mismatches exist, too. Like all representations, fictional minds necessarily have to be simplifications of their actual counterparts. A comprehensive representation would be indescribable, unreadable and, even, unknowable: Neither cognitive science nor literature have so far managed to uncover all the mysteries of the brain, and if they once do, then the resulting models are unlikely to operate on a narrativizable layer of abstractions but rather deal in neuronal activity, biochemical reactions or even quantum interactions.[11] Furthermore, fictional minds are partly teleologically motivated by plot, while actual minds are not. These differences are hard to formalize and capture in a few words, which is why I so curtly treat them in the qualification 'in most regards'. With these hedges in place, my statement can be taken as an one-line summary of Palmer's book-length argument: The science of the actual mind can be used to analyze the representation of the fictional mind. But the same statement also points towards a new direction. If the theories of cognitive science can be used to analyze fictional minds, then the corresponding computational models should also be usable in order to generate the respective phenomena in an approach like mine.

3.2.6. Objections

Before moving on to describe how an architecture for fictional minds can be implemented based on the observations in the previous sections, I would like to discuss one last line of criticism that was pointed out to me in private communication. Pablo Gervás—director of the Instituto de Tecnología del Conocimiento in Madrid and Professor at the Universidad Complutense de Madrid—expressed the concern that modelling characters based on scientific models of cognition might unnecessarily restrict the scope of what types of narratives can be computationally generated. In particular, he suggested that writers would rely on folk psychology to come up with their characters, and

---

[11]Modernist novelists have, in fact, attempted to create comprehensive representations of the mind in the form of the stream of consciousness novel, like Joyce's *Finnegans Wake* or Faulkner's *The Sound and the Fury*. However, as has been outlined above, the mind consists of more phenomena than just the consciously perceivable monologue of an inner voice that is supposed to be captured by this technique, and verbal thought might not be the most appropriate level of description for the mind.

that this folk psychology would be influenced by the prevalent theories of thought of that age. Thus, for literature predating—at the very least—the modernist period, these theories would be unscientific and unlikely to converge with our present understanding of mind. He further supported his caution with the observation that narratives would often focus on characters that are extraordinary and thus very different from the average person, while psychological and cognitive theories were developed precisely by averaging over (representative) groups of individuals.[12] Summarizing: scientific theories of cognition might not be a felicitous choice to represent *interesting* characters, and might not be suited at all to represent characters based on pre-scientific conceptions of thought. This concern is closely related to the considerations of Michael Young and Janet Murray—presented earlier—but as opposed to those, comes from a cognitive angle that is not anti-mimetic. Instead, it questions whether present day theories of cognition are necessarily the best choice to achieve a mimetic effect. It deserves pointing out that this position does not entail that the use of cognitive theories for modeling character's thought is always inappropriate, just that it limits the space of representable stories to those with a specific type of character.

I see Gervás' line of thought as very acute and tend to agree on the premise, while not on the conclusion. My working assumption is, too, that writers rely on folk psychology to construct round characters. Folk psychology is, foremost, a skill developed and trained in the real world to predict or explain the behavior of actual humans and not a cognisant approach based on formal theories. The previously introduced IIA is a perfect case in point how this process might phenomenologically manifest itself during writing. Consequently, scientific theories of cognition and folk psychology perform the same task and should both be expected to provide reasonably accurate predictions of human-seeming behavior. I agree that they can not be expected to make exactly the same predictions or offer the same explanations, and formal theories of thought surely play a role in writers' deliberations through rationalization of the folk-psychologically

---

[12] A famous quip goes that the best understood topic in psychology is the cognition of twenty year old students; that is, the subject group most readily available to psychologists. While this statement is, of course, not scientifically sound, it still points to an important issue: the effect of low diversity on the validity of legacy research.

constructed (or perhaps, simulated) behavior. But my educated guess
would be that the actual differences in predicted behavior should not
be too big. After all, the characters in a Regency novel still appear
human to us, even if their construction was influenced by Romantic
theories of thought.

Furthermore, I disagree with the point that psychological models are not well suited to model extraordinary individuals because
they are developed from mostly average subject groups. The whole
field of clinical psychology successfully relies on its models to assess
pathologies. For instance, Eysenck (2004, p. 467) reports that the
"[...] prediction that individuals with personality disorders should
have extreme scores on the Big Five factors has received much support
[...]". This entails that also other types of extraordinary individuals
could be modeled, for instance, through extreme personality scores.

In general, even if my counter arguments should prove unconvinc-
ing, I do not perceive a potential restriction of the character space as
problematic at the present state of my research. Most story composition systems restrict themselves to a specific genre or type of story,
and 'realistic character' is no worse field to explore than e.g. S. R.
Turner's (1993) Arthurian tales. If the need should arise to model
a specific sort of character at a later stage of the project, then the
suggested scientific cognitive character architecture can be replaced
with an alternative one, based e.g. on the (debunked) idea of the bicamerality of mind (Jaynes, 1976), as has, in fact, been attempted
elsewhere (Veale, 2018). The ways in which such a change of underlying architecture would affect the resulting plot is an interesting topic
for future research.

3.3. Implementing Affective Reasoning

The previous section outlined the constituent phenomena of fictional
minds, and how they can be conceptualized using the cognitive science
discourse. These insights are expected to solve the impasse encountered at the end of the previous chapter, that the character architecture realized through InBloom was not sufficient to capture the
behavior of the characters in TLRH. This hypothesis can be tested
by extending InBloom to model fictional minds, and then revisit the
case study in hope that the original plot can be finally recreated.

Of the main phenomena discussed in Sec. 3.2, the thought-action continuum has been already covered through InBloom's use of the BDI framework. Thus, the task at hand is to integrate models of personality and affect into the existing architecture. A plethora of computational models—and even whole cognitive architectures—exists, which are potential candidates for this. A compelling argument to select one over the others would be a unified treatment of both phenomena because it would simplify the temporal costs of integration considerably. In fact, such a model can be found in "A Layered Model of Affect" (ALMA), which has been proposed by Gebhard (2005) to implement real-time affective conversational agents. It views emotions as short term affect and personality as long term affect, while mood (mid-term affect) is conceptualized as an interface between the two. An integration of ALMA and BDI has been suggested previously (Alfonso et al., 2014), which is a second encouraging fact.[13]

In the following, I will first formally introduce ALMA, outline my implementation of it, and then present its integration into Jason.

3.3.1. ALMA

As pointed out, ALMA models the interactions of three different kinds of affect: emotion, mood and personality. Gebhard (2005) conceptualizes these phenomena based on the same quantifiable psychological models that have been introduced in Sec. 3.2. Thus, emotions are seen as valenced reactions to external events and their internal repercussions, using the OCC taxonomy. Mood is seen as the more stable mid-term affective state of an agent, represented using the PAD dimensions. Personality is understood as a disposition towards certain affective states, and represented using the OCEAN dimensions. The interactions of these phenomena in the ALMA model are shown in Fig. 3.3.

Every affective agent is assigned a stable *personality* on creation, which can be understood as a point in OCEAN space.

---

[13] Alfonso et al. also extend Jason in order to support ALMA-like processing. However, when working on this in early 2017, their implementation was unfortunately not yet publicly available (Alfonso, personal communication on 10.05.2017). This forced me to (reluctantly) perform an integration myself. When the authors released their code under http://gitlab.gti-ia.upv.es/balfonso/affect iveJason, my own work was well underway and its design already adapted to the needs of my project.

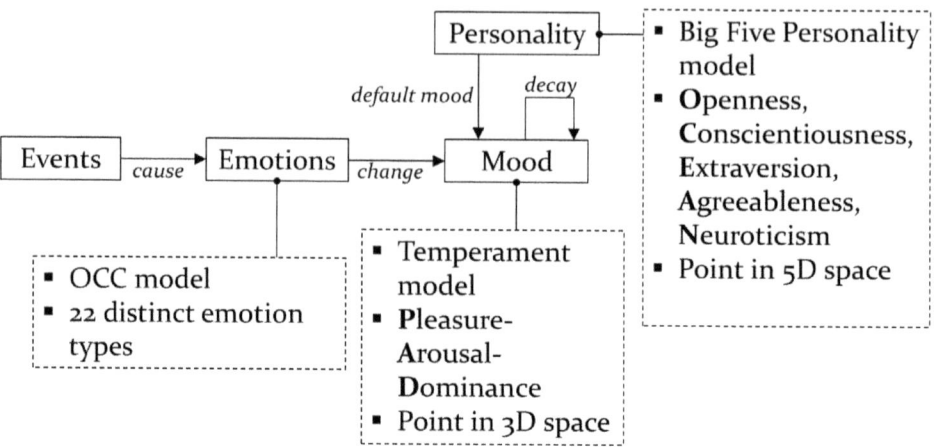

Figure 3.3: Diagram representation of the dynamics of the ALMA model.

Definition 6 (Personality). An agent's personality p is a 5-tuple of the form $(O, C, E, A, N) \in \mathbb{R}^5$, where each element is in the range $[-1, 1]$.

From personality, the agent's *default mood* can be derived. For this, Gebhard (2005) borrows some equations from Mehrabian (1996a)[14] that have been derived from correlations observed in several empirical studies of personality.

Definition 7 (Default Mood). An agent's default mood $m_d = (P, A, D) \in \mathbb{R}^3$ is a point in PAD space, which can be computed from the agent's personality p:

$$P = min(max(0.21 \cdot E + 0.59 \cdot A - 0.19 \cdot N, \ -1), 1)$$
$$A = min(max(0.15 \cdot O + 0.30 \cdot A + 0.57 \cdot N, \ -1), 1) \qquad (3.1)$$
$$D = min(max(0.25 \cdot O + 0.17 \cdot C + 0.60 \cdot E - 0.32 \cdot A, \ -1), 1)$$

To exemplify the behavior of these equations, Tab. 3.2 shows a few personality edge cases and the associated default mood. The default mood is a constant that is used to initialize the *current mood*, which

---

[14]The equations presented by Gebhard (2005) have several problems: First, Mehrabian's (1996a) original version uses trait stability, while Gebhard's uses the inverted trait neuroticism, which leads to a sign error in the computation of both P and A. Second, Gebhard confines the PAD space to the range of $[-1, 1]$ but takes no measures to enforce these boundaries on Mehrabian's equations. The decision to clip the value of the mood at 1 and -1 in my formalization (instead of normalizing it) is based on Gebhard's implementation of ALMA at https://github.com/A-L-M-A/ALMA.

represents the mid-term affective state the agent is currently in and which, consequently, changes over time.

According to ALMA, two dynamics determine the changes of the current mood. First, when the agent is experiencing emotions, that leads to a shift of the mood. Second, as long as no emotions are active but the current mood is perturbed, it slowly decays towards the default mood. To update the current mood based on emotions, the 22 OCC emotions have to be mapped into PAD space, which will allow mood updates via vector operations; Gebhard suggests the mapping in Tab. 3.3, which is partly grounded in empirical research and partly estimated by him from similarity.

Table 3.2: Personality settings and default mood.

O	C	E	A	N	P	A	D
0	0	0	0	0	0.00	0.00	0.00
1	1	1	1	1	0.61	1.00	0.70
-1	-1	-1	-1	-1	-0.61	-1.00	-0.70
0.5	0.5	0.5	0.5	0.5	0.31	0.51	0.35
0	0	0	0	1	-0.19	0.57	0.00
0	0	0	1	0	0.59	0.30	-0.32
0	0	1	0	0	0.21	0.00	0.60
0	1	0	0	0	0.00	0.00	0.17
1	0	0	0	0	0.00	0.15	0.25

When an agent appraises an event that elicits an emotion, this emotion is said to be *active*. Depending on the type and urgency of the appraised event it gets assigned an intensity, which decays over time until it reaches zero, at which point the emotion ceases to be active. Gebhard (2005) mentions that multiple decay functions are feasible. For the sake of simplicity, throughout InBloom, the simplification will be adopted that the intensity of emotions is always 1, and that the decay to 0 happens in one reasoning cycle step.[15] Since an agent can experience several emotions at the same time, an aggregation of the active emotions needs to be performed before the current mood can be updated. This is done by determining the

---

[15]This can be roughly taken to mean that InBloom, from a discourse viewpoint, operates in a "summary" mode (c.f. duration in Genette, 1983), i.e. an emotion is either present or not. To realize a dynamic that is below that of summary/plot, one could implement a switch to "scene" mode duration by adopting a slower decay function. This would allow the system to effectively 'play out' more nuanced emotional situations in real time.

Table 3.3: Mapping of OCC Emotions into PAD space, from (Gebhard, 2005).

Emotion	P	A	D
Admiration	0.5	0.3	-0.2
Anger	-0.51	0.59	0.25
Disappointment	-0.3	0.1	-0.4
Distress	-0.4	-0.2	-0.5
Fear	-0.64	0.6	-0.43
FearsConfirmed	-0.5	-0.3	-0.7
Gloating	0.3	-0.3	-0.1
Gratification	0.6	0.5	0.4
Gratitude	0.4	0.2	-0.3
HappyFor	0.4	0.2	0.2
Hate	-0.6	0.6	0.3
Hope	0.2	0.2	-0.1
Joy	0.4	0.2	0.1
Love	0.3	0.1	0.2
Pity	-0.4	-0.2	-0.5
Pride	0.4	0.3	0.3
Relief	0.2	-0.3	0.4
Remorse	-0.3	0.1	-0.6
Reproach	-0.3	-0.1	0.4
Resentment	-0.2	-0.3	-0.2
Satisfaction	0.3	-0.2	0.4
Shame	-0.3	0.1	-0.6

emotion center.

Definition 8 (Active Emotion). An emotion is a tuple (ω, ι), where $\omega \in OCC$ is the name of the emotion and $\iota \in [0, 1]$ is the emotion's intensity. The emotion is called active iff $\iota \neq 0$.

Due to the simplification outlined above, for InBloom, the following holds: If an emotion is appraised during the reasoning cycle t_j then for reasoning cycle t_i it holds that: $t_i = t_j \Rightarrow \iota = 1$ and $t_i = t_{j+1} \Rightarrow \iota = 0$. Furthermore, for convenience reasons, I will define $l_{PAD} : OCC \rightarrow [-1, 1]^3$ to be the function given by the mapping in Tab. 3.3, which determines an emotion's corresponding location in PAD space, such that $l_{PAD}(\omega) = \lambda$, where λ is a point in PAD space.

Definition 9 (Emotion Center). Let $E_t^c = \{e_1, \ldots, e_n\}$ denote the set of all active emotions for character c at reasoning cycle t. The emotion center of character c at cycle t is denoted (λ_t^c, ι_t^c). Here, λ_t^c is a point in PAD space and the centroid of all active emotions: $\lambda_t^c = \frac{\sum_{i=1}^n l_{PAD}(\pi_1(e_i))}{|E_t^c|}$.[16] While ι_t^c is the center's intensity and represents the average active emotion intensity: $\iota_t^c = \frac{\sum_{i=1}^n \pi_2(e_i)}{|E_t^c|}$. In case of $E_t = \emptyset$ the emotion center is not defined.

In our, simplified, case ι_t^c is always 1 because emotion intensity decays from one to zero in a single step.

As long as an emotion center exists, the current mood is attracted towards the outer bounds of the octant in which the emotion center is located. This results in a dynamic that Gebhard describes as pull-push (see left half of Fig. 3.4): When the zero point is located between the current mood and the emotion center, or the current mood is located between zero point and the emotion center, then the mood is attracted towards the octant of the emotion center (pull). Otherwise, when the emotion center is located between the zero point and the current mood, the mood is attracted towards the outer bounds of the emotion center's octant (push). This means that a mood always intensifies through the presence of supporting emotional experiences.

The strength of the attraction is dependent on the intensity of the emotion center (currently always 1). It is tuned in terms of a maximal update time in such a way that it would take the current mood n_{update} steps to cover the maximal distance in PAD space, given

---

[16]Let π_j denote the jth projection function.

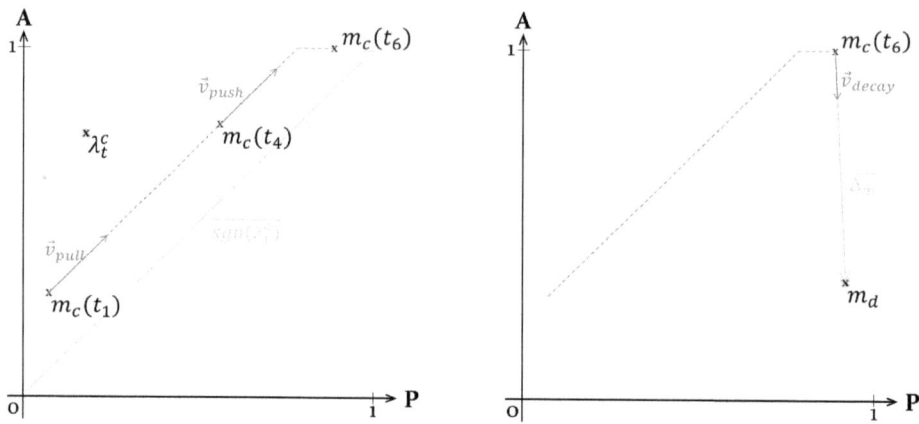

Figure 3.4: An example of mood update (left) and decay (right), projected into PA space for visualization purposes. During update, the current mood $m_c(t)$ is attracted towards the bounds of the emotion center's octant ($\vec{v}_{pull} \parallel \vec{v}_{push} \parallel \overline{sgn(\lambda_t^c)}$),[18] which results in a pull-push dynamic. During decay, the current mood is attracted towards the default mood m_d.

that an emotion center of intensity 1 would exist for that long. For all experiments throughout this thesis, $n_{update} = 5$ was employed.[17]

As has been previously discussed, trait neuroticism correlates with higher reactivity to emotional valence. This is incorporated into the mood update function by modifying the update vector by a neuroticism factor. For the sake of simplicity, the neuroticism update factor has been defined as a linear function of trait neuroticism (N) such that it increases/decreases update speed by a factor of 0.5 in case of maximal/minimal N, and leaves it unchanged at $N = 0$.

The decay of the current mood towards the default mood is defined in a comparable way, and happens in each reasoning cycle in which no emotion center exists (see right half of Fig. 3.4). Decay steps are defined in such a way that it would take the current mood at max n_{decay} steps to cover the maximal distance in PAD space. For all experiments throughout this thesis, $n_{decay} = 100$ was employed. Here, the neuroticism trait is interpreted as a general impediment for the normalization of the mood. Thus, the neuroticism decay factor has been defined in the inverse manner, as a linear function of trait

---

[17]The maximal distance in PAD space, e.g. between the points $(-1, -1, -1)$ to $(1, 1, 1)$, is $\sqrt{3 \cdot 2^2} \approx 3.46$. At $n_{update} = 5$ this means that the current mood moves approximately 0.69 per step, or $|0.4|$ in each dimension.

neuroticism such that it decreases/increases update speed by a factor of 0.5 in case of maximal/minimal N, and again leaving it unchanged at $N = 0$.

Definition 10 (Current Mood). An agent's current mood $m_c(t) = (P, A, D) \in [-1, 1]^3 \subset \mathbb{R}^3$ is a point in PAD space. It is defined in an inductive way, as a function of the reasoning cycle number t and the set of active emotions E_t.

$$m_c(t_0) = m_d \tag{3.2}$$

$$m_c(t_{n+1}) = \begin{cases} m_c(t_n) + \frac{2\iota^c_{t_{n+1}}}{n_{update}} \cdot \overrightarrow{sgn(\lambda^c_{t_{n+1}})} \cdot \upsilon_N & \text{if } E_{t_{n+1}} \neq \emptyset \\ m_c(t_n) + \frac{\sqrt{12}\delta_N}{n_{decay}} \cdot \widehat{\Delta_m} & \text{else if } |\overrightarrow{\Delta_m}| > \frac{\sqrt{12}\delta_N}{n_{decay}} \\ m_d & \text{otherwise} \end{cases} \tag{3.3}$$

Where sgn is the signum vector function[19], and $\widehat{}$ is the vector normalization operator[20]. Also, let $\upsilon_N = 1 + 0.5N$ be the update neuroticism factor, $\delta_N = 1 - 0.5N$ be the decay neuroticism factor, and $\overrightarrow{\Delta_m} = m_d - m_c(t_n)$ be a vector pointing from the current mood towards the default mood. It should be noted, that the vector additions here also have to ensure that the current mood never leaves PAD space, which in practice means that the components of $m_c(t_{n+1})$ are clipped at -1 and 1. The respective *min max* function was omitted in the formal definition for improved legibility.

This requires some unpacking. Equation 3.2 states that the initial current mood is the default mood.

The first line of equation 3.3 defines the mood updated in case of active emotions. There, $\overrightarrow{sgn(\lambda^c_{t_{n+1}})}$ can be understood as the vector representation of the emotion center's octant's attraction force. Taking the product with the scalar factor υ_N scales this vector by the neuroticism update factor. The scalar factor $\iota^c_{t_{n+1}}$ scales the resulting update vector by the intensity of the emotion center, and the scalar factor $\frac{2}{n_{update}}$ ensures that under default conditions ($\iota^c_{t_{n+1}} = 1$ and $N = 0$) at max n_{update} steps are required to reach any point in PAD space from any other point.

The second line of equation 3.3 defines the mood decay, when no active emotions are present, and the default mood is more than one

---

[18] $\|$ denotes parallelity.
[19] For $a \in \mathbb{R}^n : sgn(a) := (sgn(a_1), \ldots, sgn(a_n))$.
[20] For $a \in \mathbb{R}^n : \widehat{a} := \frac{\overrightarrow{a}}{|\overrightarrow{a}|}$

step away from the current mood ($|\overrightarrow{\Delta_m}| > \frac{\sqrt{12}\delta_N}{n_{decay}}$). First, the unit vector $\widehat{\Delta}_m$ denoting the direction between the current mood and the default mood is computed. The step length is determined by the scalar factor $\frac{\sqrt{12}\delta_N}{n_{decay}}$. It is composed of the neuroticism decay factor δ_N, and the step length factor $\frac{\sqrt{3 \cdot 2^2}}{n_{decay}} = \frac{\sqrt{12}}{n_{decay}}$, which ensures that under default conditions ($N = 0$) the longest distance in PAD space can be traversed in n_{decay} steps.

The third line of equation 3.3 defines that the current mood is set to the default mood if a regular decay step would overshoot the target.

The different formulation of the scalar products in line one and two of equation 3.3 might appear questionable at first glance. After all, if the maximal number of steps appears as the denominator in both cases, why do they differ in the numerator? The reason is that the update vectors are defined differently in the two cases: as a unit vector in the latter, and a vector from zero to one of the corners of the PAD space, in the former case. The comparability of the two formulations can be demonstrated for special cases with aligning directions, like e.g. $m_c(t_n) = 0$, $m_d = \lambda^c_{t_{n+1}} = (-1, -1, -1)$. For simplicity, lets also posit the default conditions $\iota^c_{t_{n+1}} = 1$ and $N = 0$, and assume $n_{update} = n_{decay}$.

$$\frac{2\iota^c_{t_{n+1}}}{n_{update}} \cdot \overrightarrow{sgn(\lambda^c_{t_{n+1}})} \cdot \upsilon_N \qquad \frac{\sqrt{12}\delta_N}{n_{decay}} \cdot \widehat{\Delta}_m$$

$$\equiv \frac{2}{n_{update}} \cdot \overrightarrow{sgn(\lambda^c_{t_{n+1}})} \qquad \equiv \frac{\sqrt{12}}{n_{decay}} \cdot \frac{\overrightarrow{(m_d - m_c(t_n))}}{\sqrt{3}}$$

$$\equiv \frac{2}{n_{update}} \cdot (-1, -1, -1) \qquad \equiv \frac{2}{n_{decay}} \cdot (-1, -1, -1)$$

$\square$

It is important to explicate that the definitions introduced here contain several arbitrary decisions necessary for the formalization, introduced either by the original work of Gebhard (2005), or by me. For instance, this applies to the decision to define the step length in terms of maximally necessary steps instead of e.g. steps necessary on average, the decision on how to compute the various neuroticism factors, or how these factors affect the update and decay functions. These are decisions about details on the lowest, computational level

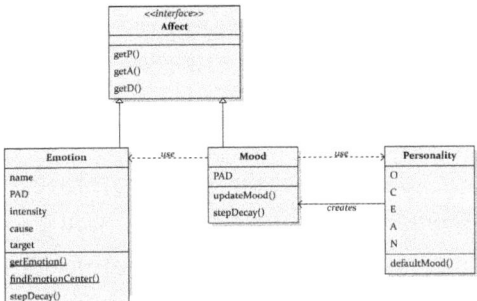

Figure 3.5: A class diagram representation of the implemented ALMA architecture. For brevity reasons attributes are represented without types and methods without parameters or return types. Static members are underlined.

of abstraction, which are rarely addressed at the higher level at which the cognitive models operate. In an ideal setting, decisions like these would be validated by comparing the behavior of the computational model with observed dynamics. Unfortunately, this lies far outside the scope of this thesis. However, the formalization introduced above has been performed in a general way, which allows a straightforward revision of any of these decisions, if the need should arise at a later stage of the project.

3.3.2. Implementing ALMA

An implementation of the formalization in the last subsection is straight forward. Since ALMA is intended as an extension of the MAS system, and is not specific to narrative semantics, it is implemented inside Jason proper. For this, the original repository was forked[21] and extended. An overview of the new classes can be found in Fig. 3.5.

The class `jason.asSemantics.Emotion` contains fields to represent the emotion instance's name, its location as a 3D point and the current intensity. Further fields are the strings `target` and `cause`, which will became relevant later on. It also implements functionality to perform one step of intensity decay, currently simply setting it to 0. This is enough to represent individual emotion instances, but further functionality is implemented on the static side. The method `static Point3D findEmotionCenter(List<Emotion> emotions)` can take a list of `Emotion` instances and returns the

---

[21]The fork is publicly available under http://github.com/cartisan/jason

PAD location of their centroid. Each appraised emotion is represented by a distinct instance of `Emotion` (instead of e.g. a singleton), and can be obtained via the method `static Emotion getEmotion(String emotion)`.

The class `jason.asSemantics.Mood` contains a field to represent a mood instance's location in PAD space. It has two relevant methods: `void updateMood(List<Emotion> emotions, Personality personality)` takes a list of active emotions and the agent's personality, and executes one update step (first line of equation 3.3), where the emotions are required to determine the emotion center and personality is required to determine the neuroticism factor, while `void stepDecay(Mood defaultMood, Personality personality)` executes one decay step (second and third line of equation 3.3) based on personality to determine the neuroticism factor, and default mood to determine the direction of decay.

The class `jason.asSemantics.Personality` contains double-typed fields to represent a personality instance's five OCEAN values. It's method `Mood defaultMood()` can be used to compute a default mood as per Def. 7.

3.3.3. Integrating ALMA and Jason

The classes introduced above implement all of the ALMA functionality, but are still separate from the BDI architecture. In order to create a unified architecture of fictional minds these two components need to be integrated. Two main interaction types can be distinguished: First, the BDI cycle influences ALMA because events perceived by the agent cause emotions to be appraised. Second, ALMA influences the BDI cycle because an agent's decision making is dependent on its affective state. But which of the three affect types should be taken into account during planning? Since personality, by definition, is understood as a disposition to act in certain ways, it seems promising to introduce this connection. However, as has been discussed on the basis of the Good Samaritan study in Sec. 3.2.2 (see p. 124), apart from personality also context plays a big role in decision making. After having analyzed the dynamics of ALMA, we can finally propose a candidate representation of context to properly account for this interaction. Emotions represent the direct link between context, seen as environment events, and affective states. However, emotions

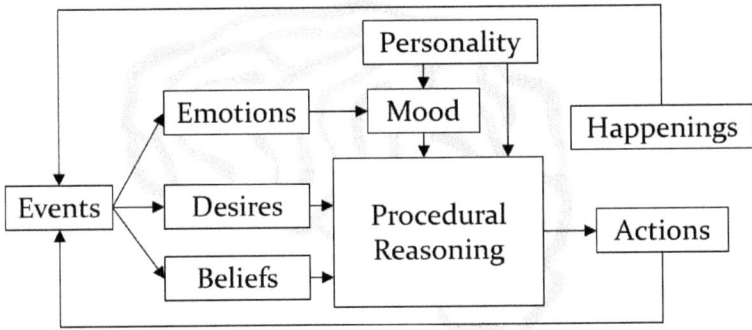

Figure 3.6: Diagram representing the integration of ALMA and BDI into a unified fictional mind architecture.

in ALMA are fleeting states, and several contradictory emotions can be present at any time. Felicitously, a time-discounted aggregate of emotions is preserved in the form of the current mood, which also has the desirable property of changing more slowly than the set of active emotions: A single negative emotion won't disturb the current mood too much, whereas a succession of negative emotions will still change it quickly enough. It is thus an auspicious proxy for an agent's current context. This led to the decision to make planning depend on both mood and personality. Fig.3.6 presents a high-level overview of the intended fictional mind architecture.

The following problems need to be addressed in order to implement the envisioned architecture:

- A mechanism is required that allows to define an agent's personality during the initialization of a narrative system.

- A mechanism is required that allows programmers to specify that a particular event triggers certain emotions.

- The BDI reasoning cycle needs to be extended to regularly keep affective phenomena up to date.

- An ASL formalism needs to be defined in order to allow mood and personality to affect plan selection, as well as to initiate new goals.

Personality Definition

Jason's `jason.asSemantics.Agent` class has no field which could be used to store personality. Following proper object oriented practice like separation of concerns, and to allow users of the framework to still use non-affective agents, the decision was made to not simply add a field to the existing `Agent` class, but instead to introduce the subclass `jason.asSemantics.AffectiveAgent` to hold this field. Because an agent's default mood is dependent on its personality, setting this field should also initialize the default mood. This functionality is implemented in the function `void initializePersonality(Personalit y personality)`.[22] If an application wants to use affective instead of vanilla Jason agents, it can configure this by setting `AffectiveAgent` as agent class in its mas2j. However, unlike other agent properties, Jason's mas2j configuration files do not support setting up personality. This has to be done by the client program during launching—after Jason created the agents but before the simulation started—using the provided `initializePersonality` method.

Emotion Appraisal

As discussed in Sec. 3.2.3, emotions can be grouped into two types: primary emotions, which are unmediated reactions to events, and secondary emotions, which are deliberative reactions. Consequently, there should be two ways for the designer of a narrative system to appraise emotions: through the environment, that is, concomitant to an event perception; and through the agent, as part of the ASL reasoning. Both methods of adding emotions have to report to the BDI interpreter which emotions have been scheduled for appraisal during the next cycle.

The environment has no way of directly affecting agent state, and its only way of transmitting information to agents is via events. Fortunately, Jason explicitly supports meta information about literals in the form of annotations (outlined on p. 68), which are accessible for the BDI interpreter when it processes an event. The annotation `emotion(X)` with $X \in OCC$ is introduced as a keyword to indicate to the reasoning cycle that a particular event should elicit the primary emotion `X`. Thus, when the need arises to schedule an unmediated emo-

---

[22]Of course this is not the only functionality of the newly introduced class. Its further responsibilities will be discussed later.

tion through the environment, it can be added through a respective emotion-annotation to the event perception. A canonical example for a primary emotion would be the immediate and involuntary bout of fear experienced upon seeing a large charging predator. Since this emotion seems not to be the result of a ponderous deliberation, but an arguably universal and instantaneous reaction, it is logical and economical to encode it as part of the environment-based event definition itself: e.g. attack(*tiger*)[emotion(*fear*), target(*tiger*)]. As becomes apparent from the example, a primary emotion can also have a target, which can be added via an appropriate annotation.

Agent-side reasoning offers a more direct route to emotion appraisal because it is conceptually permissible for ASL code to directly influence agent state. New ASL keywords can be implemented via custom internal actions, simply by adding a new class derived from jason.asSemantics.DefaultInternalAction to the package jason.stdlib. This way, a new action appraise_emotion can be defined to schedule secondary emotions from ASL code. It takes two obligatory, and two optional parameters: .appraise_emotion(emotion, source, target, type).

- The obligatory atom emotion is the name of the emotion to be scheduled.

- The obligatory string source specifies the source of the emotion, i.e. the literal that is to be preserved as its cause.

- The atom target can be added to indicate an agent at which the emotion is directed.[23]

- The integer type can be used to indicate whether the event source is the addition (0) or removal (1) of a percept, or an action/speech-act (2); it defaults to 0. This is necessary because the system can not automatically detect event types from an ASL literals, but needs to treat different event types differently.

When an internal actions is triggered in the ASL code, Jason executes its Object execute(TransitionSystem ts, Unifier un, Term[] args) method, and provides it with the internal action's arguments stored in args. What is more, it contains a reference to the

---

[23]At the moment it is not possible to denote that the emotion is targeted at an object because no use case for this has come up, so far.

respective agent's transition system. As outlined in Sec. 2.3.4 on p. 72, this class is responsible for implementing the BDI interpreter's reasoning cycle in the method `jason.asSemantics.TransitionSystem#reasoningCycle()`. To allow the reasoning cycle to manage emotions, the subclass `jason.asSemantics.AffectiveTransitionSystem` is created, and the method `scheduleForAppraisal(String emotion, String target, String source)` is implemented, which can be called as part of `appraise_emotion`'s `execute`. This method is responsible for creating appropriate instances of the `Emotion` class based on the argument `emotion`, and storing them in the field `List<Emotion> deliberative_appraisal`, where the emotions can be retrieved later, when the reasoning cycle reaches the appropriate appraisal step.

In order to notify Jason to use the newly introduced transition system instead of its vanilla counterpart, the initialization of `Affect iveAgent` is adapted by overriding the method `AffectiveAgent#initAg()` to set its transition system to an instance of `AffectiveTransitionSystem`.

Updating the Reasoning Cycle

During each reasoning cycle, the BDI interpreter has to update the agents affective state, that is: decay active emotions, appraise new emotions, and update the current mood. The transition system's method `reasoningCycle()`, in essence, implements a deterministic state machine responsible for all steps in the reasoning cycle. While a detailed depiction of the automaton can be found in Fig. 4.1 of Bordini et al. (2007), for our present purpose I present a simplified version in Fig. 3.7. To extend this automaton, the subclass `jason.asSemantics.AffectiveTransitionSystem` was introduced, in order to override the methods `applySemanticRuleSense()` as well as `applySemanticRuleDeliberate()` to insert three new states, as shown in Fig. 3.7. Speaking in the most abstract of terms, the individual steps perform the following tasks:

- **Perceive:** Use the agent architecture class to poll the environment for new percepts and update the belief base accordingly;

- **ProcMsg:** Process the next message in the queue of incoming speech acts;

- **UpMood:** Perform one mood update or decay step;

- **DeriveSEM:** Appraise secondary emotions;

- **SelEv:** Select (and remove) one event from the event queue for further processing;

- **DerivePEM:** Appraise primary emotions associated with the selected event;

- **RelPl:** Identify all relevant plans in the plan library, i.e. plans whose triggering event can be unified with the selected event;

- **ApplPl:** Determine all applicable plans, i.e. those relevant plans whose context is true according to the current belief base;

- **SelAppl:** Select one applicable plan from all applicable plans;

- **AddIM:** Determine whether the plan is part of an existing intention (i.e. a subgoal) which should wait until it is completed, or a completely new intentions (and therefore to be executed concurrently to the other existing intentions);

- **ProcAct:** Process results of previously executed actions, reported by the environment;

- **SelInt:** Select one of the concurrently active intentions, to be pursued this cycle;

- **ExecInt:** Identify the next step in the plan associated with the selected intention; if it is an action schedule it for execution by the agent architecture;

- **ClearInt:** Clear intentions that have been recognized as completed (or failed) during the course of the current cycle;

- **Act:** Use the agent architecture to execute the scheduled action in the environment;

As becomes clear, each cycle performs three main tasks: update the agent's informational state, process an internal event, and continue the execution of an intention. We will now review in detail the changes that are necessary to imbue affective reasoning capabilities into this system.

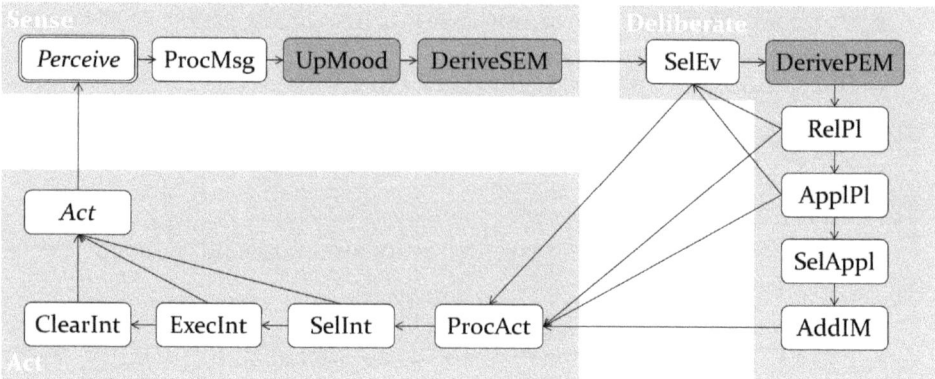

Figure 3.7: Simplified deterministic automaton representation of the extended BDI interpreter. Gray steps have been added to include affective reasoning capabilities. Italics indicate steps that are delegated to the agent's `AgArch` class, which is responsible for interactions with the environment. An explanation of individual steps can be found in Bordini et al. (2007, Chap. 4), but is not pertinent for the present thesis.

THE TRANSITORY STATE of an agent's reasoning cycle is represented in Jason using the class `jason.asSemantics.Circumstance`. To be able to also store data about its affective part, this class is subclassed by `jason.asSemantics.AffectiveCircumstance`, which has the fields `List<Emotion> PEM`, `List<Emotion> SEM` and `Mood M`. An emotion is considered active iff a respective instance is located in either of the lists, `PEM` or `SEM`, depending on whether it is primary or secondary in nature. Emotion appraisal is performed using the method `AffectiveAgent#addEmotion(Emotion emotion, S tring type)`, with `type` determining to which list of that agent's affective circumstance the emotion is added. Although actual persons are not always aware of the precise emotions they are experiencing, the decision was made to increase the algorithms expressivity by providing agents with accurate beliefs denoting the emotions that are currently active. This can be used in ASL reasoning to trigger new goals, or as plan context, which allows restricting the applicability of plans to certain emotional situations. To do so, the method `addEmotion` translates the emotion back into ASL literal representation—including its `target` and `cause` as annotations—and adds an appropriate belief of the form `emotion(X)` to the agent's belief base.[24]

---

[24]Such a reliable transmission is just the baseline solution. Creating agents that are not aware of their emotions, or whose beliefs about the emotions they experience are simply unreliable, is as easy as changing one line of code. It is well

DERIVESEM is the most straightforward of the newly introduced states. As outlined above (on p. 151), secondary emotions are added from the ASL side directly into the transition system's `deliber-ative_appraisal` list, already reified as `Emotion` instances. Thus, appraising these emotions is done by simply traversing that list, executing the method `addEmotion` for each of its items, and clearing it in the end.

DERIVEPEM works in a comparable manner but has to use another source to identify the emotions it needs to appraise. Primary emotions are attached as annotations directly to the perceptions that cause them (as has been outlined above, on p. 150), and perceptions are processed by the reasoning cycle one after another in the form of events. For this reason, DerivePEM is inserted right after the `SelEv` state which selects the event that is going to be processed by the current cycle. Thus, appraising primary emotions is done by extracting all annotations of the form `emotion(X)` and creating new `Emotion` instances. For this, `X` determines the type of emotion, the selected event determines its `cause`, and a potentially present `target(Y)` annotation determines the emotion instance's `target`. Again, each emotion can be activated by executing the method `addEmotion`.

At first glance, it might appear like secondary emotions were appraised before primary emotions because DeriveSEM is executed before DerivePEM in the automaton in Fig. 3.7. This would be incorrect, since primary emotions ipso facto should be more immediate than secondary ones. However, the appearance is deceiving. This can be demonstrated by returning to the previously mentioned example of the frightful, charging tiger. Encoded as primary emotion—using the environment perception `attack(`*`tiger`*`)[emotion(`*`fear`*`), target(`*`tiger`*`)]`—fear would be appraised during the reasoning cycle in which the corresponding event `+attack(`*`tiger`*`)[...]` is selected for processing. When the same situation is encoded using secondary emotions, the environment perception and its corresponding reasoning cycle event contain no emotion annotation: `attack(`*`tiger`*`)`. To model an appropriate affective reaction, a deliberation step would need to be added using ASL side inference rules like:

---

worth investigating which effect characters' connectedness with their emotions might have on a narrative's plot.

```
1   +attack(Being) : large(Being) <-
2       .appraise_emotion(fear, "attack(Being)", Being).
```

For fear to be actually appraised in this case, one reasoning cycle has
to select the attack event for processing, which would result in the
above inference rule being selected as applicable plan and being added
to the intention set. Even in the best case that no other intentions are
present and the newly added plan is selected as intention in the same
cycle, the resulting emotion instance is added to `deliberative_-`
`appraisal` only after `DeriveSEM` has already been executed. Thus,
it can be appraised only during the next cycle, and consequently, one
cycle later than in the primary emotion case.

UPMOOD   can use the emotions that are appraised as active by the
other two steps in order to perform mood updates according to equation 3.3. When no emotions are active (that is, `PEM` and `SEM` in `Af-`
`fectiveCircumstance` are empty), and the agent's current mood (`M`
in `AffectiveCircumstance`) is not the agent's default mood, a decay step is executed. If active emotions do exist, then an update step
is executed instead. An active emotion is considered to directly contribute to an agent's mood if their locations in PAD space agree in the
sign of at least two the three dimensions (i.e. they are located in the
same or neighboring octants). All directly contributing emotions are
checked for `targets` and `causes`, and these are preserved alongside
the new mood in the agent's `AffectiveCircumstance`. This ensures
that, for instance, an agent at whom the emotion `love` is directed
is not collaterally preserved as the target of a `hostile` mood, just
because the other emotions appraised during the same reasoning cycle happened to be negative. Whenever the current mood changes
its octant, which can be considered a change in discrete, perceivable
mood-state, these targets and causes are reset. This means that targets and causes are preserved only as long as they contribute to the
currently prevailing mood type. Like with appraised emotions, the
decision was made to make agents aware of their mood by adding
a belief of the form `mood(X)` to their belief base, which encodes the
current mood octant and consequently changes on every change of
octant. After all these updates are done, one decay step is executed
on each of the appraised emotions (which in our case means that they
are deactivated and removed from `PEM` and `SEM`).

APPLPL is an already existing state of the BDI interpreter, which has to be extended to make sure that plans are considered applicable only when their affective profile fits the agent's current affective profile. The details are explained in the coming subsection, once it has been outlined how the ASL formalism is extended to enable affective profiles for plans.

Affective Reasoning

As has been outlined in Fig. 3.6, the main interaction point of the newly introduced affective architecture and the BDI framework is the procedural reasoning step. Affective phenomena can be relevant here in two ways: First, certain plans might be applicable only under certain affective circumstances, and second, changes in affect state might change the agent's motivational state.

To denote that plans can have affective conditions in order to be applicable, the ASL syntax has to be extended. The annotation `affect` has been introduced to define these affective conditions, using a simple boolean algebra in prefix notation. It is described by the following EBNF[25]:

---

[25]Note, that in the proposed notation `affective predicate` is the abstract super-type of `personality predicate` and `mood predicate`, that is, there is only two types of concrete predicates.

$\langle$affective conditions$\rangle \models$ `affect`($\langle$predicate$\rangle$)

$\langle$predicate$\rangle \models \langle$complex predicate$\rangle \mid \langle$affective predicate$\rangle$

$\langle$complex predicate$\rangle \models$ `and`($\langle$predicate$\rangle$,$\langle$predicate$\rangle$) $\mid$

`or`($\langle$predicate$\rangle$,$\langle$predicate$\rangle$) $\mid$

`not`($\langle$predicate$\rangle$)

$\langle$affective predicate$\rangle \models \langle$personality predicate$\rangle \mid \langle$mood predicate$\rangle$

$\langle$personality predicate$\rangle \models$ `personality`($\langle$p trait$\rangle$,$\langle$value$\rangle$)

$\langle$mood predicate$\rangle \models$ `mood`($\langle$m trait$\rangle$,$\langle$value$\rangle$)

$\langle$p trait$\rangle \models$ `openness` | `conscientiousness` |

`extraversion` | `agreeableness` |

`neuroticism`

$\langle$m trait$\rangle \models$ `pleasure` | `arousal` | `dominance`

$\langle$value$\rangle \models$ `high` | `medium` | `low` | `positive` |

`negative`

A noteworthy production of this EBNF is `value`, which can produce one of five values whose denotations are presented in Tab. 3.4. This results in a discretization of the mood and personality spaces

Table 3.4: The denotations of the five different values that p `trait` and m `trait` can take.

$$\begin{array}{rl} \text{high:} & x \geq 0.7 \\ \text{medium:} & -0.7 < x < 0.7 \\ \text{low:} & x \leq -0.7 \\ \text{positive:} & x > 0 \\ \text{negative:} & x < 0 \end{array}$$

from the perspective of planning, while the actual values against which the conditions are tested remain continuous. The decision to discretize has been made to make domain-modeling easier, while maintaining expressivity. Ideally, the number of possible values and their denotation would be based on a statistical analysis of personality and mood clusters in a diverse sample. So far, however, the arbitrary decisions above have been enough for all practical concerns.

The `ApplPl` step of the BDI interpreter, which determines the subset of the relevant plans that are applicable, has been adapted to take into account these affective conditions stored in plan annotations. First, the original method is executed to identify all plans with applicable context. Then, for each of these plans, a check is performed whether an `affect` annotation is present, and if it is, the annotation is validated against the agent's affective state via the method `AffectiveAgent#checkConstraint(Literal condition)`. If the condition in the annotation is not true, the plan is removed from the list of applicable plans. This means that in, the end, the list of applicable plans contains plans that are applicable in all affective situations and those whose affective preconditions are fulfilled. Since the latter provide behavior that is more specialized and thus better suited for the particular context, the method `AffectiveAgent#selectOption(List<Option> options)` (that is responsible for selecting one of the applicable options during the Sel-Appl state) has been adapted to give precedence to plans that have `affect` annotations.

The question might arise why the extra work of introducing and processing an additional ASL formalism has been necessary, instead of simply relying on the already existing mechanism of plan contexts. After all, the applicability of plans is tested based on their context, and affective preconditions could be placed in the context. The problem with this solution is that the context is evaluated against an agent's belief base. As has been discussed, a belief base does not need to be correct, and does not need to contain all the information that is necessary to evaluate such preconditions. This makes the employed solution better suited because it evaluates affective preconditions against the objective facts of the environment instead of their subjective perception by the individual agent.

Overview

The resulting overall architecture of the affective extension of Jason can be found in Fig. 3.8.

3.3.4. Updating InBloom to use Affective Characters

Several changes have to be performed in order to allow InBloom to use the extended Jason architecture.

FIRST, AFFECTIVE PROCESSING has to be switched on, which is done by adapting the employed agent class in `inBloom.jason.Plot`

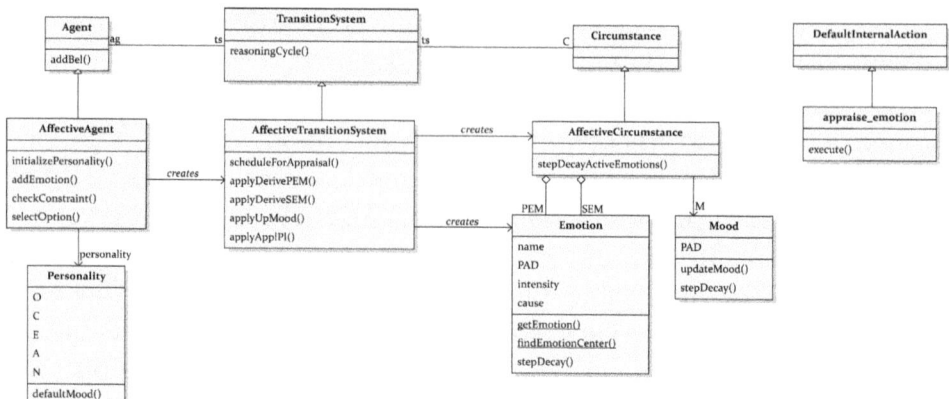

Figure 3.8: A class diagram representation of the affective extension of the Jason architecture. For brevity reasons, attributes are represented without types and methods without parameters or return types. Static members are underlined.

AwareAg to subclass **AffectiveAgent** instead of **Agent**. This entails that a narrative system implemented using InBloom has to be able to define its agents' personalities during configuration. As outlined in Sec. 2.3.4 (on p. 90), during configuration, agents' properties can be set up using the class **inBloom.LauncherAgent**. This mechanism can be extended to incorporate personality. To do so, **LauncherAgent** receives a new field **personality** of type **Personality** which can be instantiated by the narrative system with the appropriate personality when its instances are created. The personality of the respective **PlotAwareAg** is then set by the method **PlotLauncher#initializePlotAgents(List<LauncherAgent> agents)** based on the **LauncherAgent** configuration.

PREVIOUSLY, EVENT PERCEPTIONS only needed to encode the agent that perceives them, as well as their propositional content. Now, an event could potentially also be associated with a number of primary emotions, determined by the model. As has been discussed above, primary emotions need to be encoded in annotations, which are added to a perception delivered to the agent. Thus, the event implementation needs to be extended with a convenient way to add annotations. To do so, the method **PlotEnvironment#addEventPercept(String agentName, String percept, PerceptAnnotation annot)** has been implemented. Its third parameter is of the newly created type **inBloom.he** `lper.PerceptAnnotation`, a class that wraps around a list of strings that represents all the annotations that need to be added to a perception. This class offers convenience methods to add annotations of the type `emotion`, `target` and `cause`, but also a method to add annotations of arbitrary form. Its `toString()` method performs all the necessary manipulations to transform the wrapped list into a syntactically correct annotation. With this, to create an event with an emotion becomes as easy as:

```
1   environment.addPerception(
2       "hen",
3       "found(wheat)",
4       PerceptAnnotation.fromEmotion("joy")
5   );
```

A special case of event perceptions are action-result perceptions. Previously, model-side actions only needed to return true or false, depending on whether their execution succeeded (revisit Fig. 2.5 for details on how actions are processed by InBloom). Now, the result of an action could potentially also be associated with a number of primary emotions. To encapsulate all the information that an action—implemented as a method in the model—needs to return to the agent, the class `inBloom.ActionReport` is created. It contains the field `Boolean success`, which is used to encode whether the action execution succeeded, and the field `Map<String, PerceptAnnotation> perceptMap`, which can be used to store different perception annotations for different agents. This is necessary because actions are always perceived by all agents present at the same location, however, their emotional appraisal of the same action might differ. `ActionReport` is used as the return type of all model methods that implement actions. The method `PlotEnvironment#executeAction`—that receives agents' action requests and is responsible for relaying them to the model—analyzes the returned `ActionReport`, constructs event perceptions with according annotations for each present agent, and returns whether the action was successful. Its location as the interface between agents and model allows it to perform an additional analysis step: If an action is reported to fail, an additional annotation containing a disappointment emotion is constructed and attached to the perception of the executing agent. This constitutes a first step towards automatic emotion detection by InBloom.[26]

---

[26]The autonomous, domain independent detection of appropriate emotions is

Another type of events represented by InBloom are happenings, which also might need to be associated with primary emotions. Therefore, the class `Happening` is extended with the field `PerceptAnnotation annotation`, which can be used to hold any annotation, but in particular those pertaining to emotions.When the model determines that a happening has been triggered during the course of its `PlotModel#checkHappenings` method, it can now use the annotations stored in the happening to deliver a perception—complete with emotions—to the agent via the environment, in the same way as it would with actions.

THE AFFECTIVE DYNAMICS underlying the agent's behavior might be of interest to the end user, so functionality for capturing the development of mood over time in the form of line graphs has been implemented. Whenever an agent's mood value changes, the extended Jason architecture notifies `AffectiveAgent` subclasses by calling their method `updateMoodValue(Mood newMood)`. The class `PlotAwareAg` overrides this method, to store the new mood in a table-like model side structure, using the method `PlotModel#mapMood(String name, Mood mood, Integer reasoningCycleNum)`. This table—rows containing agent names, and columns containing the agent's current reasoning cycle number—is wrapped in the class `inBloom.helper.MoodMapper`. Among several auxiliary functionality it also implements the method `Mood sampleMood(String agName, Long reasoningCycleNum)`, which can determine an agent's mood at any given plot time based on the reasoning cycle numbers stored in the table. When the user wants to display a mood graph she can activate the `Show Graphs` button in the UI, effectively calling the method `PlotControlsLauncher#void drawGraphs()`. This method prompts the singleton class `inBloom.graph.MoodGraph` to analyze and visualize the mood data. The data underlying the graph is created by sampling every agent's mood data stored in the `MoodMapper`

---

a powerful tool, that has the potential to take over much responsibility from the domain modeler. How emotions can be derived from certain configurations is an open and exciting research problem, both from the AI as well as the narratology perspective. An example from narratology can be found in Dannenberg (2008, Chap. 5), who outlines how the emotions 'satisfaction' and 'regret' can be derived from downward and upward counterfactual thought. However, as the result of deliberation, they are candidates for the automatic appraisal of secondary emotions, and not primary emotions like discussed here.

in 10 millisecond steps (from the start time of the fastest agent to the stop time of the slowest agent) for a given dimension (all agents' pleasure, arousal, or dominance, or alternatively all dimensions of a single agent; which can be selected using the graph's UI). To allow for better cross-referencing with the plot graph, the x-axis of the mood graph also receives ticks indicating which reasoning cycle numbers correspond to which plot steps. The graph itself is represented as an `XYLineChart` from the Java library JFreeChart[27].

Furthermore, the plot graph is extended in order to allow it to capture the appraisal of emotions as well as changes in mood, since these internal events have become additional parts of the plot. Changes of mood are reported to the graph by a mechanisms already in place in the class `PlotCircumstanceListener`, which reports all internal events to the plot graph. This means that mood changes (the addition or removal of the belief to be in a certain mood octant) are represented in the plot graph as vertices of the generic type `PERCEPTION`. The same solution would also work for emotions, however, for further processing steps it is necessary that emotions are represented by a dedicated vertex type. Consequently, the new plot vertex type `EMOTION` was added in the class `Vertex`. Then, `PlotAwareAg`'s method `addEmotion` was extended to perform a call to `PlotGraphController#addEvent`, which adds a vertex of type `EMOTION` to the plot graph.

3.4. The Case Study Revisited

With the whole machinery for affective reasoning in place, finally, the case study from Sec. 2.4 can be revisited. The hypothesis that motivated the present chapter was that the difficulties encountered there during the modeling of the folktale TLRH, namely:

- Why does the hen normally work on the farm, while the other animals always relax?

- What triggers the hen's desire to punish the other animals?

can be resolved by taking into account characters' fictional minds. This can now be put to the test by enriching the previously outlined narrative system in three ways:

---

[27]www.jfree.org/jfreechart

1. Encoding the four characters' personalities,

2. Encoding when—and which—particular emotions are triggered,

3. Encoding the affective causes and conditions for agents' plans.

Since the original tale does not provide any explicit indications about
the characters' affective life (and even if it did, it could not be expected that such prescriptions were formulated using the conceptual
framework set up in this chapter) any such modeling must necessarily be regarded as an act of interpretation. As such, it has no claim
to universal validity: It may well be that readers' intuitions diverge
from the ones proposed below, but I would consider that not harmful
to my overall argument. What is of importance is that there exists
at least one plausible interpretation that can lead to a parametrization of the narrative system resulting in the emergence of the original
plot. Remember, that the setting of this thesis so far has been one
of generative modeling, where the goal is to reproduce phenomena
encountered 'in the wild', based on a set of first principles offered
by a particular theory. If a reconstruction has succeeded, then the
underlying theory can be considered sufficiently expressive to model
the phenomenon in question, in our case: plot.[28]

Some readers might be inclined to deny any reading that suggests
that folktale characters have personalities or experience moods, since
the classical position is that the plot of folktales is driven by the moral
and not by the characters. This is understandable, but I hope that the
previous sections have succeeded in convincing these readers to give
it the benefit of a doubt. If the silent movement of simple geometric
shapes, like employed in the Heider-Simmel experiment (see p. 44),
can create the appearance of personality in readers, then it should not
be a stretch to accept such readings in fairy tales, even if they might
not be considered overly scholarly. I concede freely that other genre
might be better suited to make my point, however, the overriding

---

[28]In fact, the argument works better in the opposite direction: If a reconstruction has not succeeded, the theory can be considered underspecified. All that a
successful reconstruction can demonstrate is that the theory is sufficient to model
one particular instance. However, for a computational approach to such a complex phenomenon like narrative even that can be considered a success. Another
indication for success is generative potential: the ability of one model to create
different instances of the modeled phenomenon based on different parametrization. This will be discussed below.

criterion here remains the simplicity of folktales, which makes them amenable to computational modeling.

3.4.1. Enriching the Narrative System of TLRH

As outlined, the narrative system needs to be enriched in three ways.

Personality

A first observation on personality is that the three farm animals behave completely the same throughout the narrative, so it is plausible to assume that their personalities are similar. It would, of course, be possible to infer differences from intertextual knowledge or social stereotypes, which would suggest different traits for e.g. the pig and the dog. However, these seem to have no relevance for TLRH since they do not lead to a difference in behavior. Hence, as a handy simplification, I will assume that their personalities are identical.

Recalling the adjectives associated with the individual personality traits presented in Tab. 3.1, the following profile can be deduced. The most prominent feature of the 'non-hen' farm animals is that they do not perform any work on the farm and are apparently not willing to be moved to do so. This suggests that they have a low level of conscientiousness, which is associated with reliability and responsibility at the high end of the scale. Another interesting feature is that the animals do not show any willingness to help the hen in her work, even when she asks them directly to do so. This would correspond to a low level of agreeableness, which on the high end would be associated with kindness and a sympathetic attitude. Also noteworthy is that the three characters spend all their time calmly relaxing in the sun, no matter the hen's antics. Foremost, this suggests a fairly low level of neuroticism, which, at the high end of the scale, is associated with instability and intolerance to stress. It also lends itself to ambivalent conclusions towards extraversion, which is associated with activity and a high energetic level on the high end, but, at the same time, also to a tendency for positive affect and cheerfulness. The animals commonly exhibit low energy behavior, but perk up when they are offered bread, and seem also to be fairly capable of enjoying positive emotions from their time in the sun. I therefore opt for a slightly low level of extraversion. None of their behavior seems to relate to the openness trait, which is associated with originality, imaginative capabilities and artistry, so I assume a neutral level. A quantified realization of this discussion can be found in Tab. 3.5.

The hen's behavior can be interpreted as the result of a different personality profile. The fact that she persistently works on the farm indicates a high level of conscientiousness. She exhibits a high level of energy, enthusiastically takes on the task of creating bread and repeatedly asks for help, which also indicates a high level of extraversion. She does not seem to react too strongly to individual rejections and setbacks but still is sufficiently stung to punish the causers after continued transgressions, which could be taken to indicate mildly negative level of neuroticism. Her level of agreeableness can't be very high, otherwise the hen would share the bread in all circumstances. However, it can't be very low, either, if the tale is taken to indicate that she would have shared the bread if the other animals did help her (see Fig. 2.3 for the reasoning behind this interpretation). For practical reasons, a somewhat negative level of agreeableness is assumed here. Again, no conclusions could be drawn about openness. A quantified realization of this discussion can be found in Tab. 3.5.

It should be noted that any mapping of qualitative assessment to quantitative representation must be arbitrary to a certain degree, unless conducted via a validated personality questionnaire averaged over several raters. This approach will, in fact, become relevant later in this section, but seemed excessive in the present context, where the relation between the two personality profiles counts more than any actual numbers. Here, the numbers were fine tuned by hand to ensure desirable dynamics.

Table 3.5: Personality profiles employed in InBloom to reproduce the plot of TLRH.

	hen	other animals
O	0	0
C	1	-1
E	0.7	-0.3
A	-0.3	-0.7
N	-0.2	-0.7

Emotion

The following (primary) emotions were implemented via the model and character classes:

- Every action that successfully changes the state of the wheat (from corn, via the preliminary stages, up until bread) elicits pride.

- Sharing an item with another agent elicits `pride` in the giver, and `gratitude` in the receiver.

- Eating an edible item elicits `joy`.

The following (secondary) emotions were implemented via the ASL reasoning file:

- When an agent realizes that a new item they dislike has come into their possession, this is appraised with `hate`[29], otherwise this situation is appraised with `love`.

- Alternatively, when a hungry agent realizes that a new edible item has come into their possession, this is instead appraised with `joy`.

- When an agent finds an item, from which a useful second item can be created, this is appraised with `hope`.

- When an agent's request for help is rejected, this is appraised with `disappointment` unless the agent's mood is `hostile`, in that case it is appraised with `anger`.

- When an agent's request for help is accepted, this is appraised with `gratitude`.

- Rejecting a request for help is appraised with `reproach` targeting the requesting agent, while accepting a request results in feeling `pride`.

- When an agent attempts to eat something but realizes that it does not possess anything edible, this is appraised with `disappointment`.

- When an agent realizes it has successfully completed its bread-making intention, this is appraised with `satisfaction`.

As attentive readers might have noticed, not all of these situations pertain directly to the ones encountered in the original plot of TLRH.

---

[29]The decision which emotion is appraised in which situation was made relying on the OCC taxonomy in Fig. 3.1. This might not always align well with an intuitive understanding of the emotions or situations in question.

Instead, they might be taken to represent situations that could arise during alternative possible plots. Since InBloom is a framework for implementing narrative systems, and narrative systems receive this name from their inherent potential to represent a plethora of possible worlds or plots, this is a desirable property of the implementation.

Affective Reasoning

Affective reasoning can take two forms: one is that plans can be supplemented with affective conditions concerning an agent's personality and current mood, while the other is that moods and emotions can be used to trigger changes in wishes and obligations. This can be used to address the two central difficulties of the initial version of the case study.

One problem was that the reason for the hen's desire to punish the other animals could not be determined and implemented. This can be now done by using a hostile mood as the triggering condition to punish those characters that caused that mood (see Lis. 3.2). When the mood lightens again, this leads to the deactivation of the respective desire.

```
1    +mood(hostile) <-
2       ?affect_target(Ags);
3       if not (.empty(Ags)) {
4          +wish(punish);
5       }.
6
7    -mood(hostile) <-
8       -wish(punish).
```

Listing 3.2: Hostile mood (de)activates punishment wish.

This seems intuitively plausible, and also follows the logic of the underlying affective reasoning framework, since the repeated rejection of the hen's requests for help will be appraised by her with negatively valenced emotions, which can lead to a drop of her mood into the hostile octant.

The other problem was that, previously, there was no way for the system to decide why the hen normally works on the farm, while the other animals usually relax in the sun. This can be addressed by leveraging their differences in trait conscientiousness: agents high on that scale should first focus on achieving their obligations, while agents closer to its lower end can freely follow their wishes instead (see Lis. 3.3).

```
1   @obligation1 [affect(personality(conscientiousness,high))]
2   +!obligation(Plan) : is_work(Plan) <-
3       !Plan;
4       !obligation(Plan).
5
6   +!obligation(Plan) : not is_work(Plan) <-
7       !Plan;
8       !obligation(Plan).
9
10  @wish1 [affect(personality(conscientiousness,high))]
11  +!wish(Plan) : obligation(Plan2) <-
12      !wish(Plan).
```

Listing 3.3: Personality dependent wish and desire management

The first plan encodes that an obligation that involves laborious tasks will be turned into an intention only when the agent is high on trait conscientiousness. This means, that non-conscientious agents' will find no plan to select in this case, and instead fail, resulting in the fallback mechanisms (see line 13 in Lis. 2.3) being activated to re-introduce the obligation. This makes sense, since an obligation does not cease to exist after being ignored once, but will be 'at the back of the agent's head' constantly. The second plan encodes that non-laborious obligations will be accepted by all agents, which is necessary to provide a plan ensuring normal obligation management behavior in case of common obligations. The third plan encodes that agents high on conscientiousness can not turn a wish into an intention, as long as they still have active obligations, instead holding on to the wish for later reconsideration.

This is sufficient to address the initial problems. However, in order for the moods and, especially, the personality traits to have a perceivable effect on the narrative system, the rest of the plan base has also to be annotated with affective conditions, wherever plausible:

- If an agent has a high value on trait agreeableness and its mood is not low on the pleasure dimension, the agent will offer to share its food with others.

- Also, if an agent has a medium value on trait agreeableness and its mood is high on the pleasure dimension, the agent will offer to share its food with others.

- An agent will ask others for help on laborious tasks only if it has a positive value on trait extraversion and its mood is not low on the dominance dimension.

- An agent will refuse a request for help if it has a low value on trait agreeableness and its mood is not low on the dominance dimension.

- An agent will also refuse a request for help if its mood is high on the dominance dimension, and its personality has a negative value on trait agreeableness.

- An agent that has a positive value on trait extraversion will loose the wish to relax, after it has executed a relax action, while having a negative value on trait extraversion means that the wish to relax remains active even after successfully executing a relax action.

- When an agent realizes that its mood switched to `relaxed`, it looses the wish to relax. Conversely, when it realizes a mood switch to `anxious`, the wish to relax becomes active again.

- If an agent has a high value on trait neuroticism, it will execute the new action `Character#fret()`—which appraises the emotion `distress`—as part of its intentions to punish someone or to reject someone's request for help.

3.4.2. Exploring a Space of Possible Plots

Recreating the Initial Plot

With the above provisions in place, all questions regarding the modeling of the narrative system and, consequently, the plot of TLRH could be resolved. This does not mean that the system is guaranteed to recreate the correct plot, since the affective dynamics of individual agents are hard to predict for the developer but crucial for the emergence of the plot. In particular, the development of the hen's mood is important here, since it has to turn hostile at the right time to activate the desire to punish the other animals. However, the above discussion of personality profiles allowed for a certain leeway with regard to their precise quantification. It should, thus, not come as a surprise that the parametrization in Tab. 3.5 can be used to successfully recreate the desired plot. The resulting plot graph, produced by InBloom, can be found in Fig. 3.9[30]. It exposes well, how the hen and the other characters behave differently due to their differences in personality: they all start out with the same wishes and obligations (step 0 in the graph), but the hen chooses to pursue her obligation, while the other animals pursue their wish. The hen's activity works as a catalyst for the plot, since it activates the happening of finding wheat (the dark blue arrow in step 2 indicates a causality relation) that sets her of on her pre-ordained path. It is also interesting to note, how she develops a desire to punish the other animals in step 5. After getting rejected for two times, her mood switches to `hostile`, which activates a wish to punish the culprits. However, she finds no plan to achieve this desire, so it leads to no consequences. After some time—and experiencing the positive emotion `pride` because she successfully planted the wheat—the hen's mood returns back to a more balanced state, which deactivates the punishment desire (step 6, omitted for brevity in Fig. 3.9). This dynamic repeats itself several times (also omitted from the graph in Fig. 3.9), and culminates with the baking of the bread. As before, the hen is in a hostile mood and has an active punishment desire. This time, however, she holds the means to put her wish into action: the intention `!punish` can be selected in step 15 because all pre-conditions of a corresponding plan are now satisfied since the hen is in possession of bread (compare with Lis. 2.7). As a result, she asks the other characters whether they would like to eat some bread, which for them activates an intention to eat bread.

---

[30]The visual representation of the graph is post processed in order to enable human readability and the computational analysis of plot quality. The details of this process, as well as the employed notation, will be introduced in detail in Chapter 4.

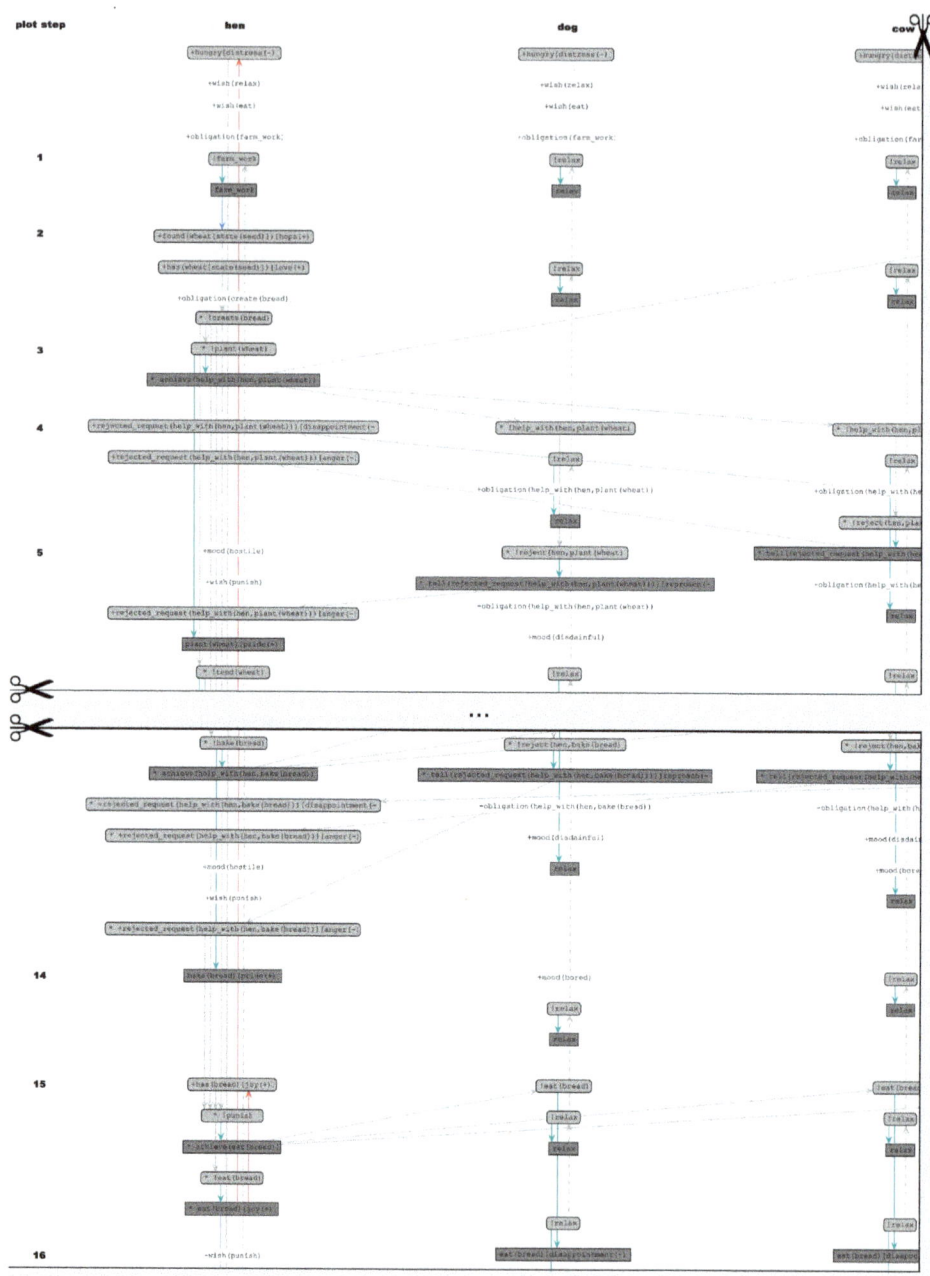

Figure 3.9: Abridged plot graph of TLRH: Parts of the `create(bread)` plan (vertical) and one and a half farm animal (horizontal) have been removed to allow a more legible rendering on the available limited space. The full plot graph can be found under https://www.home.uni-osnabrueck.de/leberov/tlrh_plot_full.pdf.

Alas, our plumed avenger does not share any of the bread, opting instead to eat it alone. Consequently, the environment determines that the other characters' `eat(bread)` actions fail, which is automatically appraised with a `disappointment` emotion. Interestingly, this solves a final puzzle that has remained open (but so far unmentioned) since the previous case study: why do the actions of the hen, in fact, constitute a punishment? For a reader who is well versed in social norms this might be trivial, but so far the InBloom system had no way of determining that the mentioned situation constituted an impairment of the other animals' state, let alone a punishment. With the introduction of emotions, the situation finally becomes comprehensible for the narrative semantics put forward in this thesis. The emotion `disappointment` results in a negative movement along the pleasure dimension of a character's current mood, which can be regarded as negative ipso facto. Furthermore, the cause of this emotion can be traced back to the hen's punishment intention, by following back the incoming light blue (indicating actualization) and gray (indicating cross-character communication) arrows.[31]

The affective dynamics of the plot can be seen more concisely in Fig. 3.10, which contains current-mood graphs, generated by In-Bloom. It is interesting to note, how these graphs are representative for the characters' personality traits. The hen's mood shows medium reactivity to events, which can be expected of a character with a non-

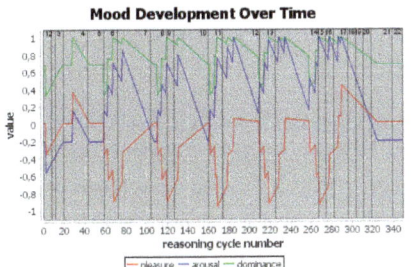
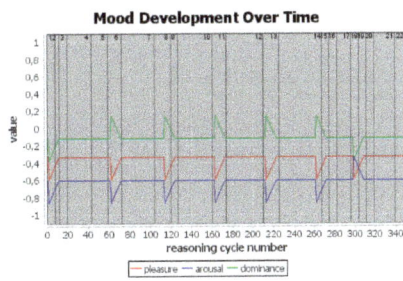

Figure 3.10: The development of the current mood in PAD space for the hen (left) and a representative farm animal (right). Black vertical lines represent environment steps and are labeled with the respective step numbers.

---

[31]In fact, following this trail even further back also reveals how the hen's punishment desire was triggered by the other characters' refusals, and so on. How InBloom is capable of detecting these connections will be presented in Chapter 4, but it should be noted that by doing so it unveils the causal structure behind the events of the story world, turning them into a coherent whole: a plot.

minimal neuroticism rating. The dog's mood (which is representative for the other non-hen animals) remains mostly constant, which can be expected of a character with a low-ish extraversion rating leading to little activity. Also, in the second case, the reactivity of the current mood is much lower than in the first, which is indicative of a lower neuroticism rating.

Exploring the Parameter Space

The previous section has demonstrated, how the right personality parameters can lead to the emergence of the original plot of TLRH. This begs the question of what will happen, when these parameters are varied. After all, InBloom is used to implement narrative systems and not individual plots, which ideally should mean that variations of the system's parameters should result in the emergence of alternative plots.

The personality parameter space of the TLRH system is fairly large, even when individual traits are considered to be discrete (low, medium, high) instead of continuous, which is a plausible simplification given how agents' planning is determined by precisely these discrete values. Already for one character, the protagonist, this results in $3^5 = 243$ possible settings, and that does not even take into account the combinations that are possible when the other three characters' parameters are varied, too. Thus, while an automatic exploration of this space would be feasible, in practice it would have little value since the system (so far) still lacks the functionality to also review the resulting plots automatically. For this reason, I preferred to conduct a manual exploration instead, performed by testing parameter combinations that seemed promising to me based on the way affective conditions were implemented in the plan base. This means that only a fraction of the possible settings could be tested, which, on the positive side, allowed me to manually review the resulting plots and evaluate their interestingness for the present discussion. The plots that could be created by the system, and the personality parameters that led to them (while keeping the happening settings unchanged), are summarized in Tab. 3.6.

Table 3.6: Personality parameter settings that lead to different plots in the narrative system of TLRH. The parameters are reported in the order: O C E A N. For convenience, in the rows containing plots number 2–8, parameter differences to plot number 1 are marked in gray. Tellability scores represented in Tab. 4.3 are referencing the plot numbers and parameter settings in this table.

Plot #	Hen	Dog	Pig	Cow	Plot Summary
1	0 1 0.7 −0.3 −0.2	0 −1 −0.3 −0.7 −0.7	0 −1 −0.3 −0.7 −0.7	0 −1 −0.3 −0.7 −0.7	Original plot
2	0 −1 0.7 −0.3 −0.2	0 −1 −0.3 −0.7 −0.7	0 −1 −0.3 −0.7 −0.7	0 −1 −0.3 −0.7 −0.7	Farm animals relax, while hen does nothing
3	0 1 0.7 −0.3 −1	0 −1 −0.3 −0.7 −0.7	0 −1 −0.3 −0.7 −0.7	0 −1 −0.3 −0.7 −0.7	Hen eats bread alone, but no punishment
4	0 1 0.7 1 −0.2	0 −1 −0.3 −0.7 −0.7	0 −1 −0.3 −0.7 −0.7	0 −1 −0.3 −0.7 −0.7	Hen shares bread despite refusals
5	0 1 0 −0.3 −0.2	0 −1 −0.3 −0.7 −0.7	0 −1 −0.3 −0.7 −0.7	0 −1 −0.3 −0.7 −0.7	Hen doesn't ask for help, shares bread
6	0 1 0 −0.2 −1	0 −1 −0.3 −0.7 −0.7	0 −1 −0.3 −0.7 −0.7	0 −1 −0.3 −0.7 −0.7	Hen doesn't ask for help, doesn't share bread
7	0 1 0.7 −0.3 −0.2	0 −1 −0.3 0.7 −0.7	0 −1 −0.3 −0.7 −0.7	0 −1 −0.3 −0.7 −0.7	Dog helps hen, no punishment, no sharing
8	0 1 0.7 −0.3 −0.2	0 −1 −0.3 0.7 −0.7	0 −1 −0.3 0.7 −0.7	0 −1 −0.3 −0.7 −0.7	Dog and pig help hen, hen shares with everyone

The first entry of the table lists the original plot for comparison. The second parametrization effectively turns the hen into a relaxed farm animal which is so content that it does nothing, while the other animals at least still actively relax. Since she does not work on the farm she can not find any wheat, and the narrative equilibrium at the beginning is never breached. In the third version, the hen's low neuroticism score makes her less responsive to the negative affect from the rejected help requests and she stoically performs her duty without getting into a hostile mood that would lead to the wish for punishment. In the fourth version, the hen's high agreeableness value forces the selection of an eating plan that includes sharing food with the other animals. Version number five sees the hen going about her business without asking for help, since this is only possible with positive extraversion traits. Curiously, the less extroverted hen is also the happier hen: never asking for help spares her the many disappointments of her alternative brethren, which results in much higher average current-mood ratings on the pleasure dimension. For this reason, she shares the bread with the other animals. The sixth parametrization shows that it is possible to combine the effects of individual parameter changes. A lower extraversion paired with a low neuroticism again sees the hen performing her tasks without requesting help. Here, her newly added stoic disposition results in much less perturbation of the current mood through her successful farming exploits, and her pleasure level never rises enough to feel compelled to share the food. The next two settings explore the influence of the other characters' personalities, while leaving the hen in her default parametrization. In the seventh version, the change in the dog's agreeableness value forces it to help the hen when she requests assistance. This means less negative emotions for the hen, and she does not develop a desire to punish the other animals. The last entry reflects a situation where both the dog and the pig help the hen, due to an increased agreeableness value, which propels her pleasure rating so high that she shares the food with everyone, including even the cow, who did not help. This is an interesting version since it, incidentally, seems to embody a very different morale, where society does not force the individual to contribute in order to secure its livelihood.[32]

3.4.3. An Empirical Evaluation of Perceived Personality

Above, I have argued that changing the personality parameters of the agents leads to a change of plot. Indeed, a change can be observed in the emergent behavior of the MAS, but is the claim justified that the changed parameters represent character personality, or are they, in the end, just arbitrary numerical levers? The argument for the representational nature of these parameters has been theoretical, so far: Since fictional minds work mostly like real minds, real minds have quasi-stable dispositions, and these dispositions can be captured using the Big Five personality trait scale in certain interactions with other reasoning phenomena, my implementation of these interactions is supposed to represent personality. However, in the setting of story composition this can only hold true if the plots that result from different parametrization also manage to convey a sense of different personality to their consumers. Even more, personality settings in the computational model should actually correlate with perceived personality in order for the parameters to be meaningful.[33] In order to evaluate, whether the proposed system is capable of modeling the personality of fictional characters, an empirical study was conducted.

Experimental Design

The study investigated whether changing the personality parameters of a character in the computational model correlated with a significant

---

[32]InBloom does not reason about the symbolic dimension of narratives, and has no means of detecting such changes at the interpretatory level. However, it is important to note that they can incidentally emerge from changes at the mimetic level, which leaves open the possibility to address this problem in future work.

[33]This should not, however, be taken to imply that modeled personality should be identical to perceived personality, since in a complex communication setting like the fictional narrative a completely faithful reconstruction of the message by the receiver should not be expected.

co-directed change of the perceived personality of this character, as judged by readers. The experiment presented below was designed to test the following null hypothesis: *Changing a personality trait of a character in the model does not correlate with a change of readers' perceptions of the same personality trait in that character.* In order to investigate whether a potential effect is diffused when multiple traits are changed at the same time, two experimental conditions were tested.

The plot of TLRH was used as the control condition, using the settings laid out in Tab. 3.5. Two experimental conditions were created by changing certain personality parameters of the protagonist:

- Condition E: the extraversion trait was lowered ($E = -0.3$),

- Condition NA: the neuroticism trait was lowered ($N = -1$) while the agreeableness trait was raised ($A = 0.7$)[34],

which resulted in plots that differed from the basic condition by at least one action executed by the protagonist. In condition E the hen doesn't request help and in the end it eats the bread alone[35], while in condition NA she requests help and is repeatedly rejected but still shares the bread in the end. The advantage of such a comparative setting is that it allows to make inferences from comparison to the control, instead of relying purely on absolute numbers, which would be the case if completely unrelated stories were to be used.

Plots in InBloom are represented only through plot graphs that contain the actions executed, the events perceived, and the emotions experienced by each character. However, no prose generation module exists that could be used to translate these graphs into story text. It is conceivable to attempt training all subjects in reading plot graphs, however, this would make the experiment more time consuming. Furthermore, the inference of character personality from text is a natural process in which readers are already proficient, and switching to an unfamiliar format might impair the quality of this ability. For these reasons, the decision was made to obtain a textualized version of the generated plot graphs of the two experimental conditions.

---

[34]Attentive readers might note that according to Tab. 3.6 the effect of increasing A subsumes the effect of decreasing N. This is true in the current system, but not at the time of conducting this study in early 2018 because the system underwent considerable refactoring in the mean time.

[35]Differences to Tab. 3.6 again due to changes implemented after the study.

To do so, a collaborator was recruited. She was presented with the system-generated plot graph for the control condition and the text of the original fairy tale, and given time to study them. Then, she was asked to translate the graphs of conditions E and NA into narrative texts based on the provided example pairing. To avoid the unconscious introduction of biased text, the collaborator was not informed about the hypothesis of the experiment or the provenance of the graphs. The crafted story text was identical to the original tale whenever the same situations were described, and only differed in the context of different actions taken by the protagonist.[36]

An online survey platform was used to carry out the study. 40 participants with English language proficiency level B2 and higher were recruited from the University of Osnabrück through e-mail and social media. A within-subject design was selected in order to reduce interpersonal differences in the data and allow meaningful results with the available number of participants. Each participant was presented with the texts of all three conditions, and each text was instantly followed by a personality survey about the protagonist. The personality survey used the 44 statements from the BFI instrument (John et al., 1991, 2008), and asked participants to indicate how much they perceived these statements as applicable to the protagonist (e.g. "Little Red Hen is helpful and unselfish with others"). Participants could provide answers to each statement using a Likert-scale ranging from 1 (strongly disagree) to 5 (strongly agree).

In order to avoid introducing a systematic bias due to carry-over effects from the first story-questions pair to following conditions, presentation order of the three conditions was randomized between participants. Feedback from a pre-trial suggested that participants found it hard to mentally separate the protagonist (Little Red Hen) of the later conditions from preceding ones. To facilitate the task, and avoid this non-systematic carry over effect, the protagonists of the three conditions were additionally assigned different names. The names were randomly selected from the top ten most common female names in the US over the last 100 years[37], in order to avoid name-related biasing. The resulting protagonist names were Little Red Hen Linda (control condition), Little Red Hen Mary (condition E) and Little

---

[36]All plot graphs and story texts can be found on www.home.uos.de/leberov/ tlrh_versions.htm.

[37]Based on https://www.ssa.gov/oact/babynames/decades/century.html.

Red Hen Susan (condition NA). As will be discussed below, these measures proved to be sufficient since the data shows no significant effect of condition order on personality judgement.

The collected data for each participant includes demographic data, the order in which conditions were presented, and the answers from three BFI inventories relating to the three conditions. The inventory data was post-processed according to the instructions provided by the instrument's authors (no ipsatization was applied). While the collected inventory data was discrete, the resulting average scores are continuous values in the range from 1.0 to 5.0. The results provide the five average personality trait scores of the protagonist as perceived by the readers, for each of the three experimental conditions (see table 3.7).

Table 3.7: Survey results: perceived personality (mean +/- std) of the protagonists of the three conditions. Asterisks indicate significant difference with control condition. *: $P \leq 0.05$, ****: $P \leq 0.0001$.

	control	condition E	condition NA
O	3.12 +/- 0.44	2.87 +/- 0.53*	3.11 +/- 0.46
C	4.50 +/- 0.37	4.26 +/- 0.56*	4.42 +/- 0.41
E	3.79 +/- 0.48	2.56 +/- 0.65****	3.72 +/- 0.54
A	3.02 +/- 0.72	2.82 +/- 0.52	4.58 +/- 0.33****
N	2.39 +/- 0.66	2.58 +/- 0.60	1.86 +/- 0.60****

Data Evaluation

The gathered experimental data allows answering the research question—formulated in the null hypothesis above—by checking for significant effects in the affected traits. This can be done by analysing whether changing a character's personality trait in the model correlates with a co-directional change in perceived personality. It is also of interest to check whether the employed personality model has the desirable property of being orthogonal, that is, whether a change in one trait also has no effect on the perception of other traits. The same approach also allows validating the employed within-subject design by checking for interaction effects between subsequently presented stories.

A Mauchly Test for all obtained trait ratings showed that the sphericity assumption was violated in the data. Therefore, in the following, all repeated measure ANOVA results are reported with a Greenhouse-Geisser correction.

Table 3.8: Results for trait *extraversion*.

ANOVA	SS	df	MS	F	P value
Between Groups	0.55	2	0.28	1.25	0.30
Within Groups	8.23	37	0.22		
Error	8.79	39	0.23		

Table 3.9: Results for trait *neuroticism*.

ANOVA	SS	df	MS	F	P value
Between Groups	3.08	2	1.54	4.11	0.02
Within Groups	13.87	37	0.37		
Error	16.95	39	0.43		

Table 3.10: Results for trait *agreeableness*.

ANOVA	SS	df	MS	F	P value
Between Groups	0.91	2	0.46	1.76	0.18
Within Groups	9.64	37	0.26		
Error	10.56	39	0.27		

Table 3.11: Results for trait *openness*.

ANOVA	SS	df	MS	F	P value
Between Groups	0.63	2	0.32	1.72	0.19
Within Groups	6.80	37	0.18		
Error	7.43	39	0.19		

CONDITION-ORDER EFFECT   It can be assumed that no interaction effects arise between subsequently presented conditions, if a condition's protagonist's perceived personality can be shown to not change significantly in dependence of the position in which the condition was presented to the participants. To determine this, the five personality trait ratings for the protagonist of the control condition were compared between three groups: participants who read the story first ($N = 16$), ones that read it second ($N = 11$), and last ($N = 13$)[38]. A single factor independent measure ANOVA was executed for each personality trait (Tabs. 3.8 through 3.12). As anticipated, no significant between-group differences were found in the O, C, E and A traits. However, a significant between-group difference was found in the N trait (at $P = 0.02$): $\mu_{N_{1st}} = 2.17$ vs. $\mu_{N_{2nd}} = 2.24$ vs. $\mu_{N_{3rd}} = 2.79$. A post-hoc pairwise comparison showed significant differences between the third group and the first group ($P = 0.04$), however, no significant difference between the first and second group ($P = 0.96$), nor between the second and the third group ($P = 0.09$).

The last result requires further analysis, since it indicates that pre-

Table 3.12: Results for trait *conscientiousness*.

ANOVA	SS	df	MS	F	P value
Between Groups	0.02	2	0.01	0.06	0.94
Within Groups	5.39	37	0.15		
Error	5.41	39	0.14		

---

[38]The unequal distribution of participants is due to a technical limitation of the employed survey software which only allows a randomized presentation order instead of true counterbalancing.

sentation order affects personality rating only for N traits and when the story is presented last. Since an ANOVA tests the assumption that all samples were drawn from the same population, the post-hoc tests suggest that the first and the second samples, as well as the second and the third samples, were drawn from the same population, while the first and the third samples originate from different populations. Since being drawn from the same population is a transitive property, this indicates inconsistent results. Furthermore, in the present case, five statistical tests were executed on the same data, of which one found a significant effect at an $\alpha = 5\%$ level. Considering that ANOVA tests are not corrected for multiple comparisons, the probability of finding at least one false positive in this setting is around 20%.[39] Taking these observations together I interpret the last finding as a random sampling effect, and not an effect of condition order.

Taking this into account I conclude that in the control condition no interaction effects take place between subsequent conditions for any of the traits, which validates the choice of a within-subject design. The same analysis could be conducted for the other two stories, but was left out due to time constraints.

PERCEPTION OF MODIFIED TRAITS   A single factor repeated measure ANOVA shows a highly significant difference (at $P = 5.85 \cdot 10^{-14}$) in the perceived extraversion between the three groups. A pairwise post-hoc comparison between the control condition ($\mu_{E_{control}} = 3.78$) and condition E ($\mu_{E_E} = 2.56$), where the parameter was lowered, demonstrates that the effect shows in the correct direction.

Single factor repeated measure ANOVAs also show a highly significant difference between the perceived neuroticism ($P = 5.48 \cdot 10^{-5}$) and agreeableness ($P = 1.29 \cdot 10^{-17}$) between groups. A pairwise post-hoc comparison between the control condition ($\mu_{N_{control}} = 2.39$, $\mu_{A_{control}} = 3.02$) and condition NA ($\mu_{N_{NA}} = 1.86$, $\mu_{A_{NA}} = 4.58$), where N was lowered while A was raised, demonstrates that the effects show in the correct direction.

This leads me to conclude that the null hypothesis can be rejected, that is, changing parameters in the model correlates with a change in perceived personality along the modified traits, and the

---

[39]This probability can be computed as the inverse probability to finding not a single false positive, i.e. $1 - 0.95^5$.

Table 3.13: Results for trait *extraversion*.

ANOVA	SS	df	MS	F	P value
Subjects	19.54	39	0.50	2.30	0.00090
Groups	37.90	2	18.95	86.00	1.37 E-20
Error	16.99	78	0.22		

Greenhouse Geisser	SS	df	MS	F	P value
Groups	37.90	1.83	20.67	86.10	5.85 E-14
Error	16.99	71.51	0.24		

Table 3.14: Results for trait *neuroticism*.

ANOVA	SS	df	MS	F	P value
Subjects	21.01	39	0.54	1.78	0.06
Groups	11.22	2	5.61	18.50	2.66 E-07
Error	23.66	78	0.30		

Greenhouse Geisser	SS	df	MS	F	P value
Groups	11.22	1.79	6.26	18.50	5.48 E-05
Error	23.66	69.92	0.34		

Table 3.15: Results for trait *agreeableness*.

ANOVA	SS	df	MS	F	P value
Subjects	21.01	39	0.54	1.78	0.06
Groups	11.22	2	5.61	18.50	2.66 E-07
Error	23.66	78	0.30		

Greenhouse Geisser	SS	df	MS	F	P value
Groups	11.22	1.79	6.26	18.50	5.48 E-05
Error	23.66	69.92	0.34		

Table 3.16: Results for trait *openness*.

ANOVA	SS	df	MS	F	P value
Subjects	16.83	39	0.43	3.51	1.19 E-06
Groups	1.60	2	0.80	6.51	0.00242
Error	9.59	78	0.12		

Greenhouse Geisser	SS	df	MS	F	P value
Groups	1.60	1.83	0.88	6.51	0.01285
Error	9.59	71.28	0.13		

effect shows in the right direction. For a statistical overview see Tables 3.13, 3.14, 3.15, 3.16, and 3.17.

PERCEPTION OF NON-MODIFIED TRAITS   The data is less conclusive on the account of trait orthogonality. Post-hoc pairwise comparisons show the following results, which indicate orthogonality:

- there is no significant difference between the O, C and E traits of the control condition and condition NA ($P_O = 1.00$, $P_C = 0.43$, $P_E = 0.79$),

- there is no significant difference between the N and A traits of the control condition and condition E ($P_N = 0.29$, $P_E = 0.23$).

At the same time, the following result indicates no orthogonality:

- there is a significant difference between the C and O traits of the control condition and condition E, although neither C nor O were changed there ($P_C = 0.0013$, $P_O = 0.0063$).

Table 3.17: Results for trait *conscientiousness*.

ANOVA	SS	df	MS	F	P value
Subjects	17.32	39	0.44	4.97	9.12 E-10
Groups	1.24	2	0.62	6.91	0.00172
Error	6.97	78	0.09		

Greenhouse and Geisser	SS	df	MS	F	P value
Groups	1.24	1.48	0.83	6.91	0.01099
Error	6.97	57.78	0.12		

A first observation is that the unintended effects are only present in condition E. This is a surprising finding, since I expected condition NA to have a higher interaction potential due to the higher number of changed personality parameters in the model (2 versus 1). Two non-mutually exclusive interpretations seem possible: (1) in the employed computational personality model the traits N and A are orthogonal to the other traits, whereas E is not orthogonal to at least O and C, (2) in this concrete narrative system a change in E trait leads to a more prominent change in behavior than a change in N and A, which propagates to stronger changes in perceived personality. The first interpretation is supported by the fact that several studies show evidence for significant intercorrelations between at least some of the five traits (Eysenck, 2004, p. 468). The second interpretation is supported by the observation that condition E differs from control by four missing actions (three times the hen doesn't ask for help and one time she doesn't offer to share the bread) whereas condition NA differs by only one action (the hen shares the bread instead of eating it alone).

It should also be noted that, while the unintended effects are significant, they are several magnitudes weaker than the intended ones. This is a desirable property since it potentially allows to counteract unintended interactions by coordinated changes in the dependent personality traits. Whether it is practically possible to negate interactions in such a way remains to be ascertained empirically.

Conclusions

The above results allow to reject the null hypothesis, which means that changes in agents' personality parameters in InBloom correlate with co-directed changes in the personality of fictional characters (represented by these agents) as perceived by readers.

This allows to draw two important conclusions: First, the employed affective agent architecture is capable of modeling personality. So far, the claim that the architecture is modeling personality was based only on the theoretical argument that it implements a psychological model of personality. However, a psychological model is necessarily an abstraction from the observed phenomenon, and an implementation of a model is necessarily a simplification. The presented results indicate that these various transformations preserved the phenomenon they modeled. This means I, now, also have a functional argument to support my claim: InBloom is capable of modeling personality because it creates plots that convey a corresponding appearance of personality in readers.

Second, cognitively inspired personality theories can be used to model the literary effect of personality. Throughout this chapter, I reported the scepticism of eminent scholars towards the idea that characters can or should be modeled through recourse to models devised to understand actual humans (voiced by Michael Young and Janet Murray). My empirical study demonstrates, that mimetic approaches are feasible. Characters based around fictional minds can be composed into a dramatic plot, and what is more, at least some of their formal properties can even be reconstructed by readers. Another line of criticism—by Pablo Gervás—has been, that it is implausible to assume that writers use scientific theories of mentation to devise their characters, but rather rely on their folk-psychological understanding. This difference might lead to problematic deviations in perceived characters, between those devised by humans and those created based on cognitive models. In particular, folk psychology would allow to generate predictions even for extreme cases, while scientific theories would work more reliably in average situations. My study, on the contrary, suggests that cognitive personality persists under narrativization. That is, personalities that can be described using the Big Five can be created in the reader's impression. As I have argued in my repudiation above, the Big Five model has been observed to correlate extreme ratings with unusual behavioral patterns, as for instance in persons with mental disorders. This is further supported by the conducted study, where some of the hen's behaviors leaned heavily towards the quixotic despite being modeled based on a cognitive architecture.

3.4.4. Discussion of the Case Study

The second iteration of generative modeling has been successful. By this I do not mean that the resulting system is sufficient to represent narratives in general. Rather, it is a bare-bones baseline, sufficient to demonstrate the general feasibility of generative modeling as an approach. In particular, it shows that the plot of one existing folktale can be reconstructed based on first principles derived from Ryan's possible worlds framework and extended by Palmer's fictional mind approach.

What is important is the observation that personality traits in the resulting system span a space of possible plots. From a computational creativity perspective this is interesting because it frames plot generation as a search problem and outlines the involved parameters. It is also interesting from a narratological perspective because it is a property of the underlying theory that has been seemingly overlooked by its creator, Mary-Laure Ryan. Her work focused on how plot is a function of beliefs, wishes, obligations and plans. Personality comes into play as a mediating factor, by determining how different characters choose between competing wishes and obligations, as well as constraining which plans they select to achieve these. The resulting choices propagate through to plot, and allow readers to develop a corresponding model of character personality. While other affective phenomena—like emotions and mood—also have been demonstrated to affect the plot, their role is less important, since they are not parameters that can be varied freely. Instead, they are a function of personality and the general ontology of the story world.

This situation is reflected clearly in Fig. 3.6. If the figure is read as a cyclic graph instead of a process model, `Personality` turns out to be a root node with no incoming edges. `Emotions` and `Mood`, on the other hand, are children nodes, dependent on other nodes connected to them via incoming edges. Reviewing the figure along these lines exposes that the affective character architecture has another root note: `Happenings`. Indeed, the happening settings of a narrative system can be arbitrarily changed (between simulations) without requiring the introduction of a justification, just like with personality parameters. The conducted case study did not explore the effect of happening variation because it would likely have transformed the resulting plots so much that they would not have been recognizable as related narratives. A system that is not an exercise in generative modeling but in computational creativity, however, would have no reasons to leave this option unused. Summarizing, the main parameters of a narrative system (that is, given a fixed environment and plan library) turn out to be: the number of characters, their five respective personality traits, as well as a variable number of happenings that can vary in type, patient and time of execution.

Some words remain to be written about the drawbacks of the extension introduced in this chapter. The biggest issue is a technical one, and reared its head during the manual exploration of the plot space. As it turns out, affective dynamics introduce a slight level of indeterminism into the system, which can lead to situations where the same personality parameter settings resulted in different plots. I hypothesize that the reason for this lies in the parallel nature of MAS, in this case, the multi-threaded implementation of Jason. The reasoning cycles of the different agents are all executed by dedicated threads. However, the order and duration of a thread's execution is determined by the thread scheduler of the operating system, where it is undefined for threads of equal priority. This means that, whenever multiple agents interact, the order in which they process these inter-actions can vary. Consequently, the reasoning cycle number, at which emotions from such interactions are appraised, is not deterministic. This can translate into noticeable changes, in particular when two emotions are appraised consecutively instead of concurrently (or vice versa). In the former case, two mood update steps are performed, while in the latter one update step is followed by one decay step, which means that one update is effectively lost (compare with the averaging operation in the equations of Def. 9). Especially in cases where the current mood is located at octant borders, this could make the difference between a new mood octant and corresponding desires being activated, or not. During my experiments, most parameter set-tings consistently yielded the same plot, even when slight differences could be observed in the mood graphs. However, some settings did ex-hibit indeterminism at the plot level, presumable when they resulted in the current mood being located at an octant border at crucial time points. What is more, I also observed differences in behavior when the operating system was running in energy saver mode, which indicates that InBloom's behavior might not always be comparable between different machines. I do not foresee any conceptual problems arising from this circumstance, but it complicates development and evaluation.

An expected issue is that affective dynamics make agent behav-ior harder to predict for the developer of narrative systems. Previ-ously, an agent's plan selection was a function of its (discrete) belief base, while now it also depends on its (continuous) current mood. This means that reproducing the behavior of existing stories becomes harder, which complicates the process of generative modeling. How-ever, in the context of computational creativity this drawback might be an advantage, since it allows for more surprising emergent behavior.

On a conceptual level it should be noted, that the cognitive approaches adopted here to represent fictional minds are neither the only possible, nor possibly the most fitting ones when seen in isolation. They were selected only because they were part of a comprehensive model outlining the interactions of all required individual phenomena. As a result, only a subset of potentially relevant affective phenomena can be represented by InBloom. This ranges from the very particular, e.g. the lack of a distinct emotion denoting surprise, to the fairly general, e.g. the lack of a coping function for emotion. Such trade-offs are inevitable, when committing to one approach over another. However, I still find it necessary to explicate their existence.

The closing observation for this chapter is that the system, in its current state, models narrative semantics only from a synthetic and a mimetic perspective. As has been convincingly argued to me in private communication by Fotis Jannidis—Professor for Computer Philology and Newer German Literary History at the University of Würzburg—this is not enough to comprehensively represent narratives, especially in the case of folktales. He illustrated his point with the question why the three farm animals do not just take the bread by force, instead of accepting to be taunted by a lone hen. The reason can not be found from the synthetic or mimetic perspectives, but lies in the symbolic teleology of the plot, its moral: Those who refuse to work hard and to plan ahead will suffer.[40] For this moral to work, the farm animals need to accept their punishment meekly, even if it were mimetically plausible for them to resort to violence. As at the end of the last iteration, we find ourselves at a point where the narratological backbone of our approach can not account for an important part of the modeled narrative, since neither Ryan nor Palmer provide us with the narratological means to address morals or messages. One way to proceed from here would be to dedicate the next iteration to expanding the narratological backing of InBloom to account for symbolic phenomena, just like we expanded it to mimetic phenomena here. However, keeping in mind that the focus of this thesis is not only on narrative theory but also on computational story

---

[40]This observation might raise the question whether folktales—a very moral-driven genre—are good case-study material for an approach like mine. I have addressed this question at the beginning of Sec. 2.2.3 and believe that the points made there are still valid.

composition, I prefer to continue with another aspect: the quality of plot. For a computational system to be able to surpass mere generation (a concept introduced in Sec. 1.3) it needs to be able to take creative responsibility for evaluating its own output. Only then can it claim to produce valuable artefacts intentionally, and not through mere fortune. Ryan's framework attempts to capture the pre-textual quality of plot using the concept of tellability, whose computational modeling will be described in the coming chapter. Although the next chapter will stay true to Ryan's work and continue to operate from a synthetic perspective, I believe that, in the end, this avenue must also converge with an analysis of the symbolic teleology of plot, as suggested by Jannidis. The original plot of TLRH is more valuable than the more violent version (in part) because it coincides with a distinct message.

4

Plot Quality Estimation

A NARRATIVE SYSTEM SPANS A SPACE OF POSSIBLE PLOTS, and the
previous chapter demonstrated that such a space can be explored by
changing personality parameters and happenings. This can be seen
as the main task of a computational story composition system. However, exploration alone is not enough. A creative system needs also to
be able to evaluate what it found, in order to establish whether it has
finished or whether it should continue searching. This is not a trivial
problem, because not every sequence of events that can be found using
a narrative system can be a priori considered a plot. Recall the manual exploration of personality parameters summarized in Tab. 3.6. In
plot version 2, lowering the conscientiousness trait of the hen to -1
resulted in a configuration, where nothing interesting happens: the
hen does nothing, while the other characters 'relax in the sun all
day'. Although this can be taken to fit our previous understanding of
plot outlined in Def. 1, and even contains virtual components in the
form of embedded narratives—after all the characters should at least
have an active wish to relax, and be able to choose actions to achieve
this wish—this still seems to hardly qualify as a plot at all, let alone
a plot worth telling. While the other parametrizations described in
Tab. 3.6 result in event sequences that seem more worthy of the title

'plot', perhaps only plot version 8 describes events that I personally would consider telling someone as a story. As Ryan puts it: "not all plots are created equal" (M.-L. Ryan, 1991, p. 148). After all, some stories disappear the moment they are told, while others have followed humanity since the dawn of civilization[1], surviving migrations, translations, and cultures. This suggests that "some configurations of facts present an intrinsic 'tellability' which precedes their textualization" (M.-L. Ryan, 1991, p. 148), and that this property is gradable, allowing plots to be compared. This view falls in the domain of narrative poetics, whose prescriptive[2] component can be divided into a poetics of discourse (i.e. "how to tell a story well") and a poetics of plot (i.e. "what makes a story worth telling") according to M.-L. Ryan (1991, p. 149). Naturally, these two components interact, since a good telling is partly determined by its ability to enhance a plot's point. But, at the same time, it is still possible to think of examples where a pointless story is presented well, or where the potential of a particular plot is botched by the telling. Thus, the separation between the two poetics is meaningful.

Following Ryan, I will refer to the poetics of plot as *tellability*. This concept was initially introduced by the social linguists Labov and Waletzky in the context of oral storytelling, where it was used to illustrate that the relevance of a story depends on the social context in which it is told: "most narratives are so designed as to emphasize the strange and unusual character of the situation" (Labov & Waletzky, [1967] 1997, p. 34). The concept was picked up by narratologists and its scope extended to other domains. In the following, I will focus on Ryan's very particular interpretation, which is concerned with formal instead of pragmatic properties.

---

[1]Recent work used linguistic phylogenetic analysis to identify the oldest story still in existence today (Da Silva & Tehrani, 2016). The plot of this story—"The Smith and the Devil" (ATU 330)—could be traced down to an original version from the Bronze Age, i.e. 3000–5000 years ago.

[2]Scholars engaged in literature studies and literary critics are sceptical about prescriptive notions of aesthetics because of their normative component. Computational modelers engaged in generation, on the other hand, are fond of such notions as they usually come with guidelines on what is prescribed, which make for excellent algorithm blue prints. For these very reasons I would like to caution computationally minded readers to scrutiny, while imploring literary minded ones for leniency on this concept.

4.1. Tellabilty

Referring back to Labov's understanding, Ryan summarizes that "in order to be tellable, a story must have a point" (M.-L. Ryan, 1991, p. 150). Following Ryan's understanding of this concept, which will be presented shortly, a story can, in fact, have multiple points, making them more akin to narrative highlights. To better understand how points could be detected, several types can be distinguished.

External points are the generous category under which Ryan groups everything that Labov would consider a point: all the possible goals of a story teller in a communicative setting. This is also the reason for the name of this category; its focus lies not inside the narrative but in its interaction with its context, i.e. the social and communicative situation of a telling. A list of such potential goals is presented in M.-L. Ryan (1991, p. 150), but since the computational part of this thesis has no access or understanding of context I will omit it here.

The more relevant counterpart are *internal points*, which are those properties of a story that have an inherent value and are of interest independent of (the social and communicative) context. Here, again, a distinction can be made. *Dynamic internal points* are events in a story that violate the expectations of at least one character. Consider the events in version 2 of the explored TLRH plots, where all animals relax or do nothing. There is no single surprise or violated expectation. This can be compared with version 5 (where the hen never asks for help due to a lower extraversion setting). There, finding a grain of wheat is an unexpected happening that can be counted as a dynamic point, and intuitively this seems to correlate with an increase in tellability. The original plot, again, contains more dynamic points since all the refused help requests can be counted as defied expectations for the hen, which could account for this version's superiority. From this, Ryan derives a general, prescriptive maxim of tellability: "seek the diversification of possible worlds in the narrative universe" (M.-L. Ryan, 1991, p. 156), which she dubs the *Principle of Diversification*. A higher diversity of the worlds of the narrative universe results in more conflicts[3]. Conflicts between a K world and TAW are a priori surprising for characters, while conflict between

---

[3]Remember, that Ryan uses an idiosyncratic notion of conflict that is equivalent to incompatibility between possible worlds. For details, revise Sec. 2.1.3.

W/O worlds and TAW instigates action and by that increases the potential for surprise. But the principle of diversification is not solely a means to ensure conflict:

> The demand for a diversified semantic universe also determines what kinds of resolutions and outcomes present the greater narrative interest. My contention is that tellability is rooted in conceptual and logical complexity, and that the complexity of a plot depends on an underlying system of purely virtual embedded narratives. [...] Among these embedded narratives, some reflect the events of the factual domain, while others delineate unactualized possibilities. The aesthetic appeal of a plot is a function of the richness and variety of the domain of the virtual, as it is surveyed and made accessible by those private embedded narratives.
>
> (M.-L. Ryan, 1991, p. 156)

In a post-closure view, this simply means that the network of the plot is more complex, which can be taken as a measure of teleological refinement, or of the richness of the corresponding narrative's semantic domain. But in a pre-closure view—which is the only one available to a reader who watches the plot unfold for the first time and does not yet know its final teleology or shape—this also corresponds to a heightened potential for curiosity. A character's intended course of action (i.e. the projected solution for a conflict) is of limited interest in itself, but demands more attention the more ways are foregrounded in which it might fail. The more forking paths are present in the virtual domain, the less expectable is a positive outcome. Remembering Jerome Bruner's assertion that "[...] narrative deals with the vicissitudes of intention" (Bruner, 1986, p. 17), discussed during the opening of Chapter 3, it becomes plausible that tellability should be tied in this way to a diversification of the narrative universe.

I would like to also draw attention to the fact that Ryan sees this diversification realized by private embedded narratives, as the main representational mechanism of the purely virtual realm (as discussed in Sec. 2.2.2). As I have observed in the last chapter, these private embedded narratives capture the whole functioning of the fictional mind, which closely ties a plot's tellability to the functioning of its fictional characters.

Static internal points are the counterpart to dynamic internal points. They are not concerned with the unfolding of a narrative's dynamics, but with properties that can be analyzed once the teleology of the whole plot becomes apparent, that is, they can be applied solely from a post-closure view on plot. Static points can be further distinguished into *substantial* and *formal*. The first type is concerned with the semantics of the story: themes and motifs. It should not come as a surprise, that semantics play a role in tellability, since some topics are of universal interest to humans, whereas others might be culture-specific or even only relevant to particular groups of individuals. Ryan quotes an example: "A French formula for successful novels lists the following ingredients: religion, sex, aristocracy, and mystery. (The last one is a [dynamic] point). According to this formula, the most tellable story reads: 'Mon Dieu, dit La Marquise, je suis enceinte et ne sais pas de qui'[4]" (M.-L. Ryan, 1991, p. 154). While this is certainly an important part of tellability, it poses no great interest to us. In a computational setting using MAS, topics and settings are almost entirely located on the environment side and rely on manual domain modeling instead of computational exploration.

Of more interest are the formal points, which are concerned with the structures that comprise tellable plots. To start her argument, Ryan, like us, observes that not all sets of events deserve the title plot. She thus formulates a pre-condition for tellability: "a [...] plot must present a conflict and at least one attempt at solving it" (M.-L. Ryan, 1991, p. 154). I would like to add, that this is a very generous pre-condition due to Ryan's specific understanding of conflict, rephrased above. Even our 'non-plot', version 2 of the TLRH plots, would still pass this criterion, as the wish to relax constitutes a conflict between the characters W world and TAW, and their intention do so is a (successful) attempt at solving it. Perhaps, a more conventional understanding of conflict would be more suitable here. At a later point in her book, M.-L. Ryan (1991, p. 227) also adds a post-condition that has to hold true for a plot to be well-formed. This closure condition holds iff every active intention in a plot has either failed or succeeded. Many narratives are open ended, which violates this condition of well-formedness, so I would consider it more as a guideline. It is against the backdrop of this guideline, however, that open endings achieve their aesthetic effect: It's the violation of an expectation for closure that results in a heightened attention.

Apart from these two general guidelines, Ryan proposes three tellability principles, that she derives from the poetics of lyric po-

---

[4]Ryan reports the following, free translation: "My God, said the Duchess, I am pregnant. Who done it?"

etry:[5]

1. *"Semantic opposition.* This principle advocates sudden turns in the plot, reversals in the fortunes of characters, and, very generally, any kind of inversion between narrative states. [...] Another form of semantic opposition contrasts the goals of characters with the result of their actions, leading to an effect known as narrative irony." (M.-L. Ryan, 1991, p. 155)

2. *"Semantic parallelism and symmetry.* This principle promotes the multiplication of narrative sequences presenting structural similarities but involving different participants." (M.-L. Ryan, 1991, p. 155)

3. *"Functional polyvalence.* Narrative highlights are formed by events entering into several distinct functional units. By functional unit I mean a grouping of states and events [...] presenting special strategic significance for the story as a whole. The principle of functional polyvalence is what accounts for the intrinsic elegance [...] of certain ways of resolving problems." (M.-L. Ryan, 1991, p. 155)

In a later chapter, Ryan returns to her tellability principles, and adds a forth one:

4. *Suspense.* "[A] delay [of] the fulfillment of the goals of characters." (M.-L. Ryan, 1991, p. 249)

Since these criteria are formal, they should be detectable in the structure (i.e. form) of the plot. Plots are represented as directed graphs in InBloom, so it is reasonable to expect that they should be also detectable in the structure of plot graphs. The detection of graph properties is a discipline with a long tradition in computer science and mathematics, which makes the four formal tellability principles the most promising points to explore in the present setting. For this to be possible, however, they need to be formalized in a much more rigorous manner than so far.

---

[5]It is not obvious to me, why lyrical principles should be translatable in this direct manner to the poetics of plot, and Ryan does not provide any arguments for this. However, from a computational perspective, her considerations are too tempting for me to be able to simply dismiss them.

4.1.1. Functional Polyvalence

Functional polyvalence captures situations where several narrative problems can be furthered by a single event, thus exposing the inherent elegance and craftsmanship of strategic economy. A high functional polyvalence is also a sign of strong narrative cohesion, which is present when the constituent parts of a narrative are closely interconnected.

Above, instances of functional polyvalence were introduced as "events entering into several distinct functional units" (M.-L. Ryan, 1991, p. 155). The notion of functional unit (FU), to which Ryan refers here, was introduced in the work of Wendy Lehnert (1981), which focused on the computational generation of abstractive plot summaries. Her summarization model still remains unimplemented because extracting the required information from the literary prose in which stories are commonly composed requires complex interpretation tasks that are mostly still outside the scope of the computationally feasible.[6] Since the natural language understanding step can be omitted in the context of computationally generated stories, where the generative algorithm can be expected (or extended) to possess the ground truth about the plots it generates, her theoretical model is relevant for the present work.

Lehnert suggests to use directed graphs to represent plots, and, as will become quickly apparent, her formalism is compatible with the one employed by InBloom. She, too, suggests to divide the plot graph into character subgraphs, where each vertex represents an event as perceived (or experienced) by that character. These vertices can have one of three types:

- $+$: Events that are pleasant for a character

- $-$: Events that are unpleasant for a character

- I: Non-affective mental events, used by Lehnert exclusively to denote intention-formation events

A vertex can be connected to an arbitrary number of other vertices in the same character subgraph by directed and labeled edges, which

---

[6]A restricted implementation attempt was recently made by Goyal, Riloff, et al. (2013), but yielded modest results.

represent causal links between events. Lehnert defines that each edge
has to have exactly one type-label, and—from observing the types of
causality involved in stories—suggests the following types[7]:

- m: Motivation links, which capture that the source event is the
  motivation for a target event (that has to be an intention)

- a: Actualization links, which capture that the source event (an
  intention) is actualized by the target event

- t: Termination links, which capture that the effect of the target
  event is supplanted by the effect of the source event[8]

- e: Equivalence links, which capture that multiple perspectives
  are possible on one affective state

It should be noted, that m and a edges follow the temporal direction, while t and e edges point in the anti-temporal direction. These
orientations have been selected by Lehnert for reasons of convenience.

From these elements (three vertex types and four edge types) 36
pair-wise combinations are possible, but only 15 are defined as legal
configurations based on semantic considerations. These 15 are called
primitive FU, are each assigned a name that captures their intended
semantics, and can be used as building blocks to assemble the actual
(complex) FUs. The original primitive FUs, as defined by Lehnert
(1981, p. 298), are depicted in Fig. 4.1. Thus, for instance, a success primitive FU is constituted by an intention that is actualized
by a positive event, while failure is constituted by an intention that
is actualized by a negative event. To illustrate each of the possible
FUs, Lehnert provides three example situations. For instance, her
three examples for success are: "You ask for a raise and you get
it. You fix a flat tire. You need a car so you steal one", while the
examples for failure are: "Your proposal of marriage is declined.
You can't find your wallet. You can't get a bank loan" (Lehnert,
1981, p. 298). In most of the cases, these examples seem plausible

---

[7]This collection of edge types will need to be adapted later, in order to be of
maximal use in the present context.

[8]For instance, a positive reaction to receiving an apple might be terminated
by the later perception that the apple is poisoned, while simply eating the apple
would not terminate the initial positive reaction (albeit terminating the apple
itself).

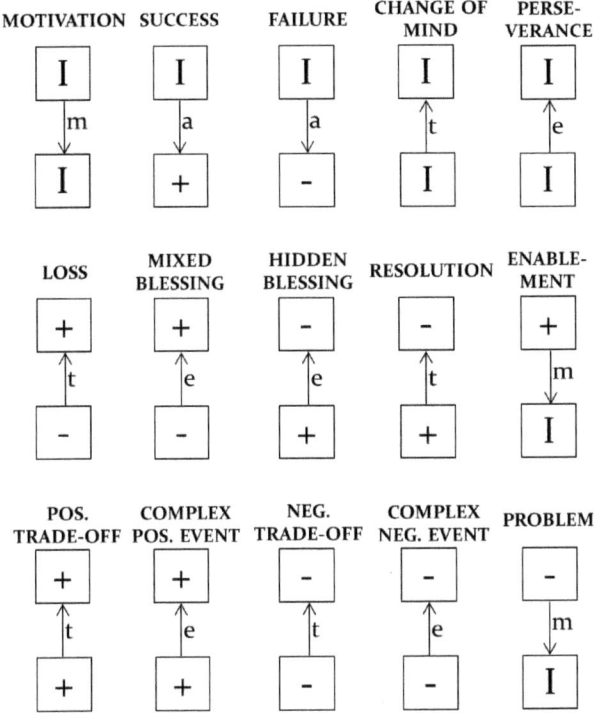

Figure 4.1: The original primitive FU defined according to Lehnert.

to me, but **hidden blessing** awoke my suspicion. The examples are: "You get audited and they owe you. You sprain an ankle and win damages. Your mother dies and you inherit a million" (Lehnert, 1981, p. 299). The sprained ankle example does not really fit the equivalence-edge situation of multiple perspectives on the same event (in InBloom-parlance this would be one event being appraised by several emotions). Rather, there seem to be two events connected by a prototypical case of causality: Spraining you ankle causes you to win damages during a subsequent event. The same perspective can be applied to the other two examples, where the first event is a happening, which is causally responsible for a second happening. This caused me to probe the other FUs that are comprised by an equivalence edge. **Mixed blessing** turns out to be a mixed bag: "You buy a car and it turns out to be a lemon. You fall in love and become insanely jealous. Your book is reviewed but they hate it" (Lehnert, 1981, p. 299). The first and the last example are in my opinion better examples of **loss**, while the remaining second one is again a case of causality between an event and a state. Also `complex positive event` ("You win respect by getting a Rolls Royce [...]") and `complex negative event` ("You break an arm in a car accident [...]") for me are better described by a causality edge. So is this just a matter of nomenclature? Apparently not, as `perseverance` would suggest: "You want to get married (again). You reapply to Yale after being rejected. You want to ski again after a bad skiing accident." Neither of these situations involves prototypical cases of causality. No one would want to go skiing again *because* they had a bad accident last time, they might consider going *despite* the accident (same holds for the marriage). And while reapplying to Yale is certainly only possible after having applied once, the cause for the application would probably remain something else, like for instance the expectation to increase one's social standing. Here, an equivalence relation is appropriate, since it marks that two intentions have the same goal. Making this difference is important for InBloom because it already contains features implementing causality relations between agent actions and happenings (see p. 13), which can be extended to detect related FUs. Hence, my solution is to keep the *e* edges, but add an additional type:

- *c*: Causality links, which capture that the source event is causally responsible[9] for the target event.

To follow intuition, *c* edges follow the temporal order (as opposed to the subset of *e* edges they replace). With this, Fig. 4.2 displays the updated primitive FUs.

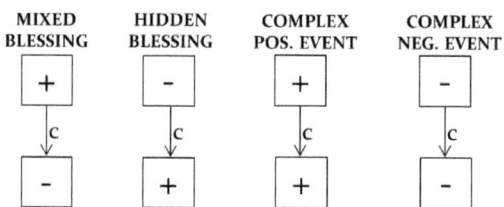

Figure 4.2: The updated primitive FUs where equality has been replaced by causality.

---

[9]My remarks on the difficulty of the notion of causality from p. 13 apply here, equally. Note, that the already introduced *m* and *a* edges can also be understood as representing causal links, however, they are specific subtypes of causality pertaining to intentionality. For this reason, *c* edges only connect vertices of types + and −, while connections pertaining to *I* vertices are already captured by the more specific *m* and *a* edges.

Another important part of narratives is interaction between different characters. This can be captured by plot graphs using cross-character edges (*cc*) that connect vertices belonging to different character subgraphs. Lehnert (1981, p. 301) does not find it useful to distinguish several types of cross-character links, and defines all possible combinations of source and target vertex types as legal (as long as they are located in different character subgraphs). This allows to uniformly represent all types of situations that affect two characters: speech acts, actions affecting an other character, but also just events that are perceived and appraised by two characters. Fig. 4.3 demonstrates the possible configurations. The first column depicts

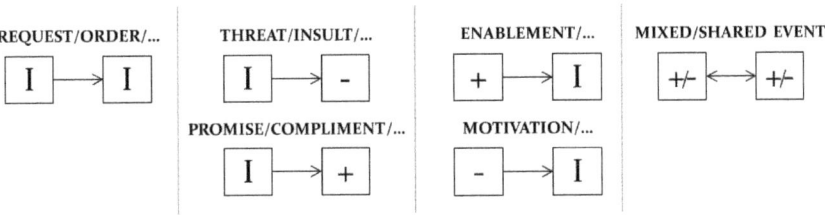

Figure 4.3: Character interactions represented using cross-character edges, along with possible interpretations.

the situation that one character communicates that it wants the other character to intend something and succeeds with this, which would constitute an order, a request or a plea, depending on the context. The second column depicts the situation that a character's speech act causes an affective reaction in the receiving character. A negative reaction might appear merely due to the content, e.g. in the case of an insult, but also due to the interpretation of this content and its consequences, for instance if a request is perceived as an imposition, or an intent is perceived as threat. The third column can be commonly taken to depict the case that a character's actions (be they perceived positively or negatively by that character) are perceived by another character and cause it to intend something itself, for instance seeing someone succeed might cause their friend to want to congratulate them. More rarely, this can be interpreted as an event merely happening to the first character, and motivating the second character in a particular way, e.g. seeing someone tumble could cause a bystander to want to help them up. The last column represents situations when the same event (or its consequences) is affecting two characters. In the case that the event has differently valenced consequences for, or is seen from different angles by, the affected characters, this constitutes a mixed event, denoted by opposed valences in the respective appraisal.

Using the primitive FUs and *cc* edges as an alphabet, complex FUs can be constructed. Ryan's interest lies in these complex FUs (simply 'FUs' from here on), which are formulated to represent units of strategic significance and are matched against actual plot graphs. Lehnert suggests a number of FUs, but notes that the lexicon is open ended. New units can be formulated when needed, and individual FUs can become arbitrarily complex. A few examples of FUs proposed by Lehnert (1981, p. 300–302, 307) can be found in Fig. 4.4. For instance, the FU `intentional problem resolution` consists of

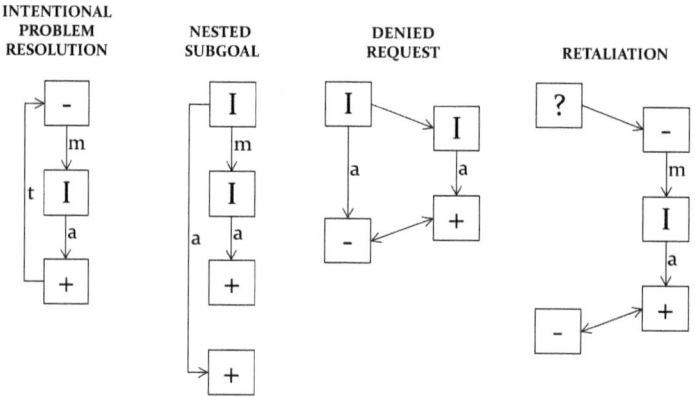

Figure 4.4: Four examples of FUs constructed by Lehnert, with the title describing which narrative function they respectively capture.

a primitive FU `problem` (where a negative perception motivates an intention), combined with a `success` (where an intention is actualized by an event that is perceived positively) and a `resolution` (where a positive event terminates a negative event). The same holds for FUs that contain two characters. A `denied request` FU is constituted by a `request` (cross-character), a `success` (the patient of the request succeeds in rejecting it) and a `failure` (of the agent to have its request fulfilled). Interactions that contain more than two characters are not supported by the formalism, and need to be split up into dyadic interactions for representation. A special case can be found in Lehnert's formalization of `retaliation`, which contains a [?] vertex. This denotes a wild-card that can match any vertex in the original plot graph.

The main task of FUs is to act as patterns that can be matched against plot graphs. This allows to decompose the plot into FU instances, which originally were used by Lehnert to create functional summaries of the plot. To provide an intuition for such matching, a very condensed and abstract version of the TLRH plot is provided in Fig. 4.5, along with an FU analysis. The depicted plot graph repre-

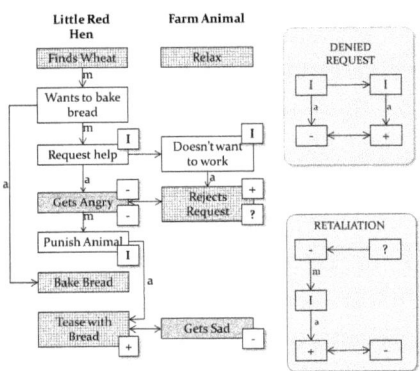

Figure 4.5: An example of FU analysis for functional polyvalence detection. On the left side: a Lehnert-style plot graph representing an abridged version of TLRH[10], where chequered vertices represent + nodes, lined vertices represent − nodes and white vertices represent I nodes. On the right side: The two FUs denied request and retaliation. A mapping of plot graph vertices to FU vertices is overlain over the graph.

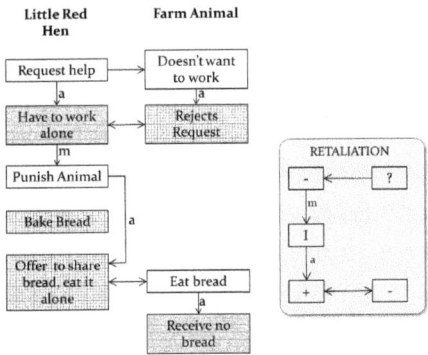

Figure 4.6: An excerpt from a Lehnert-style plot graph of TLRH (left) and Lehnert's proposed FU for retaliation (right).

sents a manual analysis of TLRH using a Lehnert style formalism. In this version, two FU instances can be matched because two structures can be found in the plot graph that are isomorphic to two of the FU graphs.

Joining Ryan's analysis of Lehnert's FUs, I too need to "[...] express some reservations as to whether some of the graphs offer a viable semantic analysis of the concepts they represent, rather than an arbitrary coding" (M.-L. Ryan, 1991, p. 215). However, I also doubt that a single "viable semantic analysis", which Ryan presupposes here, exists for any of these functions. For instance, consider Fig. 4.6 that again contains the proposed FU for `retaliation` and an excerpt from another manual plot graph of TLRH (which is, in fact, closer to what would actually be produced automatically by InBloom than the graph in Fig. 4.5).

The excerpt encodes the hen punishing a farm animal for not helping her, by offering it some bread but then eating it all alone. From an intuitive standpoint such a behavior could well be considered a retaliation, and also the structure of the graph is closely resembling that of the FU. However, close resemblance is not sufficient for Lehnert's approach to matching and the situation would be rejected as an instance of `retaliation`. Judging merely from structural properties this seems unwarranted: why should the means of retaliation be only constituted by a negative event ($[-]$, last vertex in right character subgraph of the FU), while never by inciting a `failure` ($[I] \stackrel{a}{\to} [-]$, last vertices in right character subgraph of the plot)? Yet, apart from structure there is no theory or underlying constructive principle from which an FU could draw its justification. As pointed out—rightfully—by Ryan, the FU are naught but arbitrary codings, and as such both versions should be acceptable in this case. One solution for this problem would be to define multiple alternatives for each FU, and then rely on exact matching with this enhanced lexicon. However, such an approach is inelegant because it requires uninspired labor and is susceptible for inconsistencies should changes become necessary in one of the FU originals. For this reason, it seems more prudent to me to treat FUs rather as prototypes of narrative functions, and instead adapt the matching algorithm to allow it to also match structures that are closely resembling but not completely isomorphic. Details on such an algorithm will be provided in the discussion of the implementation in Sec. 4.2.1 on p. 230.

---

[10]This graph is greatly simplified and serves only explanatory purposes, so pay no heed to details like why certain vertices have certain types; the system-generated graph for TLRH presented later in this chapter will differ from the schematic discussed here.

However FU matching is implemented in detail, in the present case we are less interested in which FUs are instantiated in a story, but rather in how these instances interact. Since an FU instance consists of multiple vertices representing individual events, functional polyvalence can be detected by identifying vertices of a plot graph that belong to multiple FU instances. For example, in the analysis depicted in Fig.4.5, the vertices `Gets Angry` and `Rejects Request` are both part of two FU instances, and for this reason can be seen as functionally polyvalent.

4.1.2. Semantic Parallelism and Symmetry

Ryan's terse summary of semantic parallelism and symmetry (P&S) outlined it as the "multiplication of narrative sequences presenting structural similarities but involving different participants" (M.-L. Ryan, 1991, p. 155). It is a feature commonly associated with western fairy tales, which often feature three similar characters or three important tasks. This demonstrates that symmetry can also appear diachronically, in relation to the same character, instead of just between different participants. As Ryan observes, this is often combined with an instance of semantic opposition on the last try or with the third character, as for instance in the well known fable "The Three Little Pigs". However, it would be rash to limit the applicability of parallelism to 'just' children's stories. For instance, O. Henry's (1905) short story *The Gift of the Magi* rests on the aesthetic effect of the two lovers—unknowingly to each other—selling their priced possession (the husband's old watch, respectively the wife's beautiful long hair) to be able to afford Christmas gifts for each other. A dramatic turn is included here again, as in the end both find out that their gifts (an elegant watch chain for the husband, and a beautiful hair comb for the wife) were meant to complement precisely those objects that the other had respectively sold.

Based on this description, P&S can be understood as properties of sequences: symmetry describes structural similarities inside one character subgraph, while parallelism describes structural similarities between two character subgraphs.[11] In the example of the "Three

---

[11]Remember that, while plots can contain events that happen in parallel, character subgraphs are by definition linearized and can hence be understood as sequences.

Little Pigs" these similarities are visible already on the story's surface, i.e. the event level: The three piglets each build a house, while the wolf huffs and puffs three times to destroy these houses. Structure proper, however, is usually considered to be formed not by the events themselves but the organizational principles behind them. For this reason, structure can be conceptualized as being located at the depth of stories (see footnote 9 on p. 58 for a short elaboration of the depth-metaphor). In *The Gift of the Magi*, on the surface, the two protagonists acquire differing items using money they procured by differing means. Yet, at a functional level, these differences become irrelevant and an underlying similarity is uncovered from the depth-level: both of them can be seen to perform a sacrifice in order to then make a gift. Since an analysis of the plot at a functional level will be available to the system (it needs to be performed in order to compute functional polyvalence) it seems appropriate to me to first attempt to compute P&S based on the plot's FU instance sequences. This has the benefit of making the aesthetic analysis more interpretative than just relying on the surface level. Only if no sufficient FUs can be detected to allow the operation at the deeper level, as a fallback, the analysis should turn to event-sequences. One might consider discounting any P&S measure computed on events instead of FUs, however, in practice I believe this will not be necessary since the higher variability encountered at the unabstracted surface level should automatically result in lower intra-character and inter-character similarity.

The term symmetry itself is often associated with geometry, where it means that an object remains invariant under certain types of transformation operations (Weisstein, 2004), most commonly translation, rotation, or reflection. Sequences are 1-dimensional objects, so rotational symmetry can be excluded a priori. Translational symmetry occurs in a sequence, when the same chain of elements occurs at several positions in that sequence, which would for instance correspond to a number of events being repeated several times during the course of a narrative. An example can be found in the sequence ABXAB, where the chain AB appears at the start, but also translated left at position three. This seems to be the canonical case for symmetry, as described in Ryan's examples. Reflectional symmetry is possible in 1D objects, too, and in our case occurs when for a chain in the sequence another chain exists, which is the inverse of that first chain. This would be the case in the sequence ABBA, where the chain AB has an inverse, but also in the sequence **ABXYBA**, where the chain **AB** appears reflected after two unrelated elements. Although no examples for reflectional symmetry in plots have been provided by Ryan, I see no reason to exclude this type of symmetry. Its poetic appeal has been recognized in the visual arts, and seeing how the tellability principles employed here have already been imported from lyrical poetics it seems not overly preposterous to motivate such a related import from another domain. Indeed, this type of symmetry seems a useful albeit not commonly employed concept. For instance, when discussing the plot of Homer's epic poem *Iliad*, classics scholar Beye (2006, p. 111) outlines in detail an inversion of action between the beginning in book one and the end in book twenty-four. He notes how this mirror symmetry acts as a "ring composition" at the core of the poem's narrative component.[12]

Parallelism's counterpart in geometry cannot be translated into one-dimensional sequences to be adapted to the present use case, like I did with symmetry. Hence, the last resort remains reasoning by analogy: Two lines are considered parallel, when they lie in the same plane but never intersect. The resulting image is one where the two lines follow each other's course into infinity. Two sequences (of events or FU instances) can be taken to follow each other's course if they are comprised of the same, or perhaps similar, events. Thus, perfect parallelism would be obtained if two character subgraphs were comprised of the same sequence. Partial parallelism, then, holds when a chain in one character subgraph can be located in another character subgraph. One might additionally impose the more strict requirement that these chains are to start at the same plot step, in order to increase the visual likeness to the analogical case of two lines following each other's course. However, I believe this would be a too literal interpretation that would exclude cases that are intuitively perceived as parallel but where the chains do not strictly align.

Multiple qualifying chains can be expected to exist for each character, for each type of P&S, and hence a value for each chain must be quantified in order to be able determine the overall score. At the very least, these values need to reflect the length of the chain and the number of times the chain is repeated. Since character subgraphs vary by

---

[12]My initial take on mirror symmetry was to only accept chains that are palindromes, but this would have excluded the example discussed by Beye (2006). It is for this reason, that I relaxed my formulation above to allow arbitrary insertions between two mirror-symmetric chains.

length but their scores should remain comparable, it seems prudent to also instantly normalize chain values by subgraph length, i.e. define chain parallelism or chain symmetry as the percentage of contributing vertices captured by that chain. In order to compute each of the sub-measures (i.e. one translational and one reflective symmetry, as well as parallelism) for a character, also the aggregation over their respective chain values needs to be decided. An incomplete selection of possible aggregation types is:

1. Average symmetry over all chains,

2. Sum of symmetry over all chains,

3. Value of best chain per character and per sub-measure,

4. Value of best chain per character and per parallelism/symmetry,[13]

5. Value of first or last chain, after temporally ordering them.[14]

The best ways to choose one of these options would be to perform a perceptual study where subjects can rate carefully selected sequences for similarity and parallelism, in order to then tune a metric to best reflect these measures. This, unfortunately, lies outside the scope of my thesis. I am wary of claiming to decide based on theoretical arguments for choosing one approach over the others, since it is my feeling that such arguments could be equally well concocted for most of them. My *intuition* here is, that the most salient chain would be the maximal chain, and that this should contribute most to perceived similarity / parallelism, such that no averaging or summation is required. Having manually compared symmetry values based on the resulting options (3 and 4) for a few example chains, my perception of similarity seems to be best reflected by 'best chain per character and per sub-measure'. As cautioned above, I view this not as a scientific but as an engineering decision, to be potentially revised in future work.

---

[13]Effectively this means looking for chains that maximize both translational and reflectional symmetry at the same time, in order to compute one overall symmetry measure. This measure can then be combined with the value of the best parallelism chain over all pairings that contain the character.

[14]Looking only at the first or last chain in a sequence could make sense considering the effects of primacy and recency on retention (Deese & Kaufman, 1957).

As outlined above, the semantic P&S measure is comprised of several sub-measures: one translational and one reflective symmetry measure per character, as well as one parallelism measure for each possible character pairing. This amounts to $2n_c + \binom{n_c}{2}$ measures, where n_c is the number of characters. Thus, after the first aggregation has been completed, still several sub-measures per character remain to be combined into one overall semantic P&S score. Again, several approaches are viable. For the time being I prefer a simple average over the sub-measures in order to be able to take into account all the different parts that could contribute to an overall sense of P&S. A disadvantage that should be pointed out here is that such an approach gives more weight to parallelism than it does to symmetry because more parallelism scores are incorporated into the mean. Should the need arise, this could be remedied by resorting to a weighted average, or by first averaging over the parallelism scores, and only then computing the overall average.

4.1.3. Semantic Opposition

Semantic opposition captures the aesthetics of a dramatic turn, which is a widely used narrative strategy that can help generate emotional engagement in the audience. Ryan's description of this principle is comprised of three related phenomena.

One is described as "sudden turns in the plot" (M.-L. Ryan, 1991, p. 150). A sudden turn can be expected to violate the expectations of at least one character, making instances of this principle an indication for the presence of a dynamic point. An example is easily found in *The Gift of The Magi*, where the two characters hold the strong conviction that they procured a great present for their partner, only to be violently confronted with the futility of both, their gifts and sacrifices; a device that only works because of violated expectations. In InBloom, expectations are encoded as agent's non-perception beliefs about the state of their environment. A violation of an expectation would then correspond to a removal or substitution of such a belief, represented by a corresponding termination edge in the analyzed plot graph. Furthermore, expectations can be also seen as beliefs related to the future. The OCC taxonomy of emotions employed by InBloom has a specific dyad of emotions that capture 'valenced reactions' to 'consequences of events' where the 'prospects are relevant' to the agent but have been 'disconfirmed' (see Fig. 3.1). These two emotions are `relief` and `disappointment`, and whenever an event is appraised by these emotions it can be assumed that this event violated an expectation.

Another manifestation of sudden turn in plot, according to Ryan, are "reversals in the fortunes of characters" (M.-L. Ryan, 1991, p. 155). 'Fortunes' are defined by the Merriam Webster online dictionary as "the turns and courses of luck accompanying one's progress (as through life)" (Merriam-Webster, 2020), and Fortuna represents the forces outside of a character's control. This can be seen akin to what I have introduced in Sec. 3.2.2 as 'context': non-dispositional factors determining the character's behavior. As discussed in Sec. 3.3.3, this is captured in InBloom through affect. Emotions are the immediate response of an agent to events in its environment, while current mood is a time-discounted aggregate of past emotions. I interpret the resolution of the *Magi* plot as a reversal in fortunes. The goals of both characters seem within their reach and at least Della is explicitly narrated as being of good spirits. The ensuing realization of failure is then connected with negative affect for both, which can be exemplified with the following passage, where Jim perceives that his wife cut her hair and thus has no use for his present:

> Jim stopped inside the door. He was as quiet as a hunting dog when it is near a bird. His eyes looked strangely at Della, and there was an expression in them that she could not understand. It filled her with fear.
>
> (Henry, 1905)

In the terminology of InBloom, Jim is experiencing deliberative emotions with negative valence, one might assume that this even leads to a change in mood. A transition from positive to negative emotions is presented more overtly for Della: "White fingers pulled off the paper. And then a cry of joy; and then a change to tears" (Henry, 1905). This occurs even before she can realize that her own gift is rendered equally futile, which can be expected to result in further (non-narrated) distress. However, not every succession of differently valenced emotions seems enough to constitute a 'reversal in fortunes'. Think of Little Red Hen joyously finding her seed, and soon after experiencing her first rejection: it seems hardly plausible to consider this a change of fortunes. Hence, I assume that changes in mood are better suited to detect this criterion: A change in fortunes can be expected to solidify as a large delta along at least one of the dimensions of the PAD space (see Sec. 3.2.3 from p. 128 onwards for details on the PAD space), combined with a crossing of the respective zero-axis (no matter in which direction). I postulate a crossing of the axis because it corresponds to a change in mood octant, the only form of mood perception available to the agent itself. Changes of fortunes seem to me significant enough events to require the realization of their occurrence by their subject. In order for this to also constitute a 'sudden turn', an additional condition would be for this change to take place over a comparatively short period of time.

Another form of semantic opposition exemplified by the ending of the *Magi*, too, is narrative irony: an effect that Ryan describes as a contrast between the goals a character has and the actual outcome of their actions. Naively, one might assume that 'contrast' is simply a failure to achieve a goal with a chosen course of action, but the irony of our example short story would not be captured by such an understanding. Both characters' goal is to make their partner a great present, in which they (in some sense) succeed. For me, the irony seems to rather reside in the fact that it is precisely the eagerness of each of the two to acquire the best possible present that undermines the value of their partner's present, and turns their success into a failure. Semantic subtleties like this go beyond simple affective analysis. Even at the FU level, which is available in InBloom for tasks requiring semantic understanding, I see no way of implementing a notion of contrast that would capture irony. For this reason, irony will be excluded from the semantic opposition measure employed in the present thesis.

Again, these diverse measures need to be aggregated and normalized. For violated expectations, the number of corresponding events can be normalized by the number of relevant events, that is, all affectively appraised events and all beliefs. The number of changes of fortunes can be normalized by the maximal number of fortune changes that could have happened throughout the plot. It can be expected, that both measures will be comparatively low since they are normalized by large numbers. For this reason, the decision was made to not aggregate them by averaging, but instead pick the larger of the two. The same holds for aggregating the opposition measures of the multiple characters of a plot. It cannot be expected that semantic opposition will be present in every secondary character, but instead will probably be focused on the protagonists, which usually are those characters that have to overcome obstacles. Simply averaging over all characters would result in an overly low score, so again the highest of the individual characters' opposition scores is taken as the overall opposition score of the plot. This focuses the analysis on the most salient hardships of one character—presumably the protagonist of the story—instead of an 'overall impression', like the previous tellability features. Given that readers' emotional investment is usually strongest with the main character, this pragmatic decision seems not overly implausible.

4.1.4. Suspense

Suspense can be seen as another way of capturing tension potential, as readers can be expected to root with protagonists and wish for the fulfillment of their goals. Ryan writes preciously little about how she envisions the mechanics of suspense: "'Suspense' may be implemented through retarding devices: delay the fulfillment of the goals of characters" (M.-L. Ryan, 1991, p. 249). This seems to indicate that suspense, for Ryan, is connected to the duration between the adoption of a goal and its fulfillment. Such issues can be addressed with the help of the analyzed plot graph, since there intentions can be traced to the actions that fulfill (or fail to fulfill) them by following actualization edges. Furthermore, intentions can contain subintentions—connected to them via motivation edges—that should be taken into account when suspense is computed.

Hence, I propose to use the term *intentional chain* to denote the sequence of vertices on the longest possible path—in an analyzed plot graph—that starts from a vertex v of type I and follows motivation or actualization edges and is not completely subsumed by any another intentional chain.[15] Suspense can then be defined in relation to intentional chains. Different ways of formalizing this are conceivable, like, for instance, the number of actions that are part of an intentional chain, or the amount of plot time (in terms of steps) that has passed between the initial intention and the last action. For now, the latter seems to be the most straightforward equivalent to Ryan's words, but future work might explore the potential benefits of alternative formulations.

It should not be forgotten, that each character subgraph can be expected to contain several intentional chains, while a plot can be

---

[15]A formal definition of intentional chains will be provided in Sec. 4.2.4, when the implementation of the suspense computation will be discussed.

expected to contain multiple characters. To compute the overall suspense of a plot, again, multiple approaches like averaging or summation of individual chains are conceivable. My intuition here is, that in a story the suspense should relate to the main events of the plot, and not be affected too much by occurrences in the exposition or denouement. This makes aggregation over all intentional chains less appropriate, and instead I opt for equating the suspense of a plot with the highest suspense observed over all intentional chains. The assumption here is that such a chain will most likely represent the main course of action. Again, future investigation of alternatives can be of interest in order to fine-tune the system.

4.1.5. Aesthetic Balance, or: Deriving Tellability

Seen in isolation, each of these principles seems to be plausible and to align with plot properties that I would deem aesthetic. Two problems need to be addressed when they are seen in combination, however.

The first is that these principles do not seem to be derived from an underlying theory, but rather from analogy to lyrics and acute observation. This means that no argument can be made to claim that Ryan's list covers all possible formal tellability principles, nor even that it covers the most important ones. This is unsettling, from a computational perspective, since it means that implementing these principles might yield only a poor approximation of a plot's tellability.

The second problem is what M.-L. Ryan (1991, p. 251) calls "aesthetic balance":

> The purpose of this [...] is to prevent any given principle from taking over and running wild. If no limits were set on the number of invocations of 'diversification', the semantic universe would reach such complexity that the reader would lose track of the worlds to be contemplated. And if 'semantic contrast' [sic] were invoked repeatedly, the tale would become a fully predictable sequence of reversals in the fortune of characters.
>
> (M.-L. Ryan, 1991, p. 251)

This is an acute observation that might get easily out of sight in a computational setting, where much focus is put on maximizing individual metrics. Consider, what a value of 1 for semantic opposition would mean: each possible interval of time that might contain a large change of mood, actually does so. The respective plot would have to be constituted by a constant flow of opposing emotions and become predictable and tiring.

Ryan suggests that aesthetic balance could "be maintained by keeping a record of the invocation and satisfaction of every principle" (M.-L. Ryan, 1991, p. 251). This seems to imply that tellability principles would be satisfied by comparable and easily locatable atomic instances, which simply need to be present in alternation. I doubt, that this is an appropriate starting point: An instance of functional polyvalence is a single event, while an instance of symmetry might be a chain that spans most of the plot. Clearly, the latter should be considered to carry more weight, and how should one decide what constitutes a healthy alternation of events and event-chains? This is the reason why above, I have opted for a quantification that is normalized and does more than simply tallying instances. In this setting, it appears judicious to rather focus on the individual scores and ensure that neither of them is too high, nor too low. This does not ensure that instances of the principles appear in a balanced manner throughout the plot, but I am unsure why this should be relevant at all. After all, plot is a concept that focuses on overarching structures instead of local details.

To quantify these considerations, we have to depart from the intuitive idea that the overall tellability of a plot is a simple average of the individual tellability principles' scores. Instead, tellability should rise whenever a score is within healthy bounds, and fall whenever individual scores go towards zero or one. The easiest way of doing so is to define tellability as the average distance of each principle from an optimal (in Ryan's terms: 'balanced') threshold. This punishes scores equally if they are too high or too low, while giving the individual metrics a comparable influence on the final tellability score, since they are already normalized (in different ways, but into the same interval).

While this approach sounds plausible for functional polyvalence, semantic P&S and semantic opposition, I am hesitant to also apply it to suspense. A high suspense, given the quantification proposed above, simply means that an intention exists that lasts throughout most of the plot. I do not see why a plot's balance should suffer from the presence of such intentions, like in the case of the other principles. In fact, suspense is different from the other principles in that its not even meaningful to speak of suspense instances, like one might of instances of functional polyvalence or instances of semantic opposition. Ryan, too, does not include suspense into her initial list of tellability principles, but adds it into the mix towards the end of her book, which encourages me to give it special treatment, too. For this reason, I see it fit to apply the balancing procedure suggested above only on the first three principles, while leaving suspense as it is.

This approach is a fairly simple and straightforward suggestion, that cannot be expected to truly do justice to a concept as elusive and complex as aesthetic balance or, perhaps even, harmony. For the present state of the system, it will suffice that it captures the rough intuition that overly high scores of the individual principles do not translate into tellable plots. A quantification that is more elaborate is surely possible, but would require a better theoretical understanding of what constitutes an aesthetic balance, and what breaks it. Its conspicuous, that Ryan does not provide any theoretic underpinning from which the necessity for aesthetic balance is derived, and which can be used to reason about its nature. Instead, like me, she seems to simply follow common sense reasoning. This might also explain why Ryan does not develop this intriguing line of thought any further, leaving it to the reader to put meat on the bones of this concept.

4.2. Implementing a Tellability Measure

The most expedient principle to start addressing is functional polyvalence, since it is based on a breakdown of the plot structure into functional units. This will help to advance the employed understanding of plot. Furthermore, the segmentation of plot into units that carry meaning can facilitate the formalization of other principles that are based on semantic structures. After that, the other principles will be addressed individually, and in the end details will follow about aggregating them into a single tellability value that can be used to compare plots of different lengths.

4.2.1. Computing Functional Polyvalence

Before FU analysis itself can be implemented, the system needs to support the underlying formalism, that is, (1) allow the emergence of affective dynamics that correspond to each of the primitive FUs, and (2) enable the generation of Lehnert-style plot graphs from these dynamics.

Def. 5, in short, described that a plot graph is a combination of character subgraphs. Character subgraphs—as per Def. 4—are vertex-labeled graphs, which contain only one type of edge that indicates temporality, and are built online (that is, while the plot unfolds in the MAS). This needs to be extended to account for the slightly different vertex types, and the variety of edge types, employed by Lehnert. While I vertices of my plot graph can be translated 1:1 into I vertices of the FU plot graph, a difficulty imminently arises with the other plot graph vertex types: P (perception), A (action), S (speech act sending) and L (speech act reception). Whether one of these events is pleasant ($+$) or unpleasant ($-$) for a character cannot be determined when the event itself is created and added to the graph, but only after it subsequently has been appraised with an emotion by the reasoning cycle of the character.[16] As described in the previous chapter, this is a process that can take some time (depending on the agent's reasoning load at that particular moment), and some events might not be emotionally appraised at all. This means that FU plot graphs cannot be built online, but instead have to be created post-hoc, by analyzing the plot graph that was assembled during MAS execution. For this reason, I will refer to Lehnert-style plot graphs that are suitable for FU analysis as *analyzed plot graphs*, and define them as being comprised by *analyzed character subgraphs*.

In order to create analyzed plot graphs, InBloom needs to perform three tasks: 1) merge emotion vertices with their respective action/perception/speech vertices, 2) create edges of appropriate types between the vertices to enable all primitive FUs, and 3) filter out irrelevant vertices that are not part of Lehnert-style plot graphs. A formal definition of analyzed plot graphs will be provided once these individual steps have been discussed below.

To allow users to start the analysis process, the button `Analyze Graph` is created by implementing the method `void PlotControlsLauncher#createAnalysisButton()` and adding it to the UI initialization routine in `void PlotControlsLauncher#createButtons()`. When the button is triggered, it creates an instance of the class `inBloom.graph.GraphAnalyzer` and provides it with an instance of the plot graph. The analyzer is responsible for analyz-

---

[16]Also emotion vertices (E) exist, where $+$ or $-$ actually can be determined, but which cannot be related to intentions by themselves, as would be required for Lehnert-style graphs.

ing the plot graph, and after it is done initiates the quantification of all tellability principles, by creating an instance of the class `inBloom.helper.Tellability` and providing it with an instance of `PlotDirectedSparseGraph`, representing the analyzed plot graph.

Since successive steps of the analysis process rely on the results of previous steps, the analysis is performed in three passes over the whole graph. Since during a pass each vertex has to be processed and the type of processing depend on the type of vertex, every pass was implemented as an individual visitor using the visitor software design pattern (see e.g. Gamma et al., 1995). The base functionality is defined in the abstract class `inBloom.graph.visitor.PlotGraphVisitor`, whose method `PlotDirectedSparseGraph apply(PlotDirectedSp arseGraph graph)` receives a plot graph, clones it, asks the clone to accept the visitor, and returns the changed clone once processing is done. To enable this, the method `void PlotDirectedSparseGraph# accept(PlotGraphVisitor visitor)` was implemented in the plot graph, which traverses the subgraph of each root vertex and, depending on the type of the currently visited vertex, calls the appropriate visitation method of `visitor`.

This means that each visitation creates a new copy of the plot graph. To be able to inspect intermediate stages of the analysis as well as the original (complete) plot graph, the UI was extended to allow to select which graph is displayed. For this, the class `PlotGraphController` receives the new member `JComboBox<PlotDi rectedSparseGraph> graphTypeList`, which is a drop-down menu that can contain plot graphs. Intermediate plot graphs are added to that menu using the method `void PlotGraphController#addG raph(PlotDirectedSparseGraph g)`, after each pass. Upon selection of a graph by the user, the method `void PlotGraphControlle r#actionPerformed(ActionEvent event)` is executed, with the selected option provided by `event`. This method changes the graph to be displayed, and updates the UI accordingly.

After the graph has been successfully transformed by the visitors into its analyzed form, the computations involved in determining the plot's tellability can be performed. The class `Tellability` encapsulates all methods required for this, as well as all the individual results that need to be combined into a holistic metric.

Vertex Merging

The merging of vertices is implemented by the visitor class `inBloom.graph.visitor.VertexMergingPPVisitor`. Three types of vertices might need to be merged, namely, `emotion`, `percept`, and `listen`.

EMOTIONS alone are of little use in the analyzed plot graph, they need to be attached to the event that caused them to thus form Lehnert-style $+$ or $-$ vertices. Due to the way emotion appraisal is implemented in InBloom, it is guaranteed that E-type vertices occur later in the graph than the event that caused them, although it is not valid to simply assume that they are a direct successor. For this reason, the causing event has to be preserved along with the emotion, until the emotion vertex is processed by the visitor. The class `jason.asSemantics.Emotion` contains the field `cause`, which can be set when the emotion instance is created, and is included as annotation into the ASL literal representation of the emotion that is used as propositional content of its vertex in the graph (example: `emotion(joy)[cause(eat(bread))]`).

As outlined in Sec. 3.3.3, InBloom distinguishes between the creation of primary and secondary emotions. Secondary emotions are created from ASL side, using the internal action `appraise_emotion`, whose second parameter `source` has to contain the event that caused the emotion. This is passed on to the method `AffectiveTransitionSystem#scheduleForAppraisal()`, which creates the emotion instance and sets its `cause` accordingly. Primary emotions are created by the environment as annotations to perceptions. These perceptions are processes as internal events by `AffectiveTransitionSystem#applyDerivePEM`, which extracts the emotions from the event annotations and creates emotion instances. Thus, the cause of these emotions is readily available—its the perception contained in the processed event. It is stripped of annotations, and set as the emotion-instance's `cause`.

Having thus ensured that all emotions are preserved along with their cause, InBloom can guarantee that all E-type plot graph vertices contain a `cause` annotation in their propositional content. The visitor has simply to extract the annotation's content, and traverse the previously visited non-intention vertices until it finds one whose propositional content matches the cause. The emotion needs then to be merged with this target vertex. Since any such target might have caused several emotions, the class `inBloom.graph.Vertex` is extended to contain a field `LinkedList<String> emotions`, which is used by the visitor to store the name of the emotion it currently processes. Since pure E vertices are not desired in the analyzed plot graph, it then deletes the emotion vertex from the plot graph and patches the resulting hole. This functionality is provided by the method `PlotDirectedSparceGraph#removeVertexAndPatchGraphA uto`, which creates a temporal edge[17] between a vertex' predecessor and its successor. As a result, all E vertices are removed from the analyzed plot graph by being merged with preceding non-intention vertices.

PERCEPTIONS can represent independent events, but also action outcomes. The reason is that actions are recorded in the plot graph when they are requested by the agent, while their outcomes are returned to the agent as perceptions from the environment later on, and are recorded only once the agent's reasoning cycle processed the internal event containing that perception. Again, the perception vertex is guaranteed to appear after the action vertex, but not necessarily as its successor.

Perceptions can carry important additional information in their annotations and might include emotions that were merged into them, while actions (as will be described later) carry information that allows to identify which intention they belong to. Thus, for a unified treatment of all aspects of an action, each action vertex needs to be merged with the corresponding outcome-perception vertex, which includes merging their annotations. Whenever a perception vertex is visited, the list of previously visited action vertices can be traversed in search for an action with the same propositional content. If one is found, the percept's annotation-content is extracted and appended to the action's annotation, after which the percept is removed from the graph and the list of visited vertices, and the graph is again patched.

LISTENS are vertices that are generated when an agent receives a speech act, and are always the target of a `cc` edge. The message passed in the speech act is placed in an internal event whose type depends on the type of the speech act (in our case either `achieve` or

---

[17]The untyped edges employed by my initial plot graph formalism have been discussed to essentially capture a temporal ordering in Sec. 2.3.4.

tell). A respective vertex (either of the type intention or perception) is added to the plot graph when the internal event is processed, thus it can be again assumed that the associated vertex will appear after the listen vertex, although not necessarily as its successor. In this case, the merging is performed through a look-ahead: the successors of the listen vertex are traversed until a vertex with the same propositional content (and appropriate format) is found. Then, the type and propositional content of the (former) listen vertex are changed to those of the found target vertex, and the target is removed from the plot graph. This approach is easier than the reverse, since it does not involve the transfer of *cc* edges. As a result, all *L* vertices are effectively removed from the analyzed plot graph by being replaced either through *I* or *P* vertices, the latter of which might potentially receive an affective valence if it is later merged with an emotion vertex.

Edge Generation

The creation of typed edges is implemented by the visitor class `inBloom.graph.visitor.EdgeGenerationPPVisitor`. Six types of edges need to be supported, namely, `equivalence`, `motivation`, `termination`, `actualization`, `causality` and `cross-character`.

EQUIVALENCE edges appear only in the primitive FU `perseverance`, where they indicate that two intentions represent the same goal (see Fig. 4.1 for graphs of all coming FUs). The most straightforward way to implement this is to test the propositional content of intentions for equality. Thus, when an *I*-type vertex is visited, the list of previously visited vertices is traversed in LIFO order, and if a match in propositional content is detected the visitor creates an *e* edge between the two, and moves on to the next vertex.

MOTIVATION edges appear in the primitive FUs `motivation`, `enablement` and `problem`, connecting any type of source vertex with an *I*-type target vertex. The information which event motivated an intention has to be preserved in the propositional content of the *I* vertex when it is created, since it is part of the agent's transient reasoning cycle state. This happens during execution of the method `PlotAwareAg#selectOption` that is called by the Jason framework to decide which applicable plan should be chosen to react to the internal event currently selected by the reasoning cycle. Once the selection is done and resulted in an appropriate achievement goal (which is the only type of goal that needs to be preserved as an intention vertex in the graph), the system can inspect the 'selected event' that was responsible for the choice of this intention. Events are preserved alongside an 'intended means stack' by Jason, which contains all (recursive) parent plans of which that event is part of. This stack is filtered for the first parent plan that is not part of the wish and obligation management system introduced in Sec. 2.3.4 because these plans are only there for the purpose of translating possible worlds semantics into a BDI form and are not part of the FU formalism. If such a plan is found then the triggering event of that plan can be treated as the event that motivated the currently generated intention. Triggering events can be either the addition or removal of beliefs (i.e. perceptions) or the introduction or termination of intentions (i.e. intentions) so that all primitive FU cases are covered. The triggering event is preserved as annotation in the propositional content of the newly created intention vertex, using the format motivation(Event).

```
1  +found(Item[Annots]) : creatable_from(Item,Y) & is_useful(Y) <-
2  //   ...
3        .appraise_emotion(hope, "found(Item[Annots])");
4        +obligation(create(Y)).
5
6  +!create(bread) : has(wheat[state(seed)]) <-
7        !plant(wheat).
```

Listing 4.1: ASL example for motivation extraction

In the example code in Lis. 4.1, the motivation of the intention !plant(wheat) would be the event +!create(bread)—the addition of the intention to create bread—because it is the triggering event of the plan that contains !plant(wheat). This corresponds to the primitive FU motivation. The motivation of the intention !create(bread), in turn, would be the belief addition +found(Item[Annots]), which will also be appraised with the secondary emotion hope, resulting in the primitive FU enablement. Note, that the intended means stack of !create(bread) will also contain plans triggered by +obligation(create(Y)), as well as the mediating +!obligation(create(Y)), but these will be ignored by the system (see Fig. 4.7 for a visual representation of the intended means stack in this example).

```
!create(bread)
+!obligation(create(bread))
+obligation(create(bread))
+found(wheat[state(seed)])
```

Figure 4.7: Example intended means stack when processing the intention !create(bread). The newer an event, the more towards the top of the stack it is located.

A special case that needs additional processing is when the identified triggering event is a mood change (for instance, changing into a hostile mood would trigger a punishment desire in the TLRH case study). The perception of a mood change itself is not an affective event in the sense of Lehnert, since it does not cause a positive or negative emotion. For this reason, preserving the mood change as the motivation of an intention would never result in a primitive FU. However, most mood changes themselves are caused by affective events (whose emotions were appraised by the agent and resulted in the mood change). These `affective_source` events for the current mood are preserved in the agent's `AffectiveCircumstance`. Whenever `PlotAwareAg#selectOption` detects a mood change as motivation, it extracts the affective source events and instead of the mood places them in the intention's motivation annotation. In the above TLRH example, this would lead to the rejected help requests being preserved as the motivations of the punishment intention, which is exactly what is desired in this situation.

When the edge visitor processes an intention vertex it thus has to extract the event(s) stored in the motivation annotation, and then traverse the list of previously visited events, creating m edges whenever a match with the annotation is found.

TERMINATION   edges appear in the primitive FUs change of mind, loss, resolution, positive trade-off and negative trade-off.

The first FU appears, when an intention is canceled out as part of another intention. This can be triggered in the ASL using the internal action `.drop_intention(I)` as part of a plan body. Whenever this is the case, Jason automatically informs InBloom by executing the method `PlotCircumstanceListener#intentionDropped(Intentio` n i). This method adds a faux intention-type vertex to the plot graph, with the propositional content `drop_intention(I)` and the annotation `termination(TriggerEvent)`. `TriggerEvent` contains the event that triggered the execution of the plan that contains the `.drop_intention` action, which can be extracted via the agent's transition system using `Circumstance#selectedOption.getTrigger()`. That way, when the edge visitor visits an intention, it can check whether its propositional content is of the above form. If it is, it traverses the list of previously visited events in search for I as well as `TriggerEvent` (that latter of which will usually be an intention addition event, i.e. an intention, too) and creates a t edge from the latter to the former. After that, the faux-intention vertex is removed from the graph, the hole is patched and the visitor moves on to the next vertex.

The next four FUs—`loss`, `resolution`, `positive trade-off` and `negative trade-off`—capture all the possible combinations in which an affectively appraised perception (either positive or negative) cancels out another affectively appraised perception (again, either positive or negative). The most direct way to detect this is to check whether the agent removed a previously held belief, or took up a belief (again) that it removed previously.Thus, whenever the edge visitor visits a perception with an attached emotion, it traverses the list of previously visited perceptions in search for a target vertex whose propositional content matches that of the visited one, whose belief base operator (either + for addition or − for removal) is different, and that also has an emotion attached. When it finds a match, it creates a t edges from the visited vertex to the target vertex. This approach will, for instance, automatically create a t edge from −`has(`*bread*`)[emotion(`*distress*`)]` to +`has(`*bread*`)[emotion(`*pride*`)]`, since the realization captured by the former terminates a state that was positive to the agent, captured by the latter.

A more interesting case can be detected when the ASL code indicates the removal of a belief. More concretely, if a mental note is removed as part of a plan that was triggered by another mental note operation, then it can be assumed that the removal is inherent to the semantics of that second mental note. Consider the example in Lis. 4.2: When an agent perceives that it dropped an item (+`is_dropped(`*bread*`)`), it removes the mental note that it posses that item (−`has(`*bread*`)`). Here, a termination edge should be created

```
1   +is_dropped(Thing)[owner(Agent)] : .my_name(Agent) <-
2       -has(Thing);
3       .appraise_emotion(remorse, "is_dropped(Thing)", Agent, 1).
```

Listing 4.2: ASL example for termination edge deduction

between +is_dropped(*bread*) and a former event, +has(*bread*).[18] Depending on which emotions are attached to +is_dropped(bread) and +has(bread), this constitutes one of the four primitive FU above. In our case, +is_dropped(bread) is appraised by a negative emotion (remorse), and +has(bread) is appraised by a positive one (joy), which makes this constellation into the primitive FU loss. To enable this functionality, mental notes should have an annotation containing the triggering event of their parent plan. This is implemented in PlotCircumstanceListener#eventAdded. If the added event is a mental note (i.e. contains the annotation source(*self*) and is not an intention) then the triggering event is extracted from that event's parent plan, and added as annotation to the newly created perception vertex, using the form cause(Trigger).[19] When the edge visitor processes an affective vertex containing the removal of a belief, and finds an annotation of the above type, it first traverses the list of previously visited events in search of the annotation content (in our case +is_dropped(bread)). It then traverses the list further in search of a vertex that contains the addition of the belief to-be-removed (here: +has(bread), and creates a *t* edge between the former and the latter.

ACTUALIZATION edges appear only in the primitive FUs success and failure, and indicate that an intention is causally responsible for an action. In the case of InBloom, the sending of speech acts can be part of an intention in exactly the same way as actions are, for which reason they will be treated similarly with regard to actualization edges. Thus, the edge visitor needs to be able to find the

---

[18]This is uncovers an additional, more interesting, connection than the rather trivial t edge between -has(*bread*) and +has(*bread*), described before.

[19]It is interesting to note what this implies: InBloom is capable of tracking the inferential chains of characters, and persist this information in the plot graph so that their role in the causal structure of the plot can be uncovered. These annotations are also relevant for the detection of several other edge types, as will be described below.

corresponding intention vertex, when visiting an action or a speech vertex. For this, each of these vertices needs to store its causally responsible intention as part of its propositional content.

When an action is requested by an agent, the method `TimeStep pedEnvironment#scheduleAction` is executed by the framework and passed the required data as a parameter. This method is overriden by `PlotEnvironment`, which extracts the intention and stores it as mapping from the agent name and the action in the field `HashMap<String , HashMap<Structure, Intention>> actionIntentionMap`. The action vertex is created later, when the requested action is actually executed by the method `PlotEnvironment#executeAction`. At this point, the intention is looked up in the `actionIntentionMap`, added as an annotation of the form `actualization(Intention)` to the content of the vertex, and the action-intention pairing is removed from the map.

The sending of a speech act, as well as the creation of the corresponding vertex, is implemented by the method `PlotAwareCentr alisedAgArch#sendMsg`. This method has access to the agent's reasoning cycle, which saves the currently selected intention. Using that information, the intention can be added to the vertex' content in the same manner as for actions.

This way, the edge visitor can simply extract the required information from any visited A or S-type vertex, and traverse the list of previously visited vertices until it finds an intention vertex whose propositional content matches the extracted intention. It then creates an a edge between the two, and moves on to the next vertex.

An unusual, but possible, case is that an agent's intention is actualized not through an action of its own, but an independent event in the environment (be it a happening, or the action of another agent). For this to be recognized, the agent needs to perceive the event and make the inference that it fulfills one of its intentions. In InBloom, such a realization would be encoded in ASL by removing a `wish` or `obligation` as reaction to the incoming perception (compare with Sec. 2.3.4 for wish and obligation management). Lis. 4.3 presents a simple example: If an agent perceives that it posses an item, then it can consider its intention to acquire such an item obsolete. As described above during the creation of termination edges, mental notes receive a cause-annotation containing the triggering event that caused its addition or removal (in our example this would be

```
1   +has(Item)   <-
2       -wish(has(Item));
```

Listing 4.3: ASL example for actualization by perception

+has(Item)). Thus, when the edge visitor processes a perception of the form -wish(X) or -obligation(X) it checks for the presence of a cause annotation. If one is present, it traverses the list of previously visited events in search for the appropriate vertex. It then moves on to locate the vertex representing the intention !X (the content of the wish/obligation to be removed, in our case !has(Item)), and creates an edge of type *a* between this intention and the previously identified cause.

CAUSALITY edges appear in the primitive FUs mixed blessing, hidden blessing, complex positive event, and complex negative event. One possible situation they capture is that the target event is an affectively appraised happening, which was triggered either by an action or another happening (also affectively appraised). InBloom can automatically detect which event is responsible for the change in environment state that caused a happening, as described in Sec. 2.3.4 on p. 79. This is implemented in PlotModel#checkHappenings, and if a cause is found it is stored in the annotations of that happening's event percept using the format cause(Event). As reader's will recall, the event percept is later delivered to the patient of the happening, and results in a perception that is subsequently added to the plot graph..

The other possible situation where this can arise is when the processing of a mental note causes the addition of another mental note; which in essence constitutes one inference step of an agent that is engaged in reasoning. A simple example can be found in Lis. 4.4. Here, the agent realizes that after successfully picking up an item (an

```
1   +collect(Thing)[success(true)] <-
2       +has(Thing).
```

Listing 4.4: ASL example for causality in mental notes

action-result perception) it is in the possession of that item (a mental note about a state). The functionality that adds the parent plan's triggering event of a mental note to its propositional content using an annotation of the form `cause(X)` is already in place, as has been described above, and can be used to preserve causality relations like these for the edge visitor.

Thus, when a perception vertex is visited, the edge visitor checks for the presence of a `cause` annotation, and if one is present traverses the list of previously visited events until it finds a perception whose propositional content matches that annotation. It then creates a c edge between the two, and moves on to the next vertex.

CROSS-CHARACTER edges can appear between any types of vertices, and thus do not form particular primitive FUs, but the potential constellations have been summarized in Fig. 4.3. Mainly, cc edges are generated by InBloom when a speech act is executed between two agents. As has been described above, the type of the receiving vertex (previously: `listen`) is changed either to I or to P (which can be affectively appraised) by the merging visitor. The sending vertex remains of the type `speech`, but can be merged with emotions by the merging visitor, or remain neutral if no emotions were appraised. This covers the cases described in Fig. 4.3 as `request`, `threat`, `promise`, `enablement` and `motivation`.

What remains are `shared event` and `mixed event`, which do not represent a communication setting but one where the same event is perceived independently by two agents. An intuitive solution would be to simply connect all vertices in different character subgraphs that have the same propositional content. This, however, would fall short. First, characters might perceive similar events but at different times, which should not result in a connection through cc edges. And second, the same event might be perceived differently by two characters[20], in which case a lookup using the propositional content would miss a required connection. The solution is to create a unique ID for each set of events that should be connected by cc edges, and attach it to the propositional content of their vertices as an annotation of the form `crosscharacter(ID)`. To gen-

---

[20]As the famous slogan goes: "One man's terrorist is another man's freedom fighter". The same aspectuality holds for events: one character might perceive an event as a terrorist attack, while another one might see the same event as a liberation attempt.

erate such an ID upon event creation, InBloom computes the hash code of (one of the alternatives for) the propositional content of the event, appended with the time stamp (in nano seconds) at which the event is created. Adding the event time avoids creating the same ID for events of the same content but happening at different times (problem one from above). This functionality is implemented in the method `PerceptAnnotation#addCrossCharAnnotation`, which creates an annotation that can be attached to each of the event perceptions that should later be connected. InBloom automatically does this for actions executed by agents because action percepts are delivered to all agents present at the acting agent's location and these perceptions should consequently be connected—a functionality implemented in `PlotEnvironment#executeAction`—as well as for percepts that are to be delivered to all agents at one location— implemented in `PlotEnvironment#addPercept(Location loc, Li teral... perceptions)`. However, custom narrative systems can also make use of this functionality whenever the logic of the story world dictates that an event is perceived by several agents.

A problem with this approach arises later, at visitation time, because the list of previously visited vertices is cleared before the visitor switches to a new character subgraph. Thus, looking up events with the same annotation in the list of previously visited vertices, like in the other cases, will not be sufficient for inter-character edges. Instead, the edge visitor maintains the hash map `ArrayListMultima p<String, Vertex> xCharIDMap`, which maps from IDs to lists of vertices. Whenever an action or perception is visited, the visitor checks whether an annotation of the required form is present in the current vertex, and if it does adds that vertex to the list to which the ID is mapped. Once all vertices in all subgraphs have been visited, the method `EdgeGenerationPPVisitor#postProcessing()` is executed, which iterates over all values in the hash map and creates bi-directional *cc* edges between all 2-combinations of each vertex-list.

Filtering

After vertices have been merged and typed edges have been created, some vertices can still be found in the plot graph that are not relevant for an FU analysis. They are removed from the analyzed plot graph by the third visitor class, `inBloom.graph.visitor.VisualizationF ilterPPVisitor`.

No emotion or listen vertices can remain in the analyzed graph by the time the filtering visitor is executed because they have been removed by the merging visitor. At the same time, intention, action and speech vertices are always considered relevant since they form part of the agents intentional state. The remaining vertex type is perception. Perceptions can be considered relevant if they are either appraised by an emotion (i.e. are of special concern for the agent) or are connected to other relevant vertices by a typed edge (i.e. form part of a network of causality). Other perceptions can a priori not be part of FUs and can hence be removed from the analyzed graph to remove clutter, and provide a more causality-centered picture.

Two exception are made here. One, for perception vertices that report the addition (respectively removal) of wishes or obligations by the agents. While these can never be part of an FU graph, I still decided to keep them in the graph to allow users to perceive the possible world semantics behind the affective reasoning. The second exception is made for vertices that represent the onset of a new mood. Even if such a vertex is not connected to relevant vertices via a typed edge it is still kept in the graph, to provide users with an easy way to track affective dynamics. Since FU analysis is not sensitive to intermitting vertices, keeping these non-relevant parts in the graph is not problematic.

ASL Programming Guidelines

As became apparent throughout the last pages, the shape of the analyzed plot graph in part depends on how the plan library is implemented in ASL. While obviously a multitude of ways exist to implement the same plan, only certain ones also ensure that InBloom is capable of automatically creating the right edges to make up FUs. For this reason, I propose the following list of ASL programming guidelines, which increase the chances of FU emergence during simulation runs:

1. The `achieveNF`-operator (!!) should be avoided, use a regular achieve-operator (!) instead.
   Reason: Events generated by `achieveNF` do not reference the triggering intention, the system would therefore be unable to create m edges.

2. The internal action `.appraise_emotion` should not be used for

appraising intentions.

Reason: Intentions are of neutral affect in Lehnert's formalism.

3. When creating a complex plan that contains sub-plans, make sure to consistently use sub-plans instead of mixing them with concrete actions.

   Reason: The FU nested goal will be created when a sub-plan is employed, but not an action.

```
1   +!create(bread) <-
2        !plant(wheat);
3        tend(wheat).
4   +!plant(wheat) <-
5        get(tools);
6        plant(wheat).
7
8
```

```
1   +!create(bread) <-
2        !plant(wheat);
3        !tend(wheat).
4   +!plant(wheat) <-
5        get(tools);
6        plant(wheat).
7   +!tend(wheat) <-
8        tend(wheat).
```

Listing 4.5: Counterexample   **Listing 4.6:** Suggestion

4. Events triggered through the reception of a speech act should be always affectively appraised.

   Reason: These events cannot receive a (primary) emotion from the environment, but require an affect label for most cross-character FUs to match.

```
1   //Agent A asks agent B for help
2   +!ask_help(X, AgentB) <-
3        .my_name(AgentA);
4        .send(AgentB, tell, request(help_with(AgentA,X))).
5
6   //Event triggered in Agent B
7   +request(help_with(AgentA, Plan)) <-
8        .appraise_emotion(reproach, "request(Plan)", AgentA);
9        .send(AgentA, tell, rejected_request(Plan)).
```

Listing 4.7: Suggestion

5. When successfully completing an action is supposed to change the agents belief base, the addition/removal of mental notes should be implemented as reaction to the action-result perception, and not as part of the original plan.

Reason: Edges of type c and t can only connect mental notes with perceptions, and not with intentions.

```
1    +!eat : has(bread) <-
2        eat(bread);
3        -has(bread).
4
```

```
1    +!eat : has(bread) <-
2        eat(bread).
3    +eat(Food)[success(true)] <-
4        -has(bread).
```

Listing 4.8: Counterexample   **Listing 4.9:** Suggestion

6. Whenever a mental note is added, make sure to ensure the consistency of the belief base by explicitly removing all beliefs that become obsolete or invalid.

   Reason: Edges of type t are created between events only if one explicitly removes the other from the belief base.

```
1    +is_dropped(Thing)[owner(Agent)] : .my_name(Agent) <-
2        -has(Thing).
```

Listing 4.10: Suggestion

Resulting Formalism

In contrast to the original formalism introduced by Lehnert, the implementation introduced above does not limit itself to $+$ and $-$ vertices that represent positive or negative affect, but instead attaches these properties in addition to the original vertex types, which can be either R, P, A, or S. In fact, some of these vertices remain in analyzed plot graphs without affective valence at all, if their relevance is due to their role in the causal structure of the plot. To account for this, my original plot graph definition needs to be adapted in such a way that vertex labels can represent not only the vertex type, but at the same time also any affective valence that was potentially merged to it during the analysis process. In the style of Definitions 4 and 5, the following describes the structure of analyzed plot graphs generated by InBloom:

Definition 11 (Analyzed Character Subgraph). An analyzed character subgraph is a directed, vertex-labeled and edge-labeled graph $G_{cha} = (V_{cha}, E_{cha}, l_v, l_e, prop)$ comprised by a set of vertices V_{cha}, a set of directed edges $E_{cha} \subseteq V_{cha}^2$, as well as the label functions $l_v : V_{cha} \rightarrow \{R, I, A, A+, A-, S, S+, S-, P, P+, P-\}$ and $l_e : E_{cha} \rightarrow$

$\{m, a, t, e, c\}$ and the propositional content function $prop : V \to Asl$, where Asl is the set of valid expressions in the AgentSpeak language. The subgraph G_{cha} is considered legal, iff $\forall \epsilon = (v_s, v_t) \in E_{cha}$ and with $\lambda_\epsilon = l_e(\epsilon)$, $\lambda_s = l_v(v_s)$ as well as $\lambda_t = l_v(v_t)$ denoting the respective edge, source and target labels:

$$\lambda_\epsilon = \begin{cases} m & \Rightarrow \lambda_t = I \\ a & \Rightarrow \lambda_s = I \wedge \lambda_t \in \{A+, A-, S+, S-, P+, P-\} \\ t & \Rightarrow \lambda_s = \lambda_t = I \vee (\lambda_s \neq I \wedge \lambda_t \neq I) \\ e & \Rightarrow \lambda_s = \lambda_t = I \\ c & \Rightarrow \lambda_s \neq I \wedge \lambda_t \neq I \end{cases}$$

and G_{cha} furthermore contains exactly one root vertex v_0—with $l_v(v_0) = R$ and $prop(v_0) = c$—which has no predecessors in the subgraph: $|E_{v_0}^-| = 0$.

Analyzed character subgraphs can be used to define analyzed plot graphs.

Definition 12 (Analyzed Plot Graph). An analyzed plot graph $G = (V, E)$ is a collection of disjoint analyzed character subgraphs and cross-character edges. Its constituents are the sets $V = \bigcup V_{c_i}$ and $E = \bigcup E_{c_i} \cup E_{cc}$, for all $c_i \in C$ where C denotes the set of all characters, and E_{cc} denotes the set of all cross-character edges. The analyzed plot graph can be said to contain the subgraphs from which it is comprised, shorthand notation: $G_{c_i} \in G$. It thus holds that: $\forall G_{c_i}, G_{c_j} \in G : i \neq j \Rightarrow V_{c_i} \cap V_{c_j} = \varnothing \wedge E_{c_i} \cap E_{c_j} = \varnothing$. The type of a vertex $v \in V$ or an edge $e \in E$ of an analyzed plot graph is a short hand way of referring to the label of that vertex or edge in the analyzed character subgraph to which it belongs:

$$type(v, G) = l_v(v) \text{ where } v \in V_c$$

$$type(e, G) = \begin{cases} l_e(e) & \text{if } \exists E_c : e \in E_c \\ cc & \text{if } e \in E_{cc} \end{cases}$$

if there exists a c such that $G_c = (V_c, E_c, l_v, l_e, prop) \in G$.

Sometimes, I will refer to vertices simply as $+$ or $-$ vertices to foreground their affective valence. This will denote vertices where the type contains $+$ or $-$ and where I do not care whether, apart from that, they are an action, perception or a speech act.

FU Matching

With the above components in place, InBloom can automatically create analyzed plot graphs with all the features that can appear in FUs, as well as the addition of A (action), P (perception), and S (speech) as part of the vertex type. This makes it possible to also expand the formalism that is used to define FUs. In the original proposal, FU vertices can either match intentions, or one type of affect. This allows only for limited discriminatory potential, especially taking into account that cross-character edges are untyped, and thus no possibility exists to distinguish cc edges that arise due to communication, and cc edges that arise because a character acts upon another character. At the same time, an FU like honored request clearly would benefit from the ability to restrict its application to cases that only involve speech acts. For this reason, I opted to also expand the FU representation formalism to allow the additional vertex types A and S.

Taking into account that FU graphs are used as patterns that are matched against analyzed plot graphs, the two should be defined comparably. The formalism needs to be adopted only to support one additional type of vertices—the wild-card vertex (denoted ?)—which are used in FUs by Lehnert (1981, p. 307) to allow matching any arbitrary plot graph vertex. While Lehnert does not mention wild-card edges (denoted ? here, too), the need for their introduction arises by necessity. Since the type of an edge depends on the type of its source and target vertices, which at the time at which an FU is defined is unclear for wild-card vertices, all incident edges of a wild-card vertex must be defined as wild-cards themselves. To account for the addition of the A and S vertex types I discussed above, I also decided to introduce a more discriminative wild-card vertex that would match any type of activity from an agent, but not intentions or perceptions, which are more deliberative in nature. These activity-vertices will be denoted A/S. In the style of Def. 12, I define an FU graph as follows:

Definition 13 (FU Graph). An FU graph is a directed, vertex-labeled, and edge-labeled graph $G_{FU} = (V_{FU}, E_{FU}, l_v, l_e)$ comprised by a set of vertices V_{FU}, a set of directed edges $E_{FU} \subseteq V_{FU}^2$, as well as the label functions $l_v : V \to \{I, +, -, A, S, A/S, ?\}$ and $l_e : E \to \{m, a, t, e, c, cc, ?\}$. The FU graph contains either one or two disjoint character subgraphs such that: $\forall G_{c_i}, G_{c_j} \in G_{FU} : i \neq j \Rightarrow V_{c_i} \cap V_{c_j} = \varnothing \wedge E_{c_i} \cap E_{c_j} = \varnothing$ and $V_{FU} = \bigcup V_{c_i}$ and $E_{FU} = \bigcup E_{c_i} \cup E_{cc}$, for all $c_i \in C$ with C being the set of all characters, and E_{cc} being the set of all cross-character edges.

FUs need to contain at least three vertices (FUs of two vertices are called primitive FU and serve as the building blocks of (complex) FU, as has been explained in Sec. 4.1.1), but no restriction is placed on their maximal size. In her paper, Lehnert proposes a number of FUs and mentions that new FUs can be defined freely. For InBloom, the 13 of her FUs which I deemed most useful have been adapted and implemented in the class `inBloom.graph.isomorphism.Functional Units`. Each unit is represented as an instance of the class `inBloom. graph.isomorphism.FunctionalUnit` which consists of a `unitGraph` of type `PlotDirectedSparseGraph`, and the `String name`. `Functi onalUnits` constructs all the defined FUs on class initialization, by assembling their respective `unitGraph`s from the required edges and vertices, and stores them in the static field `FunctionalUnit[] ALL`. The resulting FUs are depicted in Fig. 4.8. Formally, I will refer to the set of all FU graphs supported by InBloom as $\mathcal{G} = \{G_{FU_1}, \ldots, G_{FU_n}\}$.

Originally, Lehnert proposed to use the FUs as patterns that can be matched against a plot graph. Whenever a subgraph of the over-all plot graph could be identified, whose structure (including con-nections, vertex types and edge types, but excluding propositional content) was a precise match of an FU graph, this subgraph was con-sidered an *instance* of that FU. This means that it is possible for each FU to be found several times in any given plot, and that we can conceive FU analysis as a function from analyzed plot graphs to sets of subgraphs. This situation can be interpreted as an instance of the established *subgraph-isomorphism problem*, applied to the analyzed plot graph and each of the FU graphs.[21] Several recent approaches to solve this problem exist (see e.g. Bonnici et al., 2013; Cordella et al., 2004; Ullmann, 2011). However, as discussed, I deem this approach too inflexible for the present use case. Fortunately, some solutions to the subgraph isomorphism problem have been extended to also enable *inexact matching*. One such solution,Cordella et al. (1998), proposes and algorithm where "two graphs are considered similar if, by using a defined set of syntactic and semantic transformations, they can be made isomorphic to each other". This neatly captures what I have previously described as prototype based matching: The original FU graphs can be successively subjected to transformations, allowing

---

[21]While subgraph-isomorphism has been shown to be NP-complete (S. A. Cook, 1971) I do not consider this overly problematic since at present analyzed plot graphs generated by InBloom typically contain only a few hundred vertices, while all the FU graphs contain less than ten.

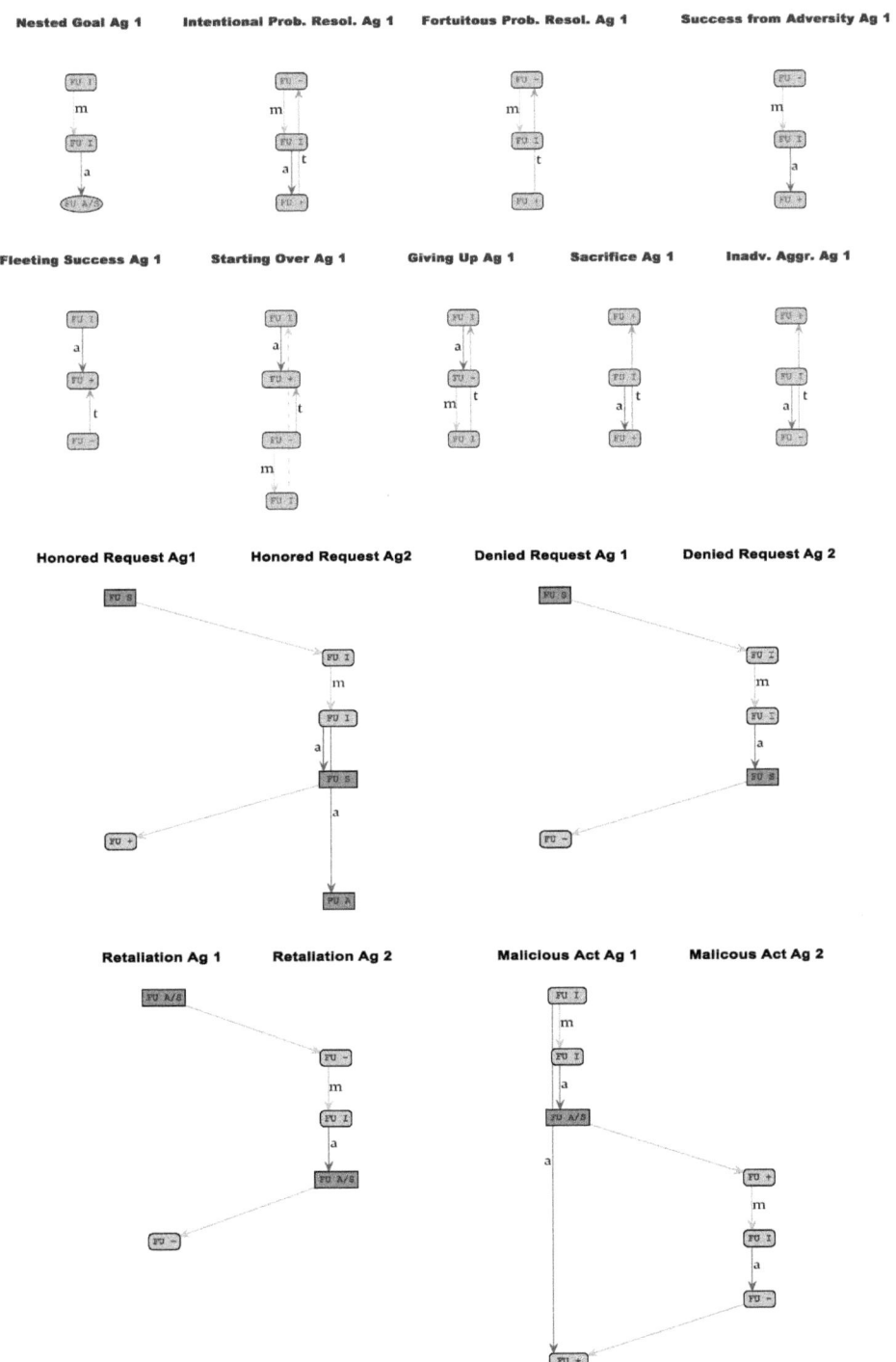

Figure 4.8: The FUs implemented in InBloom, with annotated edge types. Edges of type c do not appear in these base versions, but their relevance will become clear later.

more and more differing plot subgraphs to be matched by the FU. Thus, for the task of FU analysis, a custom version of that algorithm has been implemented in InBloom.

Cordella et al. (1998) rely on a *state space representation (SSR)* to formalize the matching process involved in solving the subgraph isomorphism problem. Let $G_1 = (V_1, E_1)$ and $G_2 = (V_2, E_2)$ be two graphs[22], and M be a mapping that associates vertices from G_2 with vertices from G_1: $M = \{(v, w) \in V_2 \times V_1 | v$ is mapped to $w\}$. Here, a mapping is a set of vertex-pairs, where each pair can be denoted as m_i. Such a mapping M can be considered a partial isomorphism if it is an injective function, where the edge structure (and labeling) as well as vertex labeling of all pairs match.

Using SSR, the matching process is described by a succession of states s_i, each of which represents a partial mapping $M(s_i) \subseteq M$, i.e. $M(s_i)$ contains some components of the final mapping M. A state transition from s_i to s_{i+1} in this formalism is possible by the addition of a new vertex mapping to $M(s_i)$. Thus, solving the inexact subgraph isomorphism problem means traversing the SSR from state s_0 with $M(s_0) = \emptyset$ until all states s_z are found, where all vertices in V_2 are part of the mapping $M(s_z)$. I will refer to the set of all these solutions for a particular pair of graphs as $\mathcal{M}_{G_1,G_2}$.

The algorithm depicted in Alg. 2 is adapted from Cordella et al. (1998) to enable such a traversal.

It starts with the current state being the empty state $s_{current} = s_0$, and generates the next state s_{next} by adding the first feasible pair[23] $p = (n, m) \in V_2 \times V_1$ to the mapping: $M(s_{next}) = M(s_{current}) \cup p$. This procedure is applied recursively on that next state (by setting $s_{current} = s_{next}$), until either a solution is found—which happens when the number of pairings in a mapping $M(s)$ is the same as the number of vertices in the subgraph G_2—or the set of feasible pairs for a state generated that way is empty. In both cases, the algorithm backtracks by removing the last feasible pair that was added to the mapping, and instead exploring the state that is created when another feasible pair is added. This amounts to a depth-first search. In a slight variation

---

[22]W.l.o.g it is assumed that $\#V_2 \leq \#V_1$, where $\#$ denotes set cardinality. This means that G_2 (the subgraph) is an FU graph, and G_1 is an analyzed plot graph.

[23]Feasible pairs will be formally defined below, on p. 238. In essence, a feasible pair is a syntactically and semantically valid mapping of a vertex from the FU graph to a vertex from the plot graph.

Algorithm 2 Inexact subgraph matching, acc. to Cordella et al. (1998, 2004)

1: **procedure** MATCH(s, $results$)
2:     *// Check whether mapping is complete*
3:     **if** $M(s)$.size() $==$ V_2.size() **then**
4:         $results$.append($M(s)$);
5:         **return** $results$
6:     **end if**
7:     *// Explore all feasible pairs that can expand the mapping*
8:     $P(s) =$ GET_CANDIDATE_PAIRS($M(s)$);
9:     **for all** p in $P(s)$ **do**
10:         **if** FEASIBLE_PAIR(p) **then**
11:             $M(s_{next}) = M(s)$.append(p);
12:             MATCH(s_{next}, $results$);
13:         **end if**
14:     **end for**
15:     **return** $results$
16: **end procedure**
17:
18: *// Initialization*
19: $M(s_0) = []$; $results = []$;
20: MATCH(s_0, $results$);

from the original, this algorithm does not terminate after it finds the first complete mapping, but instead continues to aggregate all solutions in a list.

A certain amount of complexity, including the realization of the *inexact* matching part of the algorithm, is hidden in the function `get_candidate_pairs` which is called on l. 8 of the pseudocode. Let $G_1(s) = (V_1(s), E_1(s))$ denote the projection of $M(s)$ onto G_1 (comparably for G_2). Then, let $T_1^{out}(s)$, $T_1^{in}(s)$ denote the sets of vertices that are connected to $G_1(s)$ via outgoing (respectively, incoming) edges and are not yet part of the partial mapping. $T_2^{out}(s)$, $T_2^{in}(s)$ are defined accordingly for $G_2(s)$. Also, let v_0 be a function from analyzed graphs to vertex-sets, which, given the analyzed graph $G = (V, E)$ returns a set of vertices $V_{start} \subset V$, where V_{start} contains all vertices that represent events that happened at plot step 0.[24] The (basic) candidate pairs ($P(s)$ in l. 8 of the pseudocode) are computed as follows:

$$
P(s) = \begin{cases}
v_0(G_2) \times V_1 & \text{if } \#V_2(s) = 0 \\
T_2^{out}(s) \times T_1^{out}(s) & \text{else if } T_2^{out}(s) \neq \emptyset \wedge T_1^{out}(s) \neq \emptyset \\
T_2^{in}(s) \times T_1^{in}(s) & \text{else if } T_2^{in}(s) \neq \emptyset \wedge T_1^{in}(s) \neq \emptyset \\
\emptyset & \text{else}
\end{cases}
\tag{4.1}
$$

That is, when no mapping exists yet, the algorithm suggests to match the first vertex of the FU with every vertex of the analyzed plot graph. After a successful first match, it tries to match vertices connected via outgoing edges to the current partial mapping. When no such vertices exist, incoming edges are used to identify candidates. The original algorithm employed the operation $P(s) = (V_2 \backslash V_2(s)) \times (V_1 \backslash V_1(s))$ for the `else` case, which proposes all possible pairs of not yet mapped vertices as candidates. This option is only useful for cases when G_2 contains unconnected subgraphs, which should never occur with FU graphs.[25] This makes it possible to omit it for InBloom, since under these conditions it can never detect feasible mappings, while slowing down the runtime of the algorithm considerably. According to Cordella et al. (2004, p. 1368) this approach establishes a total

---

[24]Note, that this function will be applied only on FU graphs, which are always defined in a way that exactly one such event exists.

[25]Should such FUs be added to the catalog at a later time, this decision would need to be revised. However, I would strongly discourage from introducing such FUs, since it is not clear how two causally unconnected sets of events could constitute a *unit* of functional significance.

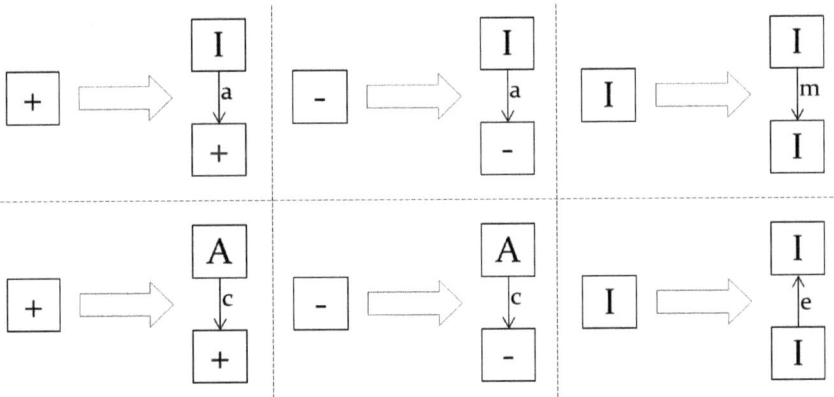

Figure 4.9: Graphical representation of the six implemented split transformations. White arrows represent the transformation, the split vertex is located on the left of that arrow, the resulting subgraph on the right.

order over the vertices in $P(s)$, which precludes the regeneration of already seen states.

So far, this only implements exact matching. For inexact matching, the generation of candidates needs to also consider legal transformations of G_2 (Cordella et al., 1998). I make the assumption that the prototype FUs encoded as part of InBloom's catalogue are the smallest viable versions of the semantics they encode. This restricts the transformations that need to be considered to *splits*, where a vertex of an FU graph is transformed into a subgraph. Formally, a split can be defined as a 4-tuple (v, E, V', E'), where v is the vertex to be split, E is the set of edges incident to v, V' is the set of vertices that are added, and E' is the set of newly introduced edges. Six possible split types have been determined by me based on the analysis of the analyzed plot graphs of several narrative systems implemented in InBloom, in comparison with the FUs that were expected to be found there based on manual interpretation. They are shown in Fig. 4.9.

Thus, before $P(s)$ is returned, each of its candidate pairs $(n, m) \in V_2 \times V_1$ needs to be tested, whether any of the possible split types can be applied to n, and all resulting mappings are also added to $P(s)$. One instance of such reasoning has been already introduced above, in Fig. 4.5. There, the actual plot graph contained a subgraph of the form $[I] \xrightarrow{a} [-]$ at a place where the FU graph for `retaliation` contained just a $[-]$ vertex. This could be resolved by the split transformation $(-, \{cc\}, \{I, -\}, \{a\})$: A negative emotion is transformed into an intention that fails (i.e. is actualized by a negatively appraised event). In fact, such a transformation can be applied to any $[-]$ vertex in the FU graph without loosing this semantic meaning, which lead to the decision to determine transformation applicability based simply on the vertex type of n. To prevent the bastardization of FUs through incremental splitting, a transformation cost was introduced, which at the moment is uniformly set to one for each transformation type.

To account for these changes, states s had to be expanded to store not only the mapping of vertices $M(s)$, but also the two complete graphs that are being mapped (since after transformations G_2 can change), as well as the accumulated transformation cost. Transformations of pairs in $P(s)$ are only added to the set if this accumulated transformation cost is smaller or equal to the maximal allowed cost. In informal experiments I conducted, already two successive splits often resulted in implausible matches, so that the maximal cost is presently set to 1.

Another noteworthy function is `feasible_pair` on l. 10 of the pseudocode. It is responsible for checking whether adding a candidate pair results in a consistent mapping $M(s_{next})$, or whether the candidate should be rejected. According to Cordella et al. (2004), a partial mapping is consistent if the partial graphs G_1 and G_2 are isomorphic. For this to be the case, the structure and the labeling of the graphs need to be compared. If a candidate state results in a consistent mapping it is called *feasible*, thus, a general feasibility function can be defined: $F(s, n, m) = F_{syn}(s, n, m) \land F_{sem}(s, n, m)$ where s is the current state, (n, m) is the candidate mapping, and F_{syn} stands for syntactic feasibility (i.e. same structure) while F_{sem} stands for semantic feasibility (i.e. same labeling).

Syntactic feasibility for a candidate pair is given, iff all predecessors/successors in the partial mapping of the first vertex are mapped to a predecessor/successor of the second mapping. Formally:

$$R_{pred}(s, n, m) \Leftrightarrow \forall n' \in V_2(s) \cap Pred(G_2, n) \tag{4.2}$$

$$\exists m' \in Pred(G_1, m) : (n', m') \in M(s)$$

$$R_{succ}(s, n, m) \Leftrightarrow \forall n' \in V_2(s) \cap Succ(G_2, n) \tag{4.3}$$

$$\exists m' \in Succ(G_1, m) : (n', m') \in M(s)$$

where $Pred(G, v)$ and $Succ(G, v)$ denote the sets that contain, respectively, the predecessors or successors of the vertex v in the graph G.[26]

Such reasoning can be applied not only to test individual states but also to prune the search tree as early as possible, since a candidate mapping can be deemed not feasible in advance, if it is clear that it has no feasible successor states. Checking the k future steps of a candidate pair for feasibility is called a k-*look-ahead*, and can be included in syntactic feasibility checks. Cordella et al. (2004, p. 1369) introduce rules that perform two 1-look-aheads: R_{in} and R_{out} as well as one 2-look-ahead: R_{new}, which check necessary but not sufficient conditions for consistency. For performance reasons these rules are included in InBloom, too, but due to the complexity of their formalization an inclusion here is forgone for readability reasons; interested readers are referred to the original publication. A last syntactic feasibility criterion is specific to InBloom: Since each FU can apply to at most two agents, the number of character subgraphs that a partial mapping graph contains has to be smaller or equal than two:

$$R_{root}(s) \Leftrightarrow \#\{c|G_c \in G_1 \wedge G_c(s) \neq \emptyset\} \leq 2 \qquad (4.4)$$

Summarizing, syntactic feasibility is given by:

$$F_{syn}(s, n, m) = R_{succ}(s, n, m) \wedge R_{pred}(s, n, m) \wedge$$
$$R_{root}(s) \wedge R_{in}(s) \wedge R_{out}(s) \wedge R_{new}(s) \qquad (4.5)$$

Semantic feasibility for a candidate pair is given when the labels of the first vertex and its incident edges match the labels of the second vertex and its incident edges. Let this be captured by a compatibility relation that is defined for vertices $\approx_v \subseteq V_{FU} \times V_{plot}$ and edges $\approx_e \subseteq E_{FU} \times E_{plot}$. Then, following Cordella et al. (2004):

$$F_{sem}(s, n, m) \Leftrightarrow n \approx_v m$$
$$\wedge \forall (n', m') \in M(s) : (n, n') \in E_2 \Rightarrow (n, n') \approx_e (m, m')$$
$$\wedge \forall (n', m') \in M(s) : (n', n) \in E_2 \Rightarrow (n', n) \approx_e (m', m) \quad (4.6)$$

---

[26]Cordella et al. (1998, 2004) also check whether the inverse is true: $\forall m' \in V_1(s) \cap Pred(G_1, m) \exists m' \in Pred(G_2, n) : (n', m') \in M(s)$; accordingly for successors. This implies that they actually address the *induced subgraph isomorphism problem*, where all edges between two mapped vertices have to match, too (see e.g. Heggernes et al., 2015). Such an additional restriction is harmful for my use case, since analyzed plot graphs are multigraphs, but edges present in a plot graph do not need to be present in an FU graph for a match. For this reason, the original conditions are relaxed as stated above.

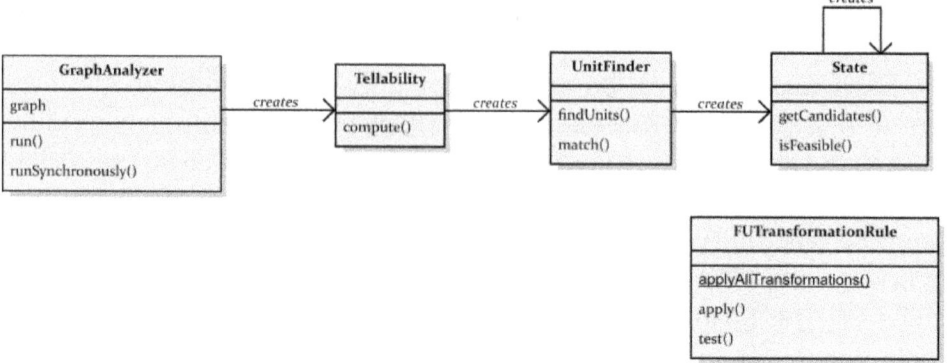

Figure 4.10: An abridged class diagram representation of the FU matching architecture in InBloom. For brevity reasons attributes are represented without types and methods without parameters or return types.

The implementation of the algorithm described here is distributed over four main classes (see Fig. 4.10). Upon instantiation by the analysis process in `GraphAnalyzer`, the class `Tellability` iterates over all the FUs contained in `FunctionalUnits.ALL`. For each FU, it executed Alg. 2, which is encapsulated in the class `inBloom.graph.isomophism.UnitFinder`. In particular, its method `Set<Map<Vertex, Vertex>> findUnits(Pl otDirectedSparseGraph unitGraph, PlotDirectedSparseG raph plotGraph, int tolerance)` performs the initialization and in turn calls method `boolean match(State s, Set<Stat e> unitList, int tolerance)`. States like *s* are implemented as instances of the class `inBloom.graph.isomophism.State`, which maintains the current mapping and a potential candidate pair. It contains the methods `boolean isFeasible()` and `Set<State> getCandidates(int tolerance)`, that implement the respective parts of the algorithm as formalized above. The list of split-transformations, which is required to compute candidate pairs, is maintained in the static initializer of the class `inBloom.graph.isomophism.FUTransformationRule`. Each transformation itself is an instance of that class, and provides the methods `boolean test(Vertex v)` and `PlotDirectedSparseGraph apply (Vertex toReplace, PlotDirectedSparseGraph fuGraph)`, which can be used to perform the split encoded by that transformation on those vertices, where it is applicable.

After the subgraph isomorphism algorithm has been executed on the analyzed plot graph $G = (V_G, E_G)$ and each of the FU graphs $G_{FU} \in \mathcal{G}$, the results are stored as a set of mappings Φ_G, where each mapping represents an FU instance (denoted ϕ from now on):

$$\Phi_G = \bigcup \mathcal{M}_{G,G_{FU}} = \{\phi|\phi = \{(v, w)|v \text{ is mapped to } w\}\} \qquad (4.7)$$

We can say that a vertex v is part of an FU instance ϕ iff $\exists x : (v, x) \in \phi \vee (x, v) \in \phi$ for some vertex x; short hand notation: $v \sqsubset \phi$.

Polyvalence Computation

All vertices of an analyzed plot graph $G = (V_G, E_G)$ that are part of more than one FU instance can be considered part of the set of polyvalent vertices: $V_G^* = \{v \in V_G|n_v > 1\}$ where $n_v = \#\{\phi \in \Phi_G|v \sqsubset \phi\}$.

To make plots of different length comparable with regard to the functional polyvalence measure, I propose to normalize the number of polyvalent vertices by the total number of vertices in the analyzed plot graph. This leads to the following density function determining a plot's functional polyvalence:

$$polyvalence(G) = \frac{\#V_G^*}{\#V_G} \qquad (4.8)$$

It might be worthwhile to explore more sophisticated versions of this equation, for instance taking into account the individual vertices' actual polyvalence scores. For my purposes, the easiest viable solution is sufficient.

4.2.2. Computing Semantic Parallelism and Symmetry

As outlined in Sec. 4.1.2, P&S are preferably computed over FU instance sequences, and only as a fallback on the actual event sequences per character.

Linearization

Thus, the first task is to create such sequences for each character. An instance is included into a character's FU instance sequence if at least one vertex that belongs to that FU instance is part of that character's subgraph. Let G be an analyzed plot graph, Φ_G the corresponding set of all FU instances, and $G_c = (V_c, E_c, l_v, l_e, prop) \in G$ be an analyzed character subgraph. The set of FU instances for character c is defined as: $Preseq_c^\phi = \{\phi \in \Phi_G | \exists v \sqsubset \phi : v \in V_c\}$. Remember, that an FU instance can contain vertices from either one, or two characters. Hence, it is possible that the same FU instance appears in two different character sequences.

Determining the order in which FU instances appear in such a set is not straight-forward, since instances span several vertices and can normally not be assigned a single plot step. In practice, an FU instance might easily span the course of the whole plot, making the question of how to assign plot steps to instances more than just a minor detail. Since an FU instance cannot be recognized by a reader until it is completed, it appears best to order instances based on their latest vertex, first. However, a vertex can be part of multiple FU instances and in practice two FU instances quite commonly end in the same vertex. In this case, their order can be compared based on their earliest vertex.

Vertex order cannot be compared easily based on the analyzed plot graph G, since it does not contain any temporal edges. However, the order can be inferred from the original plot graph. Let $G' = (V', E')$ be the plot graph from which the analyzed graph G was constructed, and $G'_c = (V'_c, E'_c, l'_v, prop') \in G'$ be the character subgraph that corresponds to G_c. Furthermore, let $v_0 \in V'_c$ be the root vertex as per Def. 4. We can define an indexing function $f_c^i : V'_c \to \mathbb{N}$ as:

$$f_c^i(v_0) = 0$$
$$f_c^i(v) = 1 + f_c^i(v_{pred}) \text{ with } v_{pred} \text{ such that } (v_{pred}, v) \in E'_c$$

Remember that plot graphs—as opposed to analyzed plot graphs— have only temporal edges, so that an edge between two vertices by necessity indicates that the former is the predecessor of the latter. Using this index function, we can define the index of the last vertex of an FU instance ϕ with regard to character subgraph c as:

$$i_{\phi,c}^{max} = \max_{v \sqsubset \phi \wedge v \in V_c} f_c^i(v)$$

Since all vertices in G_c are selected from G'_c during the analysis process, we can assume that $V_c \subseteq V'_c$ and that hence v will be part of the domain of f_c^i. The index of the first vertex of an FU instance $i_{min}^{\phi,c}$ can be defined accordingly based on the min function.

To induce a total order over $Preseq_c^\phi$ we can now define a binary relation $\succeq_{FU}: Preseq_c^\phi \times Preseq_c^\phi$ such that $\phi_1 \succeq_{FU} \phi_2$ iff[27]:

$$(i_{\phi_1,c}^{max} > i_{\phi_2,c}^{max}) \vee$$
$$((i_{\phi_1,c}^{max} = i_{\phi_2,c}^{max}) \wedge (i_{\phi_1,c}^{min} \geq i_{\phi_2,c}^{min}))$$

The total order criteria are trivially fulfilled here, since total order over FU instances is reduced to total order over natural numbers. We denote the resulting ordered set $(Preseq_c^\phi, \succeq_{FU})$, which represents what I above called a character's FU instance sequence.

In case no sufficient FU instances are present in an analyzed plot graph (the threshold I currently employ is at least three instances per character), instead, the character's event sequence is used as a basis to detect P&S. The order of events can be determined easily by the order of the respective vertices in the character subgraph, as enumerated by the function f_c^i. Thus, given the set of vertices in an analyzed character subgraph V_c, we can define a total order relation over these vertices $\succeq_V: V_c \times V_c$ such that $v_1 \succeq_V v_2$ iff: $f_c^i(v_1) > f_c^i(v_2)$. We denote the resulting ordered set $(V_c, \succ)$.

To simplify notation further on, we define the sequence on which P&S should be detected for a character c as follows:

$$Seq_c = \begin{cases} (Preseq_c^\phi, \succeq_{FU}) & \text{if } \forall c \in C : \#Preseq_c^\phi \geq 3 \\ (V_c, \succeq_V) & \text{else} \end{cases} \qquad (4.9)$$

Symmetry

TRANSLATIONAL SYMMETRY, as I outlined in Sec. 4.1.2, occurs when a chain appears n times in Seq_c, with $n > 1$. Let $Seq_c = (a_0, a_1, \ldots, a_k)$, then the ordered set $Cha = (a_i, a_{i+1}, \ldots, a_j)$ is called a chain given that $0 \leq i < j \leq k$. We define an auxiliary function f^{chain}, which takes as input a sequence Seq_c as well as the indices i, j and returns the corresponding chain Cha. The translational symmetry value of such a chain is determined by its number

---

[27] A more canonical approach would be the use of Allen's interval algebra (Allen, 1983), however, it is not applicable for FU instances because they are intervals with holes. Hence, the total order defined here is meant as a purely practical solution capable of deterministically defining an order over FU instances. It is not intended as a plausible solution to the problem of ordering intervals with holes, which would exceed the scope of this thesis.

of occurrences multiplied by its length and normalized by the overall length of the underlying sequence, computable by the function:
$v^{ts}(Seq_c, Cha) = n \times \frac{j-i+1}{k+1}$.[28]

To compute the translational symmetry value of a sequence, we first need to identify all possible chains in that sequence $Seq_c = (a_0, a_1, \ldots, a_k)$:

$$C_c = \left\{ t \mid t = \left(f^{chain}(Seq_c, i, j), i, j \right) \wedge 0 \leq i < j \leq k \text{ with } i, j \in \mathbb{N} \right\}$$

where C_c is a set of 3-tuples, each containing a chain, its start-index and end-index. Note, that $f^{chain}(Seq_c, i, j) = f^{chain}(Seq_c, m, n)$ is possible even for $(i, j) \neq (m, n)$, as long as the elements in the two chains are the same. This means that for each chain that is symmetric, C_c contains multiple elements. To be able to determine the number of occurrences of each chain, the elements of C_c need to be grouped by the actual chains:

$$C'_c = \left\{ (t_1, L) \mid (t_1, \_, \_) \in C_c \wedge L = \bigcup_{(t_1, i, j) \in C_c} \{(i, j)\} \right\}$$

which results in a set of 2-tuples, where the first element is always a chain and the second a set of (begin-index, end-index) position-pairs. A problem remains here because following the above formalization chains are allowed to overlap. For instance, the sequence $Seq_c = \{a, a, a\}$ would result in $C'_c = \left\{ \left((a, a), \{(0, 1), (1, 2)\} \right) \right\}$ because the chain (a, a) can be found at positions $(0, 1)$ and $(1, 2)$. Since I see chains as fixed units of perception, it seems more natural for me to assume that each element of a sequence can be only part of one chain instance[29], which means that such overlaps need to be filtered out from the elements of C'_c. This can be done by starting from the

---

[28] That way, a chain that covers all elements of a sequence receives the value of 1. Note, that, under this definition, a chain that covers one third of a sequence and appears three times is as valuable as a chain that covers half the sequence and appears two times. This might not correspond to human intuitions of symmetry, but is the most straight-forward approach in this scenario.

[29] As an example, inspect the sequence AABAABAA. When allowing overlap, the best translational chain would be AABAA, which covers the whole of the sequence. The best chains when disallowing it would be ABA and AA, which each cover only 75% of the sequence. The latter coincides better with my intuition that in this sequence translational symmetry should be weaker than reflectional symmetry (with chain AABA).

first position pair of each chain, and removing all subsequent position pairs whose begin-index is smaller or equal to the end-index of
that pair, until a pair is reached that does not overlap. Then, the
process is repeated with this pair, until the complete set is processed
in this way.[30] In the end, all chains that appear with only one index-
pair can be discarded, since they do not represent symmetric chains
under these more restrictive requirements. For reasons of brevity, I
omit the mathematical formalization of this procedure and simply
denote its result as $\mathcal{C}_c''$. Curious readers are referred to the implementation in `inBloom.helper.SymmetryAnalyzer#filterOverlapp`
`ingChains`. Given $\mathcal{C}_c'' = \{(t_1, L_1), (t_2, L_2), \ldots, (t_z, L_z)\}$, the translational symmetry value of each chain t_x can be computed using the
function v^{ts} introduced above, where the number of occurrences can
be determined based on the number of elements in the corresponding position-pair set: $n = \#L_x$, the position-indices are an arbitrary
position-pair $(i, j) \in L_x$ and k is the length of the underlying sequence Seq_c. As suggested in Sec. 4.1.2, the translational symmetry
of a sequence should be the value of the best chain it contains:

$$trans\_sym(Seq_c) = \max_{(t,L) \in \mathcal{C}_c''} v^{ts}(Seq_c, t) \tag{4.10}$$

REFLECTIONAL SYMMETRY, as introduced in Sec. 4.1.2, oc-
curs when a chain $Cha = (a_i, a_{i+1}, \ldots, a_j)$ exists for $Seq_c = (a_0, a_1, \ldots, a_k)$, such that its inverse $Cha^{-1} = (a_j, a_{j-1}, \ldots, a_i)$ is also
a chain for Seq_c. An additional restriction is made here, which allows
Cha and Cha^{-1} to overlap in at most one element.[31]

Again, $\mathcal{C}_c$ needs to be obtained like above, as a representation of
all possible chains in sequence Seq_c. From this, only those chains are
relevant, for which an inverse chain exists that overlaps with it in at

---

[30]We assume, that the ordering from Seq_c has been retained when constructing
$\mathcal{C}_c$ and $\mathcal{C}_c'$.

[31]The overlap is important to detect symmetry in sequences like ABA, where
the axis of symmetry runs through an element, instead of between elements. The
restriction of overlap to at most 1 element prevents overly long chains like in the
case of sequence AAAA, where AAA could be considered a mirror symmetric chain
if an overlap of 2 were allowed.

most one element:

$$C_c^* = \left\{ (t_1, L) \mid (t_1, i_1, j_1) \in C_c \wedge \exists (t_2, i_2, j_2) \in C_c : (t_2^{-1} = t_1) \wedge (i_2 \geq j_1) \right.$$

$$\wedge\, L = \bigcup_{\substack{(t_1,i_1,j_1),\\ (t_2,i_2,j_2) \in C_c:\\ (t_2^{-1}=t_1)\wedge(i_2 \geq j_1)}} \left\{ \left((i_1, j_1), (i_2, j_2) \right) \right\} \left. \right\}$$

which results in a set of 2-tuples, where the first element is a valid reflective chain, and the second element is a set of paired 2-tuples, each containing (begin-index, end-index) position-pairs of a chain instance and its reflected instance. To exemplify this, let us apply these formalizations to the sequence ABABBA with a focus only on the chain AB. The set of all chains would contain the following relevant entries: $C_c = \{((A, B), 0, 1), ((A, B), 2, 3), ((B, A), 4, 5), \dots\}$. As becomes apparent, the original chain is represented by two elements, and its inverse by another. This is combined into one object in the set of valid chains:

$$C_c^* = \left\{ \left((A, B), \{((0, 1), (4, 5)), ((2, 3), (4, 5))\} \right), \dots \right\}$$

The reflectional symmetry value of a chain is determined by the number of elements from the original sequence that are included in all instances of the chain and its inverse, normalized by the total number of elements in the sequence. Given the sequence Seq_c and the corresponding set $C_c^* = \{(t_1, L_1), (t_2, L_2), \dots\}$:

$$v^{rs}(Seq_c, t_x) = \sum_{\substack{((m_1,n_1),\\ (m_2,n_2))\\ \in L_x}} \frac{\#\left(f^{chain}(Seq_c, m_1, n_1) \cup f^{chain}(Seq_c, m_2, n_2) \right)}{\#Seq_c}$$

and the reflectional symmetry value of the whole sequence is then:

$$refl\_sym(Seq_c) = \max_{(t,L) \in C_c^*} v^{rs}(Seq_c, t) \tag{4.11}$$

Parallelism

As outlined in Sec. 4.1.2, parallelism occurs when a chain $Cha = (a_i, a_{i+1}, \dots, a_j)$ in one character's sequence $Seq_{c1} = (a_0, a_1, \dots, a_k)$

also appears in another character's sequence $Seq_{c2} = (b_0, b_1, \ldots, b_p)$.
Here, the set of all possible chains needs to be obtained for both
sequences—like above—giving us $\mathcal{C}_{c1}$ and $\mathcal{C}_{c2}$. Let's assume w.l.o.g
that $\#Seq_{c1} \leq \#Seq_{c2}$. We can define the set of all parallel chains:

$$\mathcal{C}_{c1,c2} = \{(Cha, i, j) \mid (Cha, i, j) \in \mathcal{C}_{c1} \wedge \exists (Cha, \_, \_) \in \mathcal{C}_{c2}\}$$

and compute the parallelism value of a chain using the function:
$v^p(Seq_{c1}, Cha) = \#Cha/\#Seq_{c1}$. Then, the parallelism score for a
pair of analyzed character subgraphs is:

$$para(Seq_{c1}, Seq_{c2}) = \max_{(t,\_,\_) \in \mathcal{C}_{c1,c2}} v^p(Seq_{c1}, t) \tag{4.12}$$

This value needs to be computed for each possible 2-combination of
characters.

Note, that the parallelism value is always computed with respect
to the smaller of the two sequences, it is thus possible to achieve high
parallelism values even in those cases when the best chain covers only
a small part of the larger sequence. This decision was made in order
to be able to achieve parallelism scores of one even in those (common)
cases when character sequence pairs differ in length. It remains to be
ascertained, whether this is desirable overall.

Overall

The overall semantic P&S score for a plot is the average over all of
the above values:

$$p\&s(G) = \cfrac{\displaystyle\sum_{G_c \in G} \big(trans\_sym(Seq_c) + refl\_sym(Seq_c)\big) + \displaystyle\sum_{\{c1,c2\} \in [C]^2} para(Seq_{c1}, Seq_{c2})}{2 \times \#C + \binom{\#C}{2}} \tag{4.13}$$

where C is the set of all of character participating in G, and $[C]^2$
is the set of all 2-combinations from C. The denominator, here, is
simply the number of the individual scores in the numerator: two
symmetric scores per character: $2 \times \#C$, and one parallelism score
per possible 2-combination of characters: $\binom{\#C}{2}$.

The individual computations for symmetry and parallelism
are implemented in the class `inBloom.helper.SymmetryAnalyze`
`r`, while the combination and normalization of these measures is

performed in `Tellability#detectSymmetryAndParallelism(Plot DirectedSparseGraph graph)`.

The above computation is implemented in the class `inBloom.grap h.CountingVisitor#getSuspense()` which, among others, is called by `Tellability#computeSimpleStatistics(PlotDirectedSparse Graph graph)`.

4.2.3. Computing Semantic Opposition

VIOLATED EXPECTATIONS, as I outlined in Sec. 4.1.3, is the first form of semantic opposition and consists of two parts. The number of invalid or substituted beliefs n_c^{-b} can be determined by counting the number of termination edges whose destination vertices are of the type perception. Let G be an analyzed plot graph, and $G_c = (V_c, E_c, l_v, l_e, prop) \in G$ be an analyzed character subgraph (w.l.o.g.), then:

$$n_c^{-b} = \#\{(v_1, v_2) \mid$$
$$(v_1, v_2) \in E_c \wedge l_v(v_2) \in \{P, P+, P-\} \wedge l_e((v_1, v_2)) = t\}$$

The other part is $n_c^{rel\_em}$, the number of events that have been appraised by the emotions `relief` or `disappointment`:

$$n_c^{rel\_em} = \#\{v \mid v \in V_c \wedge (\texttt{relief} \in emotion(v) \vee$$
$$\texttt{disappointment} \in emotion(v))\}$$

where $emotion : V \to \mathcal{P}(OCC)$ denotes a function that maps a vertex to the set of emotions that it was appraised with. The overall number of violated expectations $viol\_exp_c$ for character c is thus the sum of these two measures. In order to normalize it into the range between zero and one, it needs to be divided by the overall number of beliefs n_c^{*b} and the overall number of affectively appraised events n_c^{em}:

$$n_c^{*b} = \#\{v \mid v \in V_c \wedge l_v(v) \in \{P, P+, P-\}\}$$
$$n_c^{em} = \#\{v \mid v \in V_c \wedge emotion(v) \neq \emptyset\}$$

and, finally:

$$viol\_exp(c) = \frac{n_c^{-b} + n_c^{rel\_em}}{n_c^{*b} + n_c^{em}} \tag{4.14}$$

CHANGES OF FORTUNE have been introduced as the second type of semantic opposition in Sec. 4.1.3. A change of fortune occurs when a character's current mood undergoes a significant change Δ_{int}^m, during a small period of time Δ_{int}^t, and also crosses at least one of the zero-axis of the PAD space during that time. Clearly, this information cannot be obtained from a plot graph, since it only contains discrete mood information. As outlined in Sec. 3.3.4, mood data for all characters is stored in a table-like structure implemented in the class `MoodMapper`, where rows represent agents, columns represent reasoning cycle numbers, and individual cells contain a `Mood` instance if the current mood of the respective agent changed during the respective cycle. Since moods do not need to change every cycle, the table can be expected to be sparsely populated. Let $mood_c : \mathbb{N} \to PAD$ be a function that returns the current mood of agent c at any reasoning cycle number, by sampling it from the table in `MoodMapper` as per Sec. 3.3.4, which means that the value is looked up in the table and if a value is not contained for that reasoning cycle number, then the current mood at that time is determined by the last present entry before it. Furthermore, let a simulation run begin with reasoning cycle 0 and end with reasoning cycle cyc_max. We can define the set of all intervals containing changes of fortune:

$$\mathcal{I}_c = \Big\{ (i, j, mood_c(i), mood_c(j)) \mid i, j \in \mathbb{N} \wedge 0 \le i \le cyc\_max \wedge i < j < i + \Delta_{int}^t$$
$$\wedge \exists_{dim \in \{p,a,d\}} : \Big| \pi_{dim}(mood_c(i)) - \pi_{dim}(mood_c(j)) \Big| \ge \Delta_{int}^m$$
$$\wedge \operatorname{sgn}\Big(\pi_{dim}(mood_c(i))\Big) \ne \operatorname{sgn}\Big(\pi_{dim}(mood_c(j))\Big) \Big\}$$

where π_p, π_a and π_d are functions that project a mood into the respective p, a and d dimension of the PAD space. Here, $\mathcal{I}_c$ is assembled as a set of 4-tuples, where each tuple represents a change of fortunes interval that begins at reasoning cycle i and ends at reasoning cycle j, and the respective moods at these points. This is realized by finding for all possible start-cycles i all possible end-cycles j such that these two cycles are at most Δ_{int}^t apart, and where a dimension dim exists in the PAD space for which the mood difference between cycles i and j is bigger than the threshold Δ_{int}^m, and where the sign of the mood at cycle i is different from the sign at cycle j. For all experiments performed as part of this thesis, Δ_{int}^m was set to 0.5, and Δ_{int}^t to 10.

The resulting set can be expected to contain multiple overlapping intervals, whenever a mood change between a peak and a low takes longer than Δ^t_{int}. For instance, focusing on only one dimension p, given the following development of the pleasure value over reasoning cycles (cycle number, p value): $(0, 0.4)$, $(5, 0.3)$, $(8, -0.1)$, $(9, -0.2)$ the set $\mathcal{I}_c$ would contain the intervals $(0, 8, 0.4, -0.1)$, $(0, 9, 0.4, -0.2)$ and $(5, 10, 0.3, -0.2)$, which should not be counted as three separate change of fortune intervals but as one. For this reason, overlapping intervals need to be filtered out from $\mathcal{I}_c$. The procedure here is the same as for filtering out overlapping translational symmetry chains. First, a total order needs to be imposed over the set. For this, the indexing functions g_c^{start} and g_c^{end}: $(\mathbb{N}, \mathbb{N}, [-1, 1], [-1, 1]) \rightarrow \mathbb{N}$ can be defined, which map each interval to its start, respectively end, cycle:

$$g_c^{start}\big((i, j, m_i, m_j)\big) = i$$
$$g_c^{end}\big((i, j, m_i, m_j)\big) = j$$

Then, the binary relation

$$\succeq: (\mathbb{N}, \mathbb{N}, [-1, 1], [-1, 1]) \times (\mathbb{N}, \mathbb{N}, [-1, 1], [-1, 1])$$

can be defined such that $interval_1 \succeq interval_2$ iff:

$$g_c^{start}(interval_1) > g_c^{start}(interval_2) \vee$$
$$\big(g_c^{start}(interval_1) = g_c^{start}(interval_2) \wedge$$
$$g_c^{end}(interval_1) \geq g_c^{end}(interval_2)\big)$$

which is used to induce the totally ordered set $(\mathcal{I}_c, \succeq)$.

Starting from the first interval in this ordered set, all subsequent intervals are removed whose begin-index is smaller or equal to the end-index of that first interval, until an interval is reached that does not overlap. Then, the process is repeated with this interval, until the complete set is processed in this way. The resulting set is denoted $\mathcal{I}'_c$, and its cardinality represents the number of changes of fortunes. To normalize this value, it can be divided by the number of changes of fortunes that would have been possible maximally: cyc_max/Δ^t_{int}:

$$fort\_cha(c) = \frac{\#\mathcal{I}'_c \times \Delta^t_{int}}{cyc\_max} \tag{4.15}$$

OVERALL, the semantic opposition score for a character is determined as the maximum of the two measures, as motivated in Sec. 4.1.3:

$$oppo(c) = \max\{viol\_exp(c), fort\_cha(c)\} \tag{4.16}$$

and the semantic opposition value for the whole plot is the maximum of the characters' values:

$$opposition(G) = \max_{G_c \in G} oppo(c) \qquad (4.17)$$

The counting necessary to compute the violated expectations measure is performed by the `CountingVisitor`, while the changes of fortune measure, as well as the aggregations are implemented in `Tellability#detectOpposition((PlotDirectedSparse Graph graph, MoodMapper moodData))`.

4.2.4. Computing Suspense

In Sec. 4.1.4 I have proposed to determine the suspense of a plot as the highest suspense observed over all intentions of that plot. The suspense of an intention is measured as the amount of plot time that has passed since a plan to satisfy this intention has been taken up, and the latest action of that plan (recursively including all actions that were executed as part of any sub-plan that was triggered along the way). Let $G = (V, E)$ be an analyzed plot graph and $v \in V$ be a vertex in that graph. We can define a motivational path MP as follows:

$$MP_G(v) = \{v\} \cup \bigcup_{\substack{\forall v_i \in V \\ \exists e = (v, v_i) \in E: \\ type(e, G) = a \\ \vee \, (type(e, G) = m \wedge type(v, G) = I)}} MP_G(v_i)$$

Thus, a motivational path is a set of all vertices of G that can be reached from v only by following a and m edges (which, naturally, includes v itself). For technical reasons, a further restriction is placed on the m edges that are allowed in motivational paths: they have to start from an I edge. This is done to exclude edge cases like: $[I] \xrightarrow{a} [+] \xrightarrow{m} [I]$, where the action that resolves an intention motivates a completely new intention. Note, that, in practice, analyzed plot graphs are always finite, and that cycles are impossible in the present setting because m as well as a edges always point in temporal direction, which makes the recursive definition in $MP_G(v)$ uncritical.

Based on this we can define a subtype of motivational paths, called intentional chains, where $\mathcal{IC}_G$ denotes the set of all intentional chains for an analyzed plot graph:

$$\mathcal{IC}_G^{pre} = \{MP_G(v) \mid v \in V \; \wedge \; type(v, G) = I\}$$
$$\mathcal{IC}_G = \{mp \mid mp \in \mathcal{IC}_G^{pre} \; \wedge \; \nexists mp_{larger} \in \mathcal{IC}_G^{pre} : mp \subset mp_{larger}\}$$

Thus, the set of intentional chains for a graph G is the set of all motivational paths that start from an intention vertex, and are not completely subsumed by a larger motivational path starting from an intention vertex.

We can then formalize the suspense of a motivational path as the difference in plot steps between the first and the last vertex on that path. W.l.o.g. let $Path = MP_G(v)$ be the motivational path for a vertex v from graph G:

$$suspense(Path) = \max_{v_i \in Path} step(v_i) - \min_{v_j \in Path} step(v_j)$$

where $step(v)$ denotes the plot step at which the event represented by vertex v took place. The suspense of the plot represented by G, then, is the maximal suspense over all the intentional chains of G. Again, it is necessary to normalize the suspense score in order to make plots of different lengths comparable. For this, it is divided by the plot length, that is the highest plot step number observed in vertices of the analyzed plot graph:

$$suspense(G) = \frac{\max\limits_{Path \in \mathcal{IC}_G} suspense(Path)}{\max\limits_{v \in V} step(v)} \tag{4.18}$$

The above computation is implemented in the class `inBloom.grap h.CountingVisitor#getSuspense()` which, among others, is called by `Tellability#computeSimpleStatistics(PlotDirectedSparse Graph graph)`.

4.2.5. Computing Overall Tellability as Aesthetic Balance

As discussed in Sec. 4.1.5, high does not necessarily mean good with regard to tellability principles. Instead, an aesthetic balance needs to be maintained by the individual scores to ensure a high overall tellability. The scores I have derived above are the following, each normalized into the $[0, 1]$ range:

- $polyvalence(G) = \frac{\#V_G^*}{\#V_G}$

- $p\&s(G) = \dfrac{\left(\sum\limits_{G_c \in G} \big(trans\_sym(Seq_c) + refl\_sym(Seq_c) \big) + \sum\limits_{\{c1,c2\} \in [C]^2} para(Seq_{c1}, Seq_{c2}) \right)}{2 \times \#C + \binom{\#C}{2}}$

- $opposition(G) = \max\limits_{G_c \in G} oppo(c)$

- $suspense(G) = \dfrac{\max\limits_{Path_i \in \mathcal{IC}_G} suspense(Path_i)}{\max\limits_{v \in V} step(v)}$

For the first three scores, I have suggested in Sec. 4.1.5 to measure their balancedness as a distance to a predefined threshold $\theta_{balance}$ (while arguing that the last one—suspense—does not need to be balanced). Throughout the thesis, I will employ the balance threshold of $\theta_{balance} = 0.5$, since it divides the original range of the tellability scores in two equally large halves. It should be noted that a low distance to the threshold is actually preferable to a high one, and should consequently result in a higher tellability, which means that we are looking for an inverse distance measure. Postulating that a distance of 0 should result in a balanced score of 1, one possibility would be of the form: $1 - |0.5 - x|$, where x is one of the tellability score to be balanced. A problem that arises with this formalization is a bifurcation of the possible range of tellability, which becomes $[1 - \theta_{balance}, 1]$. For this reason, the distance needs to be re-normalized into $[0, 1]$, leading to the following form of the balancing function:

$$balance(x) = 1 - \frac{1}{0.5}|0.5 - x| \qquad (4.19)$$

with $balance : [0, 1] \rightarrow [0, 1]$ (for a graphical representation, see Fig. 4.11).[32]

Using the balancing function in Equation 4.19, we can define the overall tellability of a plot, represented by an analyzed plot graph G,

---

[32]Beware that this formalization only works for $\theta_{balance} = 0.5$, while the general form $balance(x) = 1 - \frac{1}{\theta_{balance}}|\theta_{balance} - x|$ does not provide the required formalization for $\theta_{balance} \neq 0.5$.

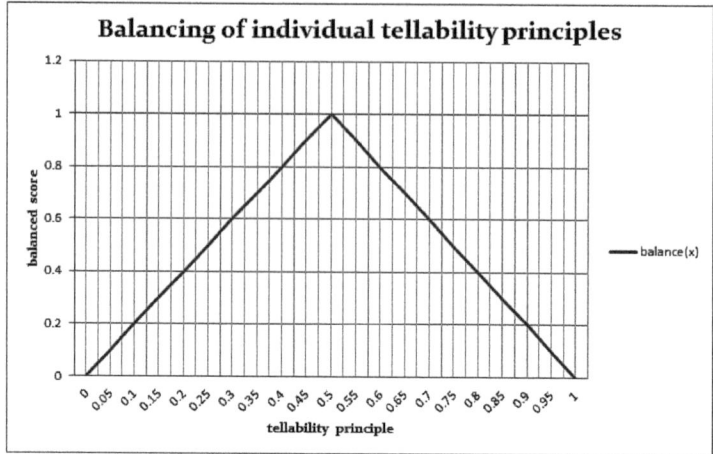

Figure 4.11: The development of the balancing function in dependence of a tellability scores that requires balancing. Note, that the function peaks at $\theta_{balance} = 0.5$.

as follows:

$$tellability(G) = \frac{\begin{array}{c} balance(polyvalence(G)) + balance(p\&g(G)) \\ + \, balance(opposition(G)) + suspense(G) \end{array}}{4}$$

$$(4.20)$$

based on Equations 4.8, 4.13, 4.17 and 4.18. This, again, results in a range of $[0, 1]$. The computation of balanced scores, as well as of the overall tellability function, is implemented in `Tellability#comp ute()`. With this, we have arrived at a quantifiable metric for plot quality and can now investigate how it fares when applied to the case study of TLRH.

4.3. The Case Study Explored

As I have admitted freely in the previous sections, Ryan's tellability principles are not derived from any sort of theoretical reasoning, and my implementation of them rests on several decisions about how to formalize underspecified concepts like 'parallelism' or 'change of fortunes' that could also be interpreted very differently. At the same time, the overall formula is fairly complicated and depends on a multitude of narratological phenomena and technological details which makes it impossible to estimate the behavior of the tellability function. It can thus not be taken for granted that the final scores computed by it will be a meaningful reflection of a plot's quality, as opposed to an arbitrary number. To quote parts of an anonymous review I received on an early version (Berov, 2017) of my tellability formalization: "I am also very sceptical that such a measure can be found at all [...]: the structure that the author describes would be too naive to provide any relevant computational measure of plot quality".

To get a feeling for the behavior of the individual tellability principles, I will first discuss in detail how the original plot of TLRH is evaluated by the system. Then, I will use tellability to rate several differing versions of the plot that can be generated by the narrative system of TLRH by varying the personality parameters of the participating agents. I share my reviewer's reservations about the existence of an objective measure of plot quality, so that the goal of this endeavor cannot be to quantifiably evaluate my implementation of tellability by comparing the ranking it produces with an ideal ranking (or even with a non-ideal, average ranking, solicited from experimental subjects). What remains to judge its worth, instead, is to qualitatively discuss whether the plot properties it condenses into different numbers are rooted in narratologically interesting structural differences, or irrelevant technical perturbations.

4.3.1. Analyzing TLRH Based on Tellability

InBloom was intentionally designed to contain no non-deterministic components because I did not want to give skeptics the option to attribute any appearance of creativity to randomness instead of intentional choice. However, the hard truth I had to learn was that in a multi-threaded MAS system some non-determinism is inevitable. While the plot generated under most parameter settings is reproducible, subtle differences in timing and agent coordination turned out to have a measurable effect on tellability. For this reason, the following scores were averaged over ten runs of InBloom's TLRH environment using the same settings (reported in Tab. 3.5), as implemented in the class `inBloom.stories.little_red_hen.Repeating RedHenLauncher`. This class executes a simulation until a narrative equilibrium is detected, automatically starts the tellability analysis and stores all the required scores. This is repeated until the desired number of runs is completed, and all the necessary statistics can be computed. For reasons that have eluded my scrutiny, the first of the simulation runs always exhibits outlier results regarding the suspense score. To pragmatically solve this problem, a dry run is always executed first, and not included into the evaluation metrics.

Tab. 4.1 shows the average and standard deviations for both, the absolute and the balanced score of each principle and the corresponding tellability: Beware, that during the runs executed by the

Table 4.1: Overview over the tellability principles' scores and the overall balanced tellability of the TLRH plot. Values are given as average ± standard deviation over 10 simulation runs.
FPo...functional   polyvalence   P&S...semantic   parallelism   and   symmetry
SOp...semantic opposition   Sus...suspense   Tell...tellability

	FPo	P&S	SOp	Sus	Tell
absolute	0.23 ±0.01	0.71 ±0.00	0.24 ±0.02	0.38 ±0.03	0.39 ±0.01
balanced	0.47 ±0.01	0.57 ±0.00	0.48 ±0.04	0.38 ±0.03	0.48 ±0.02

`RepeatingRedHenLauncher`, the GUI of the system is disabled in order to speed up the processing. This results in simulation runtime behavior and tellability scores that are different from the ones observed in a single run executed through the conventional `RedHenLauncher`. All inconsistencies attentive readers might have noted between the above numbers and the plot graph in Fig.3.9 or the mood graphs in Fig. 3.10 are due to the fact that the figures in the last chapter were produced by the latter launcher, while the current numbers were produced by the former.[33]

The value that is taken to represent the TLRH plot's quality by InBloom is balanced tellability, i.e. 0.48. Note, that the standard deviation indicates some variation in values between runs, but that these variations are fairly small. To get a better understanding of what these numbers mean, let us inspect how the system arrives at the individual absolute scores by reviewing its processing of an example run.

Functional Polyvalence

The functional unit analysis identifies an overall of 49 FU instances in the plot graph: 15 Denied Requests (DR), 26 Nested Goals (NG), 3

---

[33]It is unpleasant that an algorithmic difference like whether the GUI is displayed or not changes a narrative system's runtime behavior. However, it is an inevitable part of the multi-threaded architecture of Jason, or perhaps even all multi-threader Java programs.

Retaliations (Ret), 1 Sacrifice (Sac), 1 Fortuitous Problem Resolution (FPR) and 3 Successes from Adversity (SA).

Of the plot's overall 270 vertices, 87 are part of at least one FU instance, and of those 63 are polyvalent, resulting in an absolute functional polyvalence score of 0.23. The most polyvalent vertex is the intention `!create(bread)`, with a polyvalence score of 10.

In qualitative terms, these results are hard to place without the context of other plots. They suggest a fairly good coupling, since 72% of the vertices that are part of at least one FU instance are also polyvalent. The high polyvalence score of the vertex `!create(bread)` could be taken to suggest that this intention is a central hinging point of the plot, which connects its different parts. However, personally, I would dispute that this is as a plausible interpretation, and rather argue that it is a technical artefact, since this intention is part of each NG instance that is detected when the hen asks for help, and again for each NG instance that is detected when she performs the task herself. This, combined with the five-fold repetition of the tasks themselves artificially drives up the polyvalence score of this vertex. The second-most polyvalent vertex is the intention `!punish` with a value of 7. It is a more plausible candidate for central hinging point of the plot because it logically connects the repetitive plot part of the creation of the bread with the part where bread is withheld from the other animals as punishment, and indicates the hen's final success from adverse circumstances.

From a technological perspective, the number of detected FU instances and the number of different detected FUs is a good sign, since it indicates a reasonable flexibility of the implemented FU detection algorithm.

Semantic Parallelism and Symmetry

Since sufficient FU instances are present in the plot graph, the analysis of P&S is performed on the basis of FUs. The ordered FU instance sequence for each character is depicted in Tab. 4.2.

Table 4.2: FU sequences detected by InBloom in the TLRH plot.

Character	FU Sequence
hen	[NG, DR, DR, DR, NG, NG, DR, DR, DR, NG, NG, DR, DR, DR, NG, NG, DR, DR, DR, NG, NG, DR, DR, DR, NG, Ret, Ret, Ret, SA, SA, SA, Sac, NG, FPR]
dog	[DR, NG, DR, NG, DR, NG, DR, NG, DR, NG, Ret]
cow	[DR, NG, DR, NG, DR, NG, DR, NG, DR, NG, Ret]
pig	[DR, NG, DR, NG, DR, NG, DR, NG, DR, NG, Ret]

It clearly indicates three parallelism scores of 1.0 because the farm animals all have the same sequence of FU instances. The parallelism of the hen's sequence with each of the farm animal's sequences is computed as 0.27 based on the shared sequence: [DR, NG, Red], resulting in an average parallelism score of 0.63. The best translational chain for the hen is the sequence: [NG, DR, DR, DR, NG], which represents the hen asking for help, getting rejected by the other characters and finally performing her task herself. It is easy to see why this sequence appears multiple times and is indeed an effect of the plot's symmetry. The best reflectional chain for the hen is the FU instance sequence: [NG, DR, DR, DR, NG, NG, DR, DR, DR, NG, NG, DR, DR]. This sequence captures two and a half of the same ask-reject-do interactions as before, but instead of uncovering that they simply appear several times it focusses on the fact that also the internal structure of this interaction is mirror symmetric, combined with the fact that it appears five times in total, which allows for another level of macro-level reflectional symmetry. This results in a symmetry score of 0.75, for the hen.

The best translational chain is the same for each of the other animals: [DR, NG], capturing the events around being asked for help and rejecting that request. The best reflectional chain for the other animals is: [DR, NG, DR, NG, DR], again capturing two and a half instance of the ask-reject interaction. In terms of symmetry, for the other animals, this results in a normalized score of 0.86. All together, an average symmetry score of 0.84 is achieved, and an absolute P&S score of 0.72.

These values are fairly high, and draw attention to the parallelization and the repetitions so typical for fairy tales: The three farm animals are exact copies of each other and thus their behavior is similar. At the same time, the hen asks the animals for help five times, and gets rejected five times in much the same manner, which is responsible for the very high intra-character symmetry scores for all characters. Indeed, the absolute P&S score is by far the highest of the three absolute scores and applying the balancing reduces its value significantly, effectively punishing the plot for the high level of structural self-similarity.

Semantic Opposition

The number of violated expectations for Little Red Hen, as determined by InBloom, is 6: four times when her help request is rejected by one of the other animals while her mood is not yet hostile (which means that the rejections are appraised with `disappointment`), and two times from the terminated beliefs: `has(bread)` and `hungry`. Since the overall number of relevant events for her is 85, her normalized opposition score due to violated expectations is fairly low at 0.07. For the other characters, the only violated expectation is when the hen asks them to help her eat some bread but doesn't share any bread (resulting in an affective appraisal with `disappointment`). Combined with an overall of 33 relevant events, their opposition score from violated expectations is even lower at 0.03. The number of non-overlapping fortune change intervals for Little Red Hen is determined to be 8, starting at the reasoning cycles: $54, 105, 153, 173, 204, 224, 254$ and 274. Five of these intervals occur when the hen asks for help during each of the steps of the plan to create bread, and gets rejected by everyone, which results in a significant drop along the pleasure dimension as well as a significant rise along the arousal dimension of the PAD space. The remaining three intervals occur respectively as a result of the hen's harvest, grind and bake actions which all lead to several positive emotions that significantly drive up her mood along the pleasure dimension. The maximal number of non-overlapping interval changes that would have been possible in this plot is 32, leading to a normalized opposition score from changes of fortunes of 0.25. According to the system, the three other characters do not experience any changes of fortunes. The way InBloom aggregates semantic opposition scores means that the maximal score, i.e. the normalized number of changes of fortunes for the hen character, determines the plot's absolute opposition score.

This analysis results draw attention to several important properties of the plot. One is that Little Red Hen is the most interesting of the four characters involved because she is the one that faces the most opposition. Classically, this would indicate that she is best suited for the role of main protagonist for the plot, since it is usually the protagonist who has to face adversity. Assuming that readers of the story develop a positive emotional disposition towards the hen, choosing her as the protagonist[34] would induce the most emotional

---

[34]This is of course confounded with the question of whether the hero of the plot is also the main focalizer of the discourse, as otherwise readers might be barred from access to the hen's internal states. The generation of discourse is explicitly not addressed in this thesis, but this interaction effect is a good example of the

effect on readers, given that they experience empathy and sympathy to the main character, as discussed in the last chapter in Sec. 3.1.3. At the same time, semantic opposition helps detect parts of the plot which are characterized either by violated expectations or by strong changes of affect, and by that merit could be regarded as points of interest for the plot. It is also interesting to note that although the fundamental difference of the hen from the other characters was theoretically known to the system because of their different personalities, semantic opposition uncovers that this difference also has an important impact on the plot: while the hen exhibits fairly strong changes of affect because of what happens to her, the other animals remain stoic throughout the plot.

Suspense

The longest intentional chain detected by InBloom is located in the hen's character subgraph. It starts with the intention `!create(brea d)`, runs through the various help requests as well as farming actions and finishes with the action `bake(bread)`. This results in a path suspense of 4 plot steps and since the overall length of the plot is 10 steps, an absolute suspense of 0.4.

Given the understanding of suspense adopted by this thesis, it seems semantically plausible to assign the highest suspense value to the intention of creating bread. By this, it is highlighted as the central motivator behind the plot's action.

4.3.2. Comparing Plots Based on Tellability

In the previous chapter I reported seven manually discovered personality parameter configurations of the narrative system, which lead to alternative plots (i.e. counterfactual plots to the original TLRH plot), summarized in Tab. 3.6. These plots can be analyzed and compared based on their balanced tellability principle scores, as well as the balanced overall tellability.

Tellability Based Ranking

The first question is whether the differences in plot actually lead to significant differences in tellability, and if yes, in how far the resulting ranking coincides with an intuitive quality-ranking of these plots.

---

difficult interrelation of these two elements of narratives.

Table 4.3: Overview over the balanced tellability principles' scores and the overall balanced tellability of several plots generated by the narrative system of TLRH. Plots are generated using the parameters reported in Tab. 3.6, and the values for each plot are given as average $\pm$ standard deviation, over 10 simulation runs. Ordered by tellability in decreasing order.

FPo...functional polyvalence   P&S...semantic parallelism and symmetry   SOp...semantic opposition   Sus...suspense   Tell...tellability

Plot #	FPo	P&S	SOp	Sus	Tell	Plot Summary
8	0.46 ±0.01	0.90 ±0.00	0.72 ±0.08	0.67 ±0.01	0.69 ±0.02	Dog and pig help hen, hen shares with everyone
7	0.43 ±0.01	0.95 ±0.02	0.56 ±0.06	0.69 ±0.04	0.66 ±0.02	Dog helps hen, no punishment, no sharing
4	0.45 ±0.01	0.62 ±0.00	0.62 ±0.04	0.35 ±0.06	0.51 ±0.02	Hen shares bread despite refused help requests
1	0.47 ±0.01	0.57 ±0.01	0.48 ±0.04	0.38 ±0.03	0.48 ±0.02	Original plot
3	0.45 ±0.02	0.54 ±0.00	0.42 ±0.00	0.43 ±0.05	0.46 ±0.01	Hen eats bread alone, but no punishment
5	0.20 ±0.01	0.69 ±0.00	0.23 ±0.02	0.31 ±0.02	0.36 ±0.01	Hen doesn't ask for help, shares bread
6	0.08 ±0.00	0.79 ±0.01	0.13 ±0.00	0.40 ±0.00	0.35 ±0.00	Hen doesn't ask for help, doesn't share bread
2	0.00 ±0.00	0.82 ±0.00	0.00 ±0.00	0.00 ±0.00	0.2 ±0.00	Everyone relaxes, no plot

Tab. 4.3 reports the scores for all of the plots, including the original, ordered by balanced overall tellability. It proves that the tellability implementation of InBloom is indeed sensitive to differences in plot, and shows that four clusters of plots with roughly similar overall tellability emerge.

- The first cluster contains two plots (#8 and #7)[35], where either one or two of the farm animals help the hen instead of rejecting her requests.

- The second cluster contains the original plot (#1) as well as two other plots (#3 an #4), which run the gamut of potential reactions of the hen to being rejected by all the other animals.

- The third cluster contains the two plots where the hen doesn't ask for help (#5 and #6): one where she afterwards shares the bread with the others, and one where she doesn't.

- The last cluster contains only plot #2, where the hen does nothing while the other animals relax.

A first observation is that plots in the same cluster (i.e. with comparable overall tellability) do seem more similar than plots in different clusters, with their similarities being pointed out in the itemized list

---

[35]Remember, that the events of these plots cannot be chosen freely, but depend on the personality parameters of the involved characters. The personality parameters that lead to each of the plots are reported in Tab. 3.6.

above. Furthermore, intra-cluster differences in overall tellability are fairly low so I do not think that intra-cluster order is a meaningful reflection of differences in plot quality. Thus, a natural focus of discussion is inter-cluster order. Although this ordering is not completely in line with my intuitive expectations, it also does not strike me as implausible. I fully agree with the positioning of the last two clusters: Cluster four represents basically a non-plot, a succession of events that has no point, no cohesion and no overarching structure. Cluster three contains plots that I would rate slightly better: there is an underlying intention that drives the action forward, but the plots suffer from a lack of interaction between the characters, as well as low adversity. It is the order of clusters two and one that I would intuitively have reversed because cluster two contains the original plot of TLRH, which I would expect to exhibit the highest tellability, as it is the version that has prevailed over many oral and written retellings to become a well known folktale.[36] At the same time, I do not see any of the obvious problems of clusters three or four in cluster one, which would give me tangible reason to actively disagree with the proposed algorithmic ranking.

Analyzing Plots via Tellability

The second question, which is the more interesting of the two, is to what extent the different tellability principle scores help uncover the qualitative differences between the different plots. This will also shed more light on why—at least according to InBloom's tellability—the original plot is of lesser value than some of its alternative versions. But lets begin our analysis of the plots' qualities and shortcomings from below.

PLOT #2, AS I HAVE ARGUED REPEATEDLY, might even be considered a non-plot. So why does the system assign it a balanced

---

[36]What makes this argument problematic is that a narrative's evolutionary success is dependent on more than just the quality of its plot. Particularly with folktales, another factor of prime importance is the moral, which might well change due to differences in plot, but is not measured by tellability because it is a concept located on a completely different level of interpretation (see Sec. 1.2 for details on levels of interpretation). However, disentangling plot quality from the quality of the message conveyed by that plot might be already too analytical to be considered part of one's *intuitions* about a story, for which reason I decided to keep my justification as it is.

tellability score above zero? It should be pointed out that three of four tellability principles are actually rated zero, which captures the plot's shortcomings quite well: it contains absolutely no adversity (semantic opposition is zero), has no cohesion (functional polyvalence is zero) as well as no functional structure (no FU instances detected) and lacks a driving force (suspense is zero).

What tellability it has stems from semantic P&S: since no FU instances are detected, parallelism and symmetry are measured based simply on the actions of the participating characters, and on this superficial level the plot indeed exhibits a certain, but not excessive, level of self-similarity (i.e. organization). In fact, one might come up with a hypothetical alternative plot, where all characters would always follow random intentions that are instantly successfully actualized by their actions, which would result in a lower balanced P&S score and be even less tellable than our TLRH version #2. From this perspective, a non-zero tellability seems a justifiable reminder of that plot's meager but existing qualities.

THE PLOTS OF THE THIRD CLUSTER, #5 AND #6, differ only by the fact that in the former the hen shares her food, while in the latter she does not, and their overall tellability is nearly the same. However, the individual tellability principles paint a more nuanced picture. An interesting difference is uncovered by functional polyvalence (0.20 vs. 0.08): the act of sharing food is an interaction point between the cast of characters and a necessary cohesive element driving up both, the number of FU instances and functional polyvalence. Such a point for convergence between the different characters subgraphs is completely lacking in plot #6, which is a significant shortcoming. After all, why should several characters be included in a plot at all, if no interaction exists between their actions?

This question can be partly answered based on the semantic P&S values of the two plots (0.69 vs. 0.79): different characters can be of value even without interaction, if structural similarities exist between them. However, this insight comes with a caveat: one of the factors that contributes to the higher P&S score of the latter plot is that without the sharing-action it lacks sufficient FU instances in order to qualify for similarity analysis on the FU level, which leads to the analysis being undertaken on the event level. This makes the P&S score harder to compare to plot #5 (but easier to compare to

#2). However, sharing does lead to a break of structural similarity towards the end of plot #5, so technological details are not the only contributing factor to the higher P&S score of plot #6.

Another effect of the sharing of bread is that plot #5 takes much longer to conclude than plot #6 (18 steps vs. 11), while not affecting the actualization of both plot's main intention—the creation of bread. This leads to the lower suspense of the former plot (0.31 vs. 0.4). It seems debatable whether this is a technical artefact, or an useful indication that the latter of the two plots is more focused.

The difference in semantic opposition between the two plots (0.23 vs. 0.13), on the other hand, is only a technical artefact. It stems from the fact that the only opposition in both plots comes from two terminated beliefs: the belief to be hungry and the belief to possess bread, which are terminated when a character eats bread. In case of plot #6, this happens only to the hen who experiences many relevant events due to her prolific activity, while in plot #5 it also happens to the dog who experiences less relevant events, which leads to a higher normalized opposition (and, in fact, suggests that the protagonist of this story should be the dog and not the hen). From a narratological perspective I do not think that any of the two plots contains more than traces of semantic opposition, and that the terminated beliefs detected by the system are not valid instances of violated expectations.

A COMPARISON OF THE THREE PLOTS DISCUSSED ABOVE WITH THE FIVE REMAINING PLOTS exhibits a crucial difference in their functional polyvalence values (which lie below 0.2 for the former, but around 0.45 for the latter versions). The reason for this lies in the additional interactions between the characters in the remaining five plots, where the hen repeatedly asks for assistance with her chores. These repeating requests force the other animals to react, which results in a higher entanglement and thus higher cohesion than in the previously discussed plots. It is also a sign of tighter plotting, which means that more events form causal chains and cannot be removed without changing the remainder of the plot.[37] This causal connect-

---

[37]It is interesting to note that in order to detect such causal chains readers need to consider counterfactual plots where certain settings and events differ from the plot under consideration, in order to decide which events depend on which. By doing that they explore a space of possible plots much like the one explored

edness reaches its culmination in plot #1 (where the hen's retaliation is a consequence of the other characters' adverse behavior towards her) and plot #8 (where the sharing is a consequence of their help). Coincidentally, these are also the plots with the highest functional polyvalence scores (0.47 and 0.46), although the observed standard deviation does not allow ruling out that this is just the result of stochastic variations.

PLOTS #4 AND #1 HAVE ONE NOTEWORTHY DIFFERENCE, in their semantic opposition scores (0.62 vs. 0.48). In both cases, the opposition scores are derived from the number of change of fortunes intervals of the hen, but the former case has two more intervals than the latter. This is not an effect of differing actions or happenings between the two plots, but a direct consequence of the differing personality parameters of the hen character. Plot #4 is generated based on a higher agreeableness trait for the hen. This significantly shifts her default mood (leading to higher default pleasure and arousal values, but lower default dominance, as compared to the original version), which results in her change of fortunes intervals being based on pleasure and dominance crossing the zero-axis instead of pleasure and arousal. As I have reported in Sec. 3.4.3, readers are able to infer personality profiles that correspond to the personality parameters of InBloom from the plots it generates. It is an interesting question whether they would also be able to infer different affective reactions to comparable events based on such differences in personalities. This also draws attention to the fact that tellability was conceived by Ryan as a function not only of the actual domain, but also of the virtual M.-L. Ryan (1991, p. 156), and that this property is supported by InBloom.

THE PLOTS OF THE FIRST CLUSTER ARE EVALUATED BETTER THAN THE PLOTS OF THE SECOND CLUSTER along two tellability principles: functional P&S (~0.93 vs. ~0.58) and suspense (~0.68 vs. ~0.39). The reason for the former is that in cluster two the farm animals all share the same personality traits and exhibit the same behavior, while in cluster one at least one of the animals has different traits from the others and, consequently, behaves differently. As a result, the stories of cluster two are highly parallel (the overall parallelism sore of e.g. plot #1 is 0.64 and its normalized P&S score is 0.72), while

---

here by InBloom.

in cluster one the parallels between the farm animal are reduced (for instance plot #7 has an overall parallelism score of 0.30 and a normalized P&S of 0.53). Thus, the tellability system judges plots from cluster two as overly parallel and penalizes their P&S scores, while the P&S score of cluster one is nearly balanced and is boosted. This is also the main reason why the plots from cluster one are evaluated better by InBloom than the original plot of TLRH. I appreciate this finding, since from a purely plot-centered perspective the triplication of the farm animals in the original folktale seems superfluous. Ryan's credo is to: "seek the diversification of possible worlds in the narrative universe" (M.-L. Ryan, 1991, p. 156), and the narrative universe is diversified when the farm animals behave differently. This does not take into account genre-specific tropes and conventions, which for folktales postulated the triplication of characters and tasks, but rightly so, since this is an inter-textual concern that can affect the plot but is not governed by the rules of plot aesthetics.

Tracking down the difference in suspense is a trickier task. The most suspenseful intention remains the same in all plots of clusters one and two, but the details differ. For instance, in plot #7 the intention takes 16 steps to completion and the overall plot has a length of 23, while in plot #1 the same intention takes 4 steps and the overall plot has a length of 10. From this it is evident that whatever prolongs the plot must happen mostly during the duration of the intention to create bread. Since the personality and behavior of the hen is the same in both plots, the difference must come from the animal whose parameters were changed. My hypothesis is that the culprit is the help action that is executed by the changed animal after each help request. While the hen's activity during the creation of bread does not wait for this help to be executed, she still perceives the additional actions which forces her reasoning cycle to process additional events and delays the processing of events related to her main intention. This assumption is supported by the fact that in plot #8, where two animals execute help actions, the length of the intention as well as the overall plot is increased again. Unfortunately I see no other means of investigating this question, so the offered explanation must be viewed with caution. If it is correct, the difference would be infelicitous since it stems merely from technical details instead of valid narratological properties of the analyzed plots.

THE REMAINING DIFFERENCE IS BETWEEN PLOTS #8 AND #7, and is rooted in their semantic opposition scores (0.72 vs. 0.56) which are based on the change of fortunes intervals of the hen. In the former plot each help request is rejected once and fulfilled twice. Thus, positive emotions accumulate over time and the hen's mood oscillates around the zero-axis only along the dominance dimension. In the latter plot the situation is reversed: the hens request is accepted once and rejected twice. This leads to a mix of negative emotions from the rejections and positive emotions from successful farming, which leads to an oscillation of the hen's mood along the pleasure dimension while her dominance remains fairly high. The dynamics of the current mood are fairly complex and hard to correlate with particular events, but these differences seem to lead to more changes of fortune in the case where two animals help. I am not sure, in how far this should be regarded a valid narratological difference or a technical artefact.

SUMMARIZING, the implemented tellability measure is capable of uncovering several differences between the alternative plots that are narratologically plausible and interesting. At the same time, it also is sensitive to differences that are caused by technical properties of the implementation and should not be regarded as relevant. In the present case study, out of ten differences I analyzed five turned out to be narratologically plausible, two turned out to be implausible and the remaining three could not be placed. Furthermore, due to multi-threading the overall balanced tellability score of one and the same configuration might vary slightly between different runs.

This means that small differences in tellability should not be necessarily considered expressive. Instead, plots with similar tellability can be grouped into clusters, and the ranking can then be performed over clusters. After analyzing the reasons why the original plot has not been included in the first cluster, I also conclude that InBloom's ranking of plot clusters in the narrative system of TLRH appears plausible to me, which indicates the viability of the present implementation as well as Ryan's version of the concept itself (if only for the present case study).

4.3.3. Discussion of Tellability and its Implementation

A system that can only generate plots cannot function as a creative agent, since it lacks the means for deciding which of its outputs to scrap and which to keep, or even just when to stop generating. In computational creativity theory (see Sec. 1.3 for an overview) this creative responsibility as called *aesthetic analysis* and forms one of four main types of tasks for a CC system. Thus, the motivation behind this chapter was to find and formalize a measure of plot quality that could allow InBloom to choose the 'best' plot from a set of plots it can produce. However, it would be unreasonable to expect such a measure to represent an objective ground truth, simply because literary aesthetics are not governed by objective laws. Hence, the real value of an evaluation function for a plot composition system does not lie in the ranking it can produce, but rather in the analysis that it needs to perform in order to arrive at this ranking. If such an analysis is derived from narratologically meaningful features and is capable of detecting plausible instances of them in a plot, then it provides the system with the means to offer an explanation of why it chooses a particular story over others, and by that can contribute to its appearance of intentionality and creativity. This creative responsibility has been described as *framing*, another of the four tasks of creative systems according to CC theory, and has been recently even argued to be the new frontier of CC research (M. Cook et al., 2019). This lead me to dedicate the third cycle of generative modeling to Ryan's formal part of tellability, since it promised to be an interpretable measure of plot quality.[38] A risky endeavor, since the notion is not derived from an underlying general narratological theory, is not specified in sufficient detail to be straightforwardly quantified, was never systematically tested and—which might be worst—in the case of failure would quite likely fail in most evident and absurd ways. These problems demonstrate that potential benefits of this iteration of generative modeling lie not only on the side of computational creativity, but also on the narratological side.

Hence, before I come to an discussion of technical (de-)merits, I will first present some conceptual insights that follow for me from the performed implementation.

---

[38]This may not seem to be noteworthy from a literary perspective, but for readers from AI—who by 2020 are most likely well habituated to deep learning system that learn to magnanimously proclaim numerical qualities of texts or images based on unspeakable statistical properties learned from millions of examples and hidden in a black box of billions of parameters—this might be a welcome diversion.

Conceptual Insights

The most general (and to me, surprising) insight is that I consider the third iteration of my generative modeling process a success. Although the implemented metric was in parts sensitive to phenomena that should not be considered narratologically relevant, in general it created a plausible structuring of the plot space in terms of plot quality. The analysis it provided for favoring the plots of one cluster over the others is cogent and a plot selected on this basis could prove a reasonable foundation for a narrative. Thus, it can be used as the basis for the next iteration.

Furthermore, I want to stress the point that tellability analysis, as formalized in this chapter, is not limited to InBloom. The computation of balanced tellability scores depends on two data structures: an analyzed plot graph (as formalized in Def. 12) and a mood graph (which is a function of time into a three dimensional space over real numbers). Any system that can translate its outputs into these two graphs can use tellability to evaluate the structural quality of its plots. As a rule of thumb, applicability can be considered for plot composition systems that support the generation of at least the following narrative phenomena:

- temporality: the system needs to be able differentiate the story time at which events take place,

- intentionality: the system needs to represent characters' intentions, track which actions are associated with which intention, and realize when an event finalizes an intention,

- short-term-affectivity: the system needs to be able to identify whether characters affectively appraise pertinent events as positive or negative for them (i.e. emotions),

- mid-term-affectivity: the system needs to quantify the development of characters' affective state (i.e. mood) over time,

- causality: the system needs to be able to identify causal connections between events.

The concrete representation of these phenomena does not need to match the way they are modeled in InBloom, however, the farther they depart the more adaptations to the formalization of the individual tellability scores will be required. For instance, a change of the types of causality relations representable by a system would require a redefinition of functional unit graphs, and a departure from representing mood using the PAD space would require an adjustment in the way change of fortune intervals are computed.

FROM THIS SUCCESS, TWO INSIGHTS FOLLOW. One is that Ryan's approach proved to be justifiable. As I explained at the beginning of this chapter she developed her tellability principles by transferring formal aesthetic properties from poetry into the narrative domain, a move for which neither a reason nor a justification of its validity was provided. This justification can now be added post-hoc, since in the end it yields an operationalizable metric.

The second is that a highly underspecified and abstract narratological concept like tellability can be formalized in a way that is concrete enough to allow its quantification, without overly diluting the results through the introduction of formal or technological artefacts. This can be beneficial for narratologists for several reasons. A computational operationalization of a concept like tellability allows to analyze many more plots in much more meticulous and reproducible ways than are available to the theorist. Through this, the properties and implications of the concepts can be explored by applying it to minimally different plots and comparing the analysis results. It also opens the door to even more automatized approaches, like adversarial testing: The ability to quantify tellability allows to exploit the great capability of computers to optimize scores through machine learning. Different approaches, like reinforcement learning or genetic algorithms, can be trained to systematically vary the plot-generating system's parameters in order to identify the most tellable configurations. A manual analysis of these optimized plots can then lead to the detection of aberrant but legal configurations, and thus suggest ways how the underlying measure falls short of its goals. Performing such an exploration manually seems theoretically possible, but practically daunting and vulnerable to inconsistencies. For the claim that the computational approach is possible, on the other hands, I have anecdotal evidence. I supervised a bachelor's thesis on the topic of exploring the tellability space using nature inspired algorithms, that started out using an incomplete versions of the tellability score that only computed functional polyvalence, suspense and semantic P&S, without balancing the individual scores. Quickly, the employed algorithms learned that they could maximize tellability by interrupting the actualization of the character's first intention by presenting it again and again with the same urgent happening, effectively driving up suspense and symmetry, while doing nothing to improve the actual plot quality. From this I was reminded about the great importance of balancing the individual tellability scores (a circumstance that is treated very briefly by Ryan), and could resolve this problem by implementing the solution introduced above.

AS THE OPINION OF THE ANONYMOUS REVIEWER, that I recalled above, demonstrates, it is by no means a given that underspecified and abstract concepts from narrative theory can be operationalized at all. Decisions that have to be made at lower (implementational) levels of abstraction are often strongly governed by formal-technological constraints, which can distort properties at higher (narratological) levels. One recent instance where this problem has been observed is reported by Spendlove and Ventura (2020), who describe a machine-learning approach for the generation of six-word stories. The work represents the high-level concept 'narrative' as a hierarchically structured artifact based on the elementary structure 'word'. Based on this formalization, it applies a specialized type of Bayesian statistics to model narratives as factorized joint probability distributions over words. Training consists in inferring such a distribution from a corpus of six-word stories, and new stories can be generated by sampling from that distribution. After conducting an empirical survey, the authors conclude that it demonstrates "that a handful of [...] stories achieve coherence [...], however the majority do not. Very few of its stories are both coherent and impactful". An example coherent story reported in the work would be: "To him, 'endlessly' meant 'twenty decades"', while the only reported coherent and impactful story is: "Diamond ring. Glassy diamond. Costliest engagement". These high-quality examples only represent instances of the genus narrative (as I conceptualize it), if they are given a very benevolent reading. At the same time, human examples of this format exist that I would never hesitate to call narratives, such as the infamous "For sale: baby shoes, never worn" attributed to Ernest Hemingway, or "Goodbye, mission control. Thanks for trying" reported in the paper. My interpretation of these results is that modeling six-word narratives using Bayesian statistics lead to a focus on probabilistic surface properties that obscure latent properties of narratives rather than uncovering them.

The tellability implementation employed here, in contrast, focused primarily on underlying properties of the plot, which had to be uncovered by analyzing its causal structure. Given the nature of plot, this requires an understanding of the dynamics of concepts like event-based causality, intentionality and affectivity. Manually encoding this knowledge in declarative form as a set of rules (or even automatically extracting them from narrative texts like attempted by Goyal, Riloff, et al. (2013)) would have been a complicated and, most likely intractable, task. What allowed me to realize tellability analysis, nevertheless, was the fact that in InBloom the system that analyzes plot quality is directly connected to the system that maintains the 'objective reality' of the story world (the TAW). This way, instead of manually deriving general metaphysical rules about the story world, I enabled it to capture and pass on this information itself, via the plot graph. The insight here is that even a purely structural analysis of plot quality requires semantic knowledge about the functioning of the story world, and this does not even include what Ryan calls a substantial analysis of plot quality (which would be concerned with properties like themes, settings or motifs; see p. 193 where this difference was first introduced). My hypothesis is that this might be one of the underlying reasons why simple statistical learning approaches to story analysis and generation, like Spendlove and Ventura (2020) and Goyal, Riloff, et al. (2013), failed: the underlying corpus as well as the employed models were not sufficient to learn this kind of information. A case in point is GPT-2 (Radford et al., 2019), a very deep transformer based network that was trained to perform the language modeling task, i.e. a predicting of the most likely next word given a preceding text, on 40GB of text from varied domains. As the authors surprisingly found, the resulting network was fairly successful at several text-based tasks that test world-knowledge and common-sense reasoning (for which it was not trained). At the same time, it was the first neural network approach known to me that was capable of occasionally generating coherent and interesting multi-paragraph narratives. This success was trumped by GPT-3 (Brown et al., 2020), an even larger network of the same design, trained on an even larger corpus. Its performance on question answering and reasoning tasks led the authors to assume that the network reached a complexity where it was able to extract and encode a significant amount of world knowledge from its input data. Again, this coincides with an impressive increase in story-generating capabilities.[39] Based on these observations as well as my experience with implementing tellability I would hypothesize that generating or analyzing plots requires some sort of encoded knowledge about ontological and metaphysical properties of the underlying story world. Additionally, the way tellability was conceptualized by Ryan indicates that a crucial role is played by a particular type of world knowledge concerned with the mental functioning of fictional characters (at least for the analysis of plot quality). This interconnection between the nature of narratives and metaphysical knowledge is what makes operationalizing concepts from narratology so hard in a computational setting.

COMING BACK TO MORE CONCRETE OBSERVATIONS, exploring the behavior of the individual (unbalanced) tellability principles on a small set of plots allowed me to revise my theoretical understanding of how high scores on these principles can be interpreted narratologically:

- *Functional polyvalence*: Two metrics are relevant here. A high number of FU instances indicates a *high coherence* of the plot, since it means that its individual elements are organized in meaningful structures. A high polyvalence indicates a *high cohesion*, since it means that the individual structures are well connected. This can be also understood as strong meta-causal[40] organization.

---

[39]Despite the impressive success of GPT-3 at generating narrative prose it is important to note that the system has no explicit model of what constitutes narratives or good narratives. Although it is possible to prompt GPT-3 to generate an explanation of why it generated a certain narrative, the resulting text would not be grounded in any understanding of the narrative itself or of narrative theory. It is thus not capable of performing the aesthetic analysis or framing tasks, at least not in good faith.

[40]I refer to this as meta-causality since in the present setting plots are causally organized by default: actions are only performed to actualize intentions, intentions are triggered by perceptions, and so on. High polyvalence indicates that causality also exists at the more abstract FU level, in the interventionist sense that removing one FU instance would lead to the removal of another FU instance, simply because they share common events (i.e. vertices in a plot graph).

- *Semantic P&S*: A high P&S score indicates a high level of *structural organization* that is not causal. This can be interpreted as a foregrounding of the plot's constructedness, which is a desirable property in some genres (e.g. post modern fiction) but not others.

- *Semantic opposition*: A high opposition score indicates that the plot contains a *high level of adversity* for at least one character, which might mean that some of its plans fail, that pleasant circumstances for it are terminated or negative circumstances introduced. This increases the likelihood that a plot has dynamic points (since violated expectations normally lead to strong affect) or external points (since events describing struggle or failure are inherently of more interest than events describing smooth sailing).

- *Suspense*: A high suspense score indicates the presence of a *central driving force* that underlies most of the plot's events, and consequently a strong focus.

My take-away from this is that not all of Ryan's tellability principles are equally important. Semantic P&S certainly is a bonus when it is present, but its absence would not constitute a serious problem for a plot. The same holds, to some extent, for suspense: while a central intention can add value to a plot, it is also possible to have a tellable plot where the protagonist has to react to frequently changing demands from its circumstances instead of following one overarching goal. An example of this can be found in the adventures of the stranded Robinson Crusoe in the eponymous novel by Daniel Defoe (1719), in which the protagonist's survival depends on him mastering the various challenges life on a desert island confronts him with. A balanced level of opposition seems more important to me, than the two previous principles, since it is hard to see a point in plots without adversity. When all endeavors of the characters succeed on first try, and no sudden changes of fortunes throw them off balance, the resulting events simply fail to be noteworthy, and thus not likely to illicit in readers emotions that are important for the consumption of fiction, like curiosity, surprise, or sympathy. The most important feature, however, is functional polyvalence since it focuses on the central property that makes a plot a plot: the causal structure it superimposes on a sequence of events. This property is part of my working definition of plot outlined in Def. 1, where it says that "the plot of a narrative is any causal network of happenings, actions and mental events [...]", and has been canonically illustrated by Forster:

> We have defined a story as a narrative of events arranged in their time-sequence. A plot is also a narrative of events, the emphasis falling on causality. "The king died and then the queen died," is a story. "The king died, and then the queen died of grief" is a plot. The time-sequence is preserved, but the sense of causality overshadows it.
>
> (Forster, [1927] 2002, p. 61)

IT IS NOTEWORTHY, that it was in order to determine functional polyvalence, that an analysis of plot graphs needed to be implemented that is capable of connecting that graph's vertices with edges that indicate different types of causal connections. Revising the original definition of (unanalyzed) plot graphs in Defs. 4 and 5 with this understanding in mind reveals that they would have been more aptly named 'story graphs'(in the Forsterian sense of that word) since they contain only temporal relations between events and do not capture the causal structure that is central for plots.[41] I would, in fact, maintain that the functional analysis described in Sec. 4.2.1, and required to generate analyzed plot graphs per Defs. 11 and 12, is the most important contribution of this chapter to the overall project, since, before that, the plot generator InBloom had no proper representational format of plot. The subsequent detection of FU instances and the computation of their overlap is a valuable addition since it allows lifting the systems analytical capabilities to the more abstract level of narratological functions, but even without these steps I think that an evaluation of story graph's 'plotness' would be possible based merely on the edges generated by functional analysis. The more edges are added to a sequence of vertices and the longer the resulting chains get, the stronger a sense of causal organization can emerge from the underlying events. I do not attempt to formalize and evaluate such a measure here, anymore, since it would not further my project's progress in the right direction, but think that it's an auspicious avenue for future work. The difference, then, between the mere presence of edges and the presence of edges in certain configurations (i.e. FUs)

---

[41]I debated whether it would not be more prudent to revise the thesis and simply rename the concepts and definitions in question. If this were a more classical computer science thesis I certainly would have done so, and pretended that I knew all along. But given the decision to organize this document as a record of hermeneutic circles I decided against it. I think being able to openly disclose that the cycle completed here changed parts of my previous understanding is an advantage of the methodology of generative modeling, and a normal part of the process of modeling concepts as complex as narratives.

is that the former tells us about a plots level of organization, while the latter tells us whether this organization is coherent (i.e. meaningful).

THE PRECEDING DISCUSSION   led to a more general insight because it shifted my understanding of the levels of narratological representation that should be included in computational story composition systems. Common wisdom has it to distinguish between two levels of representation: 'what is told'—referred to as fabula or plot—and 'how it is told'—referred to as discourse (Gervás, 2009; Kybartas & Bidarra, 2017). I have come to realize that this view conflates two levels of representation into one, when it speaks of 'what is told': (1) the events that happen in the story world and (2) the abstract causal organization and roles that can be superimposed over the events as part of a meaning-making strategy.

Ryan is adamant that some events in TAW are part of the plot while some are not (M.-L. Ryan, 1991, p. 126) and that "[m]any different texts share the same plot...", but for my purposes she, too, conflates these two levels when she continues: "...(consider all the versions of 'Cinderella')." (M.-L. Ryan, 1991, p. 127). This seems to imply that there is a Cinderella plot, and different instantiations of it might differ in minor things like whether Cinderella has to sweep the floor, do the dishes, or perform some other kind of menial housework instead of going to a ball. But then it would follow that there also is a TLRH plot, a Three Little Pigs plot, as well as infinitely many more, and there is no way of judging whether a sequence of events is organized in a meaningful way or not, since there are too many plots to compare it to. In my opinion, plot should be regarded as a high-level format of representation that allows to abstract away from the details of individual events and to draw out their underlying causal structures in order to be able to compare it with structures that are meaningful. This need for abstraction is precisely what I believe forces Ryan to introduce Lehnert-style "higher semantic units" when she describes her own "Recursive Graph Model" for plot representation (M.-L. Ryan, 1991, pp.222–232), instead of merely relying on events and the changing states of character's APW.

Can there be a level of abstraction at which a few common meaningful structures emerge? Journalist and author Christopher Booker observed how seemingly very different narratives on closer inspection can be found to exhibit remarkable similarities:

> [...] a Shakespeare play, Macbeth; Vladimir Nabokov's novel Lolita;

a 1960s French film, Truffaut's Jules et Jim; the Greek myth of Icarus; and the German legend of Faust. Each begins with a hero, or heroes, in some way unfulfilled. The mood at the beginning of the story is one of anticipation, as the hero seems to be standing on the edge of some great adventure or experience. In each case he finds a focus for his ambitions or desires, and for a time seems to enjoy almost dream-like success. Macbeth becomes king; Humbert embarks on his affair with the bewitching Lolita; Jules and Jim, two young men in pre-First World War Paris, meet the girl of their dreams; Icarus discovers that he can fly; Faust is given access by the devil to all sorts of magical experiences. But gradually the mood of the story darkens. The hero experiences an increasing sense of frustration. There is something about the course he has chosen which makes it appear doomed, unable to resolve happily. More and more he runs into difficulty; everything goes wrong; until that original dream has turned into a nightmare. Finally, seemingly inexorably, the story works up to a climax of violent self-destruction.   (Booker, 2004, p. 4)

Booker calls shapes like these *basic plots*, and in a tour de force through centuries of literature identifies seven of these shapes: (1) Overcoming the Monster, (2) The Quest, (3) Voyage and Return, (4) Rags to Riches, (5) Rebirth, (6) Comedy and (7) Tragedy (the plot underlying the five examples above, according to Booker). This, however, is not the only distinction of basic plots put forward by scholars. Foster-Harris (1959) proposes three basic plots, Tobias (1993) espouses 20, while Polti (1921) raises this to 36. I do not have a stake in the question how many basic plots there should be; what is important to me is that one plot should be able to fit a wide range of event sequences. What makes this interesting is that at the same time also one sequence of events can be interpreted to adhere to several plots. One instance is observed by Gervás and León (2015), who attempt to compare the different plot-taxonomies I pointed out above from a computational perspective, and report that the difference between a narrative of 'Overcoming a Monster' and a 'Tragedy' in many cases could boil down to whether the focus is on the experiences of the hero slaying the monster, or on those of the monster being slain. The flexibility of such a many-to-many mapping is of no use in a linear generation process like the one employed by InBloom, where first the story events are generated and then a fitting plot is identified (or the events are judged untellable). In an iterative process, however, it can be exploited to the benefit of the generated narrative, if the results of one stage can be used to inform the following stage. For instance, in a first iteration a number of events is generated based on a story world. The next iteration determines that these events can be badly fit by two different plots, selects one of these plots and determines which events would be required for a better fit. The third iteration attempts to alter the story world in a way that an approximation of the missing events can emerge, which leads to a whole lot of unexpected changes, so that in the subsequent stage a different plot suggests itself... and so on, and so forth. A narrative that is generated by such a process benefits from the way two narratological forces are used to shape its content: a top-down structuring force that ensures the narrative is well formed, and a bottom-up self organizational force that ensures the characters and events are believable. Creativity, in a computational story composition system, can be derived from the way the system balances out the tension that results from these two opposing forces. This requires solving several hard problems, like identifying computational representations for story events and plots that allow bi-directional matching, developing a matching algorithm that tolerates imprecise matches, and developing an event generation process that is capable of performing a guided exploration of the system's parameters in search for ways of adding new events of certain types to a sequence of existing events. However, I believe that without addressing these problems, computational story composition is doomed to follow a linear path that is not well suited to balance out the narratological forces that shape the content plane of narratives.

Technological Considerations

The main advantage of the implementation is that it does its job, and since most design decision I have made came about to solve particular problems and have been argued when they were introduced, I do not think that a detailed review of advantages is of much worth to readers. Instead I will discuss a few problematic observations, in order to contextualize the results and insights presented above.

The most general problem is that the tellability measure implemented by InBloom is not only sensitive to narratologically plausible differences in plots, but also to differences that are rooted in technological details or the employed formalization. One part of this is that executing the same configuration several times might lead to slightly different individual tellability principle scores, as well as differing balanced overall tellability. For instance, in the ten simulation runs performed to evaluate the original plot of TLRH, the tellability determined by the system exhibited a standard deviation of 0.02. This is not a large number, but still constitutes two percent of the measure's maximal range. The reason for this seems to be that individual agent's reasoning cycles are executed as Java threads and run concurrently with the environment, which can lead to indeterminism based on race conditions. By synchronising the agent's transition systems during simulation execution and the introduction of a stepped environment I tried to remove as much indeterminism as possible, but was not completely successful. Consequently, evaluating plots on different machines might lead to different results, since the allocation of resources to threads depends on details like the processor, the operating system or the work load of the executing machine. Another instance of this is that executing the simulation without a GUI (like I did for evaluation purposes) again changes its runtime properties in a way that makes results deviate from runs executed with the GUI. This seems to be due to the increased overhead and delay required for logging the plot on the system's interface. A metric that is especially sensitive to this is the number of steps required to perform a simulation, which varied as much as four versus ten for the original plot of TLRH. This, in turn, directly affects the score of the tellability principle suspense. Overall, judging by the results of Tab. 4.3, functional poyvalence and semantic P&S seem to be affected less by technological differences than semantic opposition and suspense are. This situation is unfortunate, since it makes tellability results harder to compare and evaluate. Ideally, the implementation of a plot quality measure should be agnostic to technical details.

Another problem can be attributed to the way plot graphs are analyzed in order to insert different types of causal edges. Information that is necessary for this analysis is inserted into the original plot graph based mainly on properties of the execution of individual agents' reasoning cycles. The drawback of this solution is that it creates a strong coupling between the ASL code that models agents' reasoning and the structure of the plot graph, which means that whether an FU instance can be detected in a graph or not partly depends on how the narrative universe is modeled. This makes a hard problem (I discussed the problems connected with modeling the narrative universe in Sec. 2.4.2) even harder, since predicting whether a piece of ASL code will result in an FU instance upon execution is not easily possible, and thus the system's full potential for detecting meaningful structures might not be exhausted. I attempted to somewhat alleviate this problem, by implementing inexact instead of exact matching of FU graphs, and collecting a set of ASL programming guidelines, but this cannot solve the fundamental underlying problem.

Finally, I observed a few minor problems with the formalization and implementation of some of the tellability principles, which could be addressed in another iteration. With regards to semantic opposition, one potential part of it are terminated beliefs, which are expected to capture the semantics of violated expectations. However, in practice, it turned out that terminated beliefs, instead, are often just mental notes of state changes, like e.g. `+hungry` or `+has(bread)`, which appear when an agent realizes that it is not hungry anymore, or that it is not in the possession of bread anymore. While, usually, semantic opposition is computed based on change of fortunes intervals, in the case of plots #5 and #6 it were precisely these terminated beliefs that lead to a narratologically not justified difference in scores. I thus deem it necessary to rethink how the semantics of violated expectations could be captured by the formalism. With regards to semantic P&S, at the moment, the system computes its metrics based on FU instances when sufficient instances could be detected, and on raw events else. While this allows a wider variety of plots to be analyzed, it also makes P&S results harder to compare between plots that have sufficient FU instances and those that do not. This problem arose when comparing plots #5 and #6, too. With regards to suspense, I suspect that the measure could be easily tricked by adversarially generated examples, since all it takes to achieve a high suspense is to induce an intention in an agent that it cannot address, and then resolve it via a happening at the final step of the plot. This would yield the maximal suspense value possible, while not actually representing a suspenseful intention. One approach at addressing this would be to only count the number of steps in which an agent worked towards actualizing its intention, instead of counting all steps in which the intention was simply active.

Nearly everything I've read in the world's literature describes varieties of human failure [...] when the marriage of men and women to machines is complete, this literature will be redundant because we'll understand each other too well. [...] The lapidary haiku, the still, clear perception and celebration of things as they are, will be the only necessary form.

Ian McEwan, 'Machines Like Me'

5

Outlook: Computational Creativity

ALL THE PLOTS GENERATED AND EVALUATED BY INBLOOM, so far, have been discovered manually by me. This was sufficient for the NT side of the project, since NT is only concerned with the system's ability to represent or capture certain narratological phenomena, and by that demonstrate the expressivity of the underlying narratological theories. For the CSC side of the project, however, the computational representation of narrative is only one of the required steps. It's not enough for a computational story composition system to be able to represent narratives, it should also demonstrate that it can take over the responsibility for autonomously identifying good narratives in the search space set up by its representational formalism.

In Chap. 3, I demonstrated that narrative systems implemented in InBloom set up a space of possible plots that can be traversed by changing the personality parameters of the involved characters, and defining which happenings befall which character, and when. Then, in Chap. 4, I showed that it is possible to quantify the quality of plots created by InBloom simulations based on the tellability metric. This provides the necessary means for a computationally creative system to autonomously traverse the space spanned by any given narrative system[1], in search for plots high in tellability.

In general terms, the following approach proffers itself: An initial simulation is executed with randomly initialized characters and happenings. The resulting interactions are analyzed in order to determine the underlying plot and its tellability. As long as the tellability is below a certain threshold,

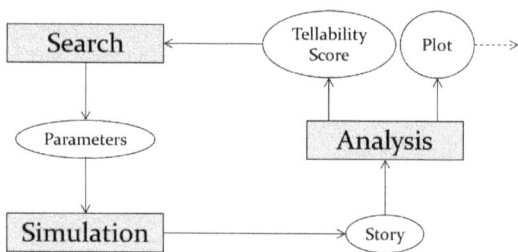

Figure 5.1: Abstract overall architecture for the realization of computational creativity in InBloom.

the plot is discarded. Then, the personality parameters of the characters are changed, and the details of the happenings are adapted, changing which happenings befall whom and when. After this, the new simulation is executed. This cycle (see Fig. 5.1) is repeated, until a sufficiently tellable plot is found, or time runs out.

The basic intuition behind this is compelling: Characters in In-Bloom are autonomous agents, whom the system cannot prescribe goals or behaviors. Thus, instead, in order to create tellable plots it attempts to *manipulate* the characters into acting in tellable ways, by finding happenings that force them into action, while calibrating their personalities in such a way that they react strongly to these happenings and their environment. This also sketches a way out of the emergent narrative paradox that I introduced in Sec. 1.4.1, and that has been leveled as criticism against emergentist strong autonomy systems like InBloom. The paradox asks how interesting plots—which consist of complex networks of conflicts between and within characters, combined with non-trivial (but believable) resolutions—can emerge solely from the interactions of autonomous characters—who in normal circumstances have mundane goals and whose behavior is

---

[1]One of the feats of writers is the ability to not only explore what plots might be possible in a given story world, but also to simultaneously modify this story world in order to facilitate the emergence of desired plots. It is the first capability for which I will transfer the responsibility to InBloom, but not the second. Without a human to hand-craft the narrative system it can explore, InBloom is helpless.

guided by the maxim of finding the path of least resistance for the satisfaction of these goals. Indeed, strong autonomy systems cannot *directly* force characters into behaving in tellable ways, since they have no direct way of dictating their behavior. However, they still can try to do this *indirectly* via manipulation.

The devil, as usual, is hiding in the details. Above, I suggested that personality settings and happening details can be iteratively changed in order to improve tellability. The tricky question is how these parameters need to be varied in order to find pockets of high tellability in this multi-dimensional search space. A naive approach would be to simply try and systematically vary these parameters in an attempt to test them all. However, this is not as straightforward as it sounds, since personality parameters are real-valued variables and are thus non-denumerable. They can be discretized to solve this problem, but even taking coarse discretization steps of 0.25 (resulting in nine discrete values), a narrative system like TLRH would result in $9^{5 \times 4} = 1.21\text{e}+19$ possible personality combinations. A number, that does not yet factor in that the one happening defined in this system can befall any subset of the four characters at any valid plot step. Given that executing a simulation and analyzing the resulting plot can take up to several seconds on a personal computer, it seems that neither systematically iterating nor randomly sampling possible settings is a viable approach. So instead, the question becomes how the plot space can be explored in an efficient way.

When faced with questions like this one, up until now, I would turn to NT in order to find theoretical answers that could be concretized and implemented by way of generative modeling. Unfortunately, NT is concerned with how narrative texts work and what they are, not how to compose them. Its lack of interest in matters of creativity, or how to search conceptual spaces, becomes evident when one searches for this term in Porter Abbott's (2002) *The Cambridge Introduction to Narrative*, where it appears exactly two times—both referring to the act of reading and interpreting narratives.

An alternative source for ways of modeling creativity could be found in the discipline of psychology, which, as I discussed in Sec. 1.3.1, does study creativity. In particular, I am aware of two process models of creative writing: Sharples (1999) and Flower and Hayes (1981), the first of which has actually been implemented by the story composition system MEXICA (Pérez y Pérez, 1999) that I introduced in

Sec. 1.4.3. However, both approaches are so general that they cannot provide insights with the particular question at hand, which is not surprising seeing how the representational format for narratives employed in this thesis is an idiosyncratic amalgamation of approaches from NT, which were not selected for cognitive plausibility. This is not problematic, since the processes employed for computational creativity do not necessarily have to resemble those in human creativity, as long as the resulting system exhibits the properties outlined in Sec. 1.3.2. However, it means that the following chapter has to part ways with the process employed by my thesis so far, i.e. generative modeling of non-computational theories. Instead, I will fall back on using a classical approach from AI, by formalizing this situation as an optimization problem, and outlining a heuristic for solving it by means of a nature inspired algorithm.

Be aware that my goal, in this chapter, is only to provide an outlook that demonstrates that it is possible to use the representational formalism for narrative, developed so far, in a computational plot composition system, in order to show that a collaboration between NT and AI is fruitful for the latter. A comprehensive investigation of CC using InBloom would have to also include empirical studies, and comparisons with existing systems, for which this thesis has already grown to lengthy.

5.1. Optimization Problems and Local Search

The situation outlined above can be described as an *optimization problem*, where we are searching for a state x in a search space (in our case, this would be a plot in a defined space of possible plots) that maximizes an objective function f (in our case, tellability). In general, optimization problems need to be formulated as:

$$\arg\max_{x \in \mathbb{R}^n} f(x)$$

Below, in Sec. 5.2, I will outline how plots can be represented to satisfy this form.

An important difference between optimization problems and simple search problems is that for the latter, any solution that can be found to satisfy the search problem can be accepted, whereas for the former a solution needs to be better than all other possible solutions, in order to be accepted. This is especially hard to verify, when the search space is so large that it is not feasible to compare all possible solutions. In such cases, approaches to solving an optimization problem cannot be expected to return the global optimum. Instead, they are expected to make an appropriate trade-off between *exploitation* (search of good solutions in promising parts of the search space) and *exploration* (search inside unexplored parts of the search space).

Optimization problems with large or continuous search spaces can be addressed by *local search* algorithms (Russell & Norvig, 2010, p. 121). Local search works by starting "[...] from some initial solution and iteratively try[ing] to replace the current solution by a better solution in an appropriately defined neighborhood of the current solution [...]" (Blum & Roli, 2003, p. 269), which means that instead of systematically trying to test all possible solutions, local search relies on heuristics in order to explore regions of interest in the search space. The heuristics that are used in order to explore the neighborhood are responsible for maintaining the balance between exploitation and exploration throughout the search process, and differ from algorithm to algorithm.

In a bachelor thesis that I supervised, Wöbkenberg (2021) investigated and compared the ability of several local search algorithms to find solutions for the optimization problem faced by InBloom (for a formalization, see Equation 5.1 below). One of the approaches that succeeded in finding the best known solution for the environment used in that work was *Genetic Algorithms* (GA).

5.2. Formalizing InBloom's Plot Search via Genetic Algorithms

GA is a probabilistic, nature inspired algorithm that is based on the intuition of evolutionary genetics (the following is based on Russell & Norvig, 2010, p. 127f): *Individuals* in a *population* compete against each other based on a *fitness function*. The fitness function measures the quality of an individual (see Sec. 5.2.1 below), and the mechanism attempts to iteratively increase the overall quality of the population. This happens, by combining the fittest individuals from a given population based on specific *crossover* principles (see Sec. 5.2.4 below), whereby a small chance exists that additional random changes called *mutations* are introduced (see Sec.5.2.5 below). These new individuals are called *offspring*. The next generation is made up proportionally by the fittest individuals from the last generation and the fittest offspring, by a selection process (see Sec. 5.2.6 below).

Thus, GA solve an optimization problem encoded in the fitness function, and each individual represents a candidate solution. Usually, these solutions consist of multiple parameters (which in this metaphor are called *allele*, and organized in *chromosomes*). GA perform a search of the so defined parameter-space, conducting exploitation by combining the parameters of successful solutions, and exploration based on the random mutation mechanism. A pseudocode representation of the algorithm can be found in Algorithm 3.

Algorithm 3 Genetic Algorithm

1: population = INITIALIZE();
2: COMPUTE_FITNESS(population);
3: **while** *time left* **do**
4:     offspring = CROSSOVER(population);
5:     offspring = MUTATION(offspring);
6:     COMPUTE_FITNESS(offspring);
7:     population = SELECTION(population, offspring);
8: **end while**
9: **return** BEST_INDIVIDUAL(population);

5.2.1. Optimization Problem and Fitness Function

The problem of finding the most tellable plot in a narrative system—as described in the beginning of this chapter—can be formalized as an optimization problem, where we are searching for an analyzed plot graph G such that it maximizes the value of the *tellability* function (as defined in Equation 4.20). We also know, that G is produced by an InBloom simulation that is defined by the set of participating characters $C = \{c_0, c_1, \ldots, c_n\}$, and the set of scheduled happenings $H = \{h_0, h_1, \ldots, h_m\}$, where each character c_i, in turn, is defined by its five personality parameters: $c_i \in [-1, 1]^5 \subset \mathbb{R}^5$, and each happening h_j by the index $p \in \{0, 1, \ldots, n\} \subset \mathbb{N}$ of its patient, the step number $s \in \mathbb{N}$ in which it is executed, and the index $t \in \mathbb{N}$ of its type[2]. Additionally, it seems useful to let an individual encode a maximum possible simulation length $L = \{l\}$ with $l \in \mathbb{N}^+$ (where $\mathbb{N}^+$ is the set of positive natural numbers), in order to allow it to control the length of the plot. I refer to this as the maximal simulation length because simulations can be automatically stopped earlier, when all participating characters die, or as soon as a narrative equilibrium is detected by InBloom, i.e. when all characters have performed the same sequence of actions for five times in a row (see p. 76 for details). Let $simulation : [-1, 1]^{5 \times n} \times \mathbb{N}^{3 \times m} \times \mathbb{N}^+ \to \mathcal{G}$—where $\mathcal{G}$ is the set of all possible analyzed plot graphs—be a function that returns the result of an InBloom simulation given a set of characters, a set of happenings, and a maximal simulation length. Then, the goal of finding the best possible plot, based on tellability, can be denoted as:

$$\underset{C, H, L}{\arg\max}\, tellability(simulation(C, H, L)) \qquad (5.1)$$

Thus, the fitness function for a GA can be formalized as:

$$fitness(I) = tellability(simulation(I)) \qquad (5.2)$$

where I is an individual that is defined by the chromosomes C, H and L.

5.2.2. Representation

IN ORDER TO APPLY GA TO AN INDIVIDUAL, its chromosomes need to be represented using a vector-based encoding. The first chromosome contains the personality parameters of all characters, and can thus be encoded as the $n \times 5$ matrix $\mathbf{C}$ defined over $[-1, 1] \in \mathbb{R}$, where each row represents a character and the columns represent the personality traits: openness to experience, conscientiousness, extraversion, agreeableness as well as neuroticism (introduced in Sec. 3.2.2). Each entry of this matrix, thus, represents a particular personality parameter of a particular character. The second chromosome contains the happening settings. It can be encoded as the $n \times m$ matrix $\mathbf{H}$ over $\mathbb{N}$, where each row represents a character and each column represents a happening type. An entry, then, can encode the earliest simulation

[2]To be able to easily represent happenings, a list containing all possible types of happenings is created and ordered at the start of a narrative system. This allows to reference each happening type by its index in that list.

step in which the respective happening can befall the respective character. The third chromosome contains the simulation length, and can be encoded as a 1×1 matrix $\mathbf{L}$ over $\mathbb{N}^+$, whose entry encodes the maximal simulation length. The complete genotype of an individual is a combination of these three chromosomes, and can be represented as a vector of length $n \times (5 + m) + 1$ by vectorizing and concatenating the individual matrices: $(vec(\mathbf{C}) \,|\, vec(\mathbf{H}) \,|\, \mathbf{L})$.[3] An example individual, encoded in this notation is provided in Fig. 5.2.

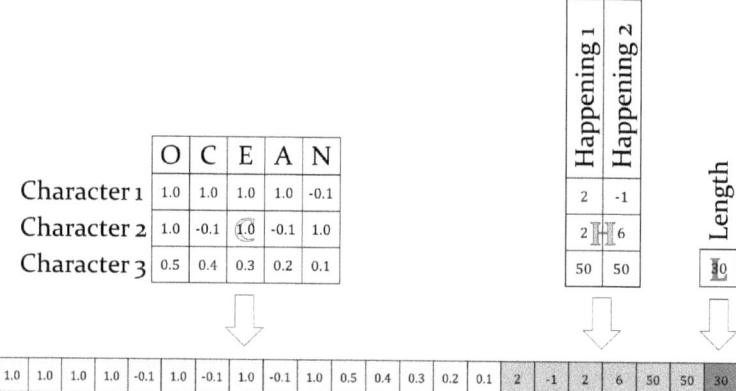

Figure 5.2: Example for a GA individual, encoded using the chromosomes $\mathbf{C}$, $\mathbf{H}$ and $\mathbf{L}$. It represents a particular simulation configuration in a narrative system with three characters and two happening types, and a maximum simulation length of 30. Note, that some happenings are disabled, by way of scheduling them to appear after the end of the simulation, or by being set to a negative value.

SOME PROPERTIES OF THIS REPRESENTATION need to be pointed out. The most important one is that the proposed representation only allows happenings to be scheduled to befall each character at most once, which results in a strong restriction of the search space. However, this decision simplifies the representation significantly, which I deem an appropriate trade-off in the context of an outlook chapter. This is especially so since the formalism leaves open an avenue for resolving this restriction in future work by a shift to three-dimensional matrices for representing $\mathbf{H}$.

Another question that needs to be addressed is how different types of entries in $\mathbf{H}$ can be interpreted. As pointed out above, they indi-

---

[3]The operator $|$ denotes vertex concatenation, and vec denotes the vectorization function, which is a linear transformation that converts a matrix into a row vector obtained by concatenating the rows of the original matrix.

cate the first plot step at which the happening can be executed by the environment. The reason why happenings cannot be guaranteed to be executed at precisely the indicated step is that they usually have associated conditions, which need to be fulfilled in the story world before the effect of the happening can take place (see Sec. 2.3.4, p. 77 for details). Since the state of a simulation cannot be predicted in advance, it is not guaranteed that the condition of a happening will be met at the scheduled step. When this is not the case, the happening will be held inactive until the condition is fulfilled, and executed only then, which actually means that scheduled happenings are not guaranteed to be executed at all.

This is further complicated by the fact that each simulation will only run for a limited number of steps, encoded by a dedicated chromosome. Consequently, entries with negative numbers, or positive numbers that are larger than the last step of a simulation, cannot be executed either. However, this is not problematic because the employed search algorithm can learn to use this behavior in order to disable happenings, which is important since not every happening that can happen necessary also needs to happen in a plot. Disabling a happening can be achieved by GA by scheduling it to appear at a step smaller or equal to zero, or after the last step of a simulation.

A last limitation of the current approach is also connected to the proposed encoding. The length of the vector representing the genotype of a solution is dependent on the number of characters. Since, classically, GA demand that the genotype of all individuals follows the same format[4], this means that the number of characters needs to be determined before the start of the algorithm. Consequently, it cannot be autonomously varied between different solutions, which further restricts the search space accessible in a single run. Theoretically, it is possible to add a chromosome to the encoding, which represents the number of agents that should be started in a simulation. However, this would make the dimensions of an individual's genotype dependent on the value of this allele, and complicate the implementation of initialization, crossover and mutation. For this reason, this avenue is left for exploration in future work.

---

[4]The rationale behind this will become clearer below, when I outline how operations like mutation and crossover are implemented.

5.2.3. Initialization

Since, in GA, most of the search is conducted by recombining existing values (only occasionally, new values are introduced via mutation), the way a population is initialized has an important influence on the performance of a run. There are multiple ways in which the chromosomes of an individual can be probabilistically initialized. When a population of size k_{pop} is initialized, one of the following strategies for personality initialization, happening initialization, and length initialization is randomly selected for each individual.

Given its personality chromosome, the following initialization procedures are introduced. For each of the $n \times 5$ alleles, based on

- *random continuous*: a random number $p \in [-1, 1] \subset \mathbb{R}$ is selected based on a continuous uniform distribution.

- *random discretized*: a random number $p \in \{-1, -0.9, -0.75, -0.5, -0.25, -0.1, 0, 0.1, 0.25, 0.5, 0.75, 0.9, 1\}$ is selected based on a discrete uniform distribution.

- *diverse random discretized*: a random number $p \in \{-1, -0.9, -0.75, -0.5, -0.25, -0.1, 0, 0.1, 0.25, 0.5, 0.75, 0.9, 1\}$ is selected without replacement, based on a discrete uniform distribution.

The first strategy allows to explore the search space most freely, but at the same time does not make use of any heuristic knowledge to improve the quality of initial individuals. The second strategy restricts the initial parameters to three different types of high and low personality, as well as seven types of medium personality (see p. 3.4 for details on high/medium/low), with a higher resolution around the notable points -1, 0 and 1. This has the potential to simplify the optimization problem by reducing the search space, but could potentially make viable solutions not reachable. The third strategy introduces another heuristic, whose aim it is to diversify the discretized gene pool as much as possible, so that subsequent recombination operations can generate a broad range of solutions.

Given its length chromosome, the following initialization strategies are introduced:

- *Random*: a random number $l \in \{1, 2, \ldots, 100\}$ is selected based on a discrete uniform distribution.

- *Discretized*: a random number $l \in \{\frac{1 \times 100}{5}, \frac{2 \times 100}{5}, \ldots, \frac{5 \times 100}{5}\}$ is selected based on a discrete uniform distribution.

Here, 100 is selected as a hard cap for maximum simulation lengths in order to prevent overly long plots that take up a lot of processing time. Hence, the first strategy allows to explore the search space most freely, while the second offers a restricted number of options that are evenly distributed through the available space and can be seen as heuristic suggestions for presumably good plot lengths.

Given an individual's happening chromosome, and assuming that a maximum simulation length L has already been initialized, the following initialization procedures are introduced:

- *Random*: for each of the $n \times m$ entries, a random number $h \in \{0, 1, \ldots, L\}$ is selected based on a discrete uniform distribution.

- *Random synchronized*: for each of the $n \times m$ entries, a random number $h \in \{\lfloor \frac{0 \times L}{5} \rfloor, \lfloor \frac{1 \times L}{5} \rfloor, \ldots, \lfloor \frac{4 \times L}{5} \rfloor\}$ is selected based on a discrete uniform distribution.

- *Random unique*: for each column in $\mathbf{H}$, exactly one entry is selected randomly based on a discrete uniform distribution and its entry is determined according to *random synchronized*, while the other entries of that column are set to 0.

Again, the first strategy allows to explore the search space most freely but does not make use of any heuristics to improve the initial population. The second strategy restricts the steps at which happenings can be scheduled to five instances that are evenly spaced throughout the L overall steps. This has the advantage, that happenings are more likely to be disabled (by being set to step 0), and also more likely to appear synchronized, which increases the likelihood of a thickening of the plot at particular times. The last strategy, on the other hand, schedules each happening at most once, which encourages leaner plots.

Ideally, the utility of each of these strategies would be determined through extensive ablation studies in order to understand whether the introduced heuristic knowledge is beneficial for the search algorithm. However, for the purpose of this thesis, it is only important to demonstrate the general ability of GA to optimize tellability, and not to optimize the search algorithm itself.

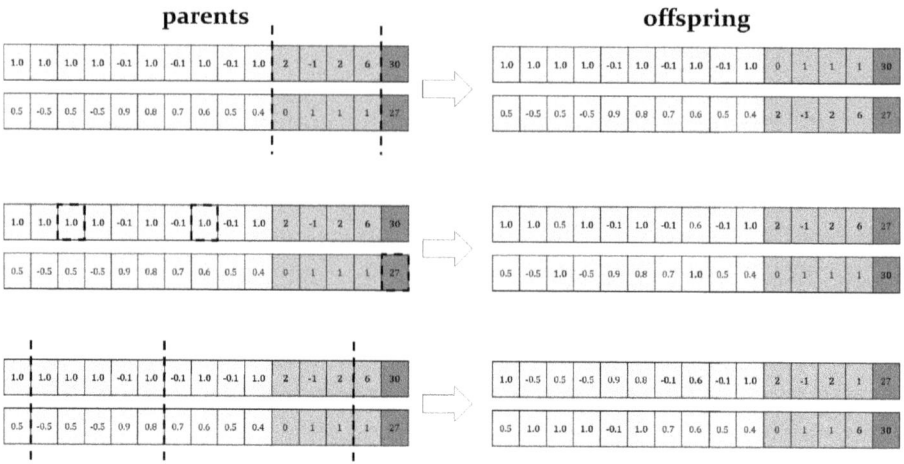

Figure 5.3: Examples of the three crossover strategies 'genetic crossover' (first row), 'uniform crossover' (second row) and 'X-point crossover' (last row). On the left side, two parent individuals are depicted for each strategy, while on the right side the offspring resulting from applying crossover to the parents is depicted. Dashed lines indicate crossover-points (or alleles to be switched, in the case of the second row) that were determined probabilistically. Note, that in the X-point crossover case (last row), the end of the genotype is implicitly treated as a crossover-point, resulting in the exchange of the last two alleles.

5.2.4. Crossover

For crossover, first, a number of parent individuals needs to be selected from which the offspring will be created. Then, the offspring is created via different types of recombination strategies.

The k_{sel} parent individuals are determined using roulette-wheel selection (Goldberg, 1989, pp. 11, 30), where population $\mathcal{P}$ is sampled k_{sel} times and the probability of individual I to be selected is $Pr(I) = \frac{fitness(I)}{\sum_{K \in \mathcal{P}} fitness(K)}$, using the fitness function defined in Equation 5.2. Thus, individuals with higher fitness are more likely to be selected for recombination, while lower fitness individuals still maintain some chance of being selected. From the set of parents, $\frac{k_{sel}}{2}$ pairs are randomly created, which will each generate two offspring.

The following crossover strategies are introduced (see Fig.5.3 for a visual example for each), some of which rely on the parameter crossover probability p_c:

- *Genetic crossover*: offspring are created by randomly deciding whether one or two chromosomes of the parents should be exchanged, and then randomly deciding which chromosomes to exchange.

- *X-point crossover*: offspring are created by iterating simultaneously over the alleles of both parent, and denoting crossover points with probability p_c. Then, all alleles between each pair of consecutive crossover points are exchanged.

- *Uniform crossover*: one offspring is created by iterating over the alleles of one parent, and replacing it with the other parent's allele at the same position with probability p_c (or simply copying the original with the inverse probability), while the other offspring is created using the same procedure based on the other parent.

The first strategy is a special case of the second one, with potential crossover points restricted to alleles separating chromosomes. Cutting an individual's genotype at these points results in the least potential for damage, since the synergies that might have developed within the characters or within the happenings are not disrupted. The second strategy follows this idea of maintaining adjacent groups of allele based on the hypothesis that these are most likely to be related, while offering the algorithm more freedom for exploring the search space by introducing the potential for more crossover points. The last strategy offers GA the most freedom to explore new settings, with the highest risk of disrupting beneficial combinations of parameters.

The crossover strategy applied to each parent pair is determined randomly. For the same reason as above, no ablation studies have been performed to compare the benefits of these different strategies.

5.2.5. Mutation

Mutation is applied to all offspring created in the last step, by iterating over each allele of each individual, and changing it with probability p_m. Commonly, p_m is selected to be much lower than p_c.

The following mutation strategies are introduced:

- *Random mutation*: for each allele a new value is selected with probability p_m. In the length chromosome, the new value is a random number $l \in \{1, 2, \ldots, 100\}$ selected based on a discrete uniform distribution. In the personality chromosome, the new value is a random number $p \in [-1, 1] \subset \mathbb{R}$, selected based on a continuous uniform distribution, while in the happening chromosome the new value is a random number $h \in \{0, 1, \ldots, l\}$ selected based on a discrete uniform distribution.

- *Toggle mutation*: each allele is toggled with probability p_m. In the length chromosome, alleles with a value smaller than the maximal simulation length cap of 100 are set to 100, while those set to cap are set to a random number $l \in \{1, 2, \ldots, 99\}$. In the personality chromosome, the value of an allele is toggled by multiplying with -1. In the happening chromosome active alleles (those with a value > 0) are toggled by setting them to zero, while inactive alleles are toggled by setting them to a random number $h \in \{1, \ldots, L'\}$.

- *Oriented mutation*: for each allele x_1 that is selected for mutation with probability p_m, another allele x_2 in the same chromosome of the same individual is randomly selected. The value of the selected allele is shifted either towards or away from that x_2: $x_1' = x_1 + \epsilon(x_2 - x_1)$ where $\epsilon \in [-1, 1] \subset \mathbb{R}$ is a random value.[5] No oriented mutation can be performed in the length chromosome, since it contains only one allele.

- *Guided mutation*: operates like *oriented mutation*, but randomly selects another individual from the population and shifts the value of the selected allele either towards or away from the value of the other individual's allele at the same position.

The first strategy offers the GA the most freedom for exploring the search space. The second strategy relies on the heuristic that interesting changes can be found by toggling the value of a parameter, and by that restricts the space explorable via this strategy to a certain dynamically defined region. The third and the forth strategy allow to gradually change the value of individual parameters, allowing to approximate information aggregated in comparable positions.

The mutation strategy applied to each offspring is determined randomly. Again, for the same reasons as above, no ablation studies have been performed to compare the benefits of these different strategies.

---

[5]Here, boundary conditions need to be respected such that no value is shifted outside the permissible range of its chromosome.

5.2.6. Selection

Elitist selection (Goldberg, 1989, p. 115) is employed, which means that the next generation of a population is to 50% comprised of the best parent individuals and to 50% of the best offspring individuals, while making sure to avoid the introduction of duplicates.

5.2.7. Implementation Details

The algorithm described above is implemented in the class `inBloo m.nia.ga.GeneticAlgorithm`, and operates on individuals that are instances of the class `inBloom.nia.ga.Individual`, comprised by three chromosomes implemented in `InBloom.nia.ChromosomeHapp enings`, `InBloom.nia.ChromosomePersonality`, and `InBloom.nia. ChromosomeLength`. Each instance of `Individual` has a reference to a dedicated instance of the class `inBloom.nia.Fitness`, which is a subclass of `PlotLauncher` and thus can start a dedicated simulation based on the parameters encoded in the individual, as well as evaluate the tellability of the resulting plot. GA can be executed by instantiating `GeneticAlgorithm`, making the desired settings using dedicated setter methods, and executing the method `GeneticAlgorithm#run()`, which will perform the search until either a timeout is reached, or the search process converges. A diagram of the resulting architecture can be found in Fig. 5.4, which also includes a set of abstract super classes that can be used to implement other nature inspired algorithms.[6]

Throughout this thesis, the following parameters have been employed: a temporal constraint of one hour, a population size of $k_{pop} = 20$, a parent selection size of $k_{sel} = 10$, a crossover probability of $p_c = 0.1$ and a mutation probability of $p_m = 0.05$.

---

[6]The bachelor thesis of Wöbkenberg (2021), conducted under my supervision, also investigated the algorithms Particle Swarm Optimization (Kennedy & Eberhart, 1995) and Quantum Swarm Optimization (Yang et al., 2004), which are also part of InBloom. Although these algorithms demonstrated that they search the space differently than GA, their results did not categorically differ from those of GA and are thus not described in this thesis.

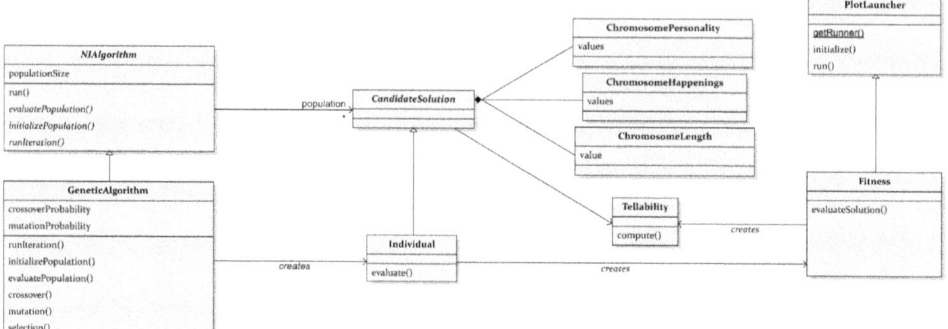

Figure 5.4: An abridged class diagram representation of the genetic algorithm architecture in InBloom, including abstract super classes that allow the implementation of alternative nature inspired algorithms. For brevity reasons attributes are represented without types, and methods without parameters or return types.

5.3. The Automated Case Study

With an implementation of the GA in place, applying it to a particular narrative system is straightforward: The algorithm needs to be informed which environment it should execute its simulations in, which types of happenings are available to be scheduled, and the number of characters that are supposed to be present in every candidate plot. For the purpose of this outlook, I will stick to the already familiar TLRH environment, its four denizens (the hen, the dog, the pig and the cow), as well as the one type of happening we also encountered before: finding a grain of wheat, which can be triggered only after some farm work has been done (see Sec. 5.2.2, p. 289, for details on the role of triggering conditions for happenings scheduled by GA). It should be clear that no radically new (or 'creative') plot can emerge from this narrative system, since there is not much room for variation with only one type of happening. On the upside, however, some manual exploration of the plot space of TLRH has been already performed in the previous chapters, which gives me the ability to judge candidate solutions proposed by the GA by comparison to the plot clusters discussed in Sec. 4.3.2. Furthermore, it means that many problems with the implementation of the environment have been already discovered and solved, which is important, given the propensity of evolutionary algorithms to exploit inconsistencies and impreciseness in the constraints of their environment, instead of searching for desired solutions.[7]

The goal of this case study is to investigate whether GA can be used as a search algorithm in the InBloom architecture sketched in Fig. 5.1. This can manifest in two non mutually-exclusive ways:

1. The solution found by the algorithm is high on tellability, i.e. comparable to the first cluster discussed in Sec. 4.3.2, or better.

2. The average tellability of populations shows an upward trend over (at least the initial) generations.

The first demonstrates that GA can explore the search space effectively, and can find desirable solutions in the available time, which cannot be just trivially assumed given the size of this space. The second demonstrates that GA can address the optimization problem[8] formulated in Equations 5.1 efficiently, which again is not trivially true given the complexity of the underlying tellability function. Both together would show that GA does not only succeed by chance, but because it can perform a directed search in the plot space. In the broader context of this chapter, it would mean that InBloom can act as a computational story composition system because it can combine creative acts of types E (generation of new exemplars) and A (aesthetic evaluation) from the FACE theory of CC (see Sec. 1.3.3 for details on this categorization), in order to autonomously compose plots it finds valuable.

Whether a proposed solution also constitutes a subjectively 'good' or 'creative' plot is a different matter altogether. If it does not, then this can provide valuable additional feedback on the viability of the employed implementation of the tellability metric, as well as on the dynamic properties of the concept of tellability itself, especially, because the present implementation can precisely attribute which properties of a plot contributed how to its tellability. As such, in fact, the present chapter could be seen as a contribution to another cycle of generative modeling, despite the reservations I have discussed at its beginning.

---

[7]A whole paper compiling the unexpected exploits of evolutionary algorithms has been recently published (Lehman et al., 2020), and makes for an entertaining (as well as humbling) read.

[8]I do not write that the algorithm can *solve* the optimization problem, simply because I do not know the most tellable plot possible in TLRH, and thus cannot discern whether a candidate solution represents a local or global maximum.

5.3.1. Empirical Evaluation

In order to empirically asses the performance of GA in searching for tellable plots, ten independent runs were executed on the TLRH environment as outlined above, with the default parameters introduced in Sec. 5.2.7. For each run, the tellability of the best individual solution found over the whole run (t_{best}), the average tellability of the whole population at the end of the last generation ($t_{average}$), and the number of generations completed during runtime (n_{gen}), are computed. Remember, that GA are probabilistic in nature, so that individual runs are not expected to exhibit the exact same behavior during search, nor return the same result (unless they reliable manage to find the global maximum).

To be able to draw comparisons to a meaningful baseline, additionally, a random-search algorithm (RA) was implemented. This algorithm simply instantiates and evaluates 20 random candidate solutions per generation, and also runs for an hour. Again, ten independent runs were executed, and the same metrics are computed as for GA.

The results of this experiment can be found in Tab. 5.1 and Tab. 5.2:

Several observations can be made. One is, that every single run of GA found a solution that exhibits a higher tellability than the maximum tellability in the best cluster I have found manually (balanced tellability of 0.69 there—see Tab. 4.3—vs. a minimum balanced tellability of 0.78, here).

RA did not manage to *consistently* outperform the best cluster found by me, however, the average tellability of its best solutions still beats it by a slight margin (0.70 vs. 0.69). One possible reason for this good performance is that RA, on average, manages to run $\overline{n_{gen}} \times k_{pop} = 131 \times 20 = 2620$ simulations during one hour, which is a considerable amount.[9] Still, RA is strongly outperformed by GA (average t_{best} of 0.82 vs. 0.70), with their difference being significant at the $p = 0.00016$ level, as determined by a two-tailed Mann-Whitney U test (Mann & Whitney, 1947).[10]

---

[9]The reason for the higher number of generations RA manages to perform in comparison to GA (56.3 vs. 131) is that RA simulations end up in a narrative equilibrium faster than GA simulations, and consequently get aborted after fewer steps.

[10]An unpaired Student's t-test could not be applied on this data because the

Table 5.1: Results of ten individual runs of GA on the TLRH environment; best run marked in bold face. Last two rows contain mean and standard deviation computed over all runs.

Run No	t_{best}	$t_{average}$	n_{gen}
1	0.81	0.58	52
2	0.81	0.79	67
3	0.87	0.77	61
4	0.81	0.54	47
5	0.79	0.65	48
6	0.83	0.70	42
7	**0.91**	**0.82**	**46**
8	0.79	0.69	64
9	0.78	0.68	52
10	0.81	0.63	84
mean:	0.82	0.68	56.3
std:	0.04	0.09	12.8

Table 5.2: Results of ten individual runs of RA on the TLRH environment; best run marked in bold face. Last two rows contain mean and standard deviation computed over all runs.

Run No	t_{best}	$t_{average}$	n_{gen}
1	0.67	0.16	128
2	0.73	0.18	130
3	0.73	0.18	128
4	0.67	0.18	125
5	0.71	0.21	115
6	0.65	0.14	136
7	0.66	0.14	136
8	**0.78**	**0.16**	**138**
9	0.71	0.18	136
10	0.64	0.19	138
mean:	0.70	0.17	131
std:	0.04	0.02	7.3

The picture becomes even clearer, when looking at the mean of the average tellability of the whole population after the last generation, $t_{average}$. Here, GA perform much better than RA (0.68 vs. 0.17), this difference being significant at the $p = 0.00016$ level, according to a two-tailed Mann-Whitney U test.[11] As can be seen in Fig. 5.5—which shows the development of the mean $t_{average}$ over all ten runs, per generation—this is grounded in the fact that GA population quality progressively increases, while RA population quality stagnates. This can be interpreted as a sign of GA being capable of performing directed search in tellability space, in contrast to RA's purely random exploration.

---

assumption of normality does not hold for any of the samples. The Mann-Whitney U test is a non-parametric alternative to the t-test, and is considered more conservative in cases of non-normality. Indeed, with the given samples, an unpaired two sample t-test with two tails returns significance at the $p = 0.000002$ level.

[11]Vigilant readers might notice that this is the same p-level as reported for the data on t_{best}. The reason for this is that the Mann-Whitney U test is a rank-sum test, and in both cases all ten data points of one group dominate all data points of the other group. Essentially this means that, in both cases, the highest significance possible with the given test and data is observed.

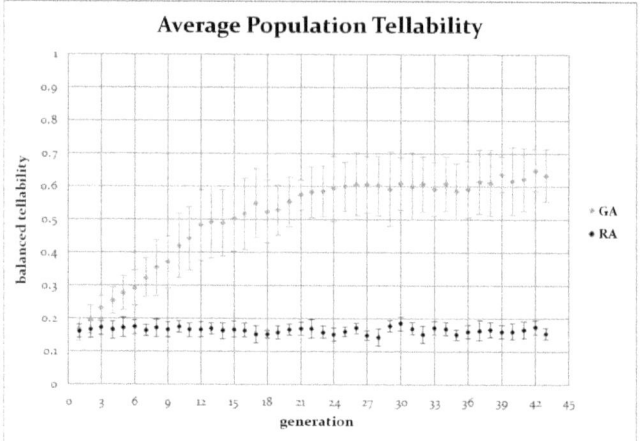

Figure 5.5: Average population tellability plotted against generation number, averaged over all 10 runs, for the first 43 generations. Gray diamonds represent development of GA and black circles that of RA, with whiskers indicating the standard deviation over all runs. The graph is restricted to 43 generations because this is the smallest n_{gen} observed over all runs.

These results clearly show that GA can be used as a search algorithm for high-tellability plots in the TLRH environment, that it performs better than random, and exhibits learning over its runtime.

5.3.2. Qualitative Evaluation

Looking purely at the tellability score, GA seems to yield remarkable results: the overall best plot found by that algorithm (no. 7 in Tab. 5.1 above) has a balanced tellability of 0.91 out of the maximally possible 1.0.[12] The break-down of this overall value into the individual sub-scores can be found in Tab. 5.3:

---

[12] As already discussed in Sec. 4.3.3, InBloom simulations have a certain amount of race-condition induced indeterminism. This problem seems exacerbated in a GA like setup, where multiple simulations are executed in quick succession. Consequently, the exact tellability score cannot be easily reproduced outside of the GA cycle, even with the same parameter settings, but values in the same ballpark have been reproduced.

Table 5.3: The balanced tellability sub-scores of the best plot found by GA in the TLRH environment. Headers are abbreviated, **FPo**: functional polyvalence, **P&S**: semantic parallelism and symmetry, **SOp**: semantic opposition, **Sus**: suspense.

FPo	P&S	SOp	Sus
0.78	0.98	0.96	0.91

The configuration of the underlying simulation is as follows: a plot length of 23 steps, and personality parameters as well as happening settings as per Tab. 5.4:

Table 5.4: Configuration summary for the best plot found by GA in the TLRH environment. First row indicates character name, the next five indicate rounded personality parameters, and the last row indicates the step at which the find-corn happening is scheduled to befall each character.

Character	O	C	E	A	N	find corn
hen	0.50	1.00	0.79	-0.5	0.83	1
dog	0.60	-0.25	0.75	0.51	0.50	1
pig	0.10	1.00	0.75	0.50	-0.75	1
cow	-0.34	0.73	0.25	0.89	0.75	2

What plot do these parameters correspond to, and how does its quality fair on a subjective level? The analyzed plot graph representation of the result can be found online[13], since it is too large to be meaningfully compressed into a single page. A natural language summary, composed manually by me for the sole purpose of reporting it here, would go like this:

> A hen, a dog, a pig and a cow live on a farm. One day, each one of them finds a grain of wheat. The dog wishes to relax in the sun and ignores this, while the other three decide that they should make use of the corn and create bread. They all ask the others for help with each laborious step of their respective plans, and even the dog assists when it is approached with a task. The plot ends when the animals are still in the middle of their work, harvesting the wheat or grinding it into flour.

FROM MY SUBJECTIVE PERSPECTIVE, this plot is pretty bad. It has no adversity which results in a lack of tension, its structure is simple so that it becomes quickly predictable, and what little difference in characters' personalities becomes apparent through their actions does not seem to be meaningful. A very obvious and important problem is, that the plot lacks a point or a moral. However, tellability was

---

[13]https://www.home.uni-osnabrueck.de/leberov/tlrh_best_ga_plot.pdf

not designed to capture symbolic concerns like these, so this issue has
to be bracketed out from subjective judgment, as much a possible.
There are a few strong points that I can come up with: The plot is
coherent, since most events seem to happen for a reason and follow a
meaningful course. It is fairly cohesive, in that characters are interconnected and the events build on each other. Furthermore, the plot
is clearly open ended, which leaves some room for speculation about
the projected course of action. It begs the question whether the three
animals will succeed with their work, and, once finished, whether the
dog's behavior will have consequences. Will they each just eat their
own bread, or will they all share the results of their work, and if yes,
will the dog also be allowed to benefit?

How can this glaring difference between a very high balanced overall tellability score and a very low subjective quality be
explained? The functional polyvalence score reported above (0.78) is
the lowest of the four, and has a decent claim to plausibility, given
that it represents the level of coherence and cohesion in the plot. It
is grounded in the FUs 'Honored Request' and 'Nested Goal' (see
Fig. 4.8 for an overview of FU types), the only two types detected in
the plot, which count 30 and 81 instances, respectively. Since there is
a natural interaction between their instances—asking for help being
part of the nested goals for labor intensive tasks like planting wheat
or tending the crops—a certain number of polyvalent vertices is only
natural.

The very high score for semantic parallelism and symmetry (0.98)
theoretically indicates a very strong balance between perceived order
and randomness. It comes into being as a mixture of a highish average symmetry score of 0.84 and a lowish parallelism score of 0.27,
which balance each other out. In practice, the high symmetry makes
sense given that each animal repeats the same course of action, while
the low parallelism is unfounded: three of the animals follow the exact same plan, and should thus have high parallelism ratings between
them. The reason the system is not capable of detecting this is indeterminism in the execution of the individual agent's reasoning cycles,
which results in differences at which points their respective succession
of nested goals is interrupted by help requests.

The high semantic opposition score (0.96) is grounded in the
change of fortune scores for the characters hen and cow: the domi-

nance of their mood component goes up every time they feel pride because of an accomplishment, and down again when they feel gratitude because they are being helped. Because of their high scores in the personality trait neuroticism (see Tab. 5.4), their mood reacts to these emotions with strong fluctuations, that are detected as changes of fortune by the system. Subjectively, I would not consider these situations important enough to be able to affect a character's fortunes.

Finally, the high suspense score (0.91) comes into being simply because the three characters' intention of creating bread starts early, as soon as they find their corn, and lasts till the end of the plot because we never see it fully actualized. This seems plausible to me, and might be taken to capture the interest that is generated by the open ended nature of the plot.

SUMMARIZING, the discrepancy between the tellability score and the plots subjective quality seems to stem, at least partly, from calibration problems. Some sub-scores are too sensitive, like semantic opposition which detects fortune changes where there are none, while others are too impervious, like semantic symmetry and parallelism which is not capable of detecting parallels due to minor, irrelevant variations. In the following section, I will discuss what this means for InBloom as a story composition algorithm, and outline suggestions on how to address this problem.

5.3.3. Discussion

The results of the case study reported above are mixed. On the one hand, the observed quantitative performance is satisfying, while the qualitative results, on the other hand, leave much to be desired.

Tellability Function

I do not see this poor qualitative performance as a fundamental problem. The work presented in this chapter can be seen as another cycle of generative modeling, resulting in the insight that the present implementation of tellability needs to be revised. As I briefly mentioned in Sec. 4.3.3, algorithms like GA can be regarded as a form of adversarial testing for the employed tellability score: They can efficiently come up with a number of example plots that are rated high on tellability, and if this rating is deemed unjustified by a human then the offending plots can inform ways in which the implementation needs to be amended. The propensity of evolutionary algorithms to exploit inconsistencies in their environments is known, as I discussed above, and can be harnessed to the benefit of this project.

Given the particular problems discovered in the case study, two avenues offer themselves for improving the tellability function. One would be to make the detection of semantic parallelism and symmetry more robust by employing some sort of inexact matching (a measure that, in fact, was already applied to functional polyvalence). The other would be to revise semantic opposition, for instance by restricting the detection of fortune change intervals to the mood domain of pleasure, which naively seems to be a more reliable indicator of a character's fortunes than arousal or dominance.

It should be noted, however, that the insights gained from the automated testing of the tellability function need not be restricted to technological considerations. They can also raise questions about Ryan's theoretical underpinnings of tellability, as the basis for my implementation. As it is standard practice in NT, Ryan developed and tested her notion based only on naturally existing, human-made narratives. Should these narratives all share some very fundamental properties that contribute to their plots' qualities, then it would be only natural to find them overlooked by an analyst, due to a lack of exemplars that do not have these properties. As a consequence, tellability would be blind to these implicit properties of narrativity, and thus CSC systems based on tellability could end up blindly endorsing plots that lack such properties. To a certain degree, this is the feeling that I get about the present case, given how the best detected plot seems to barely qualify as narrative at all. Unfortunately, at the present moment, I do not see what theoretic problem could be indicated by the observed behavior.

As an additional remark, I want to make clear that the discussed problems do not *have* to result in deviations from subjective plot quality perceptions. One instance where score and perception overlap has been reported in detail in Sec. 4.3.2, where I discussed the tellability evaluation of plots manually discovered by me. Another instance is reported in the bachelor thesis in which one of my students first experimented with nature inspired algorithms as a means for plot space exploration (Wöbkenberg, 2021). There, we employed an environment that was inspired by Defoe's (1719) *Robinson Cru-*

soe, and which fundamentally differed from TLRH in that it only had one character but ten different types of happenings (like e.g. storms, wildfires or poisonous plants). The most tellable story found by the system in that environment (with a score of 0.301) can be summarized as follows:

> The adventurer Robinson Crusoe goes on a voyage in a sailing boat. He is caught in a tropical storm that sinks his ship, but can survive by swimming to the safety of a deserted island. Hungry from his exertions he starts searching for food, but is obstructed by torrential rain. When the rain finally stops he manages to find an edible fruit, but before he can eat it he is attacked by group of monkeys that steal his food. Enfeebled, Robinson collapses and dies of hunger.

While my subjective judgment would still value Defoe's version over the one composed by the system, the latter is undeniably a much more viable exemplar of the concept plot than the best plot instance found in the TLRH environment. The point I want to make here is that any CSC algorithm can only work with the affordances it is offered by the environment it explores. Having only one type of happening at its disposal makes it that much harder for a system to find plots that not only optimize abstract structural criteria, but also appeal to subjective human predilections.

Search Algorithm

The quantitative performance of GA exhibits both properties I proposed above as indicators of its suitability as search algorithm: it finds plots high in tellability, and efficiently directs its search towards pockets of high tellability in the search space. It thus seems that GA is sufficiently powerful to effectively and efficiently explore the plot space spanned by TLRH, despite the complexity of the tellability function. Also the results of RA are remarkable, given that the algorithm does not perform any directed search, and does not even prevent the exploration of the same solutions multiple times. I take this as an indication that the optimization problem formulated in Equation 5.1 applied TLRH is tractable for computational approaches, given either enough time or appropriate algorithms.

My results do not prove that this will also be the case for other narrative systems, whose complexity can vary based on the number of characters, number of happening types, and the degree of freedom that they afford agents. It should also be remembered, that the

search space explorable by GA is somewhat restricted by design decisions regarding the chromosome representation of candidate solutions,
namely that the number of characters is fixed and that happenings
can be scheduled at most one time per character, which simplifies
the search problem at hand. However, despite these qualifications,
I consider this case study successful in making the point that the
computational representational format for narrative implemented by
InBloom can be used as the foundation for a CSC system. It allows
the system to take over responsibilities for creating candidate plots,
evaluate their value, and modify the plots in an intentional way in
order to increase their value. The way this process is realized does
not attempt to mimic, or even just resemble, human creativity, but
this is not a necessary requirement for a system do be deemed creative according to the understanding of CC introduced in Sec. 1.3.2.
What I find noteworthy, here, is that the means for computationally representing narratives employed here were not developed with
the sole purpose of being searched and optimized by a system, but
rather as a way for testing and exploring narratological theories. It is
thus anything but a given, that they should lend themselves for the
purposes of CC.

Another fact worth pointing out is that no solution was returned
more than one time, by either of the search algorithms. This is an
indication that the search terminated in local optima, and did not
reliably find the global optimum of the search space. Purely in terms
of optimization, this would be considered a shortcoming, since the
goal of optimization is to find the best possible solution. From the
perspective of CC, however, this might even be considered an advantage. For an algorithm to be deemed creative, it is not necessary for
it to find the best possible plot, as long as it finds a good-enough
one. On the contrary, being able to come up with different plots
on successive runs is actually conducive to a system's semblance of
creativity. This is an interesting observation because it implies that
when generative tasks in CC are framed as optimization problems, it
could be beneficial to solve these problems not with the most powerful
approaches at hand, but rather with ones that are on the brink of not
being capable of addressing them, in order to diversify the outputs.
This might even result in individual runs that fail to come up with
acceptable solutions in the available time, however, in humans, the
occasional failure seems to be at least conventionally considered an

expected epiphenomenon of creativity.

*It was the best of times, it was the worst of times,
it was the age of wisdom, it was the age of foolish-
ness, it was the epoch of belief, it was the epoch
of incredulity...*

Charles Dickens, 'A Tale of Two Cities'

6

Conclusion

TO CONCLUDE THE PRESENT DISSERTATION, I find it important to
accomplish two main tasks. One is to provide an overview over the
whole project—including the computational story composition (CSC)
system InBloom developed to serve as a practical case study—and
the other is to outline its contributions to the different fields that it
bridges.

The necessity to do the first arises from the unconventional,
hermeneutic structure of this thesis, which was motivated in Sec. 1.5
by the observation that for the task at hand a process is required that
combines methodologies from both Narrative Theory (NT) and Artificial Intelligence (AI). A side effect of this hermeneutic structure was
that the resulting narratological framework and computational model
were assembled incrementally, and, at no point, so far, presented in
their entirety.

The second task has been partly undertaken at the end of each
chapter, when I discussed the lessons learned during their completion. However, these insights were presented with attention to details
but no concern for a broader context because they were intended to
evaluate the work performed so far, and identify a way forward. In
this chapter, on the other hand, I want to put them in the context of
the three research questions that were introduced in Sec. 1.1:

RQ 1: Can NTs be computationally implemented using generative models? How can narratological theories benefit from such modeling?
RQ 2: Can CSC be modeled as the manipulation of a computational representation of narratives grounded in NT? What are the benefits of grounding the modeling process in NT?
RQ 3: Is a scientific/scholarly exchange between NT and CSC possible and productive? How can such an exchange be facilitated?

The first part of these RQ are yes/no questions about feasibility, which can all be answered 'yes' because the present thesis demonstrated that it is possible to implement certain narratological theories as generative models, and that these models can be used to generate novel plots, which in turn demonstrated the productivity of an exchange between NT and CSC.

These affirmations bring to the fore the respective second parts of the RQs, which I find to be the scientifically more interesting ones. First, how can NT benefit from computational generative modeling? I will address this question in Sec. 6.2.1, by summarizing the corollaries I suggest to the narrative theories considered in this thesis. Second, how can CSC benefit from a grounding in NT of the representations it operates on? This question will be addressed in Sec. 6.2.2, by summarizing the novel approaches to CSC that I explored in InBloom. And, third, how can the exchange between these two disciplines be facilitated in general, that is, what has been learned in this particular study that could aid future work at this interdisciplinary boundary? This will be addressed in Sec. 6.2.3, where I propose generative modeling as a novel research methodology and discuss it in the context of the Digital Humanities. The main contribution of my thesis, as I see it, is not in the development of a novel CSC system, but in addressing these theoretical questions.

6.1. Overview

Before I present the theoretical insights I gleaned from my work, I will provide an overview of its current state: 1) the narratological framework that I needed to assemble in order to be able to reduce the plot of my case study—the tale of *The Little Red Hen* (TLRH)—to first principles in this framework, and 2) the CSC system InBloom that implements this framework as a generative model. This section is not intended to provide a comprehensive overview over the individual parts that were developed in their respective chapters, but rather to outline how they come together to form a whole.

6.1.1. Theory: The Narratological Framework

The framework focuses on two narrative phenomena: plot and fictional characters, as well as their interactions (see Sec. 1.2.2 for an overview over narrative phenomena).

Plot is understood as a network—with virtual and actual components—in which events are connected by different types of causal relationships. The *actual domain* of this network, i.e. objective and observable parts of the plot, comprises *actions* (events that have an agent) and *happenings* (events that have no agent but patients). Its counterpart, the *virtual domain*, comprises *beliefs*, *wishes*, *obligations*, *plans*, and *affect*, i.e. the subjective, embedded narratives that individual characters build to make sense of the actual domain. The two are densely connected because mental events in embedded narratives cause characters to act, while actions and happenings are perceived by the involved characters and trigger new mental events in their embedded narratives, a dynamic that is described in detail in Sec. 2.2.

Characters are understood as affective and rational non-actual individuals. *Rational*, here, means that they follow a reasoning process in which *wishes* and *obligations* motivate characters to develop *plans* for their fulfillment. These plans are based on *beliefs* about the state of the story world, and are comprised of *actions* or sub-plans. Details on this can be found in Sec. 2.1. Their *affective* realm (as outlined in Secs. 3.2.2 and 3.2.3) is constituted by *personality* (stable dispositions to act and feel in certain ways) and *emotions* (valenced reactions to unfolding events), which interact and result in a current *mood* that captures characters' affective state at any given time in the narrative. The realms of affect and reasoning are closely intertwined: A character's personality and current mood influence what it wishes to achieve and feels obliged to do, how it prioritizes between these motivators, and the nature of the plans it can come up with for their fulfillment. Conversely, the plans and actions of a character are perceived and emotionally appraised by other characters, which then influences their affective state (for details, see Sec. 3.2.4).

Summarizing this from an internal perspective (see Sec. 1.2.4 for details on perspectives), plot emerges from the experiences and in-

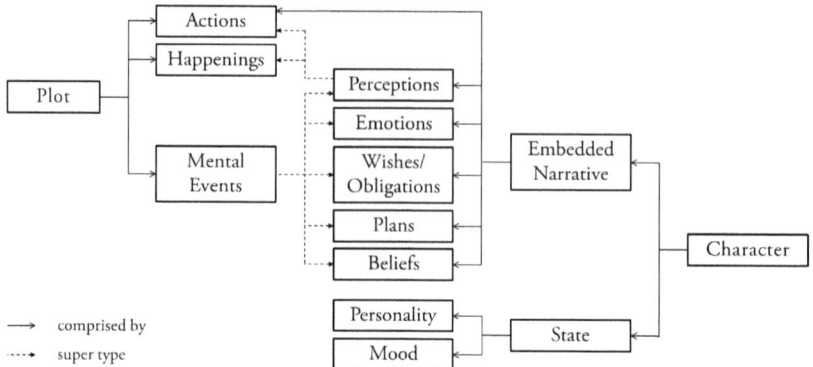

Figure 6.1: Structural relationship of the narrative phenomena plot and character in the proposed model. Normal arrows indicate a subtype relationship, open arrows a comprised-by relationship.

teractions of characters with each other and the story world in which they are spatially and temporally embedded. This is possible because a strong overlap exists between the intermediate phenomena that comprise plot and characters' embedded narratives (see Fig. 6.1). Thus, the suggested plot model is called *character-centric*: Given a narrative system that consists of the ontological rules as well as the existents of a story world, its characters' personalities and the providential happenings that befall them span a space of possible plots.

From an external perspective, these plots are not equally well suited to structure the content plane of a narrative. This circumstance is captured by *tellability*, a measure that allows to quantitatively compare and qualitatively analyze different plots. Tellability is comprised of four individual principles that gauge different types of structural properties of plot, defined based on both its actual as well as virtual components:

- *semantic opposition:* contrasts between characters' goals with the respective action outcomes, as well as reversals in the fortunes of characters

- *semantic parallelism and symmetry:* structural similarities in event-sequences pertaining to different characters, as well as to one character with itself but over time

- *functional polyvalence:* overlaps in the functions that individual events fulfill for the plot

- *suspense:* delays between the setting of a goal and its actualization or failure

Details on how this is conceptualized are outlined in Sec. 4.1.

6.1.2. Implementation: The InBloom System

Overall, InBloom is a generate-and-test architecture that performs a search over simulations (see Fig. 6.2). A *simulation* is the execution of a narrative system that has been parametrized with personality-traits for each character as well as a set of happenings. The result of this execution is a *story graph*[1], which consists of actual and mental events connected by edges denoting temporal order.

This story graph is post-processed and evaluated by the *tellability analysis* module, which creates two outputs: The *plot graph* that consists of actual and mental events connected by edges denoting causal relationships, as well as a balanced, real-valued *tellability score* be-

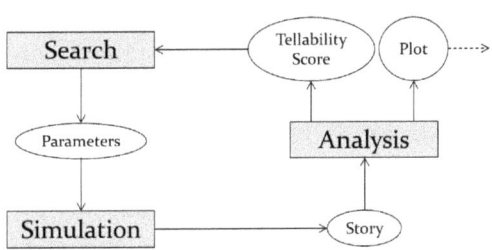

Figure 6.2: Abstract overall architecture of InBloom.

tween 0 and 1 that estimates the structural quality of the plot. Based on this score, a *search* algorithm decides whether the generated plot is good enough to finish the process, and if this is not the case decides how to change the *parameters* of the simulation, before the simulation is restarted.

Simulation

The simulation is implemented as a multi-agent system, in which autonomous agents represent fictional characters and the environment represents the story world. Plot emerges from the interactions of

---

[1]One of the conclusions presented in Sec. 4.3.3 on p. 275 was that what I called 'plot graph' in Def. 5 turned out to actually represent a 'story graph', while the 'analyzed plot graph' from Def.12 indeed represents a 'plot graph'.

these agents with each other and the environment, caused by their problem-solving behavior.

Agents are implemented as reasoning systems based on a BDI architecture, which was extended to incorporate the affective phenomena: *emotion, mood,* and *personality* as outlined in Fig. 6.3. These affective phenomena influence how *intentions* are selected from

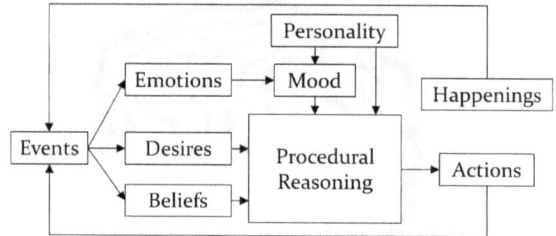

Figure 6.3: Abstract representation of the affective reasoning architecture that implements agents in InBloom.

competing *desires*, and which plans are selected to achieve these intentions. Furthermore, they can lead to the activation of new desires (for details see Sec. 3.3).

The *environment* implements *actions* that agents can take as part of their plans, *happenings* that can be scheduled by the search component of InBloom, and an initial state of the story world. It is responsible for maintaining the objective state of the story world by incorporating the effects of actions and happenings. The basic ontology supported by InBloom's environment offers restricted notions of *spatio-temporality, causality, agency* and *ownership,* which can be used and extended by individual narrative systems (for details see Sec. 2.3.4, starting from p. 74).

During the course of a simulation, all relevant events are retained in the form of a *story graph* that follows Def. 5. The vertices of this graph represent the actions taken by agents, the happenings that were triggered in the environment, and internal events generated by the affective reasoning systems of individual agents. These vertices are connected by edges that indicate a temporal order, such that each vertex has at most one predecessor and at most one successor.

Analysis

The analysis module operates on the story graph and performs two main functions: plot graph generation and tellability score computation.

The (analyzed) *plot graph*, which follows Def. 12, is generated by performing several post-processing steps over the story graph. These steps are responsible for identifying causal relations from meta-data stored in the story graph vertices as annotations (see Sec. 4.2.1). Most importantly, different types of edges are added to the graph, whenever specific types of relationships between events can be uncovered: motivation, actualization, termination, equality, causality, and cross-character interactions. These edges capture the causal structure that led to the emergence of the events on the surface of the narrative, and connect its actual with the virtual domain. This results in the analyzed plot graph, which is InBloom's main output format.

The *tellability score* is computed by quantifying instances of four specific structural properties of the plot graph, namely: functional polyvalence, semantic symmetry, semantic opposition and suspense. These values are normalized for plot length, and combined in a balanced way such that an ideal tellability is reached when no property dominates over the others (see Sec. 4.2.5). This results in a single real valued metric, the balanced tellability score, that estimates the structural quality of the plot.

Search

The plot space spanned by non-trivial narrative systems is so large, that random search is unlikely to find near-optimal plots given a realistic time frame. InBloom employs *Genetic Algorithms* (GA) to instead perform directed search. In GA, the parameters of each simulation are encoded in a vector-based format which is called the *genotype*. An initial population of 20 *individuals* with differing genotypes is created based on a number of heuristics, and each individual's tellability is analyzed. Iteratively, the worst-performing individuals are removed from the population, and replaced by *offspring* individuals whose genotype is created through *crossover*—which recombines the genotypes of the best-performing individuals in a probabilistic manner—and subsequent *mutation*—which can add random changes on top (details on these operations and the formalization can be found in Sec. 5.2). This results in a search behavior that compromises between exploitation of already identified valuable parameter combinations and exploration of novel parameter combinations, which leads to an increase of average population tellability over time.

In essence, this approach amounts to executing 20 of the cycles depicted in Fig. 6.2 in parallel, where the simulation and evaluation steps are performed independently, but the search process collects their results and derives new parameters from them.

6.1.3. Contextualization

After providing an overview over both theory and implementation, my work can be easily placed in the context of the various fields of study that were introduced in Chap. 1.

FOR THE PURPOSE OF NT, it is relevant to outline which aspects of narratives (see Sec. 1.2.4 for details) are bridged by the framework outlined in this thesis. Since it focuses on how fictional characters resemble actual persons and from this derives its notion of plot, the proposed framework can be classified as mainly concerned with the *mimetic* aspect of narrative. However, the notion of tellability adopted here is a *synthetic* one, since it quantifies how well suited a sequence of events is as a plot, which is a strictly artefactual property. No attempts are made to address symbolic or symptomatic aspects of narrative.

From the four narrative phenomena discussed in 1.2.2: *story and plot, character, discourse*, and *reader*, the present framework addresses the first two, as well as their interaction. Discourse, as a third phenomenon, can be partly tied in with the present work based on Alan Palmer's consideration about the relationship of discourse and fictional mind, which will be reiterated shortly.

IN THE CONTEXT OF CC, it is useful to locate my system on the CC continuum (see Sec. 1.3.2 for details), where I see it more on the side of the *cognitive-social* pole. The main reason for this is that my work focuses on computationally modeling theories from NT; it is interested in contributing back to that discipline rather than applying certain technologies for their own sake or in generating outstanding artefacts. This is also the reason why the plots that were explored as part of the case studies presented here are neither overly novel nor overly interesting in themselves. Their value lies in what they disclose about the theories that were used to model them. In terms of creative responsibilities (see Sec. 1.3.3), InBloom implements the A and E parts of FACE. It is capable of *generating instances of plot* (E) and of performing an *aesthetic evaluation* (A) of them. I have not mentioned it so far because it is not relevant for the narratological concepts behind InBloom, but through the use of its FU matching (which was implemented as a part of tellability analysis, see Sec. 4.1.1) the system can also be enabled to automatically generate functional summaries of the plots it produces, which I have shown elsewhere to be able to function as *framing* (Berov, 2019). While this approach would need more work to mature, it demonstrates potential for the system to also take over responsibility for F-type generative acts.

FINALLY, IN CSC, InBloom can be firmly placed as a *CC system* because it has no interactive capabilities and is directed towards composing as many tellable plots as it can find (see Sec. 1.4 for this distinction). It follows the *strong autonomy/emergent narrative approach*, since it represents characters as autonomous agents (see Sec. 1.4.1 and 1.4.2). To steer the generation of plot into more productive parts of the search space, the system does not rely on a drama manager which can assign certain goals to characters or disallow certain actions. Instead, it attempts to iteratively manipulate the autonomous characters into behaving in tellable ways by scheduling happenings that affect them, and calibrating their personalities such that they react strongly to these happenings.

6.2. Theoretical Contributions

6.2.1. Contribution to Narrative Theory

The second part of my RQ 1 asks how narratological theories can benefit from generative modeling. I think there does not exist enough practical work to inform an answer to this question in general, but will instead address it by discussing the particular narratological insights that I garnered about the two theories I based my work on: Marie-Laure Ryan's possible worlds framework, and Alan Palmer's fictional minds approach.[2]

---

[2] At the onset, this content will sound reminiscent of the framework I presented above in 6.1.1. This is only natural, since my framework is an extension and combination of these two. Differences will become apparent, once I discuss the insights.

Contribution to Ryan's Possible Worlds Approach

During the course of Chap. 2, I discussed Marie-Laure M.-L. Ryan's (1991) possible worlds based narrative semantics of plot. Ryan's theory describes the emergence and the properties of plot based on the goal-directed actions of fictional characters, which are structurally, in turn, described by a set of propositions capturing their interior state: beliefs, wishes, and obligations. Based on beliefs, characters make plans in order to fulfill their wishes and obligations (their motivators), and the actions of these plans change the state of the story world, resulting in the observable part of the plot. However, Ryan argues that also only partially actualized plans should be considered part of the plot because they are required to understand the causal structure that underlies the seemingly unfruitful actions of these thwarted plans. This means that plot is a network of actual and virtual event sequences, as well as the beliefs, wishes and obligations that drive them. However, as my implementation of a narrative system during the case study in Sec. 2.4 demonstrated, this framework is not sufficient to reconstruct the dynamics of the plot of the folktale TLRH. Based only on these principles, it is not possible to explain why the farm animals in this tale behave differently from each other: some laboriously working in the field all day long, while others are relaxing in the sun. It is also not possible to reduce the punishment of the relaxing animals by the hen to the outlined first principles: why does the hen develop the wish to punish the other animals, and why does taunting them by first offering but then withholding bread constitute a punishment? In Chap. 3 I argue that these problems can be resolved by adopting a more mimetically informed approach to the process of character reasoning, which is responsible for connecting characters' perceptions to motivators and these, in turn, to plans. In particular, I suggest that personality affects how characters select wishes or obligations to act upon, when several (perhaps conflicting) of these motivators are active, and that sufficiently strong changes in affect can induce new motivators. In the case study presented in Sec. 3.4 I demonstrate that respective refinements of the narrative system of TLRH are sufficiently expressive to allow the emergence of the desired plot dynamics: Positing different personality traits for the farm animals (high conscientiousness for the hen, low conscientiousness for the others) allows the narrative system to differentiate their initial behaviors, while the repeated experience of negative disappointment emotions by the hen due to repeated refusals of her help requests accumulate into a hostile mood that can act as a plausible trigger for her punishment wish.

Apart form describing the dynamics of plot, Ryan also introduces an idiosyncratic take on the concept of tellability, by deriving several principles from the aesthetics of lyrical poetry: functional polyvalence, semantic symmetry, and semantic opposition, as well as later adding a forth principle called suspense. She makes the individual principles plausible by presenting isolated examples from canonical works, but does not provide an in-depth analysis that would demonstrate how these principles come together into a unified whole. Furthermore, she does not demonstrate that the conclusions that can be derived from comparatively applying tellability to different works are narratologically plausible. In Chap. 4, I present a computational operationalization of the four tellability principles, which can be used to quantify the tellability of computationally represented plots following the principles I described above. This allows me to conduct a quasi-objective exploration of the properties of Ryan's tellability[3], by applying it to several minimally differing versions of the same plot and comparing the corresponding changes in tellability. The resulting analysis is, to the best of my knowledge, the first practical application of Ryan's tellability as a narratological tool.

To summarize these points, my contribution to Ryan's possible worlds based semantics of plot is the following:

- I demonstrate that the framework is underspecified, in that it does not explain how wishes or obligations arise from observed events, and how these motivators are selected as actionable in cases where they contradict each other.

- I demonstrate that this problem can be resolved by adding the mimetic character phenomena personality and affect as additional first principles affecting the dynamics of wish/obligation selection and arousal.

- I demonstrate that Ryan's tellability can be operationalized as a narratological tool for the quantitative analysis of plots, which

---

[3]Such an approach can never be objective, since any operationalization is necessarily performed by a subject, based on its interpretations of the concept. However, after its implementation, an operationalized measure can be deemed quasi objective in that it analyzes all plots in completely the same way.

leads to results that can conform to human qualitative interpretation.

Palmer's Fictional Mind Approach

Above, I explained how the problems I encountered in Ryan's approach could be solved by introducing personality and affect. The reason that led me to consider these phenomena is Alan Palmer's (2004) fictional mind approach that, in essence, states that fictional minds are represented by readers much like real minds, and thus should be narratologically constituted by similar phenomena. Although the content of Palmer's approach is fairly unconventional, the methodology that he used to argue for it is analytical modeling, the classic way of NT. Starting from the characters' actions and their presentation in the narrative's discourse, he demonstrates that the nature of the actions and the way they are presented discloses what is happening in characters' fictional minds, even when there is no explicit psycho-narration to describe it. In Sec. 3.1.3 on p. 115, I reported a canonical example from Virginia Woolf's novel *Mrs. Dalloway*, where the protagonist Clarissa Dalloway is payed an unexpected visit by her former suitor Peter Walsh. Having returned after long travels, Walsh is described as positively trembling when taking both her hands to kiss them. The natural interpretation of this passage is to assume a causative psychological state in the character's mind for this behavior, presumably excitement, instead of e.g. suspecting that he is succumbing to Parkinson's disease. Since readers are constantly presented with characters' actions and the embedded narratives that they decode from them, they start to develop expectations and mental models of these characters, which are taken to represent their personality. Palmer describes his approach as teleological because it investigates statements from the discourse and tries to uncover their purpose in fictional mind representation.. This results in an analytical reasoning chain, that starts from discursive action descriptions, derives embedded narratives from them, and finally integrates these narratives into models of personality. Thus, Palmer's general insight is that readers can (re)construct fictional minds from discourse. With the case study of Chap. 3, I demonstrated that also the inverse is true: After implementing fictional minds—using an affective BDI reasoning architecture—in my plot composition system I could empirically show that changing a character's personality parameters results in changes to their embedded narratives, which in turn can lead to significant changes in the narrative's plot. This move is in Palmer's teleological spirit because it investigates the purpose of specific parts of fictional minds. I call it inverse to Palmer's original insight for two reasons: One is that instead of analyzing how surface phenomena are integrated into deep structures, it shows through generation how changes in deep structures influence the narrative's surface. The second is that instead of arguing how fictional minds are reconstructed from discourse it argues how plot is constructed from fictional minds. It is important to note that such an inversion is difficult, if not impossible, to undertake from an analytical perspective because it is hard to isolate changes in deep structures responsible for changes on the surface in real narratives, since they normally differ in many regards at the same time. From a generative perspective, however, this is unproblematic because here the scholar has full control over the parameters of a narrative's deep structure and can thus vary them in isolation, which allows to study causal effects on the surface realization.

Summarizing, my contribution to Palmer's fictional mind approach is the following:

- I demonstrate, that not only can fictional minds be reconstructed from discourse, like Palmer argues, but that additionally fictional minds also causally influence plot.

6.2.2. Contribution to Computational Story Composition

The second part of my RQ 2 asks, how CSC can benefit from starting the modeling of story composition from grounding the employed computational representation of narratives in NT. Again, I will not attempt a general answer, but rather present the concrete insights that I gathered while working on InBloom.

Due to the nature of the narratological theories that I selected for implementation, InBloom ended up being an emergentist plot composition system. Recently, AI researcher and media artist J. Ryan (2018) published his dissertation, which goes a long way towards establishing a dedicated theory of emergent narrative systems, and that I consider an outstanding work. Some of my insights seem to align well with Ryan's ideas, while at the same time also diverging in interesting ways. For this reason, I will first outline what I consider my contributions specifically to emergentist narrative composition, in the context of Ryan's ideas. Then, I will move on to a broader topic, and outline what I consider my insights into the computational representation of narrative in general, i.e. irrespective of the particular approach.

Contribution to Emergentist Narrative Systems

The emergent narrative paradox has been leveled as a heavy charge against the viability of strong autonomy (also called emergent narrative) systems. It asks, how a structured and non-local phenomenon like plot should emerge from the interaction of autonomous characters whose decision processes are not concerned with global structures but only their personal local context. In his dissertation, James Ryan mounted a defense of emergent narrative system by demonstrating how this problem can be overcome using what he calls a *curationist approach to emergent narrative*: The simulated world and characters should be complex, the possible range of their interactions manifold and a simulation should run for a long time. The sheer complexity and abundance of the resulting material should then make sure that plot-patterns can be identified by sifting through the chronicle of the simulated world, even if their emergence is unlikely. Historians have found plenty of stories in the chronicles of the actual world, and so this should also be possible in simulated worlds. Consequently, Ryan proposes that emergentist systems should not be based on narrative theory, but rather on historiography. He argues: "the pleasure of emergent narrative is rooted primarily in its correspondences to the genre of nonfiction: when events emerge out of simulations, they feel like they really happen, and this unlocks [a] set of aesthetics [that were outlined before]" (J. Ryan, 2018, p. 220).

My position in this dissertation, from the start, was to do the exact opposite: start from narrative theory and non-dogmatically operationalize its models with any kind of generative computational model that would serve the purpose, without being much caught up with concerns of technological purity. It is thus somewhat surprising that, after having done so with models from Marie-Laure Ryan and Alan Palmer, I arrived exactly where, according to James Ryan, I should not have: in the realm of emergent narrative. This is a valuable insight in its own right, I think: the emergentist approach can stand on a broader base than what James Ryan's dissertation suggests. It *has* merit from the historiographic perspective, but *also* from the narratological. Its latter merit is this: a focus on strong autonomy and cognitively inspired agent models allows to elegantly capture essential elements of narrative semantics like knowledge, wishes, obligations, personality and affect. These phenomena are all either direct parts of plot, or indirectly affect it (as I demonstrate in Chaps. 2 and 3). They are also relevant to assess the aesthetic quality of plot (as I demonstrate in Chap. 4). A grounding of emergent narrative systems in narrative theory is important because it can shed light on the relationship between characters and plot. It can demonstrate *what sort* of complexity is relevant for character models and why, while a historiographic perspective can only argue *that* this complexity is important.

So how does my approach deal with the emergentist narrative paradox? It is all well and good that the properties of individual agents *can* come together into a plot, but this is only a *theoretical* benefit of a particular approach to the computational representation of narrative. For a story composition system, they also have to *reliably do so*, and this is where emergentist systems commonly fall short. As I glossed in Chap. 1, this problem has sometimes been approached through the use of drama managers that intervene into simulations and tell characters what their goals are, or what they can or cannot do. James Ryan refers to this approach as *interventionist emergent narrative* and argues that it is not the way forward because it works against the grain of the very approach it should rescue, by inhibiting the simulations' emergent potential and making events stand out as unnatural. In his own words, while remedying the pain of emergent narrative, it also kills its pleasure (J. Ryan, 2018, p. 221). I think that, broadly, this observation is correct. Seeing it from the historiography angle, it is understandable that interventions seem unnecessary, after all, history too unfolded without any divine intervention in order to ensure entertaining stories. However, from my narratological perspective, Ryan's solution of abolishing all intervention seems too radical. Counterfactual thought is one of the great virtues of the human mind, and as Marie-Laure Ryan demonstrated, one of the roots of narrative. Why wait for history to slowly run its course, if it is so easy to imagine how things will end, or how events might have been different if only some particular details were changed? Or, translating that into more computational parlance: Why simulate hours after hours of a complex story world in the hope of eventually generating some valuable material? Instead, one can see where the simulation is after ten minutes, adapt the parameters that define its course, and restart the simulation, until that very valuable material appears during the first ten minutes. I propose to call this approach *creationist emergent narrative* because of how it is similar but also different from Ryan's curationist approach. They are similar, because both approaches work by exploring the space of possible plots set up by a narrative system. They are different, in how this exploration works: Ryan's is a laissez-faire approach that relies on entropy and randomness to explore the space for him, while mine is more akin to the idea of intelligent design where, step by step, the 'perfect' narrative system is setup for a particular plot to emerge. This circumvents the problems of common interventionist approaches described above because characters do not need to be artificially prevented from doing certain things, or forced into doing others, while a simulation runs. Instead, if their behavior does not come together in a tellable plot, it can be changed by restarting the simulation with different personality parameters, as I have demonstrated in Chap. 4. Additionally, in Chap. 5, I have demonstrated that calibrating personality parameters with carefully orchestrated happenings allows for an indirect steering of a narrative's course of action via the manipulation of character behavior.

There is another similarity between Ryan's work and mine that I find interesting because we again arrive at it from very different directions. For Ryan, a crucial task of curationist narrative systems is what he calls *story sifting*: identifying tellable material from the chronicle of everything that was simulated. Without sifting, his approach does not work, since most of the material generated during a simulation poses no narrative interest. He suggests that there are two ways of doing this: "I differentiate between sifting patterns and sifting heuristics: the former pattern-match against the material recorded in a chronicle, while the latter encode abstract policies that may guide the sifting process" (J. Ryan, 2018, p. 237). To readers of my thesis, this may sound reminiscent of the inner workings of my tellability implementation, presented in Chap. 4. The detection of FUs in the plot graph is an instance of inexact pattern matching used to gauge the generated plot's coherence, while the four tellability principles (functional polyvalence, semantic symmetry, semantic opposition and suspense) are abstract heuristics that are used to judge whether the generated plot is tellable. Indeed, I would go as far as to claim that, when implementing tellability, I actually developed a set of sifting heuristics for InBloom (although without, at that time, knowing of the existence of this concept). There is, of course, one major difference: I use these heuristics not to sift for all tellable plots in the chronicle of a long simulation, but to test whether the one plot that was generated by a short one is worth keeping. However, I feel that this is more of a lexical difference than a functional one: I see no theoretical reasons why my implementation of tellability could not be adapted to sift instead of just test. This is a serendipitous insight since in the conclusion of his thesis James Ryan speaks highly of this challenge, and issues the following call for action:

> [...] we will likely need to develop robust sifting heuristics. This is something that is not delivered in this thesis, because I do not personally know how to do this yet, and it is a very hard challenge. I would like to issue a call to others to roll up their sleeves and get to work on this critical problem in emergent narrative—indeed, sifting heuristics could likely be the topic of another entire dissertation.
>
> (J. Ryan, 2018, p. 692)

At the risk of sounding ideological, I would like to point out that what enabled me to answer this call, with my modest contribution, was the grounding of my work in narrative theory instead of historiography. Of course, if I learned one thing from my exposure to NT then it is that several perspectives on the same phenomenon can co-exist, and that there is merit in their interaction, so I do not mean to promote one over the other.

To summarize these points, my contribution to the theory of emergent story composition is the following:

- I argue that, contrary to claims in recent work, emergent story composition can be motivated by and benefit from grounding in narrative theory.

- I expand the distinction of approaches to emergent narrative systems developed by James Ryan, which consists of interventionist and curationist approaches, with a new option called the creationist approach.

- I propose that character-personality and happenings are two types of parameters that can be varied by emergentist story composition systems in search of tellable plots, without running the danger of disrupting character believability.

- I demonstrate the viability of Marie-Laure Ryan's theoretic notion of plot tellability as a sifting heuristic for emergent storytelling systems.

Contribution to the Computational Representation of Narrative

The most concrete contribution is the formalization of tellability I developed in Chap. 4, which is not limited to use by InBloom but can be also employed by other plot composition systems in order to evaluate plot quality. In the last section, I argued that emergentist systems can use it as a sifting heuristic, but this is not the only use case. It could also be employed to guide the generation of plots in the case of strong story systems, or as an aesthetic measure in cognitive approaches. This makes it an approach-agnostic contribution to CSC. However, due to the nature of the theoretical underpinnings of tellability, not all plot composition systems can make use of the measure. In order to be able to compute tellability, systems need to represent several narrative phenomena, namely: temporality, intentionality, short-term affect, mid-term affect and causality, as I explained in Sec. 4.3.3.

At the end of Chap. 4, I observed how the need to evaluate the suitability of a sequence of InBloom-generated events as a plot resulted in the necessity to detect an "abstract causal organization and roles that can be superimposed over the events" (p. 276)—FUs, in my implementation, i.e. abstract units of meaning that can match different configurations of concrete events. From this, I argued that what researchers in the field unifyingly call the *content plane* of a narrative should rather be represented computationally using two different levels: the concrete events of the *story world plane*, and the superimposed abstract structures of the *plot plane*. The benefit of such a separation of representation is that it induces a corresponding separation of processing during composition, with dedicated processes responsible for generating the events of the story world and the structures of the plot. This is advisable because these two processes differ fundamentally: the former takes an internal perspective and exerts a bottom-up self organizational force on the content that ensures that characters and events are believable, while the latter is rooted in an external perspective and exerts a top-down structuring force that ensures the content is well formed. The two forces seem to be mutually opposing, but I believe that high potential for the composition of good narratives lies not in favoring one over the other, but in allowing them to form the narrative such that it can balance them out against each other. Less metaphorically: instead of a linear process that first generates the one and then merely tests for the presence of the other—treating it as a subordinate phenomenon—an iterative process, where a story world module and a plot module collaborate on a draft alternately, and thus mutually influencing each other, seems more promising to me (see p.277 for an example of this envisioned process, and the associated challenges). InBloom is a system that is firmly rooted in the linear tradition because its simulation first creates story world events completely autonomously, after which the tellability module checks for the presence of plot. One might argue that there is some collaboration because simulation runs with low tellability are discarded (see Chap. 5 for a description of the process), but the crux is that there is no direct influence back from plot detection to simulation. This precludes the system from realizing that e.g. the particular events of a story world have the potential to become a revenge plot, and thus the characters should be adapted such that appropriate events are more likely to emerge. An important part of this example is the capability to detect what I called 'potential': that a sequence of events partly resembles a certain basic plot, or that a certain plot is nearly instantiated by a sequence of events. Such inexact matching between the two levels of content representation would allow a story composition system to guide the exploration of the conceptual space it performs in a way that balances out the requirements for believability and structural integrity.

It is important to remember that story world and plot are not the only levels of representation that are required to model narrative. Although I bracketed them out in the present work, the levels of discourse and prose are just as important. The standard approach is to organize the generation of these levels in a linear pipeline: First, content is generated, then, it is re-arranged according to discourse principles, and finally, the discourse is rendered as narrative prose (see e.g. Callaway & Lester, 2002; Reiter & Dale, 2000). However, my observations from above seem also to apply here. As I mentioned in passing on p. 277: "the difference between a narrative of 'Overcoming a Monster' and a 'Tragedy', in many cases, could boil down to whether the focus is on the experiences of the hero slaying the monster, or on those of the monster being slain". Essentially, this implies that the same set of story world events can be seen as fitting one basic plot or another, depending on the choice of focalization, which is a decision that is firmly located on the discourse level. But if discourse level decisions can affect a narrative's plot-structure affordances then it is contra-productive to rely on a linear process where the plot is fixed before the discourse. This leads me to the hypothesis, that linear composition pipelines are generally not well suited for CSC because they can hardly do justice to the many interrelations that connect narrative phenomena (for these interrelations, refer back to Fig. 1.3). Thus, a more promising approach would be to explore iterative processes that alternate between the optimization of the different levels of representation, and do so using a multi-layered computational model of narrative that allows the content of these layers to come together via inexact matching.

Summarizing, my contribution to CSC in general is the following:

- I formalized tellability as an approach-independent measure of plot quality.

- I argue that the content-plane of a narrative should be computationally represented using at least two levels of abstraction: story-world and plot, and that such a representation should allow inexact matching of elements from one level to the other, and vice versa.

- I argue that, instead of a linear pipeline, computational story composition should be conceptualized as an iterative process that alternates between the optimization of different types of content and form.

6.2.3. Contribution to Digital Humanities

The second part of my RQ 3 asks how the exchange between NT and CSC can be facilitated. Here, I will actually propose a general answer by promoting the use of the methodology that I employed in this thesis. This falls into the interest range of the Digital Humanities (DH), a discipline that focuses on the development of computational tools and resources for the humanities, as well as the facilitation and evaluation of their usage. I consider my work an instance of DH research, and will frame the main insights gleaned in its wake once more in this broader context.

In Sec. 1.5, I outlined the challenges of interdisciplinary research between NT and generative AI: markedly differing research methodologies as well as difficulties exchanging concepts and models. I proposed an approach I called generative modeling as a methodology to address these problems. Generative modeling incorporates the linear design-implement-evaluate process of AI into hermeneutic cycles of theory formation and theory testing. Each cycle follows the same process: one starts with a narratological theory, formalizes as well as implements it using a computational generative model, and uses this model to attempt a regeneration of an existing narrative. Conclusions can be then drawn by comparing the generated narrative to its original counterpart. If the two are discernibly alike then the process can be considered a success, which makes two points: one is that the narrative in question can be reduced to the first principles put forward by the narratological theory, and the second is that the computational model is a valid implementation of the underlying theory. This addresses two important issues of the collaboration between AI and NT, namely, how to evaluate AI implementations in the NT domain where quantifiable metrics are scarce, and how to incorporate computational generative modeling in the process of NT theory formation. A more complex situation occurs, when regenerated and existing narrative are not alike (or when the narrative simply can not be regenerated at all). While it is clear that this means a failure of the respective cycle of generative modeling, the reasons for this can not be unequivocally attributed: One possibility is that the implementation of the theory is flawed, while the other is that the theory itself is not sufficient to model the narrative in question. Based on the nature of the failure, a hypothesis has to be formulated on how it can be resolved, which is then used to inform the next cycle of generative modeling. This inference is a crucial part of the methodology, since the failure of individual cycles is probable and an important source of insight. At the same time, however, this inference is the most problematic step of the process since it can rarely be made based solely on logical reasoning, but instead depends on a scholar's intuition and acumen. Still, I could demonstrate the feasibility of making such an inference with the failure of the generative modeling cycle described in Chapter 2, and its resolution through the cycle described in Chapter 3.

In the present dissertation, I employed generative modeling as the methodology driving Chaps. 2, 3 and 4, which resulted in a functioning implementation of a story composition system that is capable of generating and evaluating plots, as well as a range of theoretical contributions to NT and CSC. As I wrote on p. 40, "my thesis itself is intended to be [a] demonstration that generative modeling is a suit-

able approach for the exchange between NT and CSC". Given that I
could report several contributions above, I consider this point made.
My hope is that this encourages other researchers in DH projects,
who so far focused on implementing computational tools that support the *analysis* of literary texts, to also consider the *potential* of
generative models for their work. For NT, the gain would be that
of a radically new tool that can allow the demonstration of causal
effects that are hard to prove purely from analytical reasoning, like
the insight on the causal role of personality on plot in Palmer's fictional mind approach, presented above. For CSC, the gain could be
an influx of theoretically informed computational representation formalisms for narrative phenomena, that have so far been eschewed by
the field.[4] A long-term vision for the use of AI in NT that springs
from this idea was formulated recently by one of the working groups
of the Dagstuhl Seminar 19172[5] entitled "Computational Creativity
Meets Digital Literary Studies": Computational analysis of narrative
texts and generative modeling of narratives can ideally work hand in
hand as mutual validators in an approach called cycle consistency.
To exemplify this idea: imagine a narrative text that is translated
into some sort of well developed computational representation by an
narratological analysis system. How can the computational representation be checked for correctness? One way would be to execute a
generative system on this computational representation, and verify
that the generated narrative is isomorphic (or at least related) to the
original story. The idea is a natural descendant of the work presented
in this thesis, where the responsibility for the analysis of the narrative and its encoding in a computational representation format was
handed over to a human, while the recreation of the plot was already
the responsibility of the CSC system. 'Climbing the meta mountain'
(introduced in Sec. 1.3.3), one of the central tenets of CC research,
calls for the transfer of more and more of responsibility from the human to the machine, which, here, would culminate in exactly the cycle
consistency system sketched above. While this vision, of course, still
remains far away for NT and AI, in other fields it is already gainfully

---

[4]One such phenomenon that comes to my mind immediately is (unreliable)
narration, a long-established subject of scholarly curiosity in NT that has (to the
best of my knowledge) never been addressed by CSC systems despite its obvious
potential.

[5]https://www.dagstuhl.de/en/program/calendar/semhp/?semnr=19172

employed. In machine translation, texts often are translated into a target language and then back to the source language in order to judge the quality of the translation algorithm, and in computational style transfer it is employed as an unsupervised loss in much the same way. Enabling something similar for the computational study of narratives is a fascinating and enticing prospect.

To summarize, my contribution to the digital humanities is the following

- I propose a novel method for the computational exploration of dynamic properties of narratological theories, called generative modeling, and demonstrate its feasibility as well as ability to generate insights.

6.3. Valediction

If I were allowed to decide what impact this thesis will make, I would wish for it to encourage more collaboration between AI and NT. Both fields have the potential to benefit from an increased exchange: AI systems require the ability to tell stories in order to communicate with humans in a more natural way, and perhaps it is even one of the prerequisites for achieving human-level intelligence. NT, on the other hand, stands to gain additional tools, not only for the automated analyses of narratives but also for theory testing via generation, a practice that has already been beneficial for another domain in the humanities, linguistics. The work I presented here shows that a mutually beneficial exchange is possible, and that ways can be found to bridge the inherent methodological divide between the two disciplines. One such way, the one I laid out here, is generative modeling. If you find it appealing, by all means, include it in your own academic journeys. I would welcome for it to become a road well traveled.

7
References

Literary Works

Austen, J. (1815). *Emma*. John Murray.

de Cervantes, M. (1605). *The Ingenious Gentleman Don Quixote of La Mancha*. Francisco de Robles.

Defoe, D. (1719). *Robinson Crusoe*. William Taylor.

Dick, P. K. (1962). *The Man in the High Castle*. Putnam.

Dickens, C. (1861). *Great Expectations*.

Eliot, G. (1871). *Middlemarch, A Study of Provincial Life*. William Blackwood and Sons.

Henry, O. (1905). *The Gift of the Magi*. The New York Sunday World.

Joyce, J. (1922). *Ulysses*. Shakespeare and Company.

Poe, E. A. (1843). *The Tell-Tale Heart*. James Russell Lowell.

Shakespeare, W. (1603). *The Tragedy of Othello, the Moor of Venice*. Thomas Walkley.

Shakespeare, W. (1623). *The Tragedy of Macbeth*. Edward Blount, William and Isaac Jaggard.

Tolkien, J. R. R. (1954). *The Lord of the Rings*. Allen and Unwin.

Waugh, E. (1930). *Vile Bodies*. Chapman & Hall.

Scientific and Scholarly Works

Abbott, H. P. (2002). *The Cambridge Introduction to Narrative*. Cambridge University Press.

Akimoto, T. (2019). Theoretical framework for computational story blending: From a cognitive system perspective. *Proceedings of the 10th International Conference on Computational Creativity*, 49–56.

Alfonso, B., Vivancos, E., & Botti, V. J. (2014). An open architecture for affective traits in a BDI agent. *Proceedings of the 6th International Conference on Evolutionary Computation Theory and Applications*, 320–325. https://doi.org/10.5220/0005153603200325

Allen, J. F. (1983). Maintaining knowledge about temporal intervals. *Commun. ACM, 26*(11), 832–843.

Aylett, R. (2000). Emergent narrative, social immersion and "storification". *Proceedings of the 1st International Workshop on Narrative and Interactive Learning Environments*, 35–44.

Bahamon, J. C. (2016). *A Computational Model for the Portrayal of Personality Traits in Planning-Based Narrative Generation* [PhD Thesis]. North Carolina State University.

Bahamon, J. C., & Young, R. M. (2013). CB-POCL: A choice-based algorithm for character personality in planning-based narrative generation. *2013 Workshop on Computational Models of Narrative, 32*, 4–23. https://doi.org/10.4230/OASIcs.CMN.2013.4

Bal, M. (1997). *Narratology: Introduction to the Theory of Narrative* (Second). University of Toronto Press.

Barthes, R. (1977). *Image-Music-Text*. Macmillan.

Barthes, R. ([1970] 1974). *S/Z*. Hill & Wang.

Berov, L. (2017). Towards a computational measure of plot tellability. *Proceedings of the 10th International Workshop on Intelligent Narrative Technologies*, 169–175.

Berov, L. (2019). Summaries can frame—but no effect on creativity. *Proceedings of the Tenth International Conference on Computational Creativity*, 164–171.

Beye, C. R. (2006). *Ancient Epic Poetry: Homer, Apollonius, Virgil: With a Chapter on the Gilgamesh Poems*. Bolchazy-Carducci Publishers.

Blum, C., & Roli, A. (2003). Metaheuristics in combinatorial optimization: Overview and conceptual comparison. *ACM Comput. Surv. CSUR, 35*(3), 268–308.

Boden, M. A. (2004). *The Creative Mind: Myths and Mechanisms* (2nd edition). Routledge.

Bonnici, V., Giugno, R., Pulvirenti, A., Shasha, D., & Ferro, A. (2013). A subgraph isomorphism algorithm and its application to biochemical data. *BMC Bioinformatics, 14*(S13). https://doi.org/10.1186/1471-2105-14-S7-S13

Booker, C. (2004). *The Seven Basic Plots: Why We Tell Stories*. Continuum.

Bordini, R. H., Hübner, J. F., & Wooldridge, M. (2007). *Programming Multi-agent Systems in AgentSpeak Using Jason* (Vol. 8). John Wiley & Sons.

Brenner, M. (2010). Creating dynamic story plots with continual multiagent planning. *Proceedings of the Twenty-Fourth AAAI Conference on Artificial Intelligence}*, 1517–1522.

Brown, T. B., Mann, B., Ryder, N., Subbiah, M., Kaplan, J., Dhariwal, P., Neelakantan, A., Shyam, P., Sastry, G., Askell, A., Agarwal, S., Herbert-Voss, A., Krueger, G., Henighan, T., Child, R., Ramesh, A., Ziegler, D. M., Wu, J., Winter, C., ... Amodei, D. (2020). Language Models are Few-Shot Learners. *ArXiv200514165 Cs*. Retrieved October 5, 2020, from http://arxiv.org/abs/2005.14165

Bruner, J. S. (1986). *Actual Minds, Possible Worlds*. Harvard University Press.

Bühler, J. L., & Dunlop, W. L. (2019). The narrative identity approach and romantic relationships. *Soc. Personal. Psychol. Compass, 13*(4).

Buschmann, F., Meunier, R., Rohnert, H., Sommerlad, P., & Stal, M. (1996). *Pattern-Oriented Software Architecture - Volume 1: A System of Patterns*. Wiley Publishing.

Callaway, C. B., & Lester, J. C. (2002). Narrative prose generation. *Artif. Intell., 139*(2), 213–252.

Caracciolo, M. (2016). *Strange Narrators in Contemporary Fiction: Explorations in Readers' Engagement with Characters*. University of Nebraska Press.

Cavazza, M., & Pizzi, D. (2006). Narratology for interactive story-telling: A critical introduction. *Technol. Interact. Digit. Storytell. Entertain.*, 72–83.

Charnley, J. W., Pease, A., & Colton, S. (2012). On the notion of framing in computational creativity. *Proceedings of the 3rd International Conference on Computational Creativity*, 77–81.

Colton, S. (2008). Creativity versus the perception of creativity in computational systems. *AAAI Spring Symposium: Creative Intelligent Systems*, 14–20.

Colton, S., Charnley, J. W., & Pease, A. (2011). Computational creativity theory: The FACE and IDEA descriptive models. *Proceedings of the 2nd International Conference on Computational Creativity*, 90–95.

Colton, S., & Wiggins, G. A. (2012). Computational creativity: The final frontier? *Proceedings of the 20th European Conference on Artificial Intelligence*, *12*, 21–26.

Cook, M., Colton, S., Pease, A., & Llano, M. T. (2019). Framing in computational creativity – A survey and taxonomy. *Proceedings of the Tenth International Conference on Computational Creativity*.

Cook, S. A. (1971). The complexity of theorem-proving procedures. *Proceedings of 3rd ACM Symposium on Theory of Computing*, 151–158.

Cordella, L. P., Foggia, P., Sansone, C., & Vento, M. (1998). Subgraph transformations for the inexact matching of attributed relational graphs. In *Graph based representations in pattern recognition* (pp. 43–52). Springer.

Cordella, L. P., Foggia, P., Sansone, C., & Vento, M. (2004). A (sub)graph isomorphism algorithm for matching large graphs. *IEEE Trans. Pattern Anal. Mach. Intell.*, *26*(10), 1367–1372.

Currie, G. (2010). *Narratives and Narrators: A Philosophy of Stories*. Oxford University Press.

Da Silva, S. G., & Tehrani, J. J. (2016). Comparative phylogenetic analyses uncover the ancient roots of Indo-European folktales. *R. Soc. Open Sci.*, *3*(1).

Dannenberg, H. (2008). *Coincidence and Counterfactuality*. University of Nebraska Press.

Darley, J. M., & Batson, C. D. (1973). From jerusalem to jericho: A study of situational and dispositional variables in helping behavior. *J. Pers. Soc. Psychol.*, *27*(1), 100–108.

Deese, J., & Kaufman, R. A. (1957). Serial effects in recall of unorganized and sequentially organized verbal material. *J. Exp. Psychol.*, *54*(3), 180–187.

Doležel, L. (1998). *Heterocosmica: Fiction and Possible Worlds.* John Hopkins University Press.

Eco, U. (1984). *The Role of the Reader: Explorations in the Semiotics of Texts* (Vol. 318). Indiana University Press.

Eder, J. (2006). Ways of being close to characters. *Film Stud.*, *8*(1), 68–80.

Eder, J., Jannidis, F., & Schneider, R. (2010). *Characters in Fictional Worlds: Understanding Imaginary Beings in Literature, Film, and Other Media.* Walter de Gruyter.

Elgin, C. Z. (1999). *Considered Judgment.* Princeton University Press.

Eysenck, M. W. (2004). *Psychology: An International Perspective.* Psychology Press.

Felski, R. (2015). *The Limits of Critique.* University of Chicago Press.

Flood, A. (2011). Getting more from George RR Martin. *The Guardian.* https://www.theguardian.com/books/booksblog/2011/apr/14/more-george-r-r-martin

Flower, L., & Hayes, J. R. (1981). A cognitive process theory of writing. *Coll. Compos. Commun.*, *32*(4), 365–387.

Fludernik, M. (2009). *An Introduction to Narratology.* Routledge.

Forster, E. M. ([1927] 2002). *Aspects of the Novel* (1st electronic). RosettaBooks LLC.

Foster-Harris, W. (1959). *The Basic Patterns of Plot.* University of Oklahoma Press.

Gabriel, R. P. (2016). In the control room of the banquet. *Proceedings of the 2016 ACM International Symposium on New Ideas, New Paradigms, and Reflections on Programming and Software*, 250–268.

Gamma, E., Helm, R., Johnson, R., & Vlissides, J. (1995). *Design patterns: Elements of reusable object-oriented software.* Addison-Wesley.

Gebhard, P. (2005). ALMA: A layered model of affect. *Proceedings of the Fourth International Joint Conference on Autonomous Agents and Multiagent Systems*, 29–36.

Genette, G. (1983). *Narrative Discourse: An Essay in Method.* Cornell University Press.

Gervás, P. (2009). Computational approaches to storytelling and creativity. *AI Mag., 30*(3), 49–62.

Gervás, P. (2016). Computational drafting of plot structures for russian folk tales. *Cogn. Comput., 8*(2), 187–203.

Gervás, P., & León, C. (2015). When reflective feedback triggers goal revision: A computational model for literary creativity. *Proceedings of the First International Conference on AI and Feedback, 1407,* 32–39.

Gius, E., Reiter, N., & Willand, M. (2019). A shared task for the digital humanities: Annotating narrative levels. *J. Cult. Anal., 2*(1)
Special Issue.

Goldberg, D. E. (1989). *Genetic Algorithms in Search, Optimization, and Machine Learning.* Addison-Wesley.

Gottschall, J. (2012). *The Storytelling Animal: How Stories Make us Human.* Houghton Mifflin Harcourt.

Goyal, A., Riloff, E., et al. (2013). A computational model for plot units. *Comput. Intell., 29*(3), 466–488.

Green, M. (2017). Speech Acts (E. Zalta, Ed.; Winter 2017 Edition). *The Stanford Encyclopedia of Philosophy.* https://plato. stanford.edu/archives/win2017/entries/speech-acts/

Greimas, A. J. (1983). *Structural Semantics: An Attempt at a Method.* University of Nebraska Press.

Greimas, A. J., & Courtès, J. (1976). The cognitive dimension of narrative discourse (M. Rengstorf, Trans.). *New Lit. Hist., 7*(3), 433–447. https://doi.org/10.2307/468554

Harari, Y. N. (2014). *Sapiens: A Brief History of Humankind.* Random House.

Heggernes, P., van't Hof, P., Meister, D., & Villanger, Y. (2015). Induced subgraph isomorphism on proper interval and bipartite permutation graphs. *Theor. Comput. Sci., 562,* 252–269.

Heider, F., & Simmel, M. (1944). An experimental study of apparent behavior. *Am. J. Psychol., 57*(2), 243–259.

Herman, D., Jahn, M., & Ryan, M.-L. (Eds.). (2005). *Routledge Encyclopedia of Narrative Theory.* Routledge.

Jaynes, J. R. (1976). *The Origin of Consciousness in the Breakdown of the Bicameral Mind.* Pengin Books.

John, O. P., Donahue, E. M., & Kentle, R. L. (1991). The big five inventory–Versions 4a and 54.

John, O. P., Naumann, L. P., & Soto, C. J. (2008). Paradigm shift to the integrative Big Five trait taxonomy: History, measurement, and conceptual issues. In O. P. John, R. W. Robins, & L. A. Pervin (Eds.), *Handbook of Personality: Theory and Research* (pp. 114–158). Guilford Press.

Kahneman, D. (2011). *Thinking, Fast and Slow*. Macmillan.

Kaufman, J. C., & Sternberg, R. J. (Eds.). (2010). *The Cambridge Handbook of Creativity*. Cambridge University Press.

Keen, S. (2013). Narrative empathy. In P. Hühn, J. C. Meister, J. Pier, & W. Schmid (Eds.), *The Living Handbook of Narratology*. Hamburg University. https://www.lhn.uni-hamburg.de/node/42.html

Kelso, M. T., Weyhrauch, P., & Bates, J. (1993). Dramatic presence. *PRESENCE Teleoperators Virtual Environ.*, *2*(1), 1–15.

Kennedy, J., & Eberhart, R. (1995). Particle swarm optimization. *Proceedings of the International Conference on Neural Networks 1995*, *4*, 1942–1948. https://doi.org/10.1109/ICNN.1995.488968

Klein, S., Aeschlimann, J., & Balsiger, D. (1973). Automatic novel writing: A status report. *Wis. Univ.*

Knights, L. C. (1933). *How Many Children Had Lady Macbeth? an Essay in the Theory and Practice of Shakespearean Criticism*. Gordon Fraser, the Minority Press.

Komulainen, E., Meskanen, K., Lipsanen, J., Lahti, J. M., Jylhä, P., Melartin, T., Wichers, M., Isometsä, E., & Ekelund, J. (2014). The effect of personality on daily life emotional processes. *PLoS One*, *9*(10).

Kozbelt, A., Beghetto, R. A., & Runco, M. A. (2010). Theories of creativity. In *The Cambridge Handbook of Creativity* (pp. 20–47). Cambridge University Press.

Kybartas, B., & Bidarra, R. (2017). A survey on story generation techniques for authoring computational narratives. *IEEE Trans. Comput. Intell. Artif. Intell. Games*, *9*(3), 239–253. https://doi.org/10.1109/TCIAIG.2016.2546063

Labov, W., & Waletzky, J. ([1967] 1997). Narrative analysis: Oral versions of personal experience. *J. Narrat. Life Hist.*, *7*(1-4), 3–38.

Lahn, S., & Meister, J. C. (2013). *Einführung in die Erzähltextanalyse* (Second). J.B. Metzler.

Leclerc, Y. (1995). *Plans et Scenarios de Madame Bovary*. CNRS Editions.

in French.

Lehman, J., Clune, J., Misevic, D., Adami, C., Altenberg, L., Beaulieu, J., Bentley, P. J., Bernard, S., Beslon, G., & Bryson, D. M. (2020). The surprising creativity of digital evolution: A collection of anecdotes from the evolutionary computation and artificial life research communities. *Artif. Life, 26*(2), 274–306.

Lehnert, W. G. (1981). Plot units and narrative summarization. *Cogn. Sci., 5*(4), 293–331.

Lewis, D. (1973). *Counterfactuals*. Harvard University Press.

Mann, H. B., & Whitney, D. R. (1947). On a test of whether one of two random variables is stochastically larger than the other. *Ann. Math. Stat.*, 50–60.

Margolin, U. (1990). The what, the when, and the how of being a character in literary narrative. *Style*, 453–468.

Mateas, M., & Stern, A. (2002). Towards integrating plot and character for interactive drama. In *Socially intelligent agents* (pp. 221–228). Springer.

McCrae, R. R., & John, O. P. (1992). An introduction to the five-factor model and its applications. *J. Pers., 60*(2), 175–215.

Mead, G. (1990). The representation of fictional character. *Style*, 440–452.

Meehan, J. R. (1977). Tale-spin, an interactive program that writes stories. *Proceedings of the 5th international joint conference on Artificial Intelligence*, 91–98.

Mehrabian, A. (1996a). Analysis of the big-five personality factors in terms of the PAD temperament model. *Aust. J. Psychol., 48*(2), 86–92.

Mehrabian, A. (1996b). Pleasure-arousal-dominance: A general framework for describing and measuring individual differences in temperament. *Curr. Psychol., 14*(4), 261–292.

Meister, J. C. (2014). Narratology. In Hühn, Peter, Meister, Jan Christoph, Pier, John, & Schmid, Wolf (Eds.), *The living handbook of narratology*. Hamburg University. Retrieved May 8, 2017, from http://www.lhn.uni-hamburg.de/article/narratology

Merriam-Webster. (2020). Fortune. https://www.merriam-webster.com/dictionary/fortune

Ortony, A., Clore, G. L., & Collins, A. (1990). *The Cognitive Structure of Emotions*. Cambridge University Press.

Ozer, D. J., & Benet-Martinez, V. (2006). Personality and the prediction of consequential outcomes. *Annu Rev Psychol, 57*, 401–421.

Palmer, A. (2004). *Fictional Minds*. University of Nebraska Press.

Pérez y Pérez, R. (1999). *MEXICA : A Computer Model of Creativity in Writing* [PhD Thesis]. University of Sussex.

Pérez y Pérez, R. (2018). The computational creativity continuum. *Proceedings of the Ninth International Conference on Computational Creativity*, 177–184.

Pérez y Pérez, R., & Sharples, M. (2001). MEXICA: A computer model of a cognitive account of creative writing. *J. Exp. Theor. Artif. Intell., 13*(2), 119–139.

Plucker, J. A., & Makel, M. C. (2010). Assessment of creativity. In *The Cambridge Handbook of Creativity* (pp. 48–73). Cambridge University Press.

Polti, G. (1921). *The Thirty-Six Dramatic Situations*. Writer.

Poole, D. L., & Mackworth, A. K. (2010). *Artificial Intelligence: Foundations of computational agents*. Cambridge University Press.

Prince, G. (2003). *A Dictionary of Narratology*. U of Nebraska Press.

Propp, V. (1968). *Morphology of the Folktale* (Vol. 9). University of Texas Press.

Radford, A., Wu, J., Child, Luan, D., Amodei, D., & Sutskever, I. (2019). Language Models are Unsupervised Multitask Learners. *OpenAI Blog, 1*(8).

Rao, A. S., & Georgeff, M. P. (1991). Modeling rational agents within a BDI-Architecture. *Proceedings of the International Conference on Principles of Knowlegde Representation and Reasoning*, 473–484.

Rao, A. S., & Georgeff, M. P. (1995). BDI agents: From theory to practice. *Proceedings of the 1st International Conference on Multiagent Systems*, 312–319.

Reiter, E., & Dale, R. (2000). *Building Natural Language Generation Systems*. Cambridge University Press.

Rescher, N. (1979). The ontology of the possible. *Possible Actual Read. Metaphys. Modality*, 166–181.

Revelle, W., & Scherer, K. R. (2009). Personality and emotion. *Oxf. Companion Emot. Affect. Sci.*, 304–306.

Rhodes, M. (1961). An analysis of creativity. *Phi Delta Kappan*, *42*(7), 305–310.

Ricoeur, P. (1984). *Time and Narrative* (Vol. 1). University of Chicago Press.

Riedl, M. O., & Young, R. M. (2010). Narrative planning: Balancing plot and character. *J. Artif. Intell. Res.*, *39*, 217–268.

Riedl, M. O. (2004). *Narrative Planning: Balancing Plot and Character* [PhD Thesis]. North Carolina State University.

Riedl, M. O., & Bulitko, V. (2013). Interactive narrative: An intelligent systems approach. *AI Mag.*, *34*(1), 67.

Riegl, S., & Veale, T. (2018). Live, die, evaluate, repeat: Do-over simulation in the generation of coherent episodic stories. *Proceedings of the Ninth International Conference on Computational Creativity*, 80–87.

Russell, S., & Norvig, P. (2010). *Artificial Intelligence A Modern Approach* (Third). Prentice Hall.

Ryan, J. (2017). Grimes' fairy tales: A 1960s story generator. *International Conference on Interactive Digital Storytelling*, 89–103.

Ryan, J. (2018). *Curating Simulated Storyworlds* [PhD Thesis]. UC Santa Cruz.

Ryan, M.-L. (1991). *Possible Worlds, Artificial Intelligence, and Narrative Theory*. Indiana University Press.

Ryan, M.-L. (2013). Possible worlds. In P. Hühn, J. C. Meister, J. Pier, & W. Schmid (Eds.), *The Living Handbook of Narratology*. Hamburg University. Retrieved October 19, 2016, from http://www.lhn.uni-hamburg.de/article/possible-worlds

Schechtman, M. (2011). The narrative self. In S. Gallagher (Ed.), *The Oxford Handbook of the Self*. Oxford University Press.

Schmid, W. (2014). Implied reader. In P. Hühn, J. C. Meister, J. Pier, & W. Schmid (Eds.), *The Living Handbook of Narratology*. Hamburg University. Retrieved October 19, 2016, from http://www.lhn.uni-hamburg.de/article/implied-reader

Schneider, R. (2001). Toward a cognitive theory of literary character: The dynamics of mental-model construction. *Style*, *35*(4), 607–639.

Schneider, R. (2013). The Cognitive Theory of Character Reception: An Updated Proposal. *Anglistik*, *24*(2), 117–134.

Sengers, P. (2000). Narrative intelligence. In K. Dautenhahn (Ed.), *Human Cognition and Social Agent Technology* (pp. 1–21). John Benjamins Publishing.

Sharples, M. (1999). *How We Write: Writing as Creative Design*. Routledge.

Siebers, P.-O., & Aickelin, U. (2008). Introduction to multi-agent simulation. *Encyclopedia of Decision Making and Decision Support Technologies*, 554–564.

Spendlove, B., & Ventura, D. (2020). Creating six-word stories via inferred linguistic and semantic formats. *Proceedings of the Eleventh International Conference on Computational Creativity*, 123–130.

Swartjes, I. M. T., & Theune, M. (2008). The virtual storyteller: Story generation by simulation. *Proceedings of the 20th Belgian-Netherlands Conference on Artificial Intelligence*.

Taylor, M., Hodges, S. D., & Kohányi, A. (2003). The illusion of independent agency: Do adult fiction writers experience their characters as having minds of their own? *Imagin. Cogn. Personal.*, *22*(4), 361–380.

Theune, M., Faas, S., Heylen, D. K. J., & Nijholt, A. (2003). The virtual storyteller: Story creation by intelligent agents.

Tobias, R. B. (1993). *Master Plots: And How to Build Them*. Writer's Digest Books.

Turner, M. (1996). *The Literary Mind: The Origins of Thought and Language*. Oxford University Press.

Turner, S. R. (1993). *Minstrel: A Computer Model of Creativity and Storytelling* [PhD Thesis]. University of California at Los Angeles. Los Angeles, CA.

Ullmann, J. R. (2011). Bit-vector Algorithms for binary constraint satisfaction and subgraph isomorphism. *J. Exp. Algorithmics*, *15*. https://doi.org/10.1145/1671970.1921702

Varotsi, L. P. (2016). The authorial delusion: Counting lady Macbeth's children. *New Writ.*, 1–10.

Veale, T. (2018). Appointment in samarra: Pre-destination and bicamerality in lightweight story-telling systems. *Proceedings of the Ninth International Conference on Computational Creativity*, 128–135.

Ventura, D. (2019). Autonomous intentionality in computationally creative systems. In T. Veale & F. A. Cardoso (Eds.), *Com-*

putational Creativity: The Philosophy and Engineering of Autonomously Creative Systems (pp. 49–69). Springer.

Vermeule, B. (2010). *Why Do We Care About Literary Characters?* JHU Press.

Wadsley, T., Ryan, M., et al. (2013). A belief-desire-intention model for narrative generation. *Ninth Artificial Intelligence and Interactive Digital Entertainment Conference.*

Ware, S. G., & Young, R. M. (2014). Glaive: A state-space narrative planner supporting intentionality and conflict. *Proceedings of the Tenth Artificial Intelligence and Interactive Digital Entertainment Conference.*

Weinsheimer, J. (1979). Theory of character: Emma. *Poet. Today,* *1*(1/2), 185–211.

Weisstein, E. (2004). Symmetry. *MathWorld–A Wolfram Web Resource.* Retrieved July 10, 2020, from https://mathworld.wolfram.com/Symmetry.html

Wenzel, P. (2004). *Einführung in die Erzähltextanalyse* (Vol. 6). Wissenschaftlicher Verlag Trier.

White, H. (1981). The narrativization of real events. *Crit. Inq., 7*(4), 793–798.

Wöbkenberg, F. (2021). *A Comparison of Nature-Inspired Algorithms for Evaluation in the Context of Computational Storytelling* [Bachelor Thesis]. University of Osnabrück. Osnabrück.

Wooldridge, M. (2002). *An Introduction to MultiAgent Systems.* John Wiley & Sons.

Yang, S., Wang, M., & Jiao, L. (2004). A quantum particle swarm optimization. *Proceedings of the 2004 Congress on Evolutionary Computation, 1,* 320–324.

Zunshine, L. (2006). *Why We Read Fiction: Theory of Mind and the Novel.* Ohio State University Press.

www.ingramcontent.com/pod-product-compliance
Ingram Content Group UK Ltd.
Pitfield, Milton Keynes, MK11 3LW, UK
UKHW050044180526
471099UK00006B/207